The Editor

ROBERT S. MIOLA is the Gerard Manley Hopkins Professor of English and Lecturer in Classics at Loyola College of Maryland. His publications include *Shakespeare and Classical Tragedy*, *Shakespeare and Classical Comedy*, *Shakespeare's Reading*, and a Revels edition of Ben Jonson's *Every Man in His Humour*. He is currently editing an anthology of primary sources entitled *The Catholic Renaissance*.

A NORTON CRITICAL EDITION

William Shakespeare
MACBETH

AUTHORITATIVE TEXT
SOURCES AND CONTEXTS
CRITICISM

Edited by
ROBERT S. MIOLA
LOYOLA COLLEGE

W • W • NORTON & COMPANY • *New York* • *London*

W. W. Norton & Company has been independent since its founding in 1923, when William Warder and Mary D. Herter Norton first published lectures delivered at the People's Institute, the adult education division of New York City's Cooper Union. The Nortons soon expanded their program beyond the Institute, publishing books by celebrated academics from America and abroad. By mid-century, the two major pillars of Norton's publishing program—trade books and college texts—were firmly established. In the 1950s, the Norton family transferred control of the company to its employees, and today—with a staff of four hundred and a comparable number of trade, college, and professional titles published each year—W. W. Norton & Company stands as the largest and oldest publishing house owned wholly by its employees.

Every effort has been made to contact the copyright holders of each of the selections. Rights holders of any selections not credited should contact W. W. Norton & Company, Inc., 500 Fifth Avenue, New York, NY 10110, for a correction to be made in the next printing of our work.

The text of this book is composed in Fairfield Medium
with the display set in Bernhard Modern.
Composition by Binghamton Valley Composition, Inc.
Manufacturing by the Maple-Vail Book Group.
Book design by Antonina Krass.
Production manager: Ben Reynolds.

Library of Congress Cataloging-in-Publication Data

Shakespeare, William, 1564–1616.
Macbeth : an authoritative text, sources and contexts, criticism /
William Shakespeare; edited by Robert S. Miola.
p. cm.—(A Norton critical edition)
Includes bibliographical references.

ISBN 0-393-97786-2 (pbk.)

1. Macbeth, King of Scotland, 11th cent.—Drama.   2. Shakespeare,
William, 1564–1616. Macbeth—Sources.   3. Macbeth, King of Scotland,
11th cent.—In literature.   4. Shakespeare, William, 1564–1616. Macbeth.
5. Kings and rulers—Succession—Drama.   6. Regicides—Drama.
7. Scotland—Drama.   I. Miola, Robert S.   II. Title.

PR2823.A2M56 2003
822.3'3—dc22   2003060994

W. W. Norton & Company, Inc., 500 Fifth Avenue, New York, N.Y. 10110
www.wwnorton.com

W. W. Norton & Company Ltd., Castle House,
75/76 Wells Street, London W1T 3QT

Contents

Criticism

Introduction

Like the ancient tragedies, Shakespeare's *Macbeth* depicts a fall that evokes, according to Aristotle's prescription in the *Poetics*, both pity and terror. Though ancient playwrights believed in different deities and ethical systems, they too depicted humans struggling with the gods, with fate and free will, crime and punishment, guilt and suffering. Sophocles (fifth century B.C.E.), for example, portrays Oedipus, solver of the Sphinx's riddle and King of Thebes, who discovers that all along he has been fulfilling, not fleeing, the curse of Apollo and its dread predictions. "Lead me away, O friends, the utterly lost (*ton meg' olothrion*), most accursed (*ton kataratotaton*), and the one among mortals most hated (*exthrotaton*) by the gods!" (1341–43). In several plays that provided models for *Macbeth*, Seneca (d. 65 C.E.) presents men and women saying the unsayable, doing the unthinkable, and suffering the unimaginable. The witch Medea slays her own children in a horrifying act of revenge. In contrast to Euripides' *Medea*, which ends in a choral affirmation of Zeus's justice and order, Seneca's play concludes with Medea's transformation into something inhuman: she leaves the scene of desolation in a chariot drawn by dragons, bearing witness, wherever she goes, that there are no gods, *testare nullos esse, qua veheris, deos* (1027). Driven mad by the goddess Juno, Seneca's Hercules in *Hercules Furens* kills his children, then awakens to full recognition of his deed in suicidal grief and remorse (below, 95–97). These tragic heroes struggle against the gods and themselves.

Such classical archetypes inform tragedy in the West, Seneca especially shaping Elizabethan tragedy. *Medea* and *Hercules Furens* partly account for the child-killing so prominent in *Macbeth*. (Seneca joins with English traditions of medieval drama, represented below by Herod's massacre of holy innocents, see 85–94.) Child-killing, as many have noted, appears both in the stage action of Shakespeare's play—the murder of Macduff's children, the bloody child apparition—and in its language—for example, in Lady Macbeth's terrible hyperbole:

> I have given suck, and know
> How tender 'tis to love the babe that milks me;

> I would, while it was smiling in my face,
> Have plucked my nipple from his boneless gums
> And dashed the brains out, had I so sworn as you
> Have done to this. (1.7.54–59)

These lines, transformed, take on a contemporary urgency in William Reilly's film adaptation, *Men of Respect* (1991); there, Ruthie (Lady Macbeth) reminds her husband of her abortion: "I know what it is to have a life inside me, and squashing it out because it's not the right time, it's too difficult. I know what it is to kill for you." Like Lady Macbeth, the murdering mother here forces her husband into a guilty and awed submission.

Seneca may have directly inspired Lady Macbeth herself. When Medea invokes the gods, she asks them to "exile all foolish fear and pity" from her mind; alone, she rouses herself to a terrible deed of self creation (below, 94–95). In her famous soliloquy Lady Macbeth asks the spirits to "unsex" her, to "stop up th'access and passage to remorse," to take her "milk for gall" (1.5.36ff.). Of course, the differences between the two women loom large and important. Medea achieves a unique selfhood in *scelus* ("crime"); altering the universe by transgressing the bounds of the natural, she becomes a supernatural creation who flies away like a god. Instead of such apotheosis, however, Lady Macbeth comes crashing down. Tormented by guilt and sleeplessness, she last appears in the sleepwalking scene (5.1), a ghost of her former self, haunted, frightened, broken. Perhaps the most celebrated actress in this role, Sarah Siddons (1755–1831) portrayed Lady Macbeth washing her hands vehemently; she imagined her character, "with wan and haggard countenance, her starry eyes glazed with the ever-burning fever of remorse, and on their lids the shadows of death" (below, 236). Medea transforms herself; Lady Macbeth dies offstage.

Macbeth also experiences a breathtaking rise and crashing fall. He appears first as a classical warrior hero, "valor's minion," the bridegroom of Bellona, Roman goddess of war (1.2.19, 55). At a crucial point in the action he justifies the decision to kill Banquo in Senecan fashion: the line, "Things bad begun make strong themselves by ill" (3.2.58), echoes Seneca's proverbial saying, *per scelera semper sceleribus tutum est iter* (*Agamemnon*, 115), "The safe way for crime is through more crimes." But there is no safe way for crimes in Macbeth's world; not even Bellona's bridegroom can carve out his passage with brandished steel and bloody execution. Dagger in blood-stained hand, Macbeth suffers like no classical hero at the very moment of his triumphant murder; he hears the sleeping guards wake:

MACBETH   One cried "God bless us!" and "Amen!" the other,
   As they had seen me with these hangman's hands.
   List'ning their fear, I could not say "Amen"
   When they did say "God bless us!"
LADY MACBETH   Consider it not so deeply.
MACBETH   But wherefore could not I pronounce "Amen"?
   I had most need of blessing, and "Amen"
   Stuck in my throat. (2.2.29–36)

In David Garrick's celebrated eighteenth-century performance of
this scene, the self-reproach ("these hangman's hands") widened into
a "wonderful expression of heartfelt horror" (below, 217). Here that
reproach accompanies an urgent need for God's blessing and the
solace of prayer. Unable to say "Amen," Macbeth expresses a child-
like incomprehension and astonishment at what he has done and
become. This extraordinary moment marks the differences between
him and his classical predecessors, and from the cruel, remorseless
tyrant Shakespeare found in Holinshed's *Chronicles* (1587), the
main source of the play.

   This moment takes us into the heart of Macbeth's tragedy: he has
most need of God's blessing and cannot say "Amen." An imperfect
man in a brutal, fallen world, Macbeth needs to be saved but,
instead, chooses to save himself, and suffers miserably for his choice.
Macbeth's abortive prayer thus illuminates the moral world of the
play, the ethical universe in which he must live and die. And we
must surely share, at first, in his momentary astonishment: why, after
all, can't the man who has just butchered his guest, kinsman, and
king manage to mouth an "Amen," even if insincere? What stops
him, what sticks the word in his throat—the involuntary reflex of a
defeated conscience or some divine refusal to tolerate yet another
transgression? The play affords no window through which to look
this deeply into Macbeth's soul, but one thing is clear: Macbeth's
inability to say "Amen" signals the futility of his crime. Human action
and the will to power may prevail in Medea's world but not here,
where nature itself gives witness to the immutable order of moral
law. Macbeth fears that the very stones will prate of his whereabout
(2.1.58). The night of the King's murder is "unruly": chimneys fall,
laments and strange screams of death fill the air, the owl clamors,
the earth shakes (2.3.48–55). After, an unnatural darkness strangles
the sun, a mousing owl kills a falcon, and Duncan's horses eat each
other (2.4.5–18). In the Globe performance of 1611, Simon Forman
reports, the blood on Macbeth's hands "could not be washed off by
any means, nor from his wife's hands" (below, 205). After Banquo's
ghost returns, Macbeth says that stones move, trees speak, and birds
("maggot-pies and choughs and rooks") reveal "the secret'st man of
blood" (3.4.125–28). The mix of legend, superstition, and mirabilia

here points to providential order; the capricious pagan gods, Apollo, Juno, and Zeus, do not rule in this world, but the just Judaeo-Christian God, the God who will return at the Last Judgment, the day of the great doom, when the dead rise from their graves and walk like sprites (2.3.73–76).

This God, creator of nature and moral order, figures centrally in Holinshed's *Chronicles:* "almighty God showed himself thereby to be offended most highly for that wicked murder of King Duff, and, surely, unless the offenders were tried forth and punished for that deed, the realm should feel the just indignation of the divine judgment for omitting such punishment as was due for so grievous an offense" (below, 101). And this God makes a surprising number of appearances (fifteen total) in the language of Shakespeare's dark, bloody play, rife with scenes of evil supernaturalism and murderous ambition. Coleridge noted long ago that the witches "strike the keynote" (below, 219) of the play, but there is an insistent, if quieter, divine counterpoint. Orson Welles heard and amplified this music in his 1948 film version, often employing the symbol of the cross amid the gnarled trees and stone of his primitive Scotland, adding a Holy Father to conduct a service against Satan and oppose the rising evil. In Shakespeare's text Ross greets Duncan with unintentional irony, "God save the King!" (1.2.48). Immediately after the murder Banquo declares himself to stand "in the great hand of God" (2.3.129) against treasonous malice. Malcolm asks "God above" (4.3.121) to regulate the alliance with Macduff, echoing the lord who hoped that "Him above" (3.6.32) would ratify the rebellion against Macbeth. Witnessing Lady Macbeth sleepwalking, the Doctor does what Macbeth could not: he says a spontaneous prayer, "God, God, forgive us all" (5.1.66). The Captain compares the opening battle to Golgotha (1.2.40), place of the Crucifixion; Malcolm later praises Siward as the oldest and best soldier in "Christendom" (4.3.193). Commissioning the murderers, Macbeth pointedly asks, "Are you so gospeled to pray for this good man and for his issue, whose heavy hand hath bowed you to the grave and beggared yours for ever?" (3.1.89–91). Whether or not he alludes specifically to Matthew 5:44 ("Love your enemies and pray for those who persecute you"), Macbeth here invokes the God whom he has disobeyed and the moral order he has violated. And once again, he adverts to prayer, this time thinking it the cowardly alternative to the manly action of murder.

King Macbeth's newfound contempt for the gospel and prayer marks his moral deterioration. "Had I but died an hour before this chance, / I had lived a blessèd time" (2.3.88–89), he himself said earlier. But such blessing as he required and yearned for now lies out of reach and out of mind. Lennox, ironically, hopes that a "swift blessing" (3.6.48) in the form of divine aid and the English army will come to remove Macbeth and relieve sick, suffering Scotland. The imagery of disease runs importantly throughout the play (see Muir below, 254–66): Macbeth thinks of life as a "fitful fever" (3.2.25); "he cannot buckle his distempered cause / Within the belt of rule" (5.2.15–16). Scotland "bleeds, and each new day a gash / Is added to her wounds" (4.3.41–42); the invading Malcolm is the "med'cine of the sickly weal" (5.2.27). And the English King Edward, in purposeful contrast to King Macbeth, is a religious curer who gives "holy prayers" and the "healing benediction" to the afflicted, who has "a heavenly gift of prophecy" (4.3.155–58). "Sundry blessings hang about his throne" (4.3.159), while Macbeth becomes "a hand accursed" (3.6.50), receiving not love or honor but "curses, not loud but deep" (5.3.27).

In the Shakespeare play that most embodies the "principle of contrast" and "moves upon the verge of an abyss," in Hazlitt's fine phrasing (below, 225), other religious antitheses mark Macbeth's decline. Early on he imagines Duncan's virtues as angels pleading trumpet-tongued against the murder, and pity as heaven's cherubin blowing the horrid deed in every eye (1.7.18–24). He declares himself the kind of man who could appall the devil (3.4.61), but chooses to side with him and his minions. Too late he realizes that the witches are "juggling fiends" (5.8.19) and that he has been deceived by the "equivocation of the fiend / That lies like truth" (5.5.43–44). The association of witches, equivocation, and the devil, many have noted, draws resonance from the anti-Catholic fervor following the discovery of the Gunpowder plot; the Porter alludes to one of the convicted conspirators, the Jesuit Henry Garnet, who wrote a treatise on equivocation (below, 159–60) and was executed in 1606. "Faith here's an equivocator that could swear in both the scales against either scale, who committed treason enough for God's sake, yet could not equivocate to heaven" (2.3.7–9). Submitting to the paltering, equivocal witches, Macbeth becomes increasingly identified with the devil: Macduff wants to confront "this fiend of Scotland" (4.3.237); Malcolm calls him "devilish Macbeth" (4.3.118). Hearing Macbeth name himself, Young Siward proclaims, "The devil himself could not pronounce a title / More hateful to mine ear"; "No, nor more fearful" (5.7.9–11), Macbeth responds. Macbeth himself invokes the Prince of Darkness: "The devil damn thee black, thou cream-faced loon!" (5.3.11). He who had most need of blessing now turns the other way for curses, even threatening the witches themselves: "Deny me this [the truth about Banquo's issue] / And an eternal curse fall upon you!" (4.1.104–5).

Given the company he keeps, we should not be surprised, perhaps, that Macbeth's enemy, Hecate, leader of the witches, delivers the most telling commentary on his spiritual state: "He shall spurn fate, scorn death, and bear / His hopes 'bove wisdom, grace, and fear. / And you all know, security / Is mortals' chiefest enemy" (3.5.30–33). Hecate here plays orthodox preacher, echoing numerous homilies and popular theology pamphlets ("you all know") on the dangers of "security," i.e., spiritual overconfidence and complacency, repose in the pleasures of this world. In 1584 John Stockwood published *A Very Fruitful and Necessary Sermon* "to the wakening and stirring up of all such as be lulled asleep in the cradle of security or carelessness" (title page). The title page of Thomas Rogers' *The Enemy of Security* (1591) exhorts the reader to watch and pray, "pray continually." About the time of *Macbeth* William Est preached in *The Scourge of Security* (1609) that neglect of prayer led to the return of the unclean spirit. In the same year Thomas Draxe explained that the substance of security is contained in the words "I sleep" and the antidote in the phrase "but mine heart waketh" (*The Church's Security*, sigs. B1v–B2). This homiletic fervor motivated John Downame's *A Treatise of Security* (1622), written "to rouse up" sinners "out of this sleep or rather lethargy of security" (Epistle Dedicatory).

Hecate's precise spiritual diagnosis, then, evokes a discrete, clearly outlined, and abundantly available complex of image and exhortation. Shakespeare fully engages this familiar complex but reverses its basic logic: the sleepless Macbeth ever waketh in his cradle of security, not lulled, but racked "in the affliction of these terrible dreams / That shake us nightly" (3.2.20–21). The pervasive images of sleeplessness in the play have been well-remarked, of course—the bewitched insomniac sailor who dwindles, peaks, and pines, the mysterious cry, "Sleep no more! / Macbeth does murder sleep" (2.2.38–93), his subsequent yearning for "sleep that knits up the raveled sleave of care, / The death of each day's life" etc. (40ff.), the sleepwalking Lady Macbeth. But to contemporary audiences they must have derived their force from Shakespeare's daring inversion of conventional rhetoric and moral formula. His Macbeth is agonizingly and unremittingly awake, stung by his conscience, the agenbyte of inwit, that full, tormenting, relentless awareness of his sin.

Another terror of the play is that Macbeth's gains are negligible and indistinct, his losses large and clearly articulated: "honor, love, obedience, troops of friends, / I must not look to have" (5.3.25–26). And, correspondingly, the earthly highlands of Scotland are never so precisely mapped as the spiritual landscapes Macbeth traverses. Some of the Scottish references, Saint Colme's Inch (or Inchcolm isle) (1.2.62) and Colmekill (3.1.34), even point to the other world, where the real drama transpires: both localities pay nominal tribute to St. Columba (521–97), the abstemious missionary to northern Scotland who preached, worked miracles, and converted the pagan Picts and Druids to Christianity. Appropriately, Duncan's body is carried to the "sacred storehouse of his predecessors" (3.1.35) at Colmekill, the monastic "cell of Columba" in Iona, off the West of Scotland. The forces of Christianity thus align themselves in death as in life against the pagan barbarism of Scotland. Macbeth moves between these two opposed realms, as between blessings and curses, angels and devils, and, like one of Hamlet's crawling fellows, between heaven and hell. Lady Macbeth wants the "dunnest smoke of hell" to beshroud the world so that heaven cannot "peep through the blanket of the dark / To cry 'Hold, hold' " (1.5.49–52). "The heavens, as troubled with man's act," the murder, threaten "his bloody stage" (2.4.5–6) with natural disruptions and cosmic events. Macduff says that "new sorrows / Strike heaven on the face" (4.3.5–6). Heaven often appears as a metonym for divine providence. Lennox hopes, if it "please heaven" (3.6.19), that Macbeth will not get his hands on Duncan's heirs. The messenger says to the doomed Lady Macduff, "heaven preserve you" (4.2.68); Macduff asks if heaven looked on at the slaughter of his wife and children (4.3.227–28). Heaven grants the gifts of healing and prophecy to King Edward (4.3.150ff.). Most significantly, heaven appears in contrast to hell as the after-life abode of the blessed and just, the place of peace and happiness. Again, Macbeth himself points the moral before the murders of Duncan and Banquo: the ringing bell summons the king "to heaven or to hell" (2.1.64); and Banquo's soul "If it find heaven, must find it out tonight" (3.1.143).

On the opposing side, the Porter imagines himself keeping the gate in hell and comments on the condemned residents. Though reviled by Elizabeth Montagu ("entirely absurd," below, 215), Samuel Taylor Coleridge ("disgusting," below, 218), and others, this great serio-comic scene (2.3) appropriately gives, as Harry Levin observes, the other place a local habitation and a name. The Macbeths walk the broad and royal road to hell; in fact, they sometimes seem to live there already. Reliving her crimes over and over again, Lady Macbeth, one of the living dead, murmurs "Hell is murky" (5.1.31). In Trevor Nunn's celebrated film production, Judi Dench turned this into a discovery—"Hell *is* murky"—as she recoiled from the abyss opening for her. Hearing a night shriek, Macbeth observes: "I have supped full with horrors. / Direness, familiar to my slaughterous thoughts, / Cannot once start me" (5.5.13–15). Macduff calls Macbeth a "hell-kite" and a "hellhound" (4.3.220; 5.8.3), thus echoing his pronouncement, "Not in the legions / Of horrid hell can come a devil more damned / In evils to top Macbeth" (4.3.56–58).

Damned in evils—*Macbeth* takes us on a thrilling, terrifying journey into the heart and soul of the damned. Staging the morality-play sequence of temptation, sin, and death, Shakespeare degrades repentance in this Everyman to a melancholy remorse, leaving both Macbeths to the consequences of their actions, to the "deep damnation of his [Duncan's] taking off" (1.7.20). The resulting portraits of sin, punishment, and damnation stand worthily next to those of Dante's *Inferno*: to Ezzelino the tyrant in Phlegethon, the boiling river of blood (Canto 12); to Vanni Fucci, defiant and making an obscene gesture to God (Canto 25); to Ugolino, who eats the bodies of his dead children (Canto 33); to Fra Alberigò and Branca Doria, whose souls are already in hell though their bodies live on earth (Canto 33); to the traitors Judas, Brutus, and Cassius, writhing from the mouths of Satan in the ice of Judecca (Canto 34). Such compelling, full-bodied figures all contrast with the sterilized wraiths of the English *de casibus* tradition, tediously moralizing their histories, reciting their faults, and preaching repentance. Dante and Shakespeare portray the sinners themselves, living human beings, groaning, sweating, suffering, cursing, excusing, regretting, all their faults and imperfections on their heads, their sins in full and flagrant blossom. And, like Macbeth, the damned souls throughout the nine circles of Dante's *Inferno* are capable of every kind of speech, noise, eloquence, and remorse, save one: they cannot pray.

The play's focus on damnation inspired one recent actor, Derek Jacobi, to summarize his conception of the lead role thus: "I tried to plot his journey from the golden boy of the opening to the burnt-out loser accepting his own damnation of the conclusion" (below, 342). This journey, we should remember, Shakespeare consciously constructs from numerous possibilities in Holinshed's account. In his notes for plays and poems John Milton apparently envisioned a different kind of *Macbeth;* starting with the conference of Malcolm and Macduff (4.3) and including the ghost of Duncan, he imagined perhaps a political play in the form of a classical revenge tragedy. Shakespeare's drama of damnation, by contrast, purposefully evokes and engages contemporary theology, particularly the disputes about divine foreknowledge, human responsibility, the nature of grace, and the freedom of the human will. These disputes occupied preachers on the pulpit as well as the best theological minds of the early modern period. Asserting the total efficacy of God's foreknowledge and divine grace, the Protestant reformer Martin Luther emphatically denied the existence of free will:

> I misspoke when I said that free will before grace exists in name only; rather I should have simply said "free will is a fiction among real things, a name with no reality." For no one has it within his control to intend anything, good or evil, but rather,

as was rightly taught by the article of Wyclif which was condemned at Constance, all things occur by absolute necessity.
(below, 119)

Arguing that free will cooperates with grace, Erasmus responded to
Luther, at one point in the voice of a Bible reader speaking to God:

> "Why complain of my behaviour, when all my actions, good or
> bad, are performed by you in me regardless of my will? Why
> reproach me, when I have no power to preserve the good you
> have given me, or keep out the evil you put into me? Why entreat
> me, when everything depends on you, and happens as it pleases
> you? Why bless me, as though I had done my duty, when what-
> ever happens is your work? Why curse me, when I sinned
> through necessity?" What is the purpose of such a vast number
> of commandments if not a single person has it at all in his power
> to do what is commanded? (below, 124)

Erasmus contends that the doctrine of predestination invalidates
God's commandments and renders absurd the concept of divine
justice.

The controversy provides an illuminating context for the depiction
of witches, sin, and punishment in *Macbeth*. First, it disposes summarily the notion that the Weïrd sisters can in any sense possess or
control Macbeth. Those early Protestants and Catholics who believe
in witches never grant to them such power. Instead, they debate the
nature of God's foreknowledge and the predestination of the elect
and reprobate, the saved and the damned. Whatever his personal
convictions, Shakespeare clearly adopts a Catholic view of the action
and theology of free will in this play. Macbeth repeatedly adverts to
the terror implicit in free will, in his awesome power to choose good
or evil: "I dare do all that may become a man / Who dares do more
is none" (1.7.46–47). He never contemplates the pre-dispositions of
fate or the deity, but thinks instead on the consequences of his
choices and actions, consequences he would desperately evade and
deny. Recalling the prophecy about Banquo, he emphasizes his own
responsibility and autonomous agency:

> If't be so,
> For Banquo's issue have I filed my mind,
> For them the gracious Duncan have I murdered,
> Put rancors in the vessel of my peace
> Only for them, and mine eternal jewel
> Given to the common enemy of man
> To make them kings, the seeds of Banquo kings! (3.1.66–72)

Macbeth has chosen evil, in his words, "given" his soul to the devil.
To emphasize the point, Shakespeare departs from Holinshed in his

depiction of Banquo, who encourages him in jest to "purchase" (below, 104) the crown, and who knows in advance of the assassination. Shakespeare's Banquo, a clear foil to Macbeth, freely and steadfastly resists temptation: first he prays, "Merciful powers, / Restrain in me the cursèd thoughts that nature / Gives way to in repose" (2.1.7–9); then he confronts Macbeth directly, asserting that he must lose no honor, must keep his "bosom franchised and allegiance clear" (2.1.26–28). Rejecting the Protestant dichotomy between the elect and reprobate, Shakespeare deploys the Catholic view of free will perhaps from theological conviction, but more certainly from theatrical necessity. For the doctrine of predestination renders human action essentially undramatic: when the end is known, preordained, and absolutely just, there can be no real choice, suspense, conflict, or resolution. This conception of divine justice and human action renders pity an impertinence, terror a transgression, and tragedy an impossibility.

Consider, for example, the death of the reprobate, as described by the popular Calvinist William Perkins, *A Golden Chain, a Description of Theology containing the Order of the Causes of Salvation and Damnation* (1591): "The reprobates when they die do become without sense and astonied like unto a stone; or else they are overwhelmed with a terrible horror of conscience, and despairing of their salvation, as it were, with the gulf of the sea overturning them" (sig. V5). Perkins illustrates the first option with the story of Nabal who hears of God's judgment against him: "his heart died within him; he became like a stone. About ten days later the Lord struck Nabal, and he died" (1 Kings 23:37–38). He illustrates the second with the story of Judas, who hanged himself in despair (Matthew 27:5). However these ends may bear comparison with the death of Lady Macbeth off-stage, they contrast jarringly with Macbeth's final moments— with his somber reflections and military resurgence. Here as throughout the play, the vitality and eloquence of Macbeth distinguish him from the reprobate of the popular imagination, the heart-dead stone, Nabal, or the despairing, suicidal Judas. Shakespeare presents instead a tragedy of free will and damnation.

Another contemporary controversy, the debate over regicide, also informs *Macbeth*, just as it does, *mutatis mutandis*, Shakespeare's other history plays and tragedies. *Macbeth*, however, features not one regicide but two. The play asks that we condemn the murder of King Duncan, and, with equal conviction, applaud the murder of King Macbeth. To insure the condemnation Shakespeare denies Macbeth a coronation scene and suppresses Holinshed's notice of Duncan's inadequacies, Macbeth's possible claim to the crown, and his years of just rule. Thus Shakespeare portrays the first regicide as a monstrous rebellion, in accord with the Elizabethan *Homily against Disobedience* (below, 148–54) and the beliefs of Banquo's descendant, King James I, proponent of the divine right of kings. To portray the second regicide as virtuous restoration, Shakespeare amplifies the witches, the sinister influence of Lady Macbeth, and Macbeth's crimes. But according to the *Homily* and divine right theory, even bad kings had to be obeyed and tolerated: "let us either deserve to have a good prince, or let us patiently suffer and obey such as we deserve" (below, 150). To justify the second regicide, Shakespeare draws upon the opposing resistance theory, which holds that citizens owe obedience to kings but not to tyrants, i.e., rulers who by unlawful entrance or vicious practice forfeit their rights of sovereignty. The Jesuit Juan de Mariana, for example, argues that, under certain circumstances, anyone may depose a tyrant for the good of the commonwealth and in so doing earn gratitude and praise (below 154–59).

Accordingly, Shakespeare portrays King Macbeth as a tyrant both in the language and the action of the play. Macduff calls him "an untitled tyrant, bloody sceptred" (4.3.105), neatly alluding to both his unlawful entrance (by assassination) and vicious practice (the subsequent murders). "This tyrant holds the due of birth" (3.6.25) from Duncan's son; the "sole name" of this tyrant "blisters our tongues" (4.3.12). Like the archetypal Herod, the tyrannical Macbeth massacres the innocents. Macduff threatens to display Macbeth's picture on a pole with the legend "Here may you see the tyrant" (5.8.27). And, accordingly, Shakespeare depicts the deposer Macduff as "anyone," as an ordinary, flawed man. Macduff makes the fatal error of leaving his wife and children unprotected; he has no claim to fame except his birth by Caesarean section; and, as one Royal Shakespeare Company actor who had played the role five times observed to me, he is typically ineloquent or silent: relating Duncan's murder to others, Macduff says, "Do not bid me speak" (2.3.68); Malcolm urges him, "give sorrow words" (4.3.210); "I have no words / My voice is in my sword" (5.8.6–7), Macduff says later to Macbeth.

In this, as in other regards, the eloquent Macbeth, speaking fully thirty percent of the play's lines, stands in colossal contrast with the avenger and putative hero, Macduff. Shakespeare thus recapitulates the strategy of his previous tyrant play, *Richard III*, wherein Richmond's forgettable piety opposes Gloucester's grand and thrilling blasphemy. But both blasphemy and piety in many forms resound throughout Macbeth's speech—alternating, simultaneous, interdependent—creating memorable and musical discord. Blasphemy appears in the eerie invocation to night and "its bloody and invisible hand," which Macbeth hopes will "cancel and tear to pieces that great bond" that keeps him pale (3.2.49–53). It continues throughout the consultation with the witches (4.1). And, at the last, Macbeth, perversely mimicking his former valor instead of repenting, redefines the very terms of salvation and damnation: "Before my body / I throw my warlike shield. Lay on, Macduff, / And damned be him that first cries, Hold, enough!" (5.8.32–34). Identifying "him" as God by looking toward the heavens, Jacobi's Macbeth pointed the blasphemy with a curse against the deity. Less explicitly, an equally potent denial appears in the world-weary nihilism of Macbeth's famous meditation:

> Tomorrow, and tomorrow, and tomorrow
> Creeps in this petty pace from day to day
> To the last syllable of recorded time,
> And all our yesterdays have lighted fools
> The way to dusty death. Out, out, brief candle!
> Life's but a walking shadow, a poor player
> That struts and frets his hour upon the stage
> And then is heard no more. It is a tale
> Told by an idiot, full of sound and fury,
> Signifying nothing. (5.5.19–28)

Only those who have experienced some elevation can fall to this nadir; and the Macbeth who piously believed in evenhanded justice and heaven's cherubin, we recall, once saw life as a feast nourished by that very same progression of days, each capped by restorative sleep:

> Sleep that knits up the raveled sleeve of care,
> The death of each day's life, sore labor's bath,
> Balm of hurt minds, great nature's second course,
> Chief nourisher in life's feast—(2.2.40–43)

Here the diurnal rhythms of waking and sleeping express not meaninglessness but moral order. This belief in moral order motivates Macbeth's distinctive verse music, such piety, like blasphemy, taking various shapes. Seconds after the murder Macbeth feels an incredulous repulsion and self-alienation: "What hands are here? Ha, they pluck out mine eyes!" "To know my deed 'twere best not know myself" (2.2.62, 76). Soon after, pretending to mourn the King, he speaks truer than he intends: "from this instant / There's nothing serious in mortality. / All is but toys. Renown and grace is dead" (2.3.89–91). Racked by his guilty conscience, the man who yearned for renown and grace soon envies his victim:

> Better be with the dead,
> Whom we, to gain our peace, have sent to peace,

Than on the torture of the mind to lie
In restless ecstasy. (3.2.21–24)

There is even a clear moment of moral vision and remorse in the
final meeting with Macduff:

Of all men else I have avoided thee.
But get thee back. My soul is too much charged
With blood of thine already! (5.8.4–6)

The eloquent and elegiac register of such piety rarely survives
translation or adaptation. Plangent and moving, it arrests the hero's
descent into darkness while marking the speed and distance of his
fall. Coleridge thought *Macbeth* "the most rapid" of Shakespeare's
plays, "being wholly and purely tragic" (below, 218); Bradley called
it "the most vehement, the most concentrated" (below, 238) of the
tragedies. Consequences follow so quickly and inevitably that they
seem embedded in actions themselves, even in the thoughts preceding action. The confusion of tenses attending the verb "to do" sometimes collapses past, present, and future so that planning, acting,
and suffering become coexistent aspects of the same crime. Lady
Macbeth urges:

Thou'dst have, great Glamis,
That which cries "Thus thou must do," if thou have it,
And that which rather thou dost fear to do
Than wishest should be undone. (1.5.20–23)

And Macbeth contemplates, "If it were done when 'tis done, then
'twere well / It were done quickly" (1.7.1–2); he resolves, "I go, and
it is done" (2.1.62). The interconnectedness of conception, execution, and consequence heightens the sense of Macbeth's dizzying
plunge and, once begun, its inevitability. "I have done the deed"
(2.2.14), he says simply after the murder. "What's done is done"
(3.2.14), Lady Macbeth counsels; and then later in a rueful echo
while sleepwalking, "what's done cannot be undone" (5.1.58–59).
Writing a travesty of *Macbeth* in the nineteenth century, Francis
Talfourd shrewdly seized upon this inevitability to turn the play into
topsy-turvy burlesque. In his version Duncan returns from the dead,
nodding and winking at Macduff, and reclaims his crown. Before
Banquo and Lady Macbeth return arm-in-arm from the nether
world, Macbeth rises and addresses the King:

I tender, sir, of course, my resignation,
Since all's in train for me to leave my station.
So at your feet I lay my regal diadem
Without regret, nor wish again that I had 'em. (below, 185)

The comic fantasy strikes at the heart of Shakespeare's play, where evil freely chosen becomes a driving force, absolute, uncontrollable, irreversible, irrevocable.

Thus the play enables us to experience the thrill and misery of evil as few others do. Recoiling from this heart of darkness, William Davenant greatly expanded the role of Lady Macduff to provide a clear moral contrast to Lady Macbeth, the good wife matched against the evil one. His successful seventeenth-century adaptation also presented a Macbeth who dies not with a defiant snarl but with a belated confession of folly, "Farewell vain world, and what's most vain in it, ambition" (below, 173). Such changes diminish the evil in Shakespeare's play, reducing it to comfortable and conventional moral schema. Expanding the witches' roles, Davenant likewise transformed the evil into a spectacle located safely in the other, in the nonhuman. Such revision can constitute a strategy of evasion, modern critics remind us, for the witches release and reveal the evil in human beings and their social orderings. Janet Adelman (below, 293–315) observes that the play initially constructs maternal power as malignant and demonic then stages an exorcism of this power in a dream of masculine control; but the dream turns out to be a nightmare as such order appears finally as sterile and self-destructive. Stephen Orgel comments that witches "live outside the social order but embody its contradictions": their gender indeterminacy, women with beards, females played originally by male actors, suggest that nature is "anarchic, full of competing claims, not ordered and hierarchical" (below, 347). Evil cannot be summarily demonized, dislocated, and dismissed.

Early modern controversy supports modern critical insight about the ambivalent nature of the witches as both demonic and human, as both other and ourselves. James I depicted them as "ungodly creatures, no better than devils" (below, 138) in a pamphlet, *News from Scotland* (1591), and later in his *Daemonology* (1597). He spoke about their supernatural powers to create storms and topple kings. James was writing against such sceptics as Reginald Scot (*The Discovery of Witchcraft*, 1584), who thought witches ordinary people, either deluders or deluded themselves, "women which be commonly old, lame, blear-eyed, pale, foul, and full of wrinkles, poor, sullen, superstitious, and papists, or such as know no religion, in whose drowsy minds the devil hath gotten a fine seat; so as what mischief, mischance, calamity, or slaughter is brought to pass, they are easily persuaded the same is done by themselves" (below, 113). Shakespeare's play takes full advantage of the controversy without deciding it: *Macbeth* provides chilling testimony to the existence of supernatural evil and the forbidden black arts, well conforming to popular superstition and James' views. But, the play insists equally, Macbeth desires the crown before his first encounter with the witches. And when he later seeks them out on his own, they anticipate his arrival by saying, "Something wicked this way comes" (4.1.45). Clearly, the evil lives within Macbeth, within his human ambition; and his faith in the witches both evokes and sustains them. Their existence and power depend, as Scot insists, on human credulity and weakness. They reside in our lusts, hatreds, and sins.

Though created in a language arising from specific theological and political contexts, Shakespeare's *Macbeth* has come to new life in strange and marvelous adaptations (see Holland's survey of films below, 357–80). Akira Kurosawa's 1957 film, *Throne of Blood*, or *The Castle of the Spider's Web*, transposes the tale to medieval Japan. There the white-haired Forest Spirit sits at a spinning wheel in a hut of sticks, tempting and mocking humans. The gruff, passionate Samurai warlord, Washizu, goaded by his wife, the still, formal, precise, and menacing automaton, Asaji, slays Lord Kuniharu. Washizu then kills his friend Miki, whose spirit returns to the banquet. The labyrinthine forest finally takes spectacular revenge as volleys of hissing arrows strike and stick in Washizu, staggering desperately and defiantly on the wall of his castle. A final arrow pierces him in the neck as mist shrouds both the castle and the forest. In the early 1970s, the South African playwright Welcome Msomi staged another brilliant retelling, *uMabatha*, based partly on the life of Shaka Zulu, an early nineteenth-century chief famous for his military skill and brutality. The Sangoma, or witchdoctors, spit, beat drums, throw bones, and prophesy greatness for the warrior Mabatha. His wife, Kamadonsela, invokes her ancestors to make her heart like the devil's thorn, her blood like mamba's poison. Mabatha kills Chief Dangane and his friend Bhangane, and resolves to kill the wife and children of Mafudu: "My thoughts were children, tortoise-slow / But now I will strike / Swifter than the crouching lion / Who smells the terror of his prey" (below, 198). Mafudu returns to slay Mabatha, deceived by the Sangomas' prophecies. Such radical and daring adaptations treat the play as a myth about the mystery of evil, infinitely translatable into new series of haunting images and actions. Whether reflecting or departing from its origins, whether set in medieval Scotland or in some other land and culture, Shakespeare's *Macbeth* still stirs our deepest desires and fears.

ROBERT S. MIOLA
Loyola College of Maryland

A Note on the Text

These notes record substantive departures from the copy text, i.e., the First Folio (1623). They do not (1) present an historical collation, (2) record correction of obvious typographical errors, and (3) indicate changes in lineation and punctuation. The Act and Scene division in this edition follows the Folio, except that 5.7 in the Folio has been divided into 5.7 and 5.8 in the present text. The reading adopted for this Norton Critical Edition appears in boldface below, followed by the rejected reading from the Folio.

Abbreviations used: F the First Folio; S.D. stage direction; S.P. speech prefix; *uncorr.* uncorrected.

1.2.13 **galloglasses:** Gallowgrosses   14 **quarrel:** Quarry
1.3.33 **[and elsewhere] Weïrd:** weyward [sometimes "weyard"]   40 **Forres:** Soris   72 **Finel's:** *Sinells*   98 **hail:** Tale   99 **Came:** Can   112 **lose:** loose
1.5.1 S.P. **[and elsewhere] LADY MACBETH:** Lady   8 **lose:** *loose*
1.6.4 **martlet:** Barlet   13 **God 'ield:** God-eyld
1.7.6 **shoal:** Schoole   28 **other—:** other.   47 **do:** no
2.1.55 **strides:** sides   56 **sure:** sowre   57 **way they:** they may
2.2.66 **green one red:** Greene one, Red   76 S.D.: [after "deed"]
2.3.35 S.D.: [after 34]   69 S.D.: [after 69]   134 **nea'er:** neere
2.4.42 S.D. **all:** *omnes*
3.1.10 S.D. **LADY MACBETH, LENNOX:** *Lady Lenox*   77, 116, 140 S.P. **MURDERERS:** *Murth.*   141 S.D.: [after 143]
3.2. S.D. **LADY MACBETH:** *Macbeths Lady*
3.3.7 **and:** end
3.4.14 S.P. **[and throughout the scene] FIRST MURDERER:** *Mur.*   123 S.D. **Exeunt:** *Exit*   146 **in deed:** indeed
3.6.24 **son:** Sonnes   38 **the:** their
4.1.59 **germens:** Germaine   59 **all together:** altogether   93 **Birnam:** Byrnam [sometimes "Byrnan," "Birnan," "Byrnane," and "Birnane"]   93 **Dunsinane:** Dunsmane   94 S.D. **Descends:** *Descend*   105 S.D.: [after 106]   119 **eighth:** eight   130 **antic:** Antique
4.2.22 **none:** moue   75 S.D.: [after 75]   76, 78, 79 S.P. **A MURDERER:** *Mur.*   79 **shag-haired:** shagge-ear'd
4.3.15 **deserve:** discerne   35 **affeered:** affear'd **Fare:** Far   108 **accursed:** accust   134 **thy here-approach:** they heere approach   146 S.D.: [after "amend"]   155 **on with:** on my with [F *uncorr.*]   169 **rend:** rent
5.1.32 **fear:** feare?
5.3.40 **Cure her:** Cure   56 **senna:** Cyme   61 S.D.: [after 63]
5.4.3 **[and elsewhere] S.P. SIWARD:** *Syew.* [sometimes "*Syw.*" and "*Sey.*"]   7 S.P. **A SOLDIER:** *Sold.*
5.5.7 S.D.: [after 7]
5.7.31 S.D. **Alarums:** *Alarum*
5.8 **[not in F]**   5.8.8 S.D. **Alarums.:** *Alarum*   75 S.D.: **all** *Omnes*

The Text of
MACBETH

Dramatis Personae

WITCHES, the three Weïrd sisters and three other witches
HECATE, goddess of the moon and sorcery
APPARITIONS: an armed Head, a bloody Child, a Child crowned,
    a show of eight kings
MACBETH, Thane of Glamis, later Thane of Cawdor, later King
    of Scotland
LADY MACBETH, later Queen of Scotland
KING, Duncan, King of Scotland
MALCOLM, his son, later Prince of Cumberland
DONALDBAIN, another son
BANQUO, a thane of Scotland
FLEANCE, his son
MACDUFF, Thane of Fife
WIFE, Lady Macduff
SON, child of Macduff and Lady Macduff
LENNOX ⎫
ROSS ⎪
MENTEITH ⎬ Scottish thanes
ANGUS ⎪
CAITHNESS ⎭
SEYTON, an officer attending Macbeth
English DOCTOR
Scottish DOCTOR
GENTLEWOMAN, servant of Lady Macbeth
CAPTAIN
MURDERERS
PORTER
OLD MAN
SIWARD, English Earl of Northumberland
YOUNG SIWARD, his son
        Lords, Gentlemen, Soldiers, Officers,
        Soldiers, Attendants, Messengers, a Sewer

3

The Tragedy of Macbeth

1.1 [*Outdoors.*]

Thunder and lightning. Enter three WITCHES.

FIRST WITCH   When shall we three meet again?
  In thunder, lightning, or in rain?
SECOND WITCH   When the hurly-burly's done,
  When the battle's lost and won.
THIRD WITCH   That will be ere the set of sun.   5
FIRST WITCH   Where the place?
SECOND WITCH   Upon the heath.
THIRD WITCH   There to meet with Macbeth.
FIRST WITCH   I come, Grimalkin!
ALL   Paddock calls anon!   10
  Fair is foul, and foul is fair,
  Hover through the fog and filthy air.   *Exeunt.*

[handwritten margin note: Sets tone for entire play, fair = good, Foul = bad]

1.2 [*A camp.*]

Alarum within. Enter KING [*Duncan*], MALCOLM, DONALDBAIN,
LENNOX, *with* ATTENDANTS, *meeting a bleeding* CAPTAIN.

KING   What bloody man is that? He can report,
  As seemeth by his plight, of the revolt
  The newest state.
MALCOLM   This is the sergeant
  Who like a good and hardy soldier fought
  'Gainst my captivity.—Hail, brave friend!   5
  Say to the King the knowledge of the broil

---

3. **hurly-burly:** commotion.
7. **heath:** open, uncultivated ground with low shrubs.
9. **Grimalkin:** gray cat, the name of the witch's familiar (attendant spirit).
10. **s.p. All:** Editors have usually and unnecessarily made this line a dialogue between the Second and Third Witch; **Paddock:** toad, another familiar (spirit); **anon:** at once.
1.2 **s.d. Alarum:** a call to arms by a trumpet or other instrument; **within:** behind the back wall of the stage.
3. **sergeant:** a military officer; the rank is probably "captain," as indicated by the stage direction and speech prefixes.
6. **broil:** battle.

As thou didst leave it.
CAPTAIN　　　　　　　　Doubtful it stood,
As two spent swimmers that do cling together
And choke their art. The merciless Macdonwald—
Worthy to be a rebel, for to that　　　　　　　　　　10
The multiplying villainies of nature
Do swarm upon him—from the Western Isles
Of kerns and galloglasses is supplied;
And Fortune, on his damnèd quarrel smiling,
Showed like a rebel's whore. But all's too weak;　　15
For brave Macbeth—well he deserves that name—
Disdaining Fortune, with his brandished steel
Which smoked with bloody execution,
Like valor's minion carved out his passage
Till he faced the slave,　　　　　　　　　　　　　20
Which nev'r shook hands, nor bade farewell to him,
Till he unseamed him from the nave to th' chops,
And fixed his head upon our battlements.
KING　O valiant cousin, worthy gentleman!
CAPTAIN　As whence the sun 'gins his reflection,　　25
Shipwrecking storms and direful thunders,
So from that spring whence comfort seemed to come,
Discomfort swells. Mark, King of Scotland, mark:
No sooner justice had, with valor armed,
Compelled these skipping kerns to trust their heels,　30
But the Norweyan lord, surveying vantage,
With furbished arms and new supplies of men
Began a fresh assault.
KING　Dismayed not this our captains, Macbeth and Banquo?
CAPTAIN　Yes, as sparrows eagles, or the hare the lion.　　35

Handwritten margin notes: "Describes Macbeth + action" / "says he is brave"

8. **spent:** exhausted.
9. **choke their art:** make impossible the art of swimming.
10. **that:** that end.
11. **multiplying . . . nature:** ever-increasing numbers of villainous rebels.
12. **Western Isles:** the Hebrides and, perhaps, Ireland.
13. **kerns:** light-armed foot soldiers; **galloglasses:** soldiers armed with axes.
15. **rebel's whore:** Fortune was proverbially a strumpet.
19. **minion:** darling, favorite.
20. **slave:** Macdonwald.
21. **Which:** who.
22. Till he split him open from the navel to the jaws.
24. **cousin:** a general term of affection, here indicating a specific familial relation (see 1.7.13).
25. **whence:** from which place; **'gins his reflection:** begins its turning back across the sky.
26. **thunders:** If the verb **come** (line 27) is understood at the end of the line, there is no need to add "break" or some such word, as some editors do.
31. **surveying vantage:** seeing an advantage.
32. **furbished:** scoured, polished.

If I say sooth, I must report they were
As cannons overcharged with double cracks;
So they doubly redoubled strokes upon the foe.
Except they meant to bathe in reeking wounds,
Or memorize another Golgotha,　　　　　　　　　　40
I cannot tell—
But I am faint. My gashes cry for help.
KING　So well thy words become thee as thy wounds;
They smack of honor both.—Go get him surgeons.

　　　　　　　　　　　　　　　[*Exit Captain, attended.*]

　　　　　　　　　　　　　　Enter ROSS *and* ANGUS.

Who comes here?
MALCOLM　　　　　　The worthy Thane of Ross.　　　45
LENNOX　What a haste looks through his eyes!
So should he look that seems to speak things strange.
ROSS　God save the King!
KING　Whence cam'st thou, worthy thane?
ROSS　　　　　　　　　　　　From Fife, great King,
Where the Norweyan banners flout the sky　　　　50
And fan our people cold.
Norway himself, with terrible numbers,
Assisted by that most disloyal traitor,
The Thane of Cawdor, began a dismal conflict,
Till that Bellona's bridegroom, lapped in proof,　　55
Confronted him with self-comparisons,
Point against point, rebellious arm 'gainst arm,
Curbing his lavish spirit. And to conclude,
The victory fell on us—
KING　　　　　　　　Great happiness!—
ROSS　　　　　　　　　　　　That now Sweno,

36. **sooth:** truth.
37. **cracks:** explosives.
39. **Except:** unless.
40. **memorize another Golgotha:** make the battle as memorable as the biblical Golgotha ("the place of the skull"), where Christ was crucified (Mark 15:22).
45. **Thane:** landowner and chief of a clan, equivalent to an English earl.
46. **looks through:** is visible through.
47. **seems to:** seems about to.
49. **Fife:** county on the east coast of Scotland.
50. **flout:** mock.
52. **Norway:** the king of Norway.
54. **dismal:** ominous.
55. **Bellona:** Roman goddess of war; **lapped in proof:** (1) wearing proven armor; (2) wrapped in experience.
56. **self-comparisons:** powers comparable to his own.
58. **lavish:** wild, unrestrained.

The Norways' king, craves composition.   60
Nor would we deign him burial of his men
Till he disbursèd at Saint Colme's Inch
Ten thousand dollars to our general use.
KING   No more that Thane of Cawdor shall deceive
Our bosom interest. Go pronounce his present death,   65
And with his former title greet Macbeth.
ROSS   I'll see it done.
KING   What he hath lost noble Macbeth hath won.   *Exeunt.*

1.3 [*A heath.*]

Thunder. Enter the three WITCHES.

FIRST WITCH   Where hast thou been, sister?
SECOND WITCH   Killing swine.
THIRD WITCH   Sister, where thou?
FIRST WITCH   A sailor's wife had chestnuts in her lap,
And munched, and munched, and munched.   5
"Give me," quoth I.
"Aroint thee, witch!" the rump-fed runnion cries.
Her husband's to Aleppo gone, master o'th' *Tiger*,
But in a sieve I'll thither sail,
And like a rat without a tail,   10
I'll do, I'll do, and I'll do.
SECOND WITCH   I'll give thee a wind.
FIRST WITCH   Thou'rt kind.
THIRD WITCH   And I, another.
FIRST WITCH   I myself have all the other,
And the very ports they blow,   15
All the quarters that they know
I'th'shipman's card.

60. **Norways':** Norwegians'; **composition:** agreement, peace treaty.
61. **deign:** grant.
62. **Saint Colme's Inch:** Inchcolm, an isle near Edinburgh. **Colme's** is disyllabic, derived from St. Columba (521–597), who preached, worked miracles, and converted the Northern Picts to Christianity (see 2.4.34n.).
63. **dollars:** silver coins, probably German *thalers,* used throughout Europe.
65. **bosom interest:** heart's trust; **present:** immediate.
7. **Aroint:** be gone; **rump-fed:** (1) fed on rump meat; (2) fat-rumped; **runnion:** woman.
8. **Aleppo:** trading city in Northern Syria, part of the Turkish empire; **Tiger:** name of a ship.
9. **sieve:** Witches were commonly thought to sail in sieves.
10. **rat . . . tail:** Transformed witches sometimes had bodily defects.
11. **do:** (1) act; (2) have sexual intercourse.
16. And I control the ports where the winds blow.
17. **quarters:** directions.
18. **shipman's card:** nautical map.

I'll drain him dry as hay.
Sleep shall neither night nor day   20
Hang upon his penthouse lid;
He shall live a man forbid.
Weary sev'nnights nine times nine
Shall he dwindle, peak, and pine.
Though his bark cannot be lost,   25
Yet it shall be tempest-tossed.
Look what I have.
SECOND WITCH   Show me, show me.
FIRST WITCH   Here I have a pilot's thumb,
Wrecked as homeward he did come.   *Drum within.* 30
THIRD WITCH   A drum, a drum!
Macbeth doth come!
ALL [*Dancing in a circle*]   The Weïrd Sisters, hand in hand,
Posters of the sea and land,
Thus do go, about, about,   35
Thrice to thine, and thrice to mine,
And thrice again, to make up nine.
Peace, the charm's wound up.

Casts a spell

                    Enter MACBETH *and* BANQUO.

MACBETH   So foul and fair a day I have not seen.
BANQUO   How far is't called to Forres? What are these,   40
So withered and so wild in their attire,
That look not like th'inhabitants o'th'earth,
And yet are on't?—Live you? Or are you aught
That man may question? You seem to understand me,
By each at once her choppy finger laying   45
Upon her skinny lips. You should be women,
And yet your beards forbid me to interpret
That you are so.
MACBETH   Speak, if you can. What are you?

19. By sexual intercourse, presumably, as a succubus (demon in female form).
21. **penthouse lid:** eyelid.
22. **forbid:** cursed.
23. **sev'nnights:** weeks.
24. **peak:** waste away.
25. **bark:** ship.
30. **S.D. Drum:** a signal for the entrance of military characters.
33. **Weïrd:** fateful (from **wyrd**, "fate"), pronounced disyllabically, with a suggestion of the uncanny. Audiences might have heard "wayward" too, which appears elsewhere in the play (3.5.11).
34. **Posters of:** travelers over.
40. **Is't called:** is it said to be; **Forres:** Scottish town.
43. **aught:** anything.
45. **choppy:** chapped.

FIRST WITCH   All hail, Macbeth! Hail to thee, Thane of Glamis!
SECOND WITCH   All hail, Macbeth! Hail to thee, Thane of
  Cawdor!   50
THIRD WITCH   All hail, Macbeth, that shalt be king hereafter!
BANQUO   Good sir, why do you start and seem to fear
  Things that do sound so fair?—I'th'name of truth,
  Are ye fantastical or that indeed
  Which outwardly ye show? My noble partner   55
  You greet with present grace and great prediction
  Of noble having and of royal hope
  That he seems rapt withal. To me you speak not.
  If you can look into the seeds of time,
  ✗And say which grain will grow and which will not,✗   60
  Speak then to me, who neither beg nor fear
  Your favors nor your hate.
FIRST WITCH   Hail!
SECOND WITCH   Hail!
THIRD WITCH   Hail!   65
FIRST WITCH   Lesser than Macbeth, and greater.
SECOND WITCH   Not so happy, yet much happier.
THIRD WITCH   Thou shalt get kings, though thou be none.
  So all hail, Macbeth and Banquo!
FIRST WITCH   Banquo and Macbeth, all hail!   70
MACBETH   Stay, you imperfect speakers, tell me more.
  By Finel's death I know I am Thane of Glamis,
  But how of Cawdor? The Thane of Cawdor lives,
  A prosperous gentleman, and to be king
  Stands not within the prospect of belief,   75
  No more than to be Cawdor. Say from whence
  You owe this strange intelligence, or why
  Upon this blasted heath you stop our way
  With such prophetic greeting. Speak, I charge you.
                                              Witches vanish.
BANQUO   The earth hath bubbles, as the water has,   80

---

  49. All hail: Shakespeare identified this phrase with Judas's betrayal of Jesus (Matthew
26:49) in 3 *Henry VI* (5.7.33–4) and *Richard II* (4.1.169–71).
  52. start: flinch, recoil.
  54. fantastical: creatures of fantasy.
  58. rapt: carried away; **withal:** with it.
  68. get: beget.
  71. imperfect: unfinished.
  72. Finel: Macbeth's father.
  73–74. An apparent contradiction (explicable as an oversight or an incomplete revision)
to 1.2.54–58, which describes Macbeth's victory over Cawdor.
  75. prospect: consideration, possibility.
  77. owe: own; **intelligence:** news.
  78. blasted: blighted, often by a supernatural agent.
  79. s.D. vanish: probably by use of the trap door or smoke from burning resin.

And these are of them. Whither are they vanished?
MACBETH   Into the air. And what seemed corporal
    Melted as breath into the wind. Would they had stayed.
BANQUO   Were such things here as we do speak about?
    Or have we eaten on the insane root   85
    That takes the reason prisoner?
MACBETH   Your children shall be kings.
BANQUO   You shall be king.
MACBETH   And Thane of Cawdor too. Went it not so?
BANQUO   To the selfsame tune and words—Who's here?

                                    Enter ROSS *and* ANGUS.

ROSS   The King hath happily received, Macbeth,   90
    The news of thy success; and when he reads
    Thy personal venture in the rebels' fight,
    His wonders and his praises do contend
    Which should be thine or his. Silenced with that,
    In viewing o'er the rest o'the selfsame day,   95
    He finds thee in the stout Norweyan ranks,
    Nothing afeard of what thyself didst make,
    Strange images of death. As thick as hail
    Came post with post, and every one did bear
    Thy praises in his kingdom's great defense,   100
    And poured them down before him.
ANGUS   We are sent
    To give thee from our royal master thanks,
    Only to herald thee into his sight,
    Not pay thee.
ROSS   And for an earnest of a greater honor,   105
    He bade me, from him, call thee Thane of Cawdor;
    In which addition, hail, most worthy thane,
    For it is thine.
BANQUO   What, can the devil speak true?
MACBETH   The Thane of Cawdor lives. Why do you dress me
    In borrowed robes?
ANGUS   Who was the thane lives yet,   110

---

85. **insane root:** plant causing insanity.
91. **reads:** considers.
92. **fight:** Editors often emend to "sight."
93–94. **His . . . his:** His astonishment strikes him into awed silence and simultaneously incites his praise of you.
97. Not afraid of what you yourself created.
98. **hail:** Some defend Folio's "Tale," but **thick as hail** is proverbial (Dent H11, see Selected Bibliography) and occurs often in the drama.
99. **post with post:** messenger after messenger.
103. **herald:** usher.
105. **earnest:** token payment.
107. **addition:** title.

But under heavy judgment bears that life
Which he deserves to lose.
Whether he was combined with those of Norway,
Or did line the rebel with hidden help
And vantage, or that with both he labored   115
In his country's wrack, I know not.
But treasons capital, confessed and proved,
Have overthrown him.
MACBETH [*Aside*]   Glamis, and Thane of Cawdor!
The greatest is behind.—Thanks for your pains.
[*Aside to Banquo*] Do you not hope your children shall be
    kings,   120
When those that gave the Thane of Cawdor to me
Promised no less to them?
BANQUO [*Aside to Macbeth*]   That trusted home
Might yet enkindle you unto the crown,
Besides the Thane of Cawdor. But 'tis strange;
And oftentimes to win us to our harm,   125
The instruments of darkness tell us truths,
Win us with honest trifles, to betray's
In deepest consequence.—
Cousins, a word, I pray you.
                    [*He converses apart with Ross and Angus.*]
MACBETH [*Aside*]   Two truths are told,   130
As happy prologues to the swelling act
Of th'imperial theme.—I thank you, gentlemen.
[*Aside*] This supernatural soliciting
Cannot be ill, cannot be good. If ill,
Why hath it given me earnest of success   135
Commencing in a truth? I am Thane of Cawdor.
If good, why do I yield to that suggestion
Whose horrid image doth unfix my hair,
And make my seated heart knock at my ribs
Against the use of nature? Present fears   140
Are less than horrible imaginings.
My thought, whose murder yet is but fantastical,

114. **line the rebel:** strengthen Macdonwald.
116. **wrack:** ruin.
117. **capital:** punishable by death.
119. **behind:** still to come.
122. **home:** all the way.
126. **darkness:** evil, especially demonic.
129. **Cousins:** fellow lords.
131. **swelling act:** developing drama.
133. **soliciting:** urging.
138. **horrid:** bristling (like Macbeth's hair); **unfix:** make stand.
140. **use:** custom.
142. **whose:** in which; **fantastical:** imaginary.

Shakes so my single state of man
That function is smothered in surmise,
And nothing is but what is not.   145
BANQUO   Look how our partner's rapt.
MACBETH [*Aside*]   If chance will have me king, why, chance
   may crown me,
Without my stir.
BANQUO   New honors come upon him,
   Like our strange garments, cleave not to their mold
   But with the aid of use.
MACBETH [*Aside*]   Come what come may,   150
   Time and the hour runs through the roughest day.
BANQUO   Worthy Macbeth, we stay upon your leisure.
MACBETH   Give me your favor. My dull brain was wrought
   With things forgotten. Kind gentlemen, your pains
   Are registered where every day I turn   155
   The leaf to read them. Let us toward the King.
   [*Aside to Banquo*] Think upon what hath chanced, and at
   more time,
   The interim having weighed it, let us speak
   Our free hearts each to other.
BANQUO [*Aside to Macbeth*]   Very gladly.
MACBETH [*Aside to Banquo*]   Till then, enough.—Come, friends. 160
                                                Exeunt.

1.4 [*The King's camp or palace.*]

Flourish. Enter KING, LENNOX, MALCOLM, DONALDBAIN, *and*
ATTENDANTS.

KING   Is execution done on Cawdor?
   Or not those in commission yet returned?

143. **single . . . man:** weak human condition.
144. **function:** ability to act; **surmise:** speculation.
145. Nothing exists in the present but thoughts about the future.
146. **rapt:** entranced.
148. **stir:** stirring, effort; **come:** having come.
149. **cleave . . . mold:** do not fit the body's form.
150. **Come . . . may:** Let whatever will happen happen, a proverbial expression (Dent
C529, see Selected Bibliography).
151. Even the roughest days come to an end.
152. **stay:** wait.
153. **favor:** goodwill.
155. **registered:** recorded (in my memory).
156. **leaf:** page.
158. **The . . . it:** having considered the matter in the meantime.
1.4 S.D. **Flourish:** a trumpet signal indicating the entrance or exit of royal authority.
Flourishes honor King Duncan and later King Malcolm (5.8.34 S.D.) but never the usurper
Macbeth.
2. **Or not:** or are not; **in commission:** commissioned (to execute Cawdor).

MALCOLM   My liege,
They are not yet come back. But I have spoke
With one that saw him die, who did report   5
That very frankly he confessed his treasons,
Implored Your Highness' pardon, and set forth
A deep repentance. Nothing in his life
Became him like the leaving it. He died
As one that had been studied in his death   10
To throw away the dearest thing he owed,
As 'twere a careless trifle.
KING   There's no art
To find the mind's construction in the face.
He was a gentleman on whom I built
An absolute trust.

                    Enter MACBETH, BANQUO, ROSS, *and* ANGUS.

[*To Macbeth*]   O worthiest cousin!   15
The sin of my ingratitude even now
Was heavy on me. Thou art so far before,
That swiftest wing of recompense is slow
To overtake thee. Would thou hadst less deserved,
That the proportion both of thanks and payment   20
Might have been mine! Only I have left to say,
More is thy due than more than all can pay.
MACBETH   The service and the loyalty I owe,
In doing it, pays itself. Your Highness' part
Is to receive our duties; and our duties   25
Are to your throne and state children and servants,
Which do but what they should by doing everything
Safe toward your love and honor.
KING   Welcome hither.
I have begun to plant thee, and will labor
To make thee full of growing. Noble Banquo,   30
That hast no less deserved, nor must be known
No less to have done so, let me enfold thee,
And hold thee to my heart.

3. **liege:** superior to whom one owes service.
9. **Became:** graced, befitted.
10. **studied:** prepared by study.
11. **owed:** owned.
12. **a careless:** an uncared-for.
17. **before:** ahead (in time and in deserving).
20. **proportion:** just and satisfactory reckoning.
24. **it:** my duty.
25–26. **and . . . servants:** We owe duty to your throne and high rank just as children owe
duty to their parents, and servants to their masters.
28. **Safe toward:** to make safe.
29. **plant:** nurture.
32. **enfold:** embrace.

BANQUO   There if I grow,
  The harvest is your own.
KING   My plenteous joys,
  Wanton in fullness, seek to hide themselves   35
  In drops of sorrow.—Sons, kinsmen, thanes,
  And you whose places are the nearest, know
  We will establish our estate upon
  Our eldest, Malcolm, whom we name hereafter
  The Prince of Cumberland; which honor must   40
  Not unaccompanied invest him only,
  But signs of nobleness, like stars, shall shine
  On all deservers. [*To Macbeth*] From hence to Inverness,
  And bind us further to you.
MACBETH   The rest is labor which is not used for you.   45
  I'll be myself the harbinger and make joyful
  The hearing of my wife with your approach.
  So humbly take my leave.
KING   My worthy Cawdor.
MACBETH [*Aside*]   The Prince of Cumberland! That is a step
  On which I must fall down, or else o'erleap,   50
  For in my way it lies. Stars, hide your fires;
  Let not light see my black and deep desires.
  The eye wink at the hand; yet let that be
  Which the eye fears, when it is done, to see.   *Exit.*
KING   True, worthy Banquo, he is full so valiant,   55
  And in his commendations I am fed;
  It is a banquet to me. Let's after him,
  Whose care is gone before to bid us welcome.
  It is a peerless kinsman.   *Flourish. Exeunt.*

1.5. [*Inverness. Macbeth's castle.*]

Enter Macbeth's Wife [LADY MACBETH], *alone, with a letter.*

LADY MACBETH [*Reads*]   "They met me in the day of success, and
  I have learned by the perfect'st report they have more in them

---

35. **Wanton:** profuse.
38. **establish . . . upon:** name as heir to the throne.
40. **Prince of Cumberland:** an honorific title designating the next king.
41. **Not unaccompanied invest:** not alone adorn.
43. **Inverness:** the location of Macbeth's castle.
45. **rest:** repose.
46. **harbinger:** forerunner.
53. **The . . . hand:** Let the eye see not what the hand does.
55. **full so valiant:** fully as valiant (as you say).
56. **his commendations:** the praises of him.
2. **perfect'st report:** most reliable evidence.

than mortal knowledge. When I burnt in desire to question
them further, they made themselves air, into which they
vanished. Whiles I stood rapt in the wonder of it came missives   5
from the King, who all-hailed me 'Thane of Cawdor,' by which
title before these Weïrd Sisters saluted me, and referred me to
the coming on of time with 'Hail, king that shalt be!' This have
I thought good to deliver thee, my dearest partner of greatness,
that thou mightst not lose the dues of rejoicing by being   10
ignorant of what greatness is promised thee. Lay it to thy heart,
and farewell."
Glamis thou art, and Cawdor, and shalt be
What thou art promised. Yet do I fear thy nature;
It is too full o'th'milk of human kindness   15
To catch the nearest way. Thou wouldst be great,
Art not without ambition, but without
The illness should attend it. What thou wouldst highly,
That wouldst thou holily; wouldst not play false,
And yet wouldst wrongly win. Thou'dst have, great Glamis,   20
That which cries "Thus thou must do," if thou have it,
And that which rather thou dost fear to do
Than wishest should be undone. Hie thee hither,
That I may pour my spirits in thine ear,
And chastise with the valor of my tongue   25
All that impedes thee from the golden round,
Which fate and metaphysical aid doth seem
To have thee crowned withal.

                                    Enter MESSENGER.

                   What is your tidings?
MESSENGER   The King comes here tonight.
LADY MACBETH   Thou'rt mad to say it!
Is not thy master with him, who, were't so,   30
Would have informed for preparation?

---

5. **missives:** messengers.
6. **all-hailed:** greeted.
10. **dues:** due measure.
15. **milk . . . kindness:** compassion natural to humankind.
18. **illness:** evil that; **wouldst highly:** would have or do greatly.
20–21. **Thou'dst . . . it:** You must have, great Glamis, a voice that cries "Thus you must do" (i.e., kill the King), if you would attain the crown.
22–23. **And . . . undone:** And you would rather have Duncan dead (even though you fear killing him) than wish him alive again after he is gone.
23. **Hie:** hurry.
24. **spirits:** supernatural assistants to evil (see lines 38ff.).
26. **round:** crown.
27. **metaphysical:** supernatural.
28. **withal:** with.
31. **informed for preparation:** sent us word so that we could prepare for the visit.

MESSENGER   So please you, it is true. Our thane is coming.
   One of my fellows had the speed of him,
   Who, almost dead for breath, had scarcely more
   Than would make up his message.
LADY MACBETH   Give him tending;   35
   He brings great news.   *Exit Messenger.*
                          The raven himself is hoarse
That croaks the fatal entrance of Duncan
Under my battlements. Come, you spirits
That tend on mortal thoughts, unsex me here,
And fill me from the crown to the toe top-full   40
Of direst cruelty! Make thick my blood;
Stop up th'access and passage to remorse,
That no compunctious visitings of nature
Shake my fell purpose, nor keep peace between
Th'effect and it. Come to my woman's breasts   45
And take my milk for gall, you murd'ring ministers,
Wherever in your sightless substances
You wait on nature's mischief. Come, thick night,
And pall thee in the dunnest smoke of hell,
That my keen knife see not the wound it makes,   50
Nor heaven peep through the blanket of the dark,
To cry "Hold, hold!"

                                    Enter MACBETH.

            Great Glamis, worthy Cawdor,
   Greater than both by the all-hail hereafter!
   Thy letters have transported me beyond
   This ignorant present, and I feel now   55
   The future in the instant.
MACBETH   My dearest love,
   Duncan comes here tonight.
LADY MACBETH   And when goes hence?
MACBETH   Tomorrow, as he purposes.

---

33. had . . . him: traveled more quickly than he.
36. raven: a bird of evil portent.
37. fatal: (1) directed by fate; (2) deadly to Duncan.
39. mortal: (1) human; (2) murderous.
41. Make . . . blood: Thickened blood supposedly blocked the operation of emotions such as pity and fear.
43. compunctious visitings: feelings of compassion or guilt.
44. fell: cruel; keep peace: intervene.
46. take . . . gall: (1) replace my milk with gall, i.e., bile, associated with envy and hatred; (2) take evil from my breasts by nursing at them.
47. sightless: invisible.
48. wait on: attend, aid.
49. pall: cover (as with a funeral cloth); dunnest: darkest.
53. all-hail hereafter: the future in which everyone will salute you as king.

LADY MACBETH   Oh, never
Shall sun that morrow see!
Your face, my thane, is as a book where men   60
May read strange matters. To beguile the time,
Look like the time; bear welcome in your eye,
Your hand, your tongue. Look like th'innocent flower,
But be the serpent under't. He that's coming
Must be provided for. And you shall put   65
This night's great business into my dispatch,
Which shall to all our nights and days to come
Give solely sovereign sway and masterdom.
MACBETH   We will speak further.
LADY MACBETH   Only look up clear.
To alter favor ever is to fear.   70
Leave all the rest to me.   *Exeunt.*

1.6 [*Before Macbeth's castle.*]

Hautboys and torches. Enter KING, MALCOLM, DONALDBAIN,
BANQUO, LENNOX, MACDUFF, ROSS, ANGUS, *and* ATTENDANTS.

KING   This castle hath a pleasant seat.
The air nimbly and sweetly recommends itself
Unto our gentle senses.
BANQUO   This guest of summer,
The temple-haunting martlet, does approve
By his loved mansionry that the heavens' breath   5
Smells wooingly here. No jutty, frieze,
Buttress, nor coign of vantage, but this bird
Hath made his pendent bed and procreant cradle.
Where they must breed and haunt, I have observed,
The air is delicate.

61. **beguile the time:** deceive observers.
62. **Look . . . time:** Act the way people expect you to act.
65. **provided for:** prepared for (with sinister implication).
66. **dispatch:** management.
69. **look up clear:** look calm.
70. To change expression (**favor**) is always to show fear.
1.6 S.D. **Hautboys:** woodwind instruments, ancestors of the softer-toned oboe.
1. **seat:** site.
4. **martlet:** name used for a number of birds especially the swallow and house-martin;
approve: confirm.
5. **loved mansionry:** beloved nest building.
6. **jutty:** projection (from a building); **frieze:** painted or carved band above or at the top
of a wall.
7. **coign of vantage:** a projecting corner, affording a good observation point.
8. **pendent:** hanging.

Enter LADY MACBETH.

KING   See, see, our honored hostess!—   10
The love that follows us sometime is our trouble,
Which still we thank as love. Herein I teach you
How you shall bid God 'ield us for your pains,
And thank us for your trouble.

LADY MACBETH   All our service
In every point twice done, and then done double,   15
Were poor and single business to contend
Against those honors deep and broad wherewith
Your Majesty loads our house. For those of old,
And the late dignities heaped up to them,
We rest your hermits.

KING   Where's the Thane of Cawdor?   20
We coursed him at the heels, and had a purpose
To be his purveyor. But he rides well,
And his great love, sharp as his spur, hath holp him
To his home before us. Fair and noble hostess,
We are your guest tonight.

LADY MACBETH   Your servants ever   25
Have theirs themselves, and what is theirs in count
To make their audit at Your Highness' pleasure,
Still to return your own.

KING   Give me your hand;
Conduct me to mine host. We love him highly,
And shall continue our graces towards him.   30
By your leave, hostess.   *Exeunt.*

11–12. **The love . . . love:** The attentions of others can sometimes be a nuisance, but we still appreciate the love that motivates them.
13. **bid . . . pains:** ask God to reward me (**God 'ield us**) for putting you to trouble (because my visit is similarly motivated by love).
16. **single:** slight; **business:** exertion ("busy-ness").
16–17. **contend Against:** match, vie with.
19. **late:** recent.
20. **rest your hermits:** remain faithful petitioners to God for you, just like the hermits, i.e., beadsmen, who offered prayers for benefactors.
21. **coursed:** pursued.
22. **purveyor:** domestic officer who preceded the King or other great personages and arranged for lodging and supplies.
23. **holp:** helped.
26. **Have theirs:** have their servants; **what is theirs:** whatever they own; **count:** trust (from the King).
27. **make their audit:** render an account.
28. **Still:** always.

1.7 [*Inverness. Macbeth's castle.*]

Hautboys. Torches. Enter a SEWER, *and divers* SERVANTS *with dishes and service, [and pass] over the stage.*

Then enter MACBETH.

MACBETH   If it were done when 'tis done, then 'twere well
It were done quickly. If th'assassination
Could trammel up the consequence and catch
With his surcease success—that but this blow
Might be the be-all and the end-all!—here,   5
But here, upon this bank and shoal of time,
We'd jump the life to come. But in these cases
We still have judgment here, that we but teach
Bloody instructions, which, being taught, return
To plague th'inventor. This even-handed Justice   10
Commends th'ingredience of our poisoned chalice
To our own lips. He's here in double trust:
First, as I am his kinsman and his subject,
Strong both against the deed; then, as his host,
Who should against his murderer shut the door,   15
Not bear the knife myself. Besides, this Duncan
Hath borne his faculties so meek, hath been
So clear in his great office, that his virtues
Will plead like angels, trumpet-tongued, against
The deep damnation of his taking-off;   20
And Pity, like a naked new-born babe
Striding the blast, or heaven's cherubin, horsed
Upon the sightless couriers of the air,
Shall blow the horrid deed in every eye,
That tears shall drown the wind. I have no spur   25

1.7 S.D. **Sewer:** chief waiter; **service:** a meal and the accompanying equipment.
1–2. **If . . . quickly:** If the whole business of murder could end with the killing itself, then it would be good to kill the King quickly.
3. **trammel . . . consequence:** catch (as in a net) the consequences.
4. **his surcease:** (1) Duncan's death; (2) the cessation of consequence; **success:** (1) whatever follows; (2) a favorable outcome; (3) succession of heirs.
4. **that but:** if only.
6. **bank and shoal:** riverbank or sandbank and shallows.
7. **jump:** risk.
8. **judgment:** punishment; **that:** in that.
11. **ingredience:** contents of a mixture; **chalice:** drinking goblet, also used for the celebration of the Eucharist.
17. **faculties:** powers.
18. **clear:** blameless.
20. **taking-off:** murder.
22. **Striding the blast:** riding the wind; **cherubin:** an order of angels, sometimes represented as babies, sometimes as huge winged creatures (Ezekiel 10, Psalms 18).
23. **sightless couriers:** invisible messengers, i.e., the winds.
25. **That . . . wind:** so that the resulting tears, thick as rain, shall still the wind.

To prick the sides of my intent, but only
Vaulting Ambition, which o'erleaps itself
And falls on th'other—

Enter LADY MACBETH.

                    How now? What news?
LADY MACBETH   He has almost supped. Why have you left the
    chamber?
MACBETH   Hath he asked for me?
LADY MACBETH   Know you not he has?   30
MACBETH   We will proceed no further in this business.
    He hath honored me of late, and I have bought
    Golden opinions from all sorts of people,
    Which would be worn now in their newest gloss,
    Not cast aside so soon.
LADY MACBETH   Was the hope drunk   35
    Wherein you dressed yourself? Hath it slept since?
    And wakes it now to look so green and pale
    At what it did so freely? From this time
    Such I account thy love. Art thou afeard
    To be the same in thine own act and valor   40
    As thou art in desire? Wouldst thou have that
    Which thou esteem'st the ornament of life,
    And live a coward in thine own esteem,
    Letting "I dare not" wait upon "I would,"
    Like the poor cat i'th'adage?
MACBETH   Prithee, peace!   45
    I dare do all that may become a man;
    Who dares do more is none.
LADY MACBETH   What beast was't, then,
    That made you break this enterprise to me?
    When you durst do it, then you were a man;
    And to be more than what you were, you would   50
    Be so much more the man. Nor time, nor place
    Did then adhere, and yet you would make both.

---

28. **other:** other side. Ambition overleaps and falls down on the other side of the horse;
How now: How is it now?
32. **bought:** acquired.
34. **gloss:** luster.
37. **green and pale:** sickly, as if hung over.
42. **ornament of life:** chief acquisition and good, i.e., the crown.
44. **wait upon:** attend.
45. **cat . . . adage:** The proverb, "The cat would eat fish but she will not wet her feet"
(Dent C144, see Selected Bibliography), exhorted the idle or timorous to action.
48. **break:** broach, disclose.
50. **to be:** if you were to be.
52. **adhere:** agree, suit.

They have made themselves, and that their fitness now
Does unmake you. I have given suck, and know
How tender 'tis to love the babe that milks me;   55
I would, while it was smiling in my face,
Have plucked my nipple from his boneless gums
And dashed the brains out, had I so sworn as you
Have done to this.

MACBETH   If we should fail?

LADY MACBETH   We fail?
But screw your courage to the sticking-place,   60
And we'll not fail. When Duncan is asleep—
Whereto the rather shall his day's hard journey
Soundly invite him—his two chamberlains
Will I with wine and wassail so convince
That memory, the warder of the brain,   65
Shall be a fume, and the receipt of reason
A limbeck only. When in swinish sleep
Their drenchèd natures lies as in a death,
What cannot you and I perform upon
Th'unguarded Duncan? What not put upon   70
His spongy officers, who shall bear the guilt
Of our great quell?

MACBETH   Bring forth men-children only,
For thy undaunted mettle should compose
Nothing but males. Will it not be received,
When we have marked with blood those sleepy two   75
Of his own chamber and used their very daggers,
That they have done't?

53. **that their fitness:** their very fitness.
58. **dashed . . . out:** Psalms 137:9, anticipating the destruction of Babylon, may have contributed to this horrific image: "Blessed shall he be that taketh and dasheth thy children against the stones."
59. **We fail?:** Folio's punctuation ("?") can represent a question mark or exclamation point, and the actress must here choose among various inflections and emotions (incredulity, resignation, scorn).
60. **But:** only; **sticking-place:** the notch or place that holds the string taut on a crossbow or a musical instrument.
62. **Whereto the rather:** to which all the sooner.
63. **Soundly invite him:** (1) properly induce him; (2) invite him to sleep deeply; **chamberlains:** bedroom servants.
64. **wine and wassail:** drink in abundance (a **wassail** is a drink and drinking toast); **convince:** conquer.
65. **warder:** guardian.
66. **fume:** vapor; **receipt of reason:** receptacle of reason.
67. **limbeck:** the cap of a distilling apparatus, the cup which receives the vapors. The elaborate chemical metaphor says that the vapors rising from drink will overpower the memory and take over the reason.
71. **spongy:** absorbent (having soaked up drink).
72. **quell:** murder.
73. **mettle:** spirit, courage. There is also a pun on "metal" and perhaps on "males / mails" (line 74), **mails** referring to armor.

LADY MACBETH   Who dares receive it other,
  As we shall make our griefs and clamor roar
  Upon his death?
MACBETH   I am settled, and bend up
  Each corporal agent to this terrible feat.   80
  Away, and mock the time with fairest show;
  False face must hide what the false heart doth know. *Exeunt.*

2.1 [*Courtyard of Macbeth's castle.*]

Enter BANQUO *and* FLEANCE, *with a torch before him.*

BANQUO How goes the night, boy?
FLEANCE The moon is down; I have not heard the clock.
BANQUO And she goes down at twelve.
FLEANCE   I take't 'tis later, sir.
BANQUO Hold, take my sword. [*He gives his sword.*]
                  There's husbandry in heaven;
  Their candles are all out. Take thee that too.   5
  A heavy summons lies like lead upon me,
  And yet I would not sleep. Merciful powers,
  Restrain in me the cursèd thoughts that nature
  Gives way to in repose.

           Enter MACBETH *and a* SERVANT *with a torch.*

  Give me my sword!—Who's there? [*He takes his sword.*]   10
MACBETH A friend.
BANQUO What, sir, not yet at rest? The King's abed.
  He hath been in unusual pleasure,
  And sent forth great largess to your offices.
  This diamond he greets your wife withal,   15
  By the name of most kind hostess, and shut up
  In measureless content. [*He gives a diamond.*]

---

77. **other:** otherwise.
80. **Each corporal agent:** every part of my body.
81. **mock:** delude.
2.1 S.D. **torch:** Some have interpreted this to mean a torch-bearer.
4. **husbandry:** good management, thrift.
5. **that:** perhaps a dagger.
6. **heavy summons:** urge to sleep.
7. **powers:** an order of angels that resists demons.
14. **largess . . . offices:** gifts to your household quarters.
15. **greets . . . withal:** salutes . . . with. He honors her with the diamond and with the
name (line 16).
16. **shut up:** (1) concluded (his remarks); (2) went to bed (amidst closed curtains).

MACBETH   Being unprepared,
  Our will became the servant to defect,
  Which else should free have wrought.
BANQUO   All's well.
  I dreamt last night of the three Weïrd Sisters.   20
  To you they have showed some truth.
MACBETH   I think not of them.
  Yet, when we can entreat an hour to serve,
  We would spend it in some words upon that business,
  If you would grant the time.
BANQUO   At your kind'st leisure.
MACBETH   If you shall cleave to my consent, when 'tis,   25
  It shall make honor for you.
BANQUO   So I lose none
  In seeking to augment it, but still keep
  My bosom franchised and allegiance clear,
  I shall be counseled.
MACBETH   Good repose the while.
BANQUO   Thanks, sir; the like to you.   30
                             Exit Banquo [with Fleance].
MACBETH   Go bid thy mistress, when my drink is ready,
  She strike upon the bell. Get thee to bed.   *Exit [Servant].*
  Is this a dagger which I see before me,
  The handle toward my hand? Come, let me clutch thee.
  I have thee not, and yet I see thee still!   35
  Art thou not, fatal vision, sensible
  To feeling as to sight? Or art thou but
  A dagger of the mind, a false creation,
  Proceeding from the heat-oppressèd brain?
  I see thee yet in form as palpable
  As this which now I draw. [*He draws a dagger.*]   40
  Thou marshal'st me the way that I was going,
  And such an instrument I was to use.
  Mine eyes are made the fools o'th'other senses,
  Or else worth all the rest. I see thee still,   45

[margin, handwritten: Famous Soliloquy]

18. **will:** good will (to entertain the King); **defect:** deficient means, caused by late notice
of the visit.
19. **free:** freely.
22. **entreat . . . serve:** find a suitable time.
25. **cleave . . . consent:** agree with my opinion, i.e., go along with me; **'tis:** (1) it is my
leisure; (2) it is achieved (and I am king).
26. **honor:** external honor, i.e., wealth and station. Banquo, however, understands the
term to mean internal honor, or virtue.
28. **franchised:** free (from guilt); **clear:** stainless.
36. **sensible:** perceptible.
42. **marshal'st:** lead.
44–45. **Mine . . . rest:** My eyes are reporting a delusion, unverifiable by the other senses,
or else my eyes alone perceive truly.

And on thy blade and dudgeon gouts of blood,
Which was not so before! There's no such thing.
It is the bloody business which informs
Thus to mine eyes. Now o'er the one half world
Nature seems dead, and wicked dreams abuse   50
The curtained sleep. Witchcraft celebrates
Pale Hecate's off'rings, and withered Murder,
Alarumed by his sentinel, the wolf,
Whose howl's his watch, thus with his stealthy pace,
With Tarquin's ravishing strides, towards his design   55
Moves like a ghost. Thou sure and firm-set earth,
Hear not my steps, which way they walk, for fear
Thy very stones prate of my whereabout,
And take the present horror from the time,
Which now suits with it. Whiles I threat, he lives;   60
Words to the heat of deeds too cold breath gives.
A bell rings. I go, and it is done. The bell invites me.
Hear it not, Duncan, for it is a knell
That summons thee to heaven or to hell.   *Exit.*

2.2 [*The same.*]

Enter LADY MACBETH.

LADY MACBETH   That which hath made them drunk hath made
   me bold;
What hath quenched them hath given me fire.
   [*An owl shrieks.*]   Hark! Peace!
It was the owl that shrieked, the fatal bellman
Which gives the stern'st good-night. He is about it.
The doors are open, and the surfeited grooms   5
Do mock their charge with snores. I have drugged their
   possets,

---

46. dudgeon: handle; **gouts:** drops.
48–49. informs Thus: shapes this fantasy.
50. abuse: deceive.
52. Pale Hecate's off'rings: deeds done by or sacrifices to Hecate, goddess of sorcery and the moon (thus **pale**).
53. Alarumed: signaled.
54. his watch: the murderer's watchman.
55. Tarquin: a Roman tyrant who raped Lucrece. Shakespeare dramatized the incident in a narrative poem, *The Rape of Lucrece.*
59–60. take . . . it: break the silence appropriate to the horror of the moment.
2. quenched. (1) satisfied their thirst; (2) rendered them unconscious.
3. owl: a bird of ill omen; **bellman:** night watchman.
5. grooms: servants.
6. charge: responsibility (to guard the King); **possets:** drinks made of hot milk, liquor, and spices.

That death and nature do contend about them
Whether they live or die.

Enter MACBETH [*with bloody daggers*].

MACBETH   Who's there? What ho!
LADY MACBETH [*To herself*]   Alack, I am afraid they have
   awaked,
And 'tis not done. Th'attempt and not the deed   10
Confounds us. Hark! I laid their daggers ready;
He could not miss 'em. Had he not resembled
My father as he slept, I had done't.—My husband?
MACBETH   I have done the deed. Didst thou not hear a noise?
LADY MACBETH   I heard the owl scream and the crickets cry.   15
   Did not you speak?
MACBETH   When?
LADY MACBETH   Now.
MACBETH   As I descended?
LADY MACBETH   Ay.   20
MACBETH   Hark, who lies i'the second chamber?
LADY MACBETH   Donaldbain.
MACBETH [*Looking at his hands*]   This is a sorry sight.
LADY MACBETH   A foolish thought, to say a sorry sight.
MACBETH   There's one did laugh in's sleep, and one cried
   "Murder!"
That they did wake each other. I stood and heard them.   25
But they did say their prayers, and addressed them
Again to sleep.
LADY MACBETH   There are two lodged together.
MACBETH   One cried "God bless us!" and "Amen!" the other,
As they had seen me with these hangman's hands.   30
List'ning their fear, I could not say "Amen"
When they did say "God bless us!"
LADY MACBETH   Consider it not so deeply.
MACBETH   But wherefore could not I pronounce "Amen"?
I had most need of blessing, and "Amen"   35
   Stuck in my throat.
LADY MACBETH   These deeds must not be thought

---

8. S.D. Editors usually have Macbeth speak the next line from within, or less frequently
from above in the gallery, and move this entrance to line 13. But the Folio reading has them
miss each other (visually and auditorily) in the dark while on stage, together but each alone.
   11. **Confounds:** defeats.
   13. **husband?:** possibly an exclamation.
   27. **addressed them:** settled themselves down.
   30. **hangman's hands:** executioner's hands, hence bloody from cutting up bodies before
or after death.

After these ways; so, it will make us mad
MACBETH   Methought I heard a voice cry "Sleep no more!
Macbeth does murder sleep," the innocent sleep,
Sleep that knits up the raveled sleeve of care,   40
The death of each day's life, sore labor's bath,
Balm of hurt minds, great nature's second course,
Chief nourisher in life's feast—
LADY MACBETH   What do you mean?
MACBETH   Still it cried "Sleep no more!" to all the house;
"Glamis hath murdered sleep, and therefore Cawdor   45
Shall sleep no more! Macbeth shall sleep no more!"
LADY MACBETH   Who was it that thus cried? Why, worthy
    thane,
You do unbend your noble strength to think
So brainsickly of things. Go get some water,
And wash this filthy witness from your hand.   50
Why did you bring these daggers from the place?
They must lie there. Go carry them and smear
The sleepy grooms with blood.
MACBETH   I'll go no more.
I am afraid to think what I have done.
Look on't again I dare not.
LADY MACBETH   Infirm of purpose!   55
Give me the daggers. The sleeping and the dead
Are but as pictures; 'tis the eye of childhood
That fears a painted devil. If he do bleed,
I'll gild the faces of the grooms withal,
For it must seem their guilt.   Exit [with the daggers].

                                              Knock within.

MACBETH   Whence is that knocking?   60
How is't with me, when every noise appalls me?
What hands are here? Ha, they pluck out mine eyes!
Will all great Neptune's ocean wash this blood
Clean from my hand? No, this my hand will rather

37. so: thinking so.
40. raveled sleeve: frayed sleeve (the part of a garment that covers the arm and wrist).
Some editors prefer "raveled sleave," i.e., a tangled filament or thread, indistinguishable in
sound but less likely in sense, given the idea of repair by knitting.
42. second course: the main course.
48. unbend: slacken (as one does a bow).
50. witness: evidence.
58. he: the King. Corpses of victims were thought to bleed in the presence of their
murderers.
59. gild: cover with gold, a synonym for red (see 2.3.109). Gild here sets up the pun on
guilt (line 60).
60. s.d. within: behind the stage façade (representing the outside of the castle).

The multitudinous seas incarnadine,   65
Making the green one red.

                              Enter LADY MACBETH.

LADY MACBETH   My hands are of your color but I shame
   To wear a heart so white. (*Knock*) I hear a knocking
   At the south entry. Retire we to our chamber.
   A little water clears us of this deed.   70
   How easy is it then. Your constancy
   Hath left you unattended. (*Knock*) Hark, more knocking.
   Get on your nightgown, lest occasion call us,
   And show us to be watchers. Be not lost
   So poorly in your thoughts.   75
MACBETH   To know my deed 'twere best not know myself.
   (*Knock*)
   Wake Duncan with thy knocking. I would thou couldst!

                                            Exeunt.

2.3 [*The same.*]

Enter a PORTER. *Knocking within*

PORTER   Here's a knocking indeed! If a man were porter of hell-
   gate, he should have old turning the key. (*Knock*) Knock,
   knock, knock. Who's there, i'the name of Beelzebub? Here's a
   farmer that hanged himself on th'expectation of plenty. Come
   in time! Have napkins enough about you; here you'll sweat for't.   5
   (*Knock*) Knock, knock. Who's there, in th'other devil's name?
   Faith, here's an equivocator that could swear in both the scales
   against either scale, who committed treason enough for God's
   sake, yet could not equivocate to heaven. Oh, come in,

---

65. **multitudinous:** many and vast; **incarnadine:** turn red.
66. **green one red:** green color of the oceans a pervasive red.
72. **left you unattended:** deserted you.
74. **watchers:** awake.
75. **poorly:** dejectedly.
76. If I fully admit to this crime, I can no longer be the person I was.
1–2. **hell-gate:** the door to hell, imagined as a castle.
2. **old:** frequent.
3. **Beelzebub:** the devil.
4. **farmer . . . plenty:** The porter introduces imaginary residents of hell, beginning with the farmer who, expecting plenty but (presumably) disappointed, hanged himself.
4–5. **Come in time:** You have come in good time.
5. **napkins:** handkerchiefs (to wipe away sweat).
7. **Faith:** in faith (a mild oath).
7. **equivocator:** one who uses deceitful language. Shakespeare alludes to the doctrine of equivocation, associated with Jesuits, including Henry Garnet, recently executed (1606) for alleged complicity in the Gunpowder Plot. In his *Treatise on Equivocation*, Garnet justifies various types of verbal deceit, including, for example, the telling of a partial truth (see pp. 159–60); **both the scales:** on either side (perhaps with an allusion to the scales of Justice).

equivocator. (*Knock*) Knock, knock, knock. Who's there? Faith, 10
here's an English tailor come hither for stealing out of a French
hose. Come in, tailor. Here you may roast your goose. (*Knock*)
Knock, knock. Never at quiet? What are you? But this place is
too cold for hell. I'll devil-porter it no further. I had thought to
have let in some of all professions that go the primrose way to 15
th'everlasting bonfire. (*Knock*) Anon, anon. (*He opens the
gate.*)—I pray you, remember the porter.

Enter MACDUFF *and* LENNOX.

MACDUFF   Was it so late, friend, ere you went to bed,
That you do lie so late?
PORTER   Faith, sir, we were carousing till the second cock, and 20
drink, sir, is a great provoker of three things.
MACDUFF   What three things does drink especially provoke?
PORTER   Marry, sir, nose-painting, sleep, and urine. Lechery, sir,
it provokes and unprovokes: it provokes the desire but it takes
away the performance. Therefore, much drink may be said to 25
be an equivocator with lechery: it makes him and it mars him;
it sets him on and it takes him off; it persuades him and
disheartens him, makes him stand to and not stand to, in
conclusion, equivocates him in a sleep and, giving him the lie,
leaves him. 30
MACDUFF   I believe drink gave thee the lie last night.
PORTER   That it did, sir, i'the very throat on me. But I requited
him for his lie and, I think, being too strong for him, though
he took up my legs sometime, yet I made a shift to cast him.
MACDUFF   Is thy master stirring? 35

Enter MACBETH.

Our knocking has awaked him. Here he comes. [*Exit Porter.*]
LENNOX   Good morrow, noble sir.
MACBETH   Good morrow, both.

11–12. **English . . . hose:** The tailor has probably skimped on the fabric when making
stylish French leggings or breeches.
12. **roast . . . goose:** (1) heat your tailor's smoothing iron; (2) cook a goose.
15–16. **primrose . . . bonfire:** the pleasant path to hell.
17. **remember:** tip.
20. **second cock:** 3:00 A.M., when the cock crowed for the second time.
23. **Marry:** a mild oath ("By the Virgin Mary," originally); **nose-painting:** nose-reddening
from excessive drink.
28. **stand to:** become erect.
29. **equivocates . . . sleep:** tricks him into falling asleep; **giving . . . lie:** (1) deceiving
him; (2) making him lie down.
31. **gave . . . lie:** (1) called you a liar; (2) made you sleep.
32. **i' . . . throat:** deeply, egregiously. (Drink accused the porter of serious, deliberate
lying.)
34. **took . . . legs:** lifted me (as a wrestler would); **made a shift:** managed; **cast:** (1) toss
him as in wrestling; (2) vomit.

MACDUFF   Is the King stirring, worthy thane?
MACBETH   Not yet.
MACDUFF   He did command me to call timely on him.
   I have almost slipped the hour.
MACBETH   I'll bring you to him.   40
MACDUFF   I know this is a joyful trouble to you,
   But yet 'tis one.
MACBETH   The labor we delight in physics pain.
   This is the door.
MACDUFF   I'll make so bold to call,
   For 'tis my limited service.   *Exit Macduff.*   45
LENNOX   Goes the King hence today?
MACBETH   He does; he did appoint so.
LENNOX   The night has been unruly. Where we lay,
   Our chimneys were blown down, and, as they say,
   Lamentings heard i'th'air, strange screams of death,   50
   And prophesying with accents terrible
   Of dire combustion and confused events,
   New hatched to the woeful time. The obscure bird
   Clamored the livelong night. Some say the earth
   Was feverous and did shake.
MACBETH   'Twas a rough night.   55
LENNOX   My young remembrance cannot parallel
   A fellow to it.

                                   Enter MACDUFF.

MACDUFF   O horror, horror, horror!
   Tongue nor heart cannot conceive nor name thee!
MACBETH AND LENNOX   What's the matter?   60
MACDUFF   Confusion now hath made his masterpiece!
   Most sacrilegious murder hath broke ope
   The Lord's anointed temple and stole thence
   The life o'the building!
MACBETH   What is't you say? The life?   65
LENNOX   Mean you His Majesty?
MACDUFF   Approach the chamber and destroy your sight

---

39. **timely:** early.
40. **slipped:** let slip.
43. **physics:** relieves.
45. **limited:** appointed.
51. **accents:** utterances.
52. **combustion:** (1) fire; (2) tumult.
53. **obscure bird:** bird of darkness, the owl.
    59. The subjects and verbs are mismatched (the tongue names, the heart conceives) to
suggest the disorder and emotion.
61. **Confusion:** destruction.
63. **The . . . temple:** the King's body.

With a new Gorgon. Do not bid me speak.
See, and then speak yourselves. *Exeunt Macbeth and Lennox.*
                —Awake, awake!
Ring the alarum bell! Murder and treason!   70
Banquo and Donaldbain, Malcolm, awake!
Shake off this downy sleep, death's counterfeit,
And look on death itself! Up, up, and see
The great doom's image! Malcolm, Banquo,
As from your graves rise up and walk like sprites   75
To countenance this horror!—Ring the bell! *Bell rings.*

                        Enter LADY MACBETH.

LADY MACBETH   What's the business
That such a hideous trumpet calls to parley
The sleepers of the house? Speak, speak!
MACDUFF   O gentle lady,   80
'Tis not for you to hear what I can speak.
The repetition in a woman's ear
Would murder as it fell.

                        Enter BANQUO.

               —O Banquo, Banquo!
Our royal master's murdered!
LADY MACBETH   Woe, alas!
What, in our house?
BANQUO   Too cruel anywhere.   85
Dear Duff, I prithee, contradict thyself,
And say it is not so.

            Enter MACBETH, LENNOX, *and* ROSS.

MACBETH   Had I but died an hour before this chance,
I had lived a blessèd time, for from this instant
There's nothing serious in mortality.   90
All is but toys. Renown and grace is dead.
The wine of life is drawn, and the mere lees
Is left this vault to brag of.

            Enter MALCOLM *and* DONALDBAIN.

68. **Gorgon:** a mythical monster whose face turned beholders to stone.
74. **great doom's image:** a sight of doomsday, the Last Judgment.
75. On doomsday the spirits (**sprites**) of the dead will rise to be judged; see John 5:28:
"The hour is coming, in the which all that are in the graves shall hear his voice."
76. **countenance:** (1) act in accordance with; (2) face.
78. **parley:** conference, generally between enemies.
90. **mortality:** human life.
92. **lees:** dregs.
93. **vault:** (1) wine cellar; (2) earth, with its vault, the sky.

DONALDBAIN What is amiss?
MACBETH   You are, and do not know't.
  The spring, the head, the fountain of your blood   95
  Is stopped, the very source of it is stopped.
MACDUFF Your royal father's murdered.
MALCOLM   Oh! By whom?
LENNOX Those of his chamber, as it seemed, had done't.
  Their hands and faces were all badged with blood;
  So were their daggers, which unwiped we found   100
  Upon their pillows. They stared and were distracted;
  No man's life was to be trusted with them.
MACBETH Oh, yet I do repent me of my fury,
  That I did kill them.
MACDUFF   Wherefore did you so?
MACBETH Who can be wise, amazed, temp'rate and furious,   105
  Loyal and neutral in a moment? No man.
  Th'expedition of my violent love
  Outrun the pauser, reason. Here lay Duncan,
  His silver skin laced with his golden blood,
  And his gashed stabs looked like a breach in nature   110
  For ruin's wasteful entrance; there the murderers,
  Steeped in the colors of their trade, their daggers
  Unmannerly breeched with gore. Who could refrain
  That had a heart to love, and in that heart
  Courage to make's love known?   115
LADY MACBETH [*Fainting*] Help me hence, ho!
MACDUFF Look to the lady!
MALCOLM [*Aside to Donaldbain*] Why do we hold our tongues,
  That most may claim this argument for ours?
DONALDBAIN [*Aside to Malcolm*] What should be spoken here,
    where our fate,   120
  Hid in an auger-hole, may rush and seize us?
  Let's away. Our tears are not yet brewed.
MALCOLM [*Aside to Donaldbain*] Nor our strong sorrow upon
    the foot of motion.
BANQUO Look to the lady.   [*Exit Lady Macbeth, attended.*]
  And when we have our naked frailties hid,   125

----

99. **badged:** smeared.
105. **amazed:** shocked out of one's wits.
107. **expedition:** speedy expression.
108. **Outrun the pauser:** outran the controller.
109. **golden:** red.
110. **breach:** gap (in fortifications).
113. **Unmannerly breeched:** indecently clothed (as with breeches).
121. **auger-hole:** a hole made by an auger, or carpenter's pointer; here, a place of ambush.
123. **upon . . . motion:** ready to act.
125. **naked frailties:** (1) unclothed bodies; (2) emotional vulnerabilities.

That suffer in exposure, let us meet
And question this most bloody piece of work
To know it further. Fears and scruples shake us.
In the great hand of God I stand, and thence
Against the undivulged pretense I fight   130
Of treasonous malice.

MACDUFF   And so do I.

ALL   So, all!

MACBETH   Let's briefly put on manly readiness,
   And meet i'the hall together.

ALL   Well contented.
                     Exeunt [all but Malcolm and Donaldbain].

MALCOLM   What will you do? Let's not consort with them.
   To show an unfelt sorrow is an office   135
   Which the false man does easy. I'll to England.

DONALDBAIN   To Ireland, I. Our separated fortune
   Shall keep us both the safer. Where we are,
   There's daggers in men's smiles. The nea'er in blood,
   The nearer bloody.

MALCOLM   This murderous shaft that's shot   140
   Hath not yet lighted, and our safest way
   Is to avoid the aim. Therefore, to horse,
   And let us not be dainty of leave-taking,
   But shift away. There's warrant in that theft
   Which steals itself when there's no mercy left.   *Exeunt.* 145

2.4 [*Outside Macbeth's castle.*]

   Enter ROSS *with an* OLD MAN.

OLD MAN   Threescore and ten I can remember well,
   Within the volume of which time I have seen
   Hours dreadful and things strange, but this sore night
   Hath trifled former knowings.

127. **question:** examine.
128. **scruples:** doubts.
130. **undivulged pretense:** unrevealed purpose (of the traitor).
132. **briefly:** quickly.
135. **office:** action
139–40. **The nea'er . . . bloody:** The nearer one is to Duncan in blood, the closer he is
to being killed.
141. **lighted:** landed.
143. **dainty of:** particular about.
144. **shift:** leave stealthily; **warrant:** justification.
145. **steals:** steals away.
1. **Threescore and ten:** seventy, the biblical allotment of human life; see Psalms 90.10:
"The days of our years are threescore years and ten."
3. **sore:** severe, violent.
4. **Hath . . . knowings:** has made other experiences seem trivial.

ROSS   Ha, good father,
  Thou seest the heavens, as troubled with man's act,   5
  Threatens his bloody stage. By th'clock 'tis day,
  And yet dark night strangles the traveling lamp.
  Is't night's predominance or the day's shame
  That darkness does the face of earth entomb,
  When living light should kiss it?
OLD MAN   'Tis unnatural,   10
  Even like the deed that's done. On Tuesday last,
  A falcon, tow'ring in her pride of place,
  Was by a mousing owl hawked at and killed.
ROSS   And Duncan's horses—a thing most strange and certain!—
  Beauteous and swift, the minions of their race,   15
  Turned wild in nature, broke their stalls, flung out,
  Contending 'gainst obedience, as they would
  Make war with mankind.
OLD MAN   'Tis said they eat each other.
ROSS   They did so, to th'amazement of mine eyes
  That looked upon't.

                                        Enter MACDUFF.

                      Here comes the good Macduff.   20
  How goes the world, sir, now?
MACDUFF   Why, see you not?
ROSS   Is't known who did this more than bloody deed?
MACDUFF   Those that Macbeth hath slain.
ROSS   Alas, the day!
  What good could they pretend?
MACDUFF   They were suborned.
  Malcolm and Donaldbain, the King's two sons,   25
  Are stol'n away and fled, which puts upon them
  Suspicion of the deed.
ROSS   'Gainst nature still!
  Thriftless ambition that will ravin up
  Thine own life's means! Then, 'tis most like

    4. **father:** old man.
    6. **stage:** the earth. The metaphor continues the theatrical imagery of **heavens,** the dec-
  orated roof over the stage, and **act.**
    7. **traveling lamp:** the sun.
    8. **predominance:** superiority.
    12. **tow'ring:** soaring; **pride of place:** preeminent position.
    13. **mousing owl:** an owl that preys on mice; **hawked at:** attacked in flight.
    15. **minions:** darlings.
    16. **flung out:** kicked and bucked violently.
    18. **eat:** ate.
    24. **pretend:** put forward as a pretext; **suborned:** bribed.
    28. **thriftless:** wasteful; **ravin up:** devour hungrily.

The sovereignty will fall upon Macbeth.   30
MACDUFF   He is already named and gone to Scone
  To be invested.
ROSS   Where is Duncan's body?
MACDUFF   Carried to Colmekill,
  The sacred storehouse of his predecessors,   35
  And guardian of their bones.
ROSS   Will you to Scone?
MACDUFF   No, cousin, I'll to Fife.
ROSS   Well, I will thither.
MACDUFF   Well may you see things well done there. Adieu,
  Lest our old robes sit easier than our new.
ROSS   Farewell, father.   40
OLD MAN   God's benison go with you, and with those
  That would make good of bad, and friends of foes.
                                              Exeunt all.

3.1 [*Forres. The palace.*]

  Enter BANQUO.

BANQUO   Thou hast it now—King, Cawdor, Glamis, all
  As the Weïrd Women promised, and I fear
  Thou played'st most foully for't. Yet it was said
  It should not stand in thy posterity,
  But that myself should be the root and father   5
  Of many kings. If there come truth from them—
  As upon thee, Macbeth, their speeches shine—
  Why, by the verities on thee made good,
  May they not be my oracles as well,
  And set me up in hope? But hush, no more.   10

      Sennet sounded. Enter MACBETH *as King,* LADY MACBETH
          [*as Queen*], LENNOX, ROSS, LORDS, *and* ATTENDANTS.

MACBETH   Here's our chief guest.
LADY MACBETH   If he had been forgotten,

31. **Scone:** ancient royal city of Scotland.
32. **invested:** crowned formally as king.
34. **Colmekill:** small island (now Iona) off the West of Scotland, home of St. Columba (see 1.2.62), burial place of kings.
37. **Fife:** land ruled by Macduff.
41. **benison:** blessing.
4. **stand:** remain.
7. **shine:** shed light (of good fortune).
S.D. **Sennet:** a distinctive set of notes on a trumpet or cornet signaling a ceremonious entrance.

It had been as a gap in our great feast,
And all-thing unbecoming.
MACBETH   Tonight we hold a solemn supper, sir,
And I'll request your presence.
BANQUO   Let Your Highness   15
Command upon me, to the which my duties
Are with a most indissoluble tie
Forever knit.
MACBETH   Ride you this afternoon?
BANQUO   Ay, my good lord.   20
MACBETH   We should have else desired your good advice,
Which still hath been both grave and prosperous,
In this day's council; but we'll take tomorrow.
Is't far you ride?
BANQUO   As far, my lord, as will fill up the time   25
Twixt this and supper. Go not my horse the better,
I must become a borrower of the night
For a dark hour or twain.
MACBETH   Fail not our feast.
BANQUO   My lord, I will not.   30
MACBETH   We hear our bloody cousins are bestowed
In England and in Ireland, not confessing
Their cruel parricide, filling their hearers
With strange invention. But of that tomorrow,
When therewithal we shall have cause of state   35
Craving us jointly. Hie you to horse. Adieu,
Till you return at night. Goes Fleance with you?
BANQUO   Ay, my good lord. Our time does call upon's.
MACBETH   I wish your horses swift and sure of foot,
And so I do commend you to their backs.   40
Farewell.—   *Exit Banquo.*
Let every man be master of his time
Till seven at night. To make society
The sweeter welcome, we will keep ourself

13. **all-thing:** completely.
14. **solemn:** formal.
16. **the which:** which commandments.
22. **still:** always.
23. **take:** take it (Banquo's advice).
26. **Go . . . better:** unless my horse goes faster than I expect.
28. **twain:** two.
31. **bestowed:** lodged.
34. **invention:** falsehood (i.e., that Macbeth killed the King).
35. **therewithal:** besides that.
35–36. **cause . . . jointly:** state business requiring our joint attention.
40. **commend:** entrust.
43. **society:** company of friends.

Till suppertime alone. While then, God be with you.   45

      Exeunt Lords [and all but Macbeth and a Servant].

Sirrah, a word with you: attend those men
Our pleasure?
SERVANT   They are, my lord, without the palace gate.
MACBETH   Bring them before us.—   *Exit Servant.*
  To be thus is nothing, but to be safely thus.   50
Our fears in Banquo stick deep,
And in his royalty of nature reigns that
Which would be feared. 'Tis much he dares;
And to that dauntless temper of his mind
He hath a wisdom that doth guide his valor   55
To act in safety. There is none but he
Whose being I do fear; and under him
My genius is rebuked, as it is said
Mark Antony's was by Caesar. He chid the sisters
When first they put the name of king upon me,   60
And bade them speak to him; then prophet-like,
They hailed him father to a line of kings.
Upon my head they placed a fruitless crown,
And put a barren scepter in my grip,
Thence to be wrenched with an unlineal hand,   65
No son of mine succeeding. If't be so,
For Banquo's issue have I filed my mind,
For them the gracious Duncan have I murdered,
Put rancors in the vessel of my peace
Only for them, and mine eternal jewel   70
Given to the common enemy of man
To make them kings, the seeds of Banquo kings!
Rather than so, come fate into the list,
And champion me to th'utterance!—Who's there!

45. **While:** till.
46. **Sirrah:** a form of address to a social inferior.
50. **thus:** i.e., a King; **but:** unless.
51. **stick deep:** pierce deeply.
52. **royalty of nature:** natural royalty.
54. **to:** in addition to.
58. **genius:** attendant spirit; **rebuked:** abashed.
59. **Caesar:** Octavius Caesar (Augustus), who eventually defeated Antony in a battle
Shakespeare dramatized in *Antony and Cleopatra.*
65. **unlineal hand:** a descendant from another family line.
67. **filed:** defiled.
69. **rancors:** bitter feelings (imagined as a poison added to a **vessel,** or cup).
70. **eternal jewel:** immortal soul.
71. **common enemy:** the devil.
73. **list:** combat area, originally, jousting lanes.
74. **champion me:** (1) fight with me; (2) support me; **to th'utterance:** to the end, to death
(French, *à l'outrance*).

Enter SERVANT *and two* MURDERERS.

Now go to the door, and stay there till we call.—   75

Exit Servant.

Was it not yesterday we spoke together?

MURDERERS   It was, so please Your Highness.

MACBETH   Well then, now, have you considered of my speeches?
Know that it was he in the times past which held you so under
fortune, which you thought had been our innocent self. This I   80
made good to you in our last conference, passed in probation
with you how you were borne in hand, how crossed, the
instruments, who wrought with them, and all things else that
might to half a soul and to a notion crazed say "Thus did
Banquo."   ·85

FIRST MURDERER   You made it known to us.

MACBETH   I did so, and went further, which is now our point of
second meeting. Do you find your patience so predominant in
your nature that you can let this go? Are you so gospeled to
pray for this good man and for his issue, whose heavy hand   90
hath bowed you to the grave and beggared yours for ever?

FIRST MURDERER   We are men, my liege.

MACBETH   Ay, in the catalogue ye go for men,
As hounds and greyhounds, mongrels, spaniels, curs,
Shoughs, water-rugs, and demi-wolves are clept   95
All by the name of dogs. The valued file
Distinguishes the swift, the slow, the subtle,
The housekeeper, the hunter—every one
According to the gift which bounteous nature
Hath in him closed, whereby he does receive   100
Particular addition from the bill
That writes them all alike; and so of men.

79. **under:** out of favor with.
81–82. **passed . . . with:** proved to.
82. **borne in hand:** manipulated; **crossed:** thwarted.
83. **instruments:** means; **wrought:** worked.
84. **to . . . crazed:** to even a half-wit and unsound mind.
89. **gospeled:** influenced by gospel teachings, especially Matthew 5.44: "But I say unto you, love your enemies, bless them that curse you, do good to them that hate you, and pray for them which despitefully use you, and persecute you."
91. **yours:** your family.
93. **catalogue:** list (of human types).
94. **curs:** watch dogs or sheep dogs, sometimes used as a term of contempt.
95. **Shoughs:** lapdogs; **water-rugs:** shaggy water dogs; **demi-wolves:** dogs that are half wolf; **clept:** named.
96. **valued file:** list that records the qualities of each breed.
98. **housekeeper:** watchdog.
100. **closed:** enclosed.
101. **particular addition:** distinguishing characteristics.
101–102. **the bill . . . alike:** the general qualities common to all the dogs.

Now, if you have a station in the file,
Not i'the worst rank of manhood, say't,
And I will put that business in your bosoms   105
Whose execution takes your enemy off,
Grapples you to the heart and love of us,
Who wear our health but sickly in his life,
Which in his death were perfect.
SECOND MURDERER   I am one, my liege,
Whom the vile blows and buffets of the world   110
Have so incensed that I am reckless what
I do to spite the world.
FIRST MURDERER   And I another,
So weary with disasters, tugged with fortune,
That I would set my life on any chance
To mend it or be rid on't.
MACBETH   Both of you   115
Know Banquo was your enemy.
MURDERERS   True, my lord.
MACBETH   So is he mine, and in such bloody distance
That every minute of his being thrusts
Against my near'st of life. And though I could
With barefaced power sweep him from my sight   120
And bid my will avouch it, yet I must not,
For certain friends that are both his and mine,
Whose loves I may not drop, but wail his fall
Who I myself struck down. And thence it is
That I to your assistance do make love,   125
Masking the business from the common eye
For sundry weighty reasons.
SECOND MURDERER   We shall, my lord,
Perform what you command us.
FIRST MURDERER   Though our lives—
MACBETH   Your spirits shine through you. Within this hour, at
    most,

103. station . . . file: place in the list (of humans).
106. takes . . . off: removes, kills.
107. Grapples: seizes and attaches firmly. Grappling irons held ships to each other during
nautical battles.
108. in his life: while he lives.
114. set: risk.
115. on't: of it.
117. distance: (1) enmity; (2) striking range.
119. near'st of life: vital organs.
120. barefaced: open, without excuses.
121. And . . . it: And use my royal will as justification enough for Banquo's murder.
123. but wail: but I must lament.
125. That I request your help.

I will advise you where to plant yourselves,   130
Acquaint you with the perfect spy o'th'time,
The moment on't, for't must be done tonight,
And something from the palace, always thought
That I require a clearness. And with him—
To leave no rubs nor botches in the work—   135
Fleance, his son that keeps him company,
Whose absence is no less material to me
Than is his father's, must embrace the fate
Of that dark hour. Resolve yourselves apart.
I'll come to you anon.
MURDERERS   We are resolved, my lord.   140
MACBETH   I'll call upon you straight; abide within.
                                    Exeunt [Murderers].
It is concluded. Banquo, thy soul's flight,
If it find heaven, must find it out tonight.   [*Exit.*]

3.2 [*The palace.*]

Enter LADY MACBETH *and a* SERVANT.

LADY MACBETH   Is Banquo gone from court?
SERVANT   Ay, madam, but returns again tonight.
LADY MACBETH   Say to the King I would attend his leisure
  For a few words.
SERVANT   Madam, I will.   *Exit.*   5
LADY MACBETH   Nought's had, all's spent,
  Where our desire is got without content.
  'Tis safer to be that which we destroy
  Than by destruction dwell in doubtful joy.

                                    Enter MACBETH.

How now, my lord? Why do you keep alone,   10
Of sorriest fancies your companions making,
Using those thoughts which should indeed have died
With them they think on? Things without all remedy

---

131. **perfect spy o'th'time:** (1) best time and place for espial, or spying; (2) the perfect
spy for the job, i.e., the Third Murderer of 3.3.
133. **something:** some distance; **thought:** borne in mind.
134. **clearness:** freedom from suspicion.
135. **rubs nor botches:** rough spots nor flaws.
139. **Resolve . . . apart:** (1) determine your course of action in private; (2) gather your
courage in private.
9. **doubtful:** (1) uncertain; (2) worried.
11. **sorriest fancies:** most wretched imaginings.
13. **all:** any.

Should be without regard. What's done is done.
MACBETH   We have scorched the snake, not killed it.   15
She'll close and be herself, whilst our poor malice
Remains in danger of her former tooth.
But let the frame of things disjoint, both the worlds suffer,
Ere we will eat our meal in fear, and sleep
In the affliction of these terrible dreams   20
That shake us nightly. Better be with the dead,
Whom we, to gain our peace, have sent to peace,
Than on the torture of the mind to lie
In restless ecstasy. Duncan is in his grave.
After life's fitful fever he sleeps well.   25
Treason has done his worst; nor steel, nor poison,
Malice domestic, foreign levy, nothing,
Can touch him further.
LADY MACBETH   Come on.
Gentle my lord, sleek o'er your rugged looks.   30
Be bright and jovial among your guests tonight.
MACBETH   So shall I, love, and so, I pray, be you.
Let your remembrance apply to Banquo;
Present him eminence both with eye and tongue;
Unsafe the while that we must lave   35
Our honors in these flattering streams,
And make our faces vizards to our hearts,
Disguising what they are.
LADY MACBETH   You must leave this.
MACBETH   Oh, full of scorpions is my mind, dear wife!
Thou know'st that Banquo and his Fleance lives.   40
LADY MACBETH   But in them nature's copy's not eterne.
MACBETH   There's comfort yet; they are assailable.
Then be thou jocund. Ere the bat hath flown
His cloistered flight, ere to black Hecate's summons
The shard-born beetle with his drowsy hums   45

15. **scorched:** slashed.
16. **close:** heal; **poor:** weak.
17. **her former tooth:** her fang, just as before.
18. **frame . . . disjoint:** structure of the universe collapse; **both the worlds:** heaven and earth.
24. **ecstasy:** frenzy.
27. **domestic:** civil; **levy:** troops.
30. My noble lord, smooth over your rough look of concern.
33. **remembrance:** attention.
34. **eminence:** favor.
35. We are unsafe during this time in which we must wash.
37. **vizards:** masks.
41. **copy:** copyhold, i.e., lease (on life); **eterne:** eternal.
44. **cloistered:** enclosed
45. **shard-born:** born in dung.

Hath rung night's yawning peal, there shall be done
A deed of dreadful note.
LADY MACBETH   What's to be done?
MACBETH   Be innocent of the knowledge, dearest chuck,
Till thou applaud the deed. Come, seeling night,
Scarf up the tender eye of pitiful day,   50
And with thy bloody and invisible hand
Cancel and tear to pieces that great bond
Which keeps me pale! Light thickens,
And the crow makes wing to the rooky wood;
Good things of day begin to droop and drowse,   55
Whiles night's black agents to their preys do rouse.
Thou marvel'st at my words, but hold thee still.
Things bad begun make strong themselves by ill.
So, prithee, go with me.   *Exeunt.*

3.3. [*Outdoors, near the palace.*]

Enter three MURDERERS.

FIRST MURDERER   But who did bid thee join with us?
THIRD MURDERER   Macbeth.
SECOND MURDERER [*To First Murderer*]
He needs not our mistrust, since he delivers
Our offices and what we have to do
To the direction just.
FIRST MURDERER [*To Third Murderer*]   Then stand with us.
The west yet glimmers with some streaks of day.   5
Now spurs the lated traveler apace
To gain the timely inn, and near approaches
The subject of our watch.

46. **Hath . . . peal:** has (with its hums) announced the arrival of night and sleep. (The
image derives from the ringing of the curfew bell.)
47. **note:** notoriety.
48. **chuck:** a term of affection.
49. **seeling:** eye-closing. (Falconers seeled, i.e., stitched shut, the eyes of falcons.)
50. **Scarf up:** blindfold.
52. **bond:** contract (Banquo's lease on life).
53. **thickens:** dims.
54. **rooky:** filled with rooks, i.e., crows.
56. **rouse:** rouse themselves.
3.3 S.D. **three:** The identity of the Third Murderer has caused speculation; some have
proposed Ross, Macbeth himself in disguise, an allegorical abstraction like Destiny, or, most
probably, an unnamed extra whom Macbeth sent to make sure the others carry out the
murder.
2. **He:** the Third Murderer.
3. **offices:** duties.
4. **To . . . just:** exactly according to Macbeth's instructions.
6. **lated:** belated.
7. **timely:** arrived at in good time.

THIRD MURDERER   Hark, I hear horses.
BANQUO (*Within*)   Give us a light there, ho!
SECOND MURDERER   Then 'tis he. The rest
  That are within the note of expectation   10
  Already are i'the court.
FIRST MURDERER   His horses go about.
THIRD MURDERER   Almost a mile; but he does usually,
  So all men do from hence to the palace gate
  Make it their walk.

                Enter BANQUO *and* FLEANCE, *with a torch.*

SECOND MURDERER   A light, a light!   15
THIRD MURDERER   'Tis he.
FIRST MURDERER   Stand to't.
BANQUO   It will be rain tonight.
FIRST MURDERER   Let it come down!
                    [They attack Banquo.]
BANQUO   Oh, treachery! Fly, good Fleance, fly, fly, fly!
  Thou mayst revenge.—O slave!   20
            [Banquo dies. Fleance escapes.]
THIRD MURDERER   Who did strike out the light?
FIRST MURDERER   Was't not the way?
THIRD MURDERER   There's but one down. The son is fled.
SECOND MURDERER   We have lost best half of our affair.
FIRST MURDERER   Well, let's away, and say how much is done.

                Exeunt [with Banquo's body].

3.4 [*A room in the palace.*]

Banquet prepared. Enter MACBETH, LADY MACBETH, ROSS,
LENNOX, LORDS, *and* ATTENDANTS.

MACBETH   You know your own degrees, sit down.
  At first and last, the hearty welcome. [*They sit.*]
LORDS   Thanks to Your Majesty.
MACBETH   Ourself will mingle with society,
  And play the humble host.   5

   10. **note of expectation:** list of invited guests.
   11. **go about:** go another route, being led or ridden to the stable.
   21. **way:** right way to proceed.
   1. **degrees:** ranks, and, therefore, places at the table.
   2. **At . . . last:** to all.
   4. **mingle with society:** mix with the guests (and not remain in his special chair).

Our hostess keeps her state, but in best time
We will require her welcome.

LADY MACBETH   Pronounce it for me, sir, to all our friends,
For my heart speaks they are welcome.

Enter FIRST MURDERER [*to the door*].

MACBETH   See, they encounter thee with their hearts' thanks.   10
Both sides are even. Here I'll sit, i'the midst.
Be large in mirth; anon we'll drink a measure
The table round. [*He converses apart with the First Murderer.*]
There's blood upon thy face.

FIRST MURDERER   'Tis Banquo's, then.

MACBETH   'Tis better thee without than he within.   15
Is he dispatched?

FIRST MURDERER   My lord, his throat is cut. That I did for him.

MACBETH   Thou art the best o'the cutthroats.
Yet he's good that did the like for Fleance;
If thou didst it, thou art the nonpareil.   20

FIRST MURDERER   Most royal sir, Fleance is scaped.

MACBETH   Then comes my fit again. I had else been perfect,
Whole as the marble, founded as the rock,
As broad and general as the casing air,
But now I am cabined, cribbed, confined, bound in   25
To saucy doubts and fears. But Banquo's safe?

FIRST MURDERER   Ay, my good lord, safe in a ditch he bides,
With twenty trenchèd gashes on his head,
The least a death to nature.

MACBETH   Thanks for that.
There the grown serpent lies; the worm that's fled   30
Hath nature that in time will venom breed,
No teeth for the present. Get thee gone. Tomorrow
We'll hear ourselves again.   *Exit* [*First*] *Murderer*.

LADY MACBETH   My royal lord,

6. **keeps her state:** remains in her special chair; **in best time:** at the right time.
10. **encounter:** respond to.
11. **Both . . . even:** (1) Both sides of the table have equal numbers; (2) The guests' gratitude matches Lady Macbeth's welcome.
12. **anon:** straightway.
12–13. **measure . . . round:** toast for the whole table.
15. **thee . . . within:** on you than in him.
20. **nonpareil:** one without equal.
23. **founded:** securely established.
24. **broad and general:** free and omnipresent; **casing:** surrounding.
25. **cribbed:** enclosed in a narrow space.
26. **saucy:** sharp, insolent.
30. **worm:** small serpent.
31. **nature:** such a nature.
33. **hear ourselves:** converse together.

You do not give the cheer. The feast is sold
That is not often vouched, while 'tis a-making,   35
'Tis given with welcome. To feed were best at home;
From thence the sauce to meat is ceremony;
Meeting were bare without it.

Enter the GHOST OF BANQUO, *and sits in Macbeth's place.*

MACBETH   Sweet remembrancer!—
Now, good digestion wait on appetite,
And health on both.
LENNOX   May't please Your Highness, sit.   40
MACBETH   Here had we now our country's honor roofed,
Were the graced person of our Banquo present,
Who may I rather challenge for unkindness
Than pity for mischance.
ROSS   His absence, sir,
Lays blame upon his promise. Please't Your Highness   45
To grace us with your royal company?
MACBETH [*Seeing his place occupied*]   The table's full.
LENNOX   Here is a
place reserved, sir.
MACBETH   Where?
LENNOX   Here, my good lord. [*Macbeth starts.*] What is't that
moves Your Highness?
MACBETH   Which of you have done this?
LORDS   What, my good lord?   50
MACBETH [*To Ghost*]   Thou canst not say I did it!
Never shake thy gory locks at me!
ROSS   Gentlemen, rise. His Highness is not well.
[*They start to rise.*]
LADY MACBETH   Sit, worthy friends. My lord is often thus,
And hath been from his youth. Pray you, keep seat.   55
The fit is momentary; upon a thought
He will again be well. If much you note him,
You shall offend him and extend his passion.
Feed, and regard him not.
[*She converses apart with Macbeth.*]

34–36. The . . . welcome: The feast seems a mere duty, as if sold for a price, if not often
accompanied with assurances of welcome while the guests are eating.
36. To . . . home: Mere eating is best done at home.
37. From thence: away from home; meat: food; ceremony: courtesy.
38. Meeting: social gatherings.
39. wait on: serve, follow.
41. roofed: under one roof.
43. challenge: rebuke.
45. Lays blame: calls into question.
56. upon a thought: as quick as a thought.

                              Are you a man?

MACBETH   Ay, and a bold one that dare look on that   60
  Which might appall the devil.

LADY MACBETH   O proper stuff!
  This is the very painting of your fear!
  This is the air-drawn dagger which you said
  Led you to Duncan. Oh, these flaws and starts,
  Impostors to true fear, would well become   65
  A woman's story at a winter's fire,
  Authorized by her grandam. Shame itself!
  Why do you make such faces? When all's done,
  You look but on a stool.

MACBETH   Prithee, see there!
  Behold, look, lo! How say you?   70
  [To Ghost] Why, what care I? If thou canst nod, speak too.
  If charnel houses and our graves must send
  Those that we bury back, our monuments
  Shall be the maws of kites.   [Exit Ghost.]

LADY MACBETH   What, quite unmanned in folly?   75

MACBETH   If I stand here, I saw him.

LADY MACBETH   Fie, for shame!

MACBETH   Blood hath been shed ere now, i'th'olden time,
  Ere humane statute purged the gentle weal;
  Ay, and since too, murders have been performed,
  Too terrible for the ear. The times has been   80
  That, when the brains were out, the man would die,
  And there an end. But now they rise again,
  With twenty mortal murders on their crowns,
  And push us from our stools. This is more strange
  Than such a murder is.

LADY MACBETH   My worthy lord,   85
  Your noble friends do lack you.

MACBETH   I do forget—
  Do not muse at me, my most worthy friends.
  I have a strange infirmity, which is nothing
  To those that know me. Come, love and health to all.

61. **proper stuff:** nonsense.
63. **air-drawn:** imagined in, or moved through, the air.
64. **flaws:** outbursts of passion.
65. **to:** compared to.
67. **Authorized:** validated.
70. **lo:** look.
71. **nod:** an implicit stage direction for the ghost.
72. **charnel houses:** repositories for bones or corpses.
73–74. **monuments . . . kites:** burial places will be the stomachs of scavenging birds.
78. **Ere . . . weal:** before law (human and kindly) civilized humanity.
80. **The . . . been:** it used to be.
83. **mortal murders:** deadly wounds.

Then I'll sit down. Give me some wine; fill full.   90

                                    Enter GHOST.

I drink to the general joy o'the whole table,
And to our dear friend Banquo, whom we miss.
Would he were here! To all and him we thirst,
And all to all.
LORDS   Our duties and the pledge. [*They drink.*]
MACBETH [*To Ghost*]   Avaunt, and quit my sight! Let the earth
    hide thee!   95
Thy bones are marrowless, thy blood is cold;
Thou hast no speculation in those eyes
Which thou dost glare with.
LADY MACBETH   Think of this, good peers,
But as a thing of custom; 'tis no other,
Only it spoils the pleasure of the time.   100
MACBETH   What man dare, I dare.
Approach thou like the rugged Russian bear,
The armed rhinoceros, or th'Hyrcan tiger!
Take any shape but that, and my firm nerves
Shall never tremble. Or be alive again,   105
And dare me to the desert with thy sword.
If trembling I inhabit then, protest me
The baby of a girl. Hence, horrible shadow!
Unreal mock'ry, hence!   [*Exit Ghost.*]
                    Why, so. Being gone,
I am a man again.—Pray you, sit still.   110
LADY MACBETH   You have displaced the mirth, broke the good
    meeting
With most admired disorder.
MACBETH   Can such things be,
And overcome us like a summer's cloud,
Without our special wonder? You make me strange
Even to the disposition that I owe,   115

93. **thirst:** long for.
94. **all to all:** let all drink to all; **Our . . . pledge:** We offer our respect (**duties**) and this
toast (**pledge**).
95. **Avaunt:** go away.
97. **speculation:** sight.
99. **thing of custom:** common occurrence.
103. **armed:** armor-plated; **Hyrcan:** Hyrcanian, i.e., an ancient region on the Caspian
Sea, noted for its wildness.
104. **nerves:** tendons.
107. If I tremble then proclaim me.
108. **baby . . . girl:** a girl's baby or doll.
112. **admired:** amazing.
113. **overcome:** come over.
114–15. **You . . . owe:** You make me feel estranged from my natural courageous self (**owe**
means "own").

When now I think you can behold such sights,
And keep the natural ruby of your cheeks,
When mine is blanched with fear.
ROSS   What sights, my lord?
LADY MACBETH   I pray you, speak not; he grows worse and
    worse.
    Question enrages him. At once, good night.   120
    Stand not upon the order of your going,
    But go at once.
LENNOX   Good night, and better health
    Attend His Majesty.
LADY MACBETH   A kind good night to all.
                                   Exeunt Lords [and attendants.]
MACBETH   It will have blood; they say, "blood will have blood."
    Stones have been known to move and trees to speak;   125
    Augurs and understood relations have
    By maggot-pies and choughs and rooks brought forth
    The secret'st man of blood. What is the night?
LADY MACBETH   Almost at odds with morning, which is which.
MACBETH   How sayst thou that Macduff denies his person   130
    At our great bidding?
LADY MACBETH   Did you send to him, sir?
MACBETH   I hear it by the way, but I will send.
    There's not a one of them but in his house
    I keep a servant fee'd. I will tomorrow—
    And betimes I will—to the Weïrd Sisters.   135
    More shall they speak, for now I am bent to know
    By the worst means the worst. For mine own good,
    All causes shall give way. I am in blood
    Stepped in so far that, should I wade no more,
    Returning were as tedious as go o'er.   140
    Strange things I have in head that will to hand,

---

121. Don't insist on an orderly, ceremonious exit (cf. the ordered entrance 3.4.1).
124. Macbeth recalls the proverb, "Blood will have blood" (Dent B458, see Selected Bibliography); the idea occurs in Genesis 9:6: "Whoso sheddeth man's blood, by man shall his
blood be shed."
126. **Augurs:** predictions; **understood relations:** revealed correspondences, as between
cause and effect, for example.
127. **maggot-pies . . . rooks:** magpies, jackdaws, and crows (three types of birds that mim-
icked human speech); **brought forth:** revealed.
128. **secret'st . . . blood:** best-hidden murderer; **the night:** the time of night.
130. **How sayst thou:** what do you think.
132. **by the way:** casually; **send:** send a messenger.
133. **them:** Scottish nobles.
134. **fee'd:** paid (to spy).
135. **betimes:** (1) speedily; (2) early in the morning.
136. **bent:** determined.
140. **go o'er:** going all the way over.
141. **will to hand:** demand to be acted out.

Which must be acted ere they may be scanned.
LADY MACBETH   You lack the season of all natures, sleep.
MACBETH   Come, we'll to sleep. My strange and self-abuse
  Is the initiate fear that wants hard use.   145
  We are yet but young in deed.   *Exeunt.*

3.5 [*A heath.*]

Thunder. Enter the three WITCHES, *meeting* HECATE.

FIRST WITCH   Why, how now, Hecate? You look angerly.
HECATE   Have I not reason, beldams as you are?
  Saucy and overbold, how did you dare
  To trade and traffic with Macbeth
  In riddles and affairs of death,   5
  And I, the mistress of your charms,
  The close contriver of all harms,
  Was never called to bear my part,
  Or show the glory of our art?
  And, which is worse, all you have done   10
  Hath been but for a wayward son,
  Spiteful and wrathful, who, as others do,
  Loves for his own ends, not for you.
  But make amends now. Get you gone,
  And at the pit of Acheron   15
  Meet me i'the morning. Thither he
  Will come to know his destiny.
  Your vessels and your spells provide,
  Your charms and everything beside.
  I am for th'air. This night I'll spend   20
  Unto a dismal and a fatal end.
  Great business must be wrought ere noon.
  Upon the corner of the moon
  There hangs a vap'rous drop profound;
  I'll catch it ere it come to ground.   25

---

142. **scanned:** analyzed.
143. **season:** seasoning, preservative.
144. **strange and self-abuse:** unnatural violation of who I am.
145. **wants hard use:** lacks experience.
  3.5 Most scholars agree that this scene and parts of 4.1 were written by another author, perhaps Thomas Middleton.
  1. **angerly:** angrily, angry.
  2. **beldams:** hags, witches.
  7. **close:** secret.
11. **wayward:** self-willed, disobedient.
15. **Acheron:** a river in Hades.
  24. **vap'rous drop:** lunar foam, supposedly gathered for enchantments; **profound:** with deep, hidden properties.

And that, distilled by magic sleights,
Shall raise such artificial sprites
As by the strength of their illusion
Shall draw him on to his confusion.
He shall spurn fate, scorn death, and bear   30
His hopes 'bove wisdom, grace, and fear.
And you all know, security
Is mortals' chiefest enemy. *Music and a song.*
Hark, I am called. My little spirit, see,
Sits in a foggy cloud and stays for me.   *[Exit.]* 35

         Sing within: "Come away, come away," *etc.*

FIRST WITCH   Come, let's make haste. She'll soon be back
    again.   *Exeunt.*

3.6 [*Unlocalized.*]

Enter LENNOX *and another* LORD.

LENNOX   My former speeches have but hit your thoughts,
Which can interpret farther. Only I say
Things have been strangely borne. The gracious Duncan
Was pitied of Macbeth; marry, he was dead.
And the right valiant Banquo walked too late,   5
Whom you may say, if't please you, Fleance killed,
For Fleance fled; men must not walk too late.
Who cannot want the thought how monstrous
It was for Malcolm and for Donaldbain
To kill their gracious father? Damnèd fact,   10
How it did grieve Macbeth! Did he not straight
In pious rage the two delinquents tear,
That were the slaves of drink and thralls of sleep?
Was not that nobly done? Ay, and wisely too,
For 'twould have angered any heart alive   15
To hear the men deny't. So that I say

26. **sleights:** tricks.
27. **artificial:** constructed by art.
29. **confusion:** destruction.
32. **security:** spiritual overconfidence and complacency.
35.1 S.D. For an early text of the song see below, pp. 168–69.
1. **hit:** touched upon.
2. **interpret:** develop the ideas, draw the logical inferences.
3. **borne:** endured.
4. **of:** by.
8. **cannot . . . thought:** can help thinking.
10. **fact:** crime.
13. **thralls:** prisoners.

He has borne all things well. And I do think
That had he Duncan's sons under his key—
As an't please heaven, he shall not—they should find
What 'twere to kill a father. So should Fleance.   20
But, peace! For from broad words and 'cause he failed
His presence at the tyrant's feast, I hear
Macduff lives in disgrace. Sir, can you tell
Where he bestows himself?

LORD   The son of Duncan,
From whom this tyrant holds the due of birth,   25
Lives in the English court, and is received
Of the most pious Edward with such grace
That the malevolence of fortune nothing
Takes from his high respect. Thither Macduff
Is gone to pray the holy King, upon his aid,   30
To wake Northumberland and warlike Siward,
That by the help of these, with Him above
To ratify the work, we may again
Give to our tables meat, sleep to our nights,
Free from our feasts and banquets bloody knives,   35
Do faithful homage, and receive free honors—
All which we pine for now. And this report
Hath so exasperate the King that he
Prepares for some attempt of war.

LENNOX   Sent he to Macduff?   40

LORD   He did, and with an absolute "Sir, not I,"
The cloudy messenger turns me his back,
And hums, as who should say "You'll rue the time
That clogs me with this answer."

17. **borne:** carried out.
19. **an't:** if it.
21. **from broad words:** as a result of his plain speaking.
24. **son of Duncan:** Malcolm.
27. **Edward:** Edward the Confessor (king of England, 1042–66)
28–29. **nothing Takes:** does not detract.
30. **upon his aid:** with his assistance.
31. **Northumberland:** a northern English county; **Siward:** the family name of some Northumberland earls.
35. Free our feasts and banquets from bloody knives.
36. **free:** untainted.
37. **this report:** (1) news of Macduff's flight (though this is in apparent contradiction with Macbeth's surprise at 4.1.142); (2) news of Malcolm's reception and purpose in England.
38. **exasperate the King:** exasperated Macbeth. Those who do not emend the Folio's "their" to the take "their" to refer to Northumberland's and Siward's king, Edward; in this reading the **report** (line 37) refers to Malcolm's report of Scotland's troubles to Edward. But the he following (line 40), which must refer to Macbeth, argues strongly for emendation.
41. **absolute:** certain, unconditional; **Sir . . . I:** In these words Macduff refuses Macbeth's request (to return?).
42. **cloudy:** gloomy; **turns me:** turns (**me** is colloquial).
44. **clogs:** burdens.

LENNOX   And that well might
  Advise him to a caution, t'hold what distance   45
  His wisdom can provide. Some holy angel
  Fly to the court of England and unfold
  His message ere he come, that a swift blessing
  May soon return to this our suffering country
  Under a hand accursed.
LORD   I'll send my prayers with him.   50

                                                    Exeunt.

4.1 [*A cavern.*]

Thunder. Enter the three WITCHES [*with a cauldron*].

FIRST WITCH   Thrice the brinded cat hath mewed.
SECOND WITCH   Thrice, and once the hedge-pig whined.
THIRD WITCH   Harpier cries, "'Tis time, 'tis time!"
FIRST WITCH   Round about the cauldron go;
  In the poisoned entrails throw.   5
  Toad, that under cold stone
  Days and nights has thirty-one
  Sweltered venom sleeping got,
  Boil thou first i'th'charmèd pot.
ALL   Double, double, toil and trouble;   10
  Fire burn, and cauldron bubble.
SECOND WITCH   Fillet of a fenny snake
  In the cauldron boil and bake;
  Eye of newt and toe of frog,
  Wool of bat and tongue of dog,   15
  Adder's fork and blind-worm's sting,
  Lizard's leg and howlet's wing,
  For a charm of powerful trouble,
  Like a hell-broth boil and bubble.
ALL   Double, double, toil and trouble;   20
  Fire burn, and cauldron bubble.
THIRD WITCH   Scale of dragon, tooth of wolf,

---

45. **t'hold**: to keep.
47. **unfold**: reveal.
1. **brinded**: streaked or spotted.
2. **hedge-pig**: hedgehog.
3. **Harpier**: perhaps a familiar spirit.
7–8. **Days . . . got**: for thirty-one days and nights has exuded venom like sweat during
sleep.
12. **Fillet**: slice; **fenny**: inhabiting fens or swamps.
16. **fork**: forked tongue; **blind-worm**: an adder, a small venomous snake.
17. **howlet**: a small owl.

Witches' mummy, maw and gulf
Of the ravined salt-sea shark,
Root of hemlock digged i'the dark,   25
Liver of blaspheming Jew,
Gall of goat, and slips of yew
Slivered in the moon's eclipse,
Nose of Turk and Tartar's lips,
Finger of birth-strangled babe   30
Ditch-delivered by a drab,
Make the gruel thick and slab.
Add thereto a tiger's chawdron,
For th'ingredience of our cauldron.
ALL   Double, double, toil and trouble;   35
Fire burn, and cauldron bubble.
SECOND WITCH   Cool it with a baboon's blood,
Then the charm is firm and good.

Enter HECATE *and the other three* WITCHES.

HECATE   Oh, well done! I commend your pains,
And every one shall share i'th'gains.   40
And now about the cauldron sing,
Live elves and fairies in a ring,
Enchanting all that you put in.

Music and a song, "Black spirits," *etc.*

SECOND WITCH   By the pricking of my thumbs,
Something wicked this way comes.   45
Open, locks,
Whoever knocks!

Enter MACBETH.

MACBETH   How now, you secret, black, and midnight hags?
What is't you do?
ALL   A deed without a name.
MACBETH   I conjure you by that which you profess,   50

23. **mummy:** mummified human flesh; **maw and gulf:** throat and stomach.
24. **ravined:** (1) ravenous; (2) glutted with prey.
26. **blaspheming:** Jews were so called for denying Christ's divinity.
27. **slips:** cuttings.
29. **Turk:** In the popular imagination the Turk threatened Europe and Christian civilization and often appeared as a figure of evil; **Tartar:** inhabitant of Central Asia, often considered
as a Turk or violent pagan.
31. **drab:** whore.
32. **slab:** semi-solid.
33. **chawdron:** entrails.
39–43. Most consider these lines non-Shakespearean. For an early text of the song "Black
spirits," see p. 170.

Howe'er you come to know it, answer me.
Though you untie the winds and let them fight
Against the churches, though the yeasty waves
Confound and swallow navigation up,
Though bladed corn be lodged and trees blown down,   55
Though castles topple on their warders' heads,
Though palaces and pyramids do slope
Their heads to their foundations, though the treasure
Of nature's germens tumble all together
Even till destruction sicken, answer me   60
To what I ask you.

FIRST WITCH   Speak.
SECOND WITCH   Demand.
THIRD WITCH   We'll answer.
FIRST WITCH   Say if thou'dst rather hear it from our mouths,
Or from our masters?
MACBETH   Call 'em; let me see 'em.
FIRST WITCH   Pour in sow's blood, that hath eaten
Her nine farrow; grease that's sweaten   65
From the murderer's gibbet throw
Into the flame.
ALL   Come high or low,
Thyself and office deftly show!

            Thunder. FIRST APPARITION, *an armed Head.*

MACBETH   Tell me, thou unknown power—
FIRST WITCH   He knows thy thought.
Hear his speech, but say thou nought.   70
FIRST APPARITION   Macbeth! Macbeth! Macbeth! Beware
    Macduff,
Beware the Thane of Fife. Dismiss me. Enough.
                                    He descends.
MACBETH   Whate'er thou art, for thy good caution, thanks;
Thou hast harped my fear aright. But one word more—

---

53. yeasty: frothy.
55. bladed corn: leafed grain (**corn** is a generic term); **lodged:** laid on the ground (by the wind).
56. warders: guards.
57. slope: bend.
59. germens: seeds from which all life springs.
60. sicken: gets sick from excess.
65. nine farrow: litter of nine; **sweaten:** sweated (rhymes with **eaten**).
66. gibbet: gallows, from which criminals were hanged.
68. office: function.
S.D. armed Head: helmeted head, foreshadowing Macbeth's decapitation by Macduff.
72. S.D. descends: The stage had a trap-door for such effects.
74. harped: given voice to; **aright:** exactly.

FIRST WITCH   He will not be commanded. Here's another,   75
  More potent than the first.

                  Thunder. SECOND APPARITION, *a bloody Child.*

SECOND APPARITION   Macbeth! Macbeth! Macbeth!
MACBETH   Had I three ears, I'd hear thee.
SECOND APPARITION   Be bloody, bold, and resolute; laugh to
  scorn
  The pow'r of man, for none of woman born   80
  Shall harm Macbeth.   *Descends.*
MACBETH   Then live, Macduff. What need I fear of thee?
  But yet I'll make assurance double sure,
  And take a bond of fate. Thou shalt not live,
  That I may tell pale-hearted fear it lies,   85
  And sleep in spite of thunder.

           Thunder. THIRD APPARITION, *a Child crowned,*
                      with a tree in his hand.

                What is this
  That rises like the issue of a king,
  And wears upon his baby brow the round
  And top of sovereignty?
ALL   Listen, but speak not to't.
THIRD APPARITION   Be lion-mettled, proud, and take no care   90
  Who chafes, who frets, or where conspirers are.
  Macbeth shall never vanquished be until
  Great Birnam Wood to high Dunsinane Hill
  Shall come against him.   *Descends.*
MACBETH   That will never be.
  Who can impress the forest, bid the tree   95
  Unfix his earth-bound root? Sweet bodements, good.
  Rebellious dead, rise never till the wood
  Of Birnam rise, and our high-placed Macbeth
  Shall live the lease of nature, pay his breath

---

   76. S.D. bloody Child: This image suggests the infanticides in the imagery (1.7.54–58)
and the action (4.2), and also the retribution in the person of Macduff, untimely ripped from
his mother's womb.
   80. of woman born: a human being. The phrase echoes biblical pronouncements (see Job
14:1, 15:14, 25:4).
   84. take . . . fate: get a guarantee from fate; **Thou:** Macduff.
   86. S.D. Child: This figure may represent Malcolm, true heir to the throne, or Banquo's
issue, future heirs. The tree suggests Birnam Wood.
   88–89. round And top: crown.
   95. impress: draft into service.
   96. bodements: omens, prophecies.
   97. Rebellious dead: Banquo and his ghost.

To time and mortal custom. Yet my heart   100
Throbs to know one thing: tell me, if your art
Can tell so much, shall Banquo's issue ever
Reign in this kingdom?
ALL   Seek to know no more.
MACBETH   I will be satisfied. Deny me this,
And an eternal curse fall on you! Let me know.   105

                    [*The cauldron descends.*] *Hautboys.*

Why sinks that cauldron? And what noise is this?
FIRST WITCH   Show!
SECOND WITCH   Show!
THIRD WITCH   Show!
ALL   Show his eyes, and grieve his heart;   110
Come like shadows, so depart.

                    A show of eight KINGS, *and* BANQUO *last;*
                    [*the eighth King*] *with a glass in his hand.*

MACBETH   Thou art too like the spirit of Banquo. Down!
Thy crown does sear mine eyeballs! And thy hair,
Thou other gold-bound brow, is like the first.
A third is like the former.—Filthy hags,   115
Why do you show me this?—A fourth! Start, eyes!
What, will the line stretch out to the crack of doom?
Another yet? A seventh! I'll see no more.
And yet the eighth appears, who bears a glass
Which shows me many more; and some I see   120
That two-fold balls and treble scepters carry.
Horrible sight! Now, I see, 'tis true,
For the blood-boltered Banquo smiles upon me,
And points at them for his.   [*The apparitions vanish.*]
                    What, is this so?
FIRST WITCH   Ay, sir, all this is so. But why   125
Stands Macbeth thus amazedly?
Come, sisters, cheer we up his sprites,
And show the best of our delights.

---

100. **mortal custom:** the custom of mortality.
111. S.D. The eight kings represent descendants of Banquo, the ancestors of the Stuart line culminating in King James (1603–25), reigning at the time of the play.
111.2. S.D. **glass:** magic mirror.
114. **other:** second.
116. **Start:** bulge from eye sockets.
121. **two-fold . . . scepters:** two orbs and three scepters, symbolic accoutrements of royalty, perhaps alluding to James I, king of Scotland and Ireland. The three scepters may refer to James' assumed authority over Great Britain, France, and Ireland.
123. **blood-boltered:** having hair matted with blood.
125–32. usually regarded as non-Shakespearean.

I'll charm the air to give a sound,
While you perform your antic round,   130
That this great king may kindly say,
Our duties did his welcome pay.

                    Music. The Witches dance and vanish.

MACBETH   Where are they? Gone? Let this pernicious hour
Stand aye accursèd in the calendar!
Come in, without there!

                                        Enter LENNOX.

LENNOX   What's Your Grace's will?   135
MACBETH   Saw you the Weïrd Sisters?
LENNOX   No, my lord.
MACBETH   Came they not by you?
LENNOX   No, indeed, my lord.
MACBETH   Infected be the air whereon they ride,
And damned all those that trust them! I did hear
The galloping of horse. Who was't came by?   140
LENNOX   'Tis two or three, my lord, that bring you word
Macduff is fled to England.
MACBETH   Fled to England!
LENNOX   Ay, my good lord.
MACBETH [*Aside*]   Time, thou anticipat'st my dread exploits.
The flighty purpose never is o'ertook   145
Unless the deed go with it. From this moment
The very firstlings of my heart shall be
The firstlings of my hand. And even now,
To crown my thoughts with acts, be it thought and done.
The castle of Macduff I will surprise,   150
Seize upon Fife, give to th'edge o'th'sword
His wife, his babes, and all unfortunate souls
That trace him in his line. No boasting like a fool;
This deed I'll do before this purpose cool.
But no more sights!—Where are these gentlemen?   155
Come, bring me where they are.   *Exeunt.*

---

130. **antic round:** fantastic circle dance.
134. **aye:** ever.
144. **anticipat'st:** foresee (and thus prevent).
145–46. **The . . . it:** The swift resolution to do something never amounts to anything unless accompanied by action.
147. **firstlings:** first children. Macbeth promises to turn his impulses to deeds.
150. **surprise:** attack unexpectedly.
153. **trace . . . line:** follow him in his family line.
155. **these gentlemen:** the two or three messengers (line 141).

4.2 [*Fife. Macduff's castle.*]

Enter Macduff's WIFE, *her* SON, *and* ROSS.

WIFE   What had he done to make him fly the land?
ROSS   You must have patience, madam.
WIFE   He had none;
  His flight was madness. When our actions do not,
  Our fears do make us traitors.
ROSS   You know not
  Whether it was his wisdom or his fear.   5
WIFE   Wisdom? To leave his wife, to leave his babes,
  His mansion, and his titles in a place
  From whence himself does fly? He loves us not;
  He wants the natural touch. For the poor wren,
  The most diminutive of birds, will fight,   10
  Her young ones in her nest, against the owl.
  All is the fear and nothing is the love,
  As little is the wisdom, where the flight
  So runs against all reason.
ROSS   My dearest coz,
  I pray you, school yourself. But, for your husband,   15
  He is noble, wise, judicious, and best knows
  The fits o'the season. I dare not speak much further,
  But cruel are the times when we are traitors
  And do not know ourselves, when we hold rumor
  From what we fear, yet know not what we fear,   20
  But float upon a wild and violent sea,
  Each way and none. I take my leave of you;
  Shall not be long but I'll be here again.
  Things at the worst will cease, or else climb upward
  To what they were before. [*To the Son*] My pretty cousin, 25
  Blessing upon you!
WIFE   Fathered he is, and yet he's fatherless.
ROSS   I am so much a fool, should I stay longer
  It would be my disgrace and your discomfort.
  I take my leave at once.   *Exit Ross.*

3–4. **When . . . traitors:** Even when we commit no acts of treason, our fears can make
us treasonous. (Macduff, she suggests, has betrayed his family and country by running away.)
9. **wants:** lacks.
14. **coz:** cousin, kinswoman (a term of affection).
15. **school:** discipline.
17. **fits . . . season:** violent conditions of the time.
19. **know ourselves:** know ourselves to be such (traitors); **hold:** believe.
20. About what we fear, though we don't know what we fear exactly.
22. **Each . . . none:** in every direction at once and in none specifically.
29. My staying (and weeping) would disgrace me and distress you.

WIFE   Sirrah, your father's dead.   30
  And what will you do now? How will you live?
SON   As birds do, mother.
WIFE   What, with worms and flies?
SON   With what I get, I mean; and so do they.
WIFE   Poor bird, thou'dst never fear the net nor lime,
  The pitfall nor the gin.   35
SON   Why should I, mother? Poor birds they are not set for.
  My father is not dead, for all your saying.
WIFE   Yes, he is dead. How wilt thou do for a father?
SON   Nay, how will you do for a husband?
WIFE   Why, I can buy me twenty at any market.   40
SON   Then you'll buy 'em to sell again.
WIFE   Thou speak'st with all thy wit, and yet, i'faith, with wit
  enough for thee.
SON   Was my father a traitor, mother?
WIFE   Ay, that he was.   45
SON   What is a traitor?
WIFE   Why, one that swears and lies.
SON   And be all traitors that do so?
WIFE   Every one that does so is a traitor and must be hanged.
SON   And must they all be hanged that swear and lie?   50
WIFE   Every one.
SON   Who must hang them?
WIFE   Why, the honest men.
SON   Then the liars and swearers are fools, for there are liars and
  swearers enough to beat the honest men and hang up them.   55
WIFE   Now, God help thee, poor monkey! But how wilt thou do
  for a father?
SON   If he were dead, you'd weep for him; if you would not, it
  were a good sign that I should quickly have a new father.
WIFE   Poor prattler, how thou talk'st!   60

                                  Enter a MESSENGER.

MESSENGER   Bless you, fair dame. I am not to you known,
  Though in your state of honor I am perfect.

---

  30. Sirrah: an affectionate form of address to a child.
  34–35. net . . . gin: These are traps for birds; **lime:** birdlime, a sticky substance; **gin:** a snare or trap.
  36. they: traps.
  47. swears and lies: swears an oath to a sovereign (or wife) and breaks it.
  58–59. if . . . father: The son suggests that the mother's lack of tears would indicate a new love interest.
  62. Though I know well your nobility.

I doubt some danger does approach you nearly.
If you will take a homely man's advice,
Be not found here. Hence with your little ones!   65
To fright you thus, methinks, I am too savage;
To do worse to you were fell cruelty,
Which is too nigh your person. Heaven preserve you.
I dare abide no longer.   *Exit Messenger.*
WIFE   Whither should I fly?
I have done no harm. But I remember now   70
I am in this earthly world, where to do harm
Is often laudable, to do good sometime
Accounted dangerous folly. Why then, alas,
Do I put up that womanly defense,
To say I have done no harm?

                              Enter MURDERERS.

                    What are these faces?   75
A MURDERER   Where is your husband?
WIFE   I hope in no place so unsanctified
Where such as thou mayst find him.
A MURDERER   He's a traitor.
SON   Thou liest, thou shag-haired villain!
A MURDERER   What, you egg!
Young fry of treachery! [*He stabs him.*]
SON   He has killed me, mother!   80
Run away, I pray you! [*He dies.*]

        Exit [*Wife*] *crying* "Murder!" [*followed by Murderers with
                              Son's body*].

4.3 [*England. At the court of King Edward the Confessor.*]

        Enter MALCOLM *and* MACDUFF.

MALCOLM   Let us seek out some desolate shade, and there
    Weep our sad bosoms empty.
MACDUFF   Let us rather
    Hold fast the mortal sword, and like good men

    63. doubt: fear.
    64. homely: plain (speaking).
    67. fell: vicious.
    68. Which . . . person: such cruelty is too near you now.
    80. fry: offspring (of fish).
    3. mortal: deadly.

Bestride our downfall birthdom. Each new morn
New widows howl, new orphans cry, new sorrows   5
Strike heaven on the face, that it resounds
As if it felt with Scotland and yelled out
Like syllable of dolor.

MALCOLM   What I believe, I'll wail;
What know, believe; and what I can redress,
As I shall find the time to friend, I will.   10
What you have spoke, it may be so, perchance.
This tyrant, whose sole name blisters our tongues,
Was once thought honest. You have loved him well;
He hath not touched you yet. I am young, but something
You may deserve of him through me, and wisdom   15
To offer up a weak, poor, innocent lamb
T'appease an angry god.

MACDUFF   I am not treacherous.

MALCOLM   But Macbeth is.
A good and virtuous nature may recoil   20
In an imperial charge. But I shall crave your pardon.
That which you are my thoughts cannot transpose;
Angels are bright still, though the brightest fell.
Though all things foul would wear the brows of grace,
Yet grace must still look so.

MACDUFF   I have lost my hopes.   25

MALCOLM   Perchance even there where I did find my doubts.
Why in that rawness left you wife and child,
Those precious motives, those strong knots of love,
Without leave-taking? I pray you,
Let not my jealousies be your dishonors,   30
But mine own safeties. You may be rightly just,

4. **Bestride . . . birthdom:** stand over and protect our fallen native land.
6. **that:** so that.
8. **Like . . . dolor:** the same cry of pain.
10. **the . . . friend:** the opportune time.
12. **sole:** mere.
14–15. **something . . . me:** something you may get from him as a reward for betraying me.
15. **wisdom:** it is wise.
20–21. **recoil . . . charge:** give way, or go in a reverse motion, because of imperial force or command. (The image is of a gun springing back by force of the firing.)
22. **transpose:** transform.
23. **the brightest:** Lucifer.
24. **brows:** appearance.
25. **look so:** like grace. Though foul things put on good appearances, in other words, good things still appear good and may be trusted.
26. **there:** in the general climate of suspicion and fear.
27. **rawness:** (1) vulnerable position; (2) rudeness (referring to Macduff's abrupt departure).
30–31. **Let . . . safeties:** Assume that I ask such questions not for your dishonor but for my safety.

Whatever I shall think.
MACDUFF   Bleed, bleed, poor country!
Great tyranny, lay thou thy basis sure,
For goodness dare not check thee; wear thou thy wrongs,
The title is affeered. Fare thee well, lord.   35
I would not be the villain that thou think'st
For the whole space that's in the tyrant's grasp,
And the rich East to boot.
MALCOLM   Be not offended.
I speak not as in absolute fear of you.
I think our country sinks beneath the yoke;   40
It weeps, it bleeds, and each new day a gash
Is added to her wounds. I think withal
There would be hands uplifted in my right,
And here from gracious England have I offer
Of goodly thousands. But, for all this,   45
When I shall tread upon the tyrant's head,
Or wear it on my sword, yet my poor country
Shall have more vices than it had before,
More suffer and more sundry ways than ever,
By him that shall succeed.
MACDUFF   What should he be?   50
MALCOLM   It is myself I mean, in whom I know
All the particulars of vice so grafted
That, when they shall be opened, black Macbeth
Will seem as pure as snow, and the poor state
Esteem him as a lamb, being compared   55
With my confineless harms.
MACDUFF   Not in the legions
Of horrid hell can come a devil more damned
In evils to top Macbeth.
MALCOLM   I grant him bloody,
Luxurious, avaricious, false, deceitful,
Sudden, malicious, smacking of every sin   60

33. **basis sure:** foundation securely.
34. **wear:** display (as on a heraldic shield).
35. **title is affeered:** The tyranny is confirmed, settled.
39. **absolute fear:** complete mistrust.
42. **withal:** in addition.
43. **in my right:** in support of my claim to the throne.
44. **England:** the king of England.
45. **goodly:** considerable in respect to size.
50. **succeed:** succeed to the throne.
52. **grafted:** implanted into his character.
53. **opened:** revealed, as a bud is opened (continues the plant imagery).
56. **confineless:** limitless.
59. **Luxurious:** lecherous.
60. **Sudden:** rash.

That has a name. But there's no bottom, none,
In my voluptuousness; your wives, your daughters,
Your matrons, and your maids could not fill up
The cistern of my lust, and my desire
All continent impediments would o'erbear   65
That did oppose my will. Better Macbeth
Than such an one to reign.
MACDUFF   Boundless intemperance
In nature is a tyranny. It hath been
Th'untimely emptying of the happy throne,
And fall of many kings. But fear not yet   70
To take upon you what is yours. You may
Convey your pleasures in a spacious plenty,
And yet seem cold; the time you may so hoodwink.
We have willing dames enough. There cannot be
That vulture in you to devour so many   75
As will to greatness dedicate themselves,
Finding it so inclined.
MALCOLM   With this there grows
In my most ill-composed affection such
A stanchless avarice that, were I king,
I should cut off the nobles for their lands,   80
Desire his jewels and this other's house,
And my more-having would be as a sauce
To make me hunger more, that I should forge
Quarrels unjust against the good and loyal,
Destroying them for wealth.
MACDUFF   This avarice   85
Sticks deeper, grows with more pernicious root
Than summer-seeming lust, and it hath been
The sword of our slain kings. Yet do not fear;
Scotland hath foisons to fill up your will
Of your mere own. All these are portable,   90

65. **continent**: containing, restraining.
66. **will**: lust.
68. **nature**: human nature.
70. **yet**: nevertheless.
72. **Convey**: manage in secret.
73. **cold**: chaste; **hoodwink**: blindfold, deceive.
78. **ill-composed affection**: (1) evil disposition; (2) poorly managed passion.
79. **stanchless**: insatiable.
81. **his**: one man's.
82. **more-having**: having more.
87. **summer-seeming**: (1) seeming like summer, i.e., hot and transitory; (2) summer beseeming, i.e., appropriate to youth.
88. **sword . . . slain**: sword that slew our.
89. **foisons**: resources.
90. **Of . . . own**: from your royal supplies alone; **portable**: endurable.

With other graces weighed.
MALCOLM   But I have none. The king-becoming graces,
As justice, verity, temp'rance, stableness,
Bounty, perseverance, mercy, lowliness,
Devotion, patience, courage, fortitude—   95
I have no relish of them, but abound
In the division of each several crime,
Acting it many ways. Nay, had I pow'r, I should
Pour the sweet milk of concord into hell,
Uproar the universal peace, confound   100
All unity on earth.
MACDUFF ·   O Scotland, Scotland!
MALCOLM   If such a one be fit to govern, speak.
I am as I have spoken.
MACDUFF   Fit to govern?
No, not to live! O nation miserable,
With an untitled tyrant, bloody-sceptered!   105
When shalt thou see thy wholesome days again,
Since that the truest issue of thy throne
By his own interdiction stands accursed,
And does blaspheme his breed? Thy royal father
Was a most sainted king; the queen that bore thee,   110
Oft'ner upon her knees than on her feet,
Died every day she lived. Fare thee well.
These evils thou repeat'st upon thyself
Have banished me from Scotland. O my breast,
Thy hope ends here.
MALCOLM   Macduff, this noble passion,   115
Child of integrity, hath from my soul
Wiped the black scruples, reconciled my thoughts
To thy good truth and honor. Devilish Macbeth
By many of these trains hath sought to win me
Into his power, and modest wisdom plucks me   120
From over-credulous haste. But God above
Deal between thee and me. For even now

91. **weighed:** counterbalanced.
94. **lowliness:** humility.
97. **division:** variations; **several:** distinct.
100. **Uproar:** throw into confusion.
105. **untitled:** usurping.
108. **interdiction:** prohibition.
109. **blaspheme:** slander.
112. **Died . . . lived:** died to this world by daily religious practices.
113–14. **These . . . Scotland:** Your self-confessed evil makes it impossible for me to
return (with you) to Scotland.
117. **scruples:** doubts.
119. **trains:** tricks.
120. **modest . . . plucks:** prudence restrains.

I put myself to thy direction and
Unspeak mine own detraction, here abjure
The taints and blames I laid upon myself   125
For strangers to my nature. I am yet
Unknown to woman, never was forsworn,
Scarcely have coveted what was mine own,
At no time broke my faith, would not betray
The devil to his fellow, and delight   130
No less in truth than life. My first false speaking
Was this upon myself. What I am truly
Is thine and my poor country's to command,
Whither, indeed, before thy here-approach,
Old Siward with ten thousand warlike men   135
Already at a point was setting forth.
Now we'll together, and the chance of goodness
Be like our warranted quarrel. Why are you silent?
MACDUFF   Such welcome and unwelcome things at once,
'Tis hard to reconcile.   140

                                    Enter a DOCTOR.

MALCOLM   Well, more anon. [*To the Doctor*] Comes the King
    forth, I pray you?
DOCTOR   Ay, sir. There are a crew of wretched souls
    That stay his cure. Their malady convinces
    The great assay of art, but at his touch—
    Such sanctity hath heaven given his hand!—   145
    They presently amend.
MALCOLM   I thank you, Doctor.   *Exit* [*Doctor*].
MACDUFF   What's the disease he means?
MALCOLM   'Tis called the Evil.
    A most miraculous work in this good king,
    Which often, since my here-remain in England,
    I have seen him do. How he solicits heaven,   150

124. **mine own detraction:** my former self-condemnation.
126. **For:** as.
127. **Unknown to woman:** a virgin.
132. **upon:** against.
134. **Whither:** to which place.
135. **warlike:** armed.
136. **at a point:** resolved.
137. **we'll:** we'll go; **chance of goodness:** (1) chance of a favorable outcome; (2) fortune of the good.
138. **Be . . . quarrel:** match the justice of our cause.
143. **stay:** await; **convinces:** conquers.
144. **assay of art:** attempts of medical science.
146. **amend:** get better.
147. **Evil:** scrofula, a disease characterized by chronic enlargement of the lymphatic glands and ulcers, supposedly cured by the royal touch.
149. **here-remain:** stay.

Himself best knows; but strangely-visited people,
All swoll'n and ulcerous, pitiful to the eye,
The mere despair of surgery, he cures,
Hanging a golden stamp about their necks,
Put on with holy prayers; and, 'tis spoken,   155
To the succeeding royalty he leaves
The healing benediction. With this strange virtue,
He hath a heavenly gift of prophecy,
And sundry blessings hang about his throne
That speak him full of grace.

                                                    Enter ROSS.

MACDUFF   See who comes here?   160
MALCOLM   My countryman, but yet I know him not.
MACDUFF   My ever gentle cousin, welcome hither.
MALCOLM   I know him now. Good God, betimes remove
   The means that makes us strangers.
ROSS   Sir, amen.
MACDUFF   Stands Scotland where it did?
ROSS   Alas, poor country,   165
   Almost afraid to know itself. It cannot
   Be called our mother, but our grave; where nothing
   But who knows nothing is once seen to smile;
   Where sighs and groans and shrieks that rend the air
   Are made, not marked; where violent sorrow seems   170
   A modern ecstasy. The deadman's knell
   Is there scarce asked for who, and good men's lives
   Expire before the flowers in their caps,
   Dying or ere they sicken.
MACDUFF   O relation
   Too nice and yet too true!
MALCOLM   What's the newest grief?   175
ROSS   That of an hour's age doth hiss the speaker;
   Each minute teems a new one.
MACDUFF   How does my wife?

151. **strangely-visited:** strangely afflicted.
153. **mere:** absolute.
154. **stamp:** coin. Elizabeth and James gave a gold coin to those they touched.
157. **healing benediction:** this power to heal; **virtue:** power.
163. **betimes:** immediately.
167. **nothing:** nobody.
168. **who:** one who; **once:** ever.
170. **marked:** noticed.
171. **modern ecstasy:** common state of emotion.
174. **or ere:** before; **relation:** report.
175. **nice:** precise.
176. A report only one hour old is hissed as old news.
177. **teems:** brings forth.

ROSS   Why, well.
MACDUFF   And all my children?
ROSS   Well too.
MACDUFF   The tyrant has not battered at their peace?
ROSS   No, they were well at peace when I did leave 'em.   180
MACDUFF   Be not a niggard of your speech. How goes't?
ROSS   When I came hither to transport the tidings
   Which I have heavily borne, there ran a rumor
   Of many worthy fellows that were out,
   Which was to my belief witnessed the rather   185
   For that I saw the tyrant's power afoot.
   Now is the time of help. [*To Malcolm*] Your eye in Scotland
   Would create soldiers, make our women fight
   To doff their dire distresses.
MALCOLM   Be't their comfort
   We are coming thither. Gracious England hath   190
   Lent us good Siward and ten thousand men—
   An older and a better soldier none
   That Christendom gives out.
ROSS   Would I could answer
   This comfort with the like. But I have words
   That would be howled out in the desert air,   195
   Where hearing should not latch them.
MACDUFF   What concern they?
   The general cause, or is it a fee-grief
   Due to some single breast?
ROSS   No mind that's honest
   But in it shares some woe, though the main part
   Pertains to you alone.
MACDUFF   If it be mine,   200
   Keep it not from me; quickly let me have it.
ROSS   Let not your ears despise my tongue forever,
   Which shall possess them with the heaviest sound
   That ever yet they heard.
MACDUFF   Hum, I guess at it.
ROSS   Your castle is surprised, your wife and babes   205

181. **niggard:** miser.
184. **out:** in the field, in arms.
185. **witnessed the rather:** made more credible.
186. **afoot:** mobilized for action.
187. **eye:** person, i.e., yourself.
189. **doff:** take off (like clothing).
190. **England:** King Edward.
192. **none:** is no one.
193. **gives out:** tells of.
196. **latch:** catch.
197–98. **fee-grief . . . breast:** grief belonging to a particular person. The phrase derives from "fee-simple," an estate belonging to the owner and his heirs forever.

Savagely slaughtered. To relate the manner
Were, on the quarry of these murdered deer,
To add the death of you.
MALCOLM   Merciful heaven!
What, man, ne'er pull your hat upon your brows.
Give sorrow words. The grief that does not speak   210
Whispers the o'er-fraught heart and bids it break.
MACDUFF   My children too?
ROSS   Wife, children, servants—all that could be found.
MACDUFF   And I must be from thence! My wife kill'd too?
ROSS   I have said.   215
MALCOLM   Be comforted.
Let's make us med'cines of our great revenge,
To cure this deadly grief.
MACDUFF   He has no children. All my pretty ones?
Did you say all? O hell-kite! All?   220
What, all my pretty chickens and their dam
At one fell swoop?
MALCOLM   Dispute it like a man.
MACDUFF   I shall do so.
But I must also feel it as a man.   225
I cannot but remember such things were
That were most precious to me. Did heaven look on
And would not take their part? Sinful Macduff,
They were all struck for thee! Naught that I am,
Not for their own demerits but for mine,   230
Fell slaughter on their souls. Heaven rest them now.
MALCOLM   Be this the whetstone of your sword. Let grief
Convert to anger; blunt not the heart, enrage it.
MACDUFF   Oh, I could play the woman with mine eyes
And braggart with my tongue. But, gentle heavens,   235
Cut short all intermission! Front to front
Bring thou this fiend of Scotland and myself!
Within my sword's length set him! If he scape,
Heaven forgive him too.

207. **quarry:** heap of slaughtered deer (with a pun on "dear").
209. **pull . . . brows:** hide your grief.
211. **Whispers:** whispers to; **o'erfraught:** overburdened.
214. **from thence:** away from home.
219. **He . . . children:** (1) Macbeth has no children (and therefore cannot suffer a fitting retribution); (2) Malcolm has no children (and therefore cannot understand this pain).
220. **hell-kite:** kite (bird of prey) from hell.
221. **dam:** mother.
223. **Dispute:** fight against.
229. **Naught:** wicked man.
232. **whetstone:** sharpening stone.
234. **play . . . eyes:** weep.
236. **intermission:** delay; **Front to front:** face to face.

MALCOLM   This time goes manly.
  Come, go we to the King. Our power is ready;   240
  Our lack is nothing but our leave. Macbeth
  Is ripe for shaking, and the powers above
  Put on their instruments. Receive what cheer you may;
  The night is long that never finds the day.   *Exeunt.*

5.1 [*Dunsinane. Macbeth's castle.*]

Enter a DOCTOR OF PHYSIC *and a* WAITING-GENTLEWOMAN.

DOCTOR   I have two nights watched with you, but can perceive
  no truth in your report. When was it she last walked?
GENTLEWOMAN   Since His Majesty went into the field, I have
  seen her rise from her bed, throw her nightgown upon her,
  unlock her closet, take forth paper, fold it, write upon't, read   5
  it, afterwards seal it, and again return to bed, yet all this while
  in a most fast sleep.
DOCTOR   A great perturbation in nature, to receive at once the
  benefit of sleep, and do the effects of watching. In this slumbery
  agitation, besides her walking and other actual performances,   10
  what at any time have you heard her say?
GENTLEWOMAN   That, sir, which I will not report after her.
DOCTOR   You may to me, and 'tis most meet you should.
GENTLEWOMAN   Neither to you nor any one, having no witness
  to confirm my speech.   15

                    Enter LADY MACBETH, *with a taper.*

  Lo, you, here she comes. This is her very guise and, upon my
  life, fast asleep. Observe her; stand close.   [*They stand aside.*]
DOCTOR   How came she by that light?
GENTLEWOMAN   Why, it stood by her. She has light by her
  continually; 'tis her command.   20
DOCTOR   You see her eyes are open.
GENTLEWOMAN   Ay, but their sense are shut.

  239. time: time of resolution and action. Some editors have plausibly emended to "tune,"
referring to the new mood of resolution.
  241. Our . . . leave: We have only to take leave of the English King.
  243. Put . . . instruments: (1) arm themselves for action; (2) take us as their agents.
  S.D. Physic: medicine; **Waiting-gentlewoman:** personal servant.
  5. closet: cabinet.
  9. do . . . watching: act as if she were awake.
  13. meet: fitting.
  15. S.D. taper: candle.
  16. guise: custom.
  17. close: concealed.

DOCTOR   What is it she does now? Look how she rubs her hands.

GENTLEWOMAN   It is an accustomed action with her to seem thus washing her hands. I have known her continue in this a quarter 25 of an hour.

LADY MACBETH   Yet here's a spot.

DOCTOR   Hark, she speaks. I will set down what comes from her to satisfy my remembrance the more strongly.

LADY MACBETH   Out, damned spot! Out, I say! One, two, why, 30 then, 'tis time to do't. Hell is murky. Fie, my lord, fie, a soldier, and afeard? What need we fear who knows it, when none can call our power to account? Yet who would have thought the old man to have had so much blood in him?

DOCTOR   Do you mark that?   35

LADY MACBETH   The Thane of Fife had a wife. Where is she now? What, will these hands ne'er be clean? No more o'that, my lord, no more o'that. You mar all with this starting.

DOCTOR   Go to; go to. You have known what you should not.

GENTLEWOMAN   She has spoke what she should not, I am sure of 40 that. Heaven knows what she has known.

LADY MACBETH   Here's the smell of the blood still. All the perfumes of Arabia will not sweeten this little hand. Oh, oh, oh!

DOCTOR   What a sigh is there! The heart is sorely charged.   45

GENTLEWOMAN   I would not have such a heart in my bosom for the dignity of the whole body.

DOCTOR   Well, well, well.

GENTLEWOMAN   Pray God it be, sir.

DOCTOR   This disease is beyond my practice. Yet I have known 50 those which have walked in their sleep who have died holily in their beds.

LADY MACBETH   Wash your hands; put on your nightgown; look not so pale. I tell you yet again, Banquo's buried; he cannot come out on's grave.   55

DOCTOR   Even so?

LADY MACBETH   To bed, to bed. There's knocking at the gate. Come, come, come, come, give me your hand. What's done cannot be undone. To bed, to bed, to bed.   *Exit Lady.*

36. Thane of Fife: Macduff.
38. starting: flinching.
39. Go to: come on (a mild reprimand).
43. Arabia: known for its spices.
45. charged: burdened.
47. dignity: high rank (as Queen).
55. on's: of his.

DOCTOR   Will she go now to bed?   60
GENTLEWOMAN   Directly.
DOCTOR   Foul whisp'rings are abroad. Unnatural deeds
  Do breed unnatural troubles. Infected minds
  To their deaf pillows will discharge their secrets.
  More needs she the divine than the physician.   65
  God, God forgive us all. Look after her;
  Remove from her the means of all annoyance,
  And still keep eyes upon her. So, good night.
  My mind she has mated, and amazed my sight.
  I think, but dare not speak.
GENTLEWOMAN   Good night, good Doctor.   70

                                           Exeunt.

5.2 [*Country near Dunsinane.*]

Drum and colors. Enter MENTEITH, CAITHNESS, ANGUS, LENNOX,
SOLDIERS.

MENTEITH   The English pow'r is near, led on by Malcolm,
  His uncle Siward, and the good Macduff.
  Revenges burn in them, for their dear causes
  Would to the bleeding and the grim alarm
  Excite the mortified man.
ANGUS   Near Birnam Wood   5
  Shall we well meet them; that way are they coming.
CAITHNESS   Who knows if Donaldbain be with his brother?
LENNOX   For certain, sir, he is not. I have a file
  Of all the gentry. There is Siward's son,
  And many unrough youths that even now   10
  Protest their first of manhood.
MENTEITH   What does the tyrant?
CAITHNESS   Great Dunsinane he strongly fortifies.
  Some say he's mad; others that lesser hate him
  Do call it valiant fury. But for certain
  He cannot buckle his distempered cause   15

  65. **divine:** clergyman.
  67. **annoyance:** harm, injury The Doctor seeks to prevent suicide.
  69. **mated:** stupefied.
  s.D. **Drum and colors:** drummers and flag-carriers.
  3. **dear:** deeply felt.
  4–5. **Would . . . man:** would stir the dead (**mortified**) man to bloody (**bleeding**) and grim
  battle.
  8. **file:** list.
  10. **unrough:** unbearded, young.
  11. **protest:** assert publicly; **first:** first evidence.
  15. **distempered:** diseased and swollen.

Within the belt of rule.

ANGUS   Now does he feel
His secret murders sticking on his hands;
Now minutely revolts upbraid his faith-breach.
Those he commands move only in command,
Nothing in love. Now does he feel his title   20
Hang loose about him, like a giant's robe
Upon a dwarfish thief.

MENTEITH   Who then shall blame
His pestered senses to recoil and start,
When all that is within him does condemn
Itself for being there?

CAITHNESS   Well, march we on   25
To give obedience where 'tis truly owed.
Meet we the med'cine of the sickly weal,
And with him pour we in our country's purge
Each drop of us.

LENNOX   Or so much as it needs
To dew the sovereign flower and drown the weeds.   30
Make we our march towards Birnam.   *Exeunt, marching.*

5.3 [*Dunsinane. Macbeth's castle.*]

Enter MACBETH, DOCTOR, *and* ATTENDANTS.

MACBETH   Bring me no more reports. Let them fly all!
Till Birnam Wood remove to Dunsinane,
I cannot taint with fear. What's the boy Malcolm?
Was he not born of woman? The spirits that know
All mortal consequences have pronounced me thus: 5
"Fear not, Macbeth! No man that's born of woman
Shall e'er have power upon thee." Then fly, false thanes,
And mingle with the English epicures!
The mind I sway by and the heart I bear
Shall never sag with doubt nor shake with fear.   10

18. **minutely:** every minute; **faith-breach:** violation of faith and trust.
19. **in command:** out of obligation.
23. **pestered:** tormented.
27. **weal:** commonweal.
28. **him:** Malcolm (the medicine for sick Scotland); **pour we:** we pour ourselves (as part of the bloodletting, or **purge,** of the country).
30. **sovereign:** (1) royal; (2) curative. Malcolm is the **sovereign flower.**
1. **them:** deserting thanes.
3. **taint:** become weak.
5. **mortal consequences:** human eventualities.
8. **epicures:** lovers of pleasure.
9. **sway:** rule.

Enter SERVANT.

The devil damn thee black, thou cream-faced loon!
Where gott'st thou that goose look?
SERVANT   There is ten thousand—
MACBETH   Geese, villain?
SERVANT   Soldiers, sir.
MACBETH   Go prick thy face, and over-red thy fear,
   Thou lily-livered boy. What soldiers, patch?   15
   Death of thy soul! Those linen cheeks of thine
   Are counselors to fear. What soldiers, whey-face?
SERVANT   The English force, so please you.
MACBETH   Take thy face hence.   [*Exit Servant.*]
                     Seyton!—I am sick at heart,
   When I behold—Seyton, I say!—This push   20
   Will cheer me ever or disseat me now.
   I have lived long enough. My way of life
   Is fall'n into the sere, the yellow leaf,
   And that which should accompany old age,
   As honor, love, obedience, troops of friends,   25
   I must not look to have, but in their stead
   Curses, not loud but deep, mouth-honor, breath,
   Which the poor heart would fain deny and dare not.
   —Seyton!

Enter SEYTON.

SEYTON   What's your gracious pleasure?
MACBETH   What news more?   30
SEYTON   All is confirmed, my lord, which was reported.
MACBETH   I'll fight till from my bones my flesh be hacked.
   Give me my armor.
SEYTON   'Tis not needed yet.
MACBETH   I'll put it on.   35
   Send out more horses, skirr the country round,

11. **black**: the color of damned souls; **loon**: idler.
12. **goose**: stupid.
14. **over-red**: redden over. The servant is pale with fear (**cream-faced**, line 11, having **linen cheeks,** line 16).
15. **lily-livered**: cowardly. Blood has vacated the servant's liver, seat of passions such as courage; **patch**: fool.
16. **of thy**: on thy.
17. **Are . . . fear**: advise others to fear; **whey**: pale (as milk).
20. **behold**: Macbeth does not finish this thought; **push**: enemy advance.
21. **disseat**: dethrone.
23. **sere**: withered.
27. **mouth-honor**: honors given only with the mouth (and not the heart).
28. **fain**: gladly.
36. **skirr**: scour.

Hang those that talk of fear. Give me mine armor.—
How does your patient, doctor?
DOCTOR   Not so sick, my lord,
  As she is troubled with thick-coming fancies
  That keep her from her rest.
MACBETH   Cure her of that.   40
  Canst thou not minister to a mind diseased,
  Pluck from the memory a rooted sorrow,
  Raze out the written troubles of the brain,
  And with some sweet, oblivious antidote
  Cleanse the stuffed bosom of that perilous stuff   45
  Which weighs upon the heart?
DOCTOR   Therein the patient
  Must minister to himself.
MACBETH   Throw physic to the dogs! I'll none of it.—
  Come put mine armor on; give me my staff.
  Seyton, send out. Doctor, the thanes fly from me.—   50
  Come, sir, dispatch.—If thou couldst, Doctor, cast
  The water of my land, find her disease,
  And purge it to a sound and pristine health,
  I would applaud thee to the very echo
  That should applaud again.—Pull't off, I say.—   55
  What rhubarb, senna, or what purgative drug,
  Would scour these English hence? Hear'st thou of them?
DOCTOR   Ay, my good lord. Your royal preparation
  Makes us hear something.
MACBETH   Bring it after me.—
  I will not be afraid of death and bane,   60
  Till Birnam forest come to Dunsinane.
                                    Exeunt [all but the Doctor].
DOCTOR   Were I from Dunsinane away and clear,
  Profit again should hardly draw me here.   [*Exit.*]

---

43. **Raze out:** erase.
44. **oblivious:** causing forgetfulness.
48. **physic:** medicine.
51. **dispatch:** hurry, finish the job (of arming me).
51–52. **cast . . . land:** discover the disease of Scotland. To "cast water" was to diagnose
by inspecting urine.
56. **rhubarb, senna:** medicinal plants.
57. **scour:** clear out, purge.
59. **it:** the armor, not yet put on.
60. **bane:** destruction.
63. No profit or fee could lure me back here again.

5.4 [*Country near Birnam Wood.*]

Drum and colors. Enter MALCOLM, SIWARD, MACDUFF, SIWARD'S
SON, MENTEITH, CAITHNESS, ANGUS, *and* SOLDIERS, *marching.*

MALCOLM   Cousins, I hope the days are near at hand
  That chambers will be safe.
MENTEITH   We doubt it nothing.
SIWARD   What wood is this before us?
MENTEITH   The Wood of Birnam.
MALCOLM   Let every soldier hew him down a bough
  And bear't before him. Thereby shall we shadow   5
  The numbers of our host, and make discovery
  Err in report of us.
A SOLDIER   It shall be done.
SIWARD   We learn no other but the confident tyrant
  Keeps still in Dunsinane, and will endure
  Our setting down before't.
MALCOLM   'Tis his main hope.   10
  For where there is advantage to be given,
  Both more and less have given him the revolt,
  And none serve with him but constrainèd things
  Whose hearts are absent too.
MACDUFF   Let our just censures
  Attend the true event, and put we on   15
  Industrious soldiership.
SIWARD   The time approaches
  That will with due decision make us know
  What we shall say we have and what we owe.
  Thoughts speculative their unsure hopes relate,
  But certain issue strokes must arbitrate—   20
  Towards which, advance the war.   *Exeunt, marching.*

2. **chambers:** bedchambers, i.e., the homes of citizens; **nothing:** not at all.
5. **shadow:** conceal.
6. **discovery:** reports.
8. **other:** other news.
9. **Keeps still:** remains yet.
10. **setting . . . before't:** besieging the castle.
11. **advantage . . . given:** opportunity (to escape).
12. **more and less:** soldiers greater and lesser in rank.
14–15. **Let . . . event:** Let our impartial judgment await the actual outcome.
18. **owe:** own.
19–20. Thoughts now can relate only our hopes; blows must decide the real outcome.
21. **war:** army.

5.5 [*Dunsinane. Macbeth's castle.*]

Enter MACBETH, SEYTON, *and* SOLDIERS, *with drum and colors*

MACBETH   Hang out our banners on the outward walls.
The cry is still, "They come!" Our castle's strength
Will laugh a siege to scorn. Here let them lie
Till famine and the ague eat them up.
Were they not forced with those that should be ours,   5
We might have met them dareful, beard to beard,
And beat them backward home.   *A cry within of women.*
                              What is that noise?
SEYTON   It is the cry of women, my good lord.   [*Exit.*]
MACBETH   I have almost forgot the taste of fears.
The time has been my senses would have cooled   10
To hear a night-shriek, and my fell of hair
Would at a dismal treatise rouse and stir
As life were in't. I have supped full with horrors.
Direness, familiar to my slaughterous thoughts,
Cannot once start me.

                              [*Enter* SEYTON.]

                    Wherefore was that cry?   15
SEYTON   The Queen, my lord, is dead.
MACBETH   She should have died hereafter;
There would have been a time for such a word.
Tomorrow, and tomorrow, and tomorrow
Creeps in this petty pace from day to day   20
To the last syllable of recorded time,
And all our yesterdays have lighted fools
The way to dusty death. Out, out, brief candle!
Life's but a walking shadow, a poor player
That struts and frets his hour upon the stage   25

4. **ague:** fever.
5. **forced:** reinforced.
6. **dareful:** full of daring and defiance.
10. **my . . . cooled:** would have felt cold fear.
11. **fell:** covering, i.e., the hair on my head.
12. **dismal treatise:** dreadful story.
14. **Direness:** horror.
15. **start:** startle.
17. **should . . . hereafter:** (1) ought to have died at some better time; (2) would have died anyway.
21. **syllable:** smallest portion; **recorded time:** recordable time.
23. **dusty death:** perhaps echoing Genesis 3:19: "for dust thou art, and unto dust shalt thou return"; **candle:** a traditional symbol of life (see Job 18:6, 21:17; Dent CC1, see Selected Bibliography).
24. **Life's . . . shadow:** There are many classical and biblical precedents for the idea, including Job 8.9: "We are but of yesterday and know nothing because our days upon earth are a shadow." (Dent L249.1, see Selected Bibliography.)
25. **stage:** The world as stage is another common metaphor.

And then is heard no more. It is a tale
Told by an idiot, full of sound and fury,
Signifying nothing.

                                    Enter a MESSENGER.

Thou com'st to use thy tongue; thy story quickly.
MESSENGER   Gracious my lord,   30
  I should report that which I say I saw,
  But know not how to do't.
MACBETH   Well, say, sir.
MESSENGER   As I did stand my watch upon the hill,
  I looked toward Birnam, and anon methought
  The wood began to move.
MACBETH   Liar and slave!   35
MESSENGER   Let me endure your wrath if't be not so.
  Within this three mile may you see it coming;
  I say, a moving grove.
MACBETH   If thou speak'st false,
  Upon the next tree shall thou hang alive,
  Till famine cling thee; if thy speech be sooth,   40
  I care not if thou dost for me as much.
  I pull in resolution, and begin
  To doubt th'equivocation of the fiend
  That lies like truth. "Fear not, till Birnam Wood
  Do come to Dunsinane," and now a wood   45
  Comes toward Dunsinane. Arm, arm, and out!
  If this which he avouches does appear,
  There is nor flying hence nor tarrying here.
  I 'gin to be aweary of the sun,
  And wish th'estate o'the world were now undone.   50
  Ring the alarum bell! [*Alarums.*] Blow, wind, come, wrack!
  At least we'll die with harness on our back.   *Exeunt.*

5.6 [*Dunsinane. Before the castle.*]

Drum and colors. Enter MALCOLM, SIWARD, MACDUFF, *and their*
ARMY, *with boughs.*

MALCOLM   Now near enough. Your leafy screens throw down,
  And show like those you are. [*They throw down the boughs*]
                          You, worthy uncle,

40. **cling:** shrivel; **sooth:** truth.
42. **pull in:** rein in.
50. **estate:** order.
51. **wrack:** ruin
52. **harness:** armor.
2. **show:** show yourselves; **uncle:** Siward (a term of respect).

Shall with my cousin, your right noble son,
Lead our first battle. Worthy Macduff and we
Shall take upon's what else remains to do,   5
According to our order.
SIWARD   Fare you well.
Do we but find the tyrant's power tonight,
Let us be beaten if we cannot fight.
MACDUFF   Make all our trumpets speak. Give them all breath,
Those clamorous harbingers of blood and death!   *Exeunt.* 10
                                        Alarums continued.

5.7. [*The battlefield.*]

Enter MACBETH.

MACBETH   They have tied me to a stake. I cannot fly,
But bear-like I must fight the course. What's he
That was not born of woman? Such a one
Am I to fear, or none.

                                        Enter YOUNG SIWARD.

YOUNG SIWARD   What is thy name?   5
MACBETH   Thou'lt be afraid to hear it.
YOUNG SIWARD   No, though thou call'st thyself a hotter name
Than any is in hell.
MACBETH   My name's Macbeth.
YOUNG SIWARD   The devil himself could not pronounce a title
More hateful to mine ear.
MACBETH   No, nor more fearful.   10
YOUNG SIWARD   Thou liest, abhorrèd tyrant! With my sword
I'll prove the lie thou speak'st. *Fight, and Young Siward slain.*
MACBETH   Thou wast born of woman.
But swords I smile at, weapons laugh to scorn,
Brandished by man that's of a woman born.   15
                                        Exit [*with the body*].

                                        Alarums. Enter MACDUFF.

MACDUFF   That way the noise is. Tyrant, show thy face!
If thou be'st slain and with no stroke of mine,

---

4. **battle:** battalion.
6. **order:** battle plan.
7. **power:** army.
10. **harbingers:** forerunners.
2. **course:** a round in bearbaiting, wherein dogs attacked a bear tied to a stake.
12. **prove . . . speak'st:** prove that you speak a lie.

My wife and children's ghosts will haunt me still.
I cannot strike at wretched kerns, whose arms
Are hired to bear their staves. Either thou, Macbeth,   20
Or else my sword with an unbattered edge
I sheathe again, undeeded. There thou shouldst be;
By this great clatter one of greatest note
Seems bruited. Let me find him, Fortune,
And more I beg not.   *Exit. Alarums.* 25

                    Enter MALCOLM *and* SIWARD.

SIWARD   This way, my lord. The castle's gently rendered.
  The tyrant's people on both sides do fight;
  The noble thanes do bravely in the war;
  The day almost itself professes yours,
  And little is to do.
MALCOLM   We have met with foes   30
  That strike beside us.
SIWARD   Enter, sir, the castle.   *Exeunt. Alarums.*

[5.8 *The battlefield or in the castle.*]

                    Enter MACBETH.

MACBETH   Why should I play the Roman fool and die
  On mine own sword? Whiles I see lives, the gashes
  Do better upon them.

                              Enter MACDUFF.

MACDUFF   Turn, hellhound, turn!
MACBETH   Of all men else I have avoided thee.
  But get thee back. My soul is too much charged   5
  With blood of thine already!
MACDUFF   I have no words.
  My voice is in my sword, thou bloodier villain
  Than terms can give thee out!   *Fight. Alarums.*
MACBETH   Thou losest labor.

19. **kerns:** light-armed foot soldiers.
20. **staves:** lances.
22. **undeeded:** having done nothing.
24. **bruited:** noised, indicated.
26. **rendered:** surrendered.
29. **itself professes:** proclaims itself.
31. **strike beside:** fight on our side.
1. **play . . . fool:** imitate those foolish Romans who commit suicide.
2. **lives:** living enemies.
8. **terms:** words; **give . . . out:** describe you.

As easy mayst thou the intrenchant air
With thy keen sword impress as make me bleed. 10
Let fall thy blade on vulnerable crests.
I bear a charmèd life which must not yield
To one of woman born.

MACDUFF   Despair thy charm
And let the angel whom thou still hast served
Tell thee, Macduff was from his mother's womb 15
Untimely ripped.

MACBETH Accursèd be that tongue that tells me so,
For it hath cowed my better part of man!
And be these juggling fiends no more believed,
That palter with us in a double sense, 20
That keep the word of promise to our ear,
And break it to our hope. I'll not fight with thee.

MACDUFF Then yield thee, coward,
And live to be the show and gaze o'the time.
We'll have thee, as our rarer monsters are, 25
Painted upon a pole and underwrit,
"Here may you see the tyrant."

MACBETH   I will not yield,
To kiss the ground before young Malcolm's feet,
And to be baited with the rabble's curse.
Though Birnam Wood be come to Dunsinane, 30
And thou opposed, being of no woman born,
Yet I will try the last. Before my body
I throw my warlike shield. Lay on, Macduff,
And damned be him that first cries, "Hold, enough!"

                    Exeunt, fighting. Alarums.

        Enter [MACBETH *and* MACDUFF] *fighting, and
                    Macbeth slain.*

        [*Exit Macduff, with Macbeth's body.*]

9. **intrenchant:** incapable of being cut.
10. **impress:** mark.
11. **crests:** heads.
13. **charm:** magic.
14. **angel:** evil spirit (said ironically).
16. **Untimely:** prematurely, by Caesarean section.
18. **better . . . man:** courage.
19. **juggling:** deceiving.
20. **palter:** equivocate.
24. **gaze:** spectacle.
26. Macbeth's picture will be painted on a pole and displayed with an accompanying description.
29. **baited:** attacked (as by dogs).
32. **last:** (1) my last reserves of strength and courage; (2) the last battle.

Retreat and flourish. Enter, with drum and colors,
MALCOLM, SIWARD, ROSS, THANES, *and* SOLDIERS.

MALCOLM   I would the friends we miss were safe arrived.   35
SIWARD   Some must go off; and yet, by these I see
  So great a day as this is cheaply bought.
MALCOLM   Macduff is missing, and your noble son.
ROSS   Your son, my lord, has paid a soldier's debt.
  He only lived but till he was a man,   40
  The which no sooner had his prowess confirmed
  In the unshrinking station where he fought,
  But like a man he died.
SIWARD   Then, he is dead?
ROSS   Ay, and brought off the field. Your cause of sorrow
  Must not be measured by his worth, for then   45
  It hath no end.
SIWARD   Had he his hurts before?
ROSS   Ay, on the front.
SIWARD   Why, then, God's soldier be he.
  Had I as many sons as I have hairs,
  I would not wish them to a fairer death.
  And so, his knell is knolled.
MALCOLM   He's worth more sorrow,   50
  And that I'll spend for him.
SIWARD   He's worth no more.
  They say he parted well and paid his score,
  And so, God be with him. Here comes newer comfort.

Enter MACDUFF, *with Macbeth's head.*

MACDUFF   Hail, King! For so thou art. Behold where stands
  Th'usurper's cursèd head. The time is free.   55
  I see thee compassed with thy kingdom's pearl,
  That speak my salutation in their minds,
  Whose voices I desire aloud with mine:
  Hail, King of Scotland!
ALL   Hail, King of Scotland!   *Flourish.*

---

  34. s.d. The **Retreat** is a sound from a trumpet or drum signaling the concluding stage
of battle.
  36. go off: die, by these: by the survivors present.
  42. unshrinking station: place where he refused to back down.
  46. before: on his front (from facing the enemy).
  50. knolled: rung.
  52. score: reckoning.
  55. time is free: a proclamation of liberty from tyranny and the restoration of order in
Scotland.
  56. compassed . . . pearl: surrounded by the treasures of your kingdom, the Scottish
nobles.

MALCOLM We shall not spend a large expense of time   60
    Before we reckon with your several loves,
    And make us even with you. My thanes and kinsmen,
    Henceforth be earls, the first that ever Scotland
    In such an honor named. What's more to do,
    Which would be planted newly with the time,   65
    As calling home our exiled friends abroad
    That fled the snares of watchful tyranny,
    Producing forth the cruel ministers
    Of this dead butcher and his fiend-like queen—
    Who, as 'tis thought, by self and violent hands   70
    Took off her life—this, and what needful else
    That calls upon us, by the grace of grace,
    We will perform in measure, time and place.
    So, thanks to all at once and to each one
    Whom we invite to see us crowned at Scone.   75

                              Flourish. Exeunt all.

                                       Finis.

---

61. **reckon:** settle accounts.
65. **planted . . . time:** established in this new age.
68. **Producing forth:** leading to justice; **ministers:** agents.
70. **self and violent:** her own violent.
72. **grace of grace:** favor of divine grace.

SOURCES AND CONTEXTS

Sources

N-TOWN CYCLE

[The Slaughter of the Holy Innocents and the Death of Herod, 14th Century]†

[*Enter* KING HEROD, STEWARD, SOLDIERS.]

Then, looking back, the Steward goes to Herod and speaks.

STEWARD:　Lord, I have walked by dale and hill,
　　And waited as it is your will.
　　The kings three steal away full still
　　Through Bethlehem land.
　　They will never, so may I the,[1]
　　Come in the land of Galilee
　　For to see your fair city,
　　Nor deeds of your hand.
KING HEROD:　I ride on my rowel,[2] rich in my reign!
　　Ribs full red with rape[3] shall I rend!
　　Poppets and pap-hawks[4] I shall put in pain,
　　With my spear proven pichen and to pend.[5]
　　The gomes with gold crowns ne get never geyn![6]
　　To seek those sots, sondes[7] shall I send.

---

† From *The N-Town Play: Cotton MS Vespasian D.8*, ed. Stephen Spector (Oxford: Oxford University Press, 1991), 1:187–97. Reprinted by permission of Oxford University Press. Footnotes are by the editor of this Norton Critical Edition. Spelling and punctuation have also been modernized by the editor. The popular medieval cycle plays, presenting biblical scenes in lively Middle English verse, influenced much later drama. The ranting, murderous Herod, for example, lurks behind the tyrants of Elizabethan drama, including Macbeth. Both Herod and Macbeth boast, kill children, throw a feast, and suddenly face death.
1. thrive.
2. spur point.
3. blows.
4. puppets, i.e., children, and suckling infants.
5. to thrust and to stab.
6. The gold-crowned children will never thrive. (Here and in the next line Herod may refer to the children or the three kings.)
7. soldiers; **sots:** fools.

Do owlet hoot, Hoberd and Hein,[8]
When her bairns bleed under cradle-band?[9]
Sharply I shall them shend![1]
The knave[2] children that be
In all Israel country,
They shall have bloody blee[3]
For one I called unkind.[4]
It is told in Gru[5]
His name should be Jesu.
I found[6]
To have him you gone,
Hew the flesh with the bone,
And give him wound!
Now keen knights, kithe[7] your crafts,
And killeth knave children and casteth them in clay!
Showeth on your shoulders shields and shafts,
Shapeth among schelchowns a shrilling shray![8]
Doth rounces run with raking raftes[9]
Till ribs be to-rent with a red array![1]
Let no bairn be left unbeat baftes[2]
Till a beggar bleed by beasts' bay.[3]
Mahound, that best may![4]
I warn you, my knights,
A bairn is born, I plights,[5]
Would climb[6] king and knights,
And let my lordly lay.[7]
Knights wise,
Chosen, full choice,[8]
Arise, arise,
And take your tool!

8. The hooting owlet refers proleptically to the bereaved mothers of the Innocents; **hoberd** and **hein** mean "knave," "rascal," though used as proper names.
9. When their babies bleed in their swaddling clothes.
1. destroy.
2. boy.
3. appearance.
4. wicked (i.e., Jesus Christ).
5. Greek.
6. decided.
7. show.
8. Create among women a piercing outcry!
9. Let horses run with thrusting spears.
1. torn in pieces and covered in blood.
2. behind.
3. stall. (The beggar is Christ in the stable.)
4. Mahound (a shortening of Mahomet, the principal devil and false god of English mystery cycles), who is most powerful.
5. promise.
6. climb above.
7. diminish my lordly way of life.
8. excellent.

And every page,[9]
Of two-year age,
Ere ever you swage,[1]
Slayeth ilk a fool![2]
One of them all
Was born in stall;
Fools him call
King in crown!
With bitter gall
He shall down fall!
My might in hall
Shall never go down!

FIRST SOLDIER: I shall slay churls,
And queans with thirls;[3]
Her knave-girls[4]
I shall stick!
Forth will I speed
To do[5] them bleed.
Though girls grede,[6]
We shall be wreak![7]

SECOND SOLDIER: For swords sharp
As an harp
Queans shall carp,[8]
And of sorrow sing.
Bairns young,
They shall be stung!
Through liver and lung,
We shall them sting!   [Exeunt all.]

[Enter ANGEL, JOSEPH, MARY, with BABY JESUS.]

ANGEL: Awake, Joseph, and take thy wife,
Thy child also—ride belife![9]
For King Herod with sharp knife,
His knights he doth send.
The Father of Heaven hath to thee sent[1]
Into Egypt that thou be bent,[2]

9. boy.
1. cease.
2. Slayeth each a child.
3. harlots with piercings.
4. male children.
5. make.
6. harlots shall cry out (another insulting reference to the mothers of the infants).
7. avenged.
8. harlots shall talk.
9. at once.
1. commanded.
2. headed.

For cruel knights thy child have meant
With sword to slay and shend![3]
JOSEPH: Awake, good wife, out of your sleep,
And of your child taketh good keep,[4]
While I your clothes lay on heap,
And truss[5] them on the ass.
King Herod the child will slay,
Therefore to Egypt must we go—
An angel of God said me so,
And therefore let us pass.   [*Exeunt all.*]

[*Enter* SOLDIERS, *and* WOMEN *carrying babies.*]

*Then the soldiers will go to kill the boys and the First
Woman will speak.*

FIRST WOMAN: Long lulling have I lorn![6]
Alas, why was my bairn born?
With swapping[7] sword now is he shorn
The head right from the neck!
Shank and shoulder is all to-torn.[8]
Sorrow I see behind and before,
Both midnight, midday, and at morn.
Of my life I not reck.[9]
SECOND WOMAN: Certainly I say the same,
Gone is all my good game!
My little child lieth all lame,
That lulled on my paps.
My forty weeks' groaning
Hath sent me seven-year sorrowing.
Mickle[1] is my mourning,
And right hard are mine haps![2]
FIRST SOLDIER: Lord in throne,
Maketh no moan!
Queans 'gin groan
In world about.
Upon my spear
A girl[3] I bear,

3. destroy.
4. care.
5. pack.
6. Long singing of lullabyes have I lost.
7. smiting.
8. torn to pieces.
9. care.
1. much.
2. misfortunes.
3. boy.

I dare well swear,
Let mothers hoot!   [*Exeunt all.*]

                                        [*Enter* KING HEROD, SOLDIERS.]

SECOND SOLDIER: Lord, we have sped
   As you bade:
   Bairns been bled,
   And lie in ditch,
   Flesh and vein
   Have tholed[4] pain,
   And you shall reign
   Evermore rich.
KING HEROD: You shall have steeds
   To your meeds,[5]
   Lands and ledes,[6]
   Frith and fee.[7]
   Well have you wrought,
   My foe is sought,
   To death is he brought!
   Now come up to me!
   In seat now am I set as king of mights most;
   All this world for their love to me shall they lout,[8]
   Both of heaven and of earth, and of hell coast.
   For digne[9] of my dignity they have of me doubt![1]
   There is no lord like on life to me worth a toast,[2]
   Neither king nor kaiser in all this world about!
   If any briber[3] do brag or blow against my boast,
   I shall rap those ribalds and rake them on rout[4]
   With my bright brond![5]
   There shall be neither kaiser nor king
   But that I shall them down ding,[6]
   Less than[7] he at my bidding
   Be buxom[8] to mine hand.

4. suffered.
5. for your rewards.
6. people.
7. landed and movable property.
8. bow.
9. because of the greatness.
1. fear.
2. like me alive worth a piece of toast.
3. scoundrel.
4. I shall smite those rogues and destroy them as a group.
5. sword.
6. beat.
7. unless
8. obedient.

Now my gentle and courteous knights, hark to me this
  stound.[9]
Good time soon, methinketh, at dinner that we were.
Smartly, therefore, set a table anon here full sound,
Covered with a curious[1] cloth and with rich, worthy fare,
Service for the loveliest lord that living is on ground.
Best meats and worthiest wines look that you none spare,
Though that a little pint should cost a thousand pound!
Bring always of the best; for cost take you no care.
Anon that it be done!

[A table is set. Enter STEWARD, a MINSTREL.]

STEWARD: My lord, the table is ready dight,[2]
Here is water; now wash forthright.
Now blow up,[3] minstrel, with all your might!
The service[4] cometh in soon.

[Herod and the soldiers sit at table; food is served.]

KING HEROD: Now am I set at meat
And worthily served at my degree.[5]
Come forth, knights, sit down and eat,
And be as merry as you can be!
FIRST SOLDIER: Lord, at your bidding we take our seat,
With hearty[6] will obey we thee.
There is no lord of might so great,
Through all this world in no country,
In worship[7] to abide.
KING HEROD: I was never merrier herebeforn,[8]
Sith[9] that I was first born,
Than I am now right in this morn.
In joy I 'gin to glide.

[Enter DEATH in tattered garments, covered with worms.]

DEATH: Ow! I heard a page[1] make praising of pride!
All princes he passeth, he weeneth, of pousty.[2]
He weeneth to be the worthiest of all this world wide;

9. time.
1. elaborate.
2. prepared.
3. sound the fanfare.
4. meal.
5. as befits my station.
6. heartfelt.
7. honor.
8. before now.
9. since.
1. servant.
2. in power; **weeneth**: thinks.

King over all kings, that page weeneth to be!
He sent into Bethlehem to seek on every side
Christ for to quell,[3] if they might him see.
But of his wicked will, lurdan,[4] yet he lied!
God's Son doth live; there is no lord but he.
Over all lords he is king.
I am Death, God's messenger.
Almighty God hath sent me here
Yon lurdan to slay, without dwere,[5]
For his wicked working.
I am sent from God. Death is my name.
All thing that is on ground I wield at my will:
Both man and beast, and birds wild and tame.
When that I come them to with death I do them kill,
Herb, grass, and trees strong, take them all in-same.[6]
Yea, the great, mighty oaks with my dent I spill.[7]
What man that I wrestle with, he shall right soon have shame;
I give him such a trippet[8] he shall evermore lie still
For Death kan[9] no sport!
Where I smite there is no grace,
For after my stroke man hath no space
To make amends for his trespass,
But[1] God him grant comfort.
Ow! see how proudly yon caitiff[2] sits at meat!
Of death hath he no doubt;[3] he weeneth to live evermore.
To him will I go and give him such an hit[4]
That all the leeches[5] of the land his life shall never restore.
Against my dreadful dents it vaileth[6] never to plead.
Ere I him part from, I shall him make full poor.
All the blood of his body I shall him out-sweat,[7]
For now I go to slay him with strokes sad[8] and sore,
This tide,[9]
Both him and his knights all,

3. kill.
4. rogue.
5. doubt.
6. together.
7. blow I kill.
8. tripping up.
9. knows.
1. unless.
2. wretch.
3. fear.
4. The word **hete** also could refer to "heat," as in fever.
5. doctors.
6. blows it avails.
7. sweat out of him.
8. vigorous.
9. time.

I shall them make to me but thrall;[1]
With my spear slay them I shall,
And so cast down his pride!

KING HEROD: Now, kind[2] knights, be merry and glad!
With all good diligence show now some mirth!
For, by gracious Mahound, more mirth never I had,
Nor never more joy was in from time of my birth.
For now my foe is dead and prended as a pad.[3]
Above me is no king, on ground nor on garth,[4]
Mirths, therefore, make you and be right nothing sad!
Spare neither meat nor drink, and spare for no dearth
Of wine nor of bread.
For now am I a king alone.
So worthy as I, may there be none.
Therefore, knights be merry each one,
For now my foe is dead.

FIRST SOLDIER: When the boys sprawled at my spear's end,
By Satan, our sire, it was a goodly sight!
A good game it was that boy for to shend,[5]
That would have been our king and put you from your right.

SECOND SOLDIER: Now truly, my lord the King, we had been
   unhend[6]
And never none of us able for to be a knight,
If that any of us to them had been a friend,
And had saved any life against thy mickle[7] might,
From death them to flit.[8]

KING HEROD: Amongst all that great rout
He is dead, I have no doubt.
Therefore, minstrel, round about,
Blow up a merry fit![9]

> *Here, while they play trumpets, let Death kill Herod and
> two soldiers immediately, and let the Devil [emerging
> from hell-mouth] receive them.*

DEVIL: All ours! all ours! This chattel[1] is mine!
I shall them bring unto my cell,

1. captives.
2. noble.
3. taken as a toad.
4. in open or enclosed space, i.e., anywhere.
5. destroy.
6. discourteous.
7. great.
8. deliver.
9. tune.
1. property.

I shall them teach plays[2] fine,
And show such mirth as is in hell.
It were more better amongst swine,
That evermore stink thereby to dwell!
For in our lodge[3] is so great pain
That no earthly tongue can tell.
[*To the victims*] With you I go my way.
I shall you bear forth with me,
And show you sports of our glee.
Of our mirths now shall you see,
And ever sing "Welaway!"

                    [*The Devil takes their souls to hell.*]

DEATH: Of King Herod all men beware,
That hath rejoiced in pomp and pride.
For all his boast of bliss, full bare
He lieth now dead here on his side.
For when I come I cannot spare.
From me no wight may him[4] hide.
Now is he dead and cast in care,
In hell pit ever to abide;
His lordship is all lorn.[5]
Now is he as poor as I,
Worms' meat is his body;
His soul in hell full painfully
Of devils is all to-torn.[6]
All men dwelling upon the ground,
Beware of me, by mine counsel,
For faint fellowship in me is found.
I kan[7] no courtesy, as I you tell,
For be a man never so sound,
Of health in heart never so well,
I come suddenly within a stound.[8]
Me withstand may no castle!
My journey will I speed.[9]
Of my coming no man is ware,[1]
For when men make most merry fare,

2. games.
3. prison.
4. person may himself.
5. lost.
6. torn to pieces.
7. know.
8. short time.
9. accomplish.
1. aware

Then suddenly I cast them in care,
And slay them even in deed!
Though I be naked and poor of array,
And worms gnaw me all about,
Yet look you dread me night and day,
For when Death cometh you stand in doubt.
Even like to me, as I you say,
Shall all you be here in this rout.[2]
When I you challenge, at my day,
I shall you make right low to lout,[3]
And naked for to be.
Amongst worms, as I you tell,
Under the earth shall you dwell,
And they shall eat both flesh and fell,[4]
As they have done me.   [*Exeunt all.*]

SENECA

Medea†

Medea: Then at the altars of the gods my children shall be slain,
With crimson-colored blood of babes their altars will I stain,
Through[1] livers, lungs, the lights,[2] and heart, through every gut and
    gall,[3]
For vengeance break away, perforce, and spare no blood at all,
If any lusty life as yet within thy soul do rest,
If aught of ancient courage still do dwell within my breast,
Exile all foolish female fear and pity from thy mind,
And as th'untamed tigers use to rage and rave unkind,
That haunt the croaking, cumbrous caves and clumpered[4] frozen
    climes,

2. crowd.
3. bow.
4. skin.
† From *Seneca His Tenne Tragedies, Translated into Englysh,* ed. Thomas Newton (London, 1581), sigs. R2v, D2v, C4, D3v, D4–D4v, T8–T8v. *Medea* is translated by John Studley. Footnotes are by the editor of this Norton Critical Edition. Spelling and punctuation have been modernized by the editor. A Stoic philosopher, Lucius Annaeus Seneca (4?B.C.E–65 C.E.) wrote plays that served as models of tragic language and action for Elizabethans. In this first selection the witch Medea rouses herself to a terrible revenge on her unfaithful husband by murdering their children. Compare Lady Macbeth (1.5.38–52) urging herself to *scelus,* "crime," in a highly charged monologue of self-creation.
1. by means of. Medea uses her children's vital organs as the beast entrails of a sacrifice.
2. eyes.
3. liver, here used generically for internal organ.
4. congealed (with ice); **cumbrous:** difficult to access.

And craggy rocks of Caucasus,[5] whose bitter cold deprives
The soil of all inhabitors, permit to lodge and rest
Such savage, brutish tyranny within thy brazen breast.
Whatever hurly-burly wrought doth Phasis[6] understand,
What mighty, monstrous, bloody feat I wrought by sea or land,
The like in Corinth[7] shall be seen in most outrageous guise,
Most hideous, hateful, horrible to hear or see with eyes,
Most devilish, desperate, dreadful deed, yet never known before,
Whose rage shall force heaven, earth, and hell to quake and tremble
    sore.
My burning breast that rolls in wrath and doth in rancor boil,
Sore thirsteth after blood and wounds with slaughter, death, and
    spoil,
By renting[8] racked limbs from limbs to drive them down to grave.
Tush, these be but as flea-bitings that mentionèd I have;
As weighty things as these I did in greener girlish age.
Now sorrow's smart doth rub the gall[9] and frets with sharper rage.
But sith my womb hath yielded fruit, it doth me well behove,[1]
The strength and parlous puissance[2] of weightier ills to prove.
Be ready, Wrath, with all thy might that fury kindle may,
Thy foes to their destruction be ready to assay.[3]

Hercules Furens†

Theseus: In one appointed judgment place is Gnossian Minos hard,
And in another, Rhadamanth; this crime doth Aeac hear.[1]
What each man once hath done he feels, and guilt to th'author there
Returns,[2] and th'hurtful with their own example punished be.
The bloody, cruel captains I in prison shut did see,
And back of tyrant impotent even with his people's hand
All torn and cut. What man of might with favor leads his land,

5. mountain-range between the Black and Caspian seas, a symbol of remoteness and deso-
    lation.
6. Whatever disturbance has occurred near Phasis, a river in Colchis, Medea's homeland
    (present-day Russia).
7. ancient Greek city, home of Medea's husband Jason, and scene of the present tragedy.
8. tearing.
9. chafe the wound.
1. behoove, suit.
2. dangerous power.
3. attempt (to bring about).
† Translated by Jasper Heywood. Recalling his journey to Hades in the first passage from
    Hercules Furens, Theseus articulates a pagan conception of justice and the afterlife impor-
    tant to Elizabethan tragedy and Shakespeare.
1. Minos, Rhadamanthus, and Aecus, the three judges in Hades.
2. a popular Senecan sentence, *auctorem scelus / repetit* (735–36), "crime returns to its own
    author"; compare *Macbeth,* 1.7.8–12.

And, of his own life lord, reserves his hurtless hands to good,[3]
And gently doth his empire guide without the thirst of blood,
And spares his soul, he, having long led forth the ling'ring days
Of happy age, at length to heaven doth either find the ways,
Or joyful, happy places else of fair Elysius wood.[4]

* * *

Hercules:[5] Take mercy, father; lo, I lift to thee my humble hands.
What meaneth this? My hand fleeth back. Some privy[6] guilt there
    stands.
Whence comes this blood? Or what doth mean, flowing with death
    of child,
The shaft imbrued with slaughter once of Lerney monster killed?[7]
I see my weapons now; the hand I seek no more to wit.[8]
Whose hand could bend this bow but mine? Or what right arm but
    it
Could string the bow that unto me even scantly[9] doth obey?
To you I turn: O father dear, is this my guilt,[1] I pray?
They held their peace;[2] it is mine own.

* * *

Hercules: Wherefore I longer should[3] sustain my life yet in this light
And linger here, no cause there is; all good lost have I quite—
My mind, my weapons, my renown, my wife, my sons, my hands,
And fury too; no man may heal and loose from guilty bands
My mind defiled.

* * *

Hercules: What place shall I seek, runagate,[4] for rest?
Where shall I hide myself? Or in what land myself engrave?[5]
What Tanais, or what Nilus else, or with his Persian wave
What Tigris violent of stream, or what fierce Rhenus flood,

---

3. And, though is lord of life (*dominusque vitae*, 740), uses his harmless hands only to do
    good.
4. the abode of the blessed and virtuous.
5. The next selections feature the hero of the tragedy, Hercules, realizing that he has slain
    his own children in a mad rage set upon him by the goddess Juno. His anguished rhetoric
    of recognition and remorse echoes through Shakespeare's great tragedies; the imagery of
    blood-stained hands is especially important for *Macbeth* (see 2.2.62–66).
6. private.
7. The arrow stained formerly with the slaughter of the Lernaean Hydra (a monster Hercules
    slew as one of his labors).
8. know.
9. hardly.
1. with a pun on "gilt," a gold or red covering.
2. His father and Theseus kept silent.
3. Why I should longer. Compare *Macbeth* 5.3.22–28.
4. fugitive.
5. bury myself in.

Or Tagus troublesome that flows with Iber's treasures good,
May my right hand now wash from guilt? Although Maeotis cold[6]
The waves of all the northern sea on me shed out now would,
And all the water thereof should now pass by my two hands,
Yet will the mischief deep remain. Alas, into what lands
Wilt thou, O wicked man, resort? To east or western coast?
Each were well known; all place I have of banishment quite lost.

Agamemnon†

Chorus: O Fortune, that dost fail[1] the great estate[2] of kings,
On slippery, sliding seat thou placest lofty things,
And setst on tott'ring sort,[3] where perils do abound.
Yet never kingdom calm nor quiet could be found;
No day to scepters sure doth shine,[4] that they might say,
"Tomorrow shall we rule as we have done today."
One clod of crooked care another bringeth in,
One hurly-burly[5] done, another doth begin.

*   *   *

O how doth Fortune toss and tumble in her wheel[6]
The stagg'ring states of kings that ready be to reel!
Fain[7] would they dreaded be, and yet not settled so,[8]
When as they fearèd are, they fear and live in woe.
The silent lady, Night, so sweet to man and beast,
Cannot bestow on them her safe and quiet rest;
Sleep that doth overcome and break the bonds of grief,
It cannot ease their hearts nor minister relief.
What castle strongly built, what bulwark, tower, or town,
Is not by mischief's means brought topsy-turvy down?
What rampart[9] walls are not made weak by wicked war?
From stately courts of kings doth justice fly afar;

---

6. The exotic waters include the Tanais, a river of ancient Scythia (Southern Russia); the Nile river in Egypt; the Tigris river (in present-day Turkey and Iraq); the Rhine river in Western Europe; the Tagus river of golden sands in Spain (Iber); and Lake Maeotis in ancient Scythia.
† Translated by John Studley. This Choral song about Fortune's power and sleeplessness echoes throughout *Macbeth* (see 2.2.39–43; 5.5.17–28).
1. make fail.
2. power and position.
3. set in motion wavering fate.
4. No day shines surely to rulers.
5. commotion.
6. Fortune was often depicted as a wheel upon which all rose and fell in ceaseless motion.
7. gladly.
8. They are not settled, or content, when they are feared (*metui cupiunt / metuique timent*, 72–73, "they want to be feared, they dread to be feared").
9. fortified.

In princely places, of honesty the lore,
And wedlock vow devout, is set by little store.[1]
The bloody Bellon[2] those doth haunt with gory hand,
Whose light and vain conceit[3] in painted pomp doth stand.

RAPHAEL HOLINSHED

[Duff and Duncan]†

Duff

Amongst them there were also certain young gentlemen, right beautiful and goodly personages, being near of kin unto Donwald, captain of the castle, and had been persuaded to be partakers with the other rebels more through the fraudulent counsel of divers wicked persons than of their own accord. Whereupon the foresaid Donwald, lamenting their case, made earnest labor and suit to the King to have begged their pardon; but having a plain denial, he conceived such an inward malice towards the King (though he showed it not outwardly at the first) that the same continued still boiling in his stomach and ceased not till, through setting on of his wife[1] and in revenge of such unthankfulness, he found means to murder the King within the foresaid castle of Forres where he used to sojourn. For the King, being in that country, was accustomed to lie most commonly within the same castle, having a special trust in Donwald as a man whom he never suspected.

But Donwald, not forgetting the reproach which his lineage[2] had sustained by the execution of those his kinsmen whom the King for a spectacle to the people had caused to be hanged, could not but show manifest tokens of great grief at home amongst his family, which his wife, perceiving, ceased not to travail[3] with him till she

1. The doctrine (**lore**) of honesty and marital fidelity are little valued at court.
2. Bellona, Roman goddess of war.
3. self-conception.
† From Raphael Holinshed; *The First and Second Volumes of Chronicles* (London, 1587), vol. 2, *The History of Scotland,* fols. 150–52, 168–76. Footnotes are by the editor of this Norton Critical Edition. Spelling and punctuation have been modernized by the editor. Raphael Holinshed (d. 1580) gathered various legends and accounts into a bulky chronicle of England, Scotland, and Ireland (1577, 1587), which became the main source of Shakespeare's English history plays. In *Macbeth* Shakespeare combines the assassinations of Duff and Duncan from the *Chronicles,* greatly expanding the supernatural elements and the role of Lady Macbeth. He alters Holinshed's Banquo, a conspirator, and his Duncan, a weak ruler, and suppresses all mention of Macbeth's ten years of good rule. Shakespeare makes his greatest changes to Macbeth himself, endowing Holinshed's cruel tyrant with a voice of moral sensibility, poetic self-consciousness, and regret.
1. because of his wife's encouragement.
2. family.
3. labor.

understood what the cause was of his displeasure. Which at length when she had learned by his own relation, she, as one that bare no less malice in her heart towards the King for the like cause on her behalf than her husband did for his friends', counseled him (sith[4] the King oftentimes used to lodge in his house without any guard about him other than the garrison of the castle, which was wholly at his commandment) to make him away,[5] and showed him the means whereby he might soonest accomplish it.

Donwald, thus being the more kindled in wrath by the words of his wife, determined to follow her advice in the execution of so heinous an act. Whereupon, devising with himself for a while which way he might best accomplish his cursed intent, at length gat[6] opportunity and sped his purpose as followeth. It chanced that the King, upon the day before he purposed to depart forth of the castle, was long in his oratory[7] at his prayers and there continued till it was late in the night. At the last, coming forth, he called such afore him as had faithfully served him in pursuit and apprehension of the rebels, and, giving the hearty thanks, he bestowed sundry honorable gifts amongst them, of the which number Donwald was one, as he that had been ever accounted a most faithful servant to the King.

At length, having talked with them a long time, he got him[8] into his privy chamber only with two of his chamberlains[9] who, having brought him to bed, came forth again and then fell to banqueting with Donwald and his wife, who had prepared divers delicate dishes and sundry sorts of drinks for their rear supper or collation;[1] whereat they sat up so long till they had charged their stomachs with such full gorges[2] that their heads were no sooner got to the pillow but asleep they were so fast that a man might have removed the chamber over them sooner than to have awaked them out of their drunken sleep.

Then Donwald, though he abhorred the act greatly in heart, yet through instigation of his wife he called four of his servants unto him, whom he had made privy to his wicked intent before and framed[3] to his purpose with large gifts, and now declaring unto them after what sort[4] they should work the feat, they gladly obeyed his instructions. And speedily going about the murder, they enter[ed] the chamber in which the King lay a little before cock's crow, where

---

4. since.
5. to kill him.
6. got.
7. chapel.
8. himself
9. personal servants.
1. final meal of the day.
2. large ingestions.
3. shaped.
4. in what manner.

they secretly cut his throat as he lay sleeping, without any buskling[5] at all. And immediately, by a postern[6] gate, they carried forth the dead body into the fields, and, throwing it upon an horse there provided ready for that purpose, they convey[ed] it unto a place about two miles distant from the castle, where they stayed and gat certain laborers to help them to turn the course of a little river running through the fields there; and digging a deep hole in the channel, they burie[d] the body in the same, ramming it up with stones and gravel so closely that, setting the water in the right course again, no man could perceive that anything had been newly digged there. This they did by order appointed them by Donwald (as is reported), for that the body should not be found and, by bleeding when Donwald should be present, declare him to be guilty of the murder. For such an opinion men have that the dead corpse of any man, being slain, will bleed abundantly if the murderer be present. But for what consideration soever they buried him there, they had no sooner finished the work but that they slew them whose help they used herein and straightways thereupon fled into Orkney.

Donwald, about the time that the murder was in doing, got him amongst them that kept the watch and so continued in company with them all the residue of the night. But in the morning, when the noise was raised in the King's chamber how the King was slain, his body conveyed away, and the bed all berayed[7] with blood, he with the watch ran thither as though he had known nothing of the matter and, breaking into the chamber and finding cakes[8] of blood in the bed and on the floor about the sides of it, he forthwith slew the chamberlains as guilty of that heinous murder. And then, like a madman, running to and fro, he ransacked every corner within the castle as though it had been to have seen if he might have found either the body or any of the murderers hid in any privy[9] place. But at length coming to the postern gate and finding it open, he burdened the chamberlains whom he had slain with all the fault, they having the keys of the gates committed to their keeping all the night, and therefore it could not be otherwise (said he) but that they were of counsel[1] in the committing of that most detestable murder.

Finally, such was his over-earnest diligence in the severe inquisition and trial of the offenders herein that some of the lords began to mislike the matter and to smell forth shrewd tokens[2] that he should not be altogether clear himself. But forsomuch as they were

5. scuffling, commotion.
6. back.
7. befouled.
8. clots.
9. private.
1. agreed.
2. detect ominous signs.

in that country where he had the whole rule, what by reason of his friends and authority together, they doubted[3] to utter what they thought till time and place should better serve thereunto, and hereupon got them away, every man to his home. For the space of six months together after this heinous murder thus committed, there appeared no sun by day nor moon by night in any part of the realm, but still[4] was the sky covered with continual clouds, and sometimes such outrageous winds arose, with lightnings and tempests, that the people were in great fear of present destruction.

In the meantime, Culain, Prince of Cumberland, the son (as I have said) of King Indulph, accompanied with a great number of lords and nobles of the realm, came unto Scone, there to receive the crown according to the manner. But at his coming thither he demanded of the bishops what the cause should be of such untemperate weather. Who made answer that undoubtedly almighty God showed himself thereby to be offended most highly for that wicked murder of King Duff, and, surely, unless the offenders were tried forth and punished for that deed, the realm should feel the just indignation of the divine judgement for omitting such punishment as was due for so grievous an offense.

* * *

Monstrous sights also that were seen within the Scottish kingdom that year were these: Horses in Lothian, being of singular beauty and swiftness, did eat their own flesh and would in no wise taste any other meat. In Angus there was a gentlewoman brought forth a child without eyes, nose, hand, or foot. There was a sparhawk[5] also strangled by an owl. Neither was it any less wonder that the sun, as before is said, was continually covered with clouds for six months' space. But all men understood that the abominable murder of King Duff was the cause hereof, which being revenged by the death of the authors (in manner as before is said), Cullen was crowned as lawful successor to the same Duff at Scone, with all due honor and solemnity, in the year of our Lord 972.

* * *

Duncan

After Malcolm, succeeded his nephew[6] Duncan, the son of his daughter Beatrice. For Malcolm had two daughters; the one, which was this Beatrice, being given in marriage unto one Abbanath

3. feared.
4. continually.
5. sparrow-hawk.
6. grandson.

Crinen, a man of great nobility and thane of the Isles and west parts of Scotland, bare of that marriage the foresaid Duncan. The other, called Doada, was married unto Sinel, the Thane of Glamis, by whom she had issue one Macbeth, a valiant gentleman and one that, if he had not been somewhat cruel of nature, might have been thought most worthy the government of a realm. On the other part, Duncan was so soft and gentle of nature that the people wished the inclinations and manners of these two cousins to have been so tempered[7] and interchangeably bestowed betwixt them that, where the one had too much of clemency and the other of cruelty, the mean virtue betwixt these two extremities might have reigned by indifferent partition[8] in them both; so should Duncan have proved a worthy king and Macbeth an excellent captain. The beginning of Duncan's reign was very quiet and peaceable, without any notable trouble; but after it was perceived how negligent he was in punishing offenders, many misruled[9] persons took occasion thereof to trouble the peace and quiet state of the commonwealth by seditious commotions which first had their beginnings in this wise.

Banquo, the Thane of Lochaber, of whom the House of the Stuarts[1] is descended, the which by order of lineage hath now for a long time enjoyed the crown of Scotland even till these our days, as he gathered the finances due to the King and further punished somewhat sharply such as were notorious offenders, being assailed by a number of rebels inhabiting in that country and spoiled[2] of the money and all other things, had much ado to get away with life after he had received sundry grievous wounds amongst them. Yet, escaping their hands, after he was somewhat recovered of his hurts and was able to ride, he repaired[3] to the court, where, making his complaint to the King in most earnest wise, he purchased[4] at length that the offenders were sent for by a sergeant-at-arms to appear to make answer unto such matters as should be laid to their charge. But they, augmenting their mischievous act with a more wicked deed, after they had misused the messenger with sundry kinds of reproaches, they finally slew him also.

Then, doubting not but for such contemptuous demeanor against the King's regal authority they should be invaded with all the power[5] the King could make, Macdowald, one of great estimation among

7. mixed.
8. equal distribution.
9. disorderly.
1. royal family governing England from the time of King James I (1603–25) to 1688.
2. robbed.
3. returned.
4. arranged.
5. army.

them, making first a confederacy with his nearest friends and kinsmen, took upon him to be chief captain of all such rebels as would
stand against the King in maintenance of their grievous offenses
lately committed against him. Many slanderous words also and rail-
ing taunts this Macdowald uttered against his prince, calling him a
fainthearted milksop more meet to govern a sort[6] of idle monks in
some cloister than to have the rule of such valiant and hardy men
of war as the Scots were. He used also such subtle persuasions and
forged allurements that in a small time he had gotten together a
mighty power of men; for out of the Western Isles there came unto
him a great multitude of people offering themselves to assist him in
that rebellious quarrel, and out of Ireland in hope of the spoil came
no small number of kerns and galloglasses,[7] offering gladly to serve
under him whither it should please him to lead them.

Macdowald, thus having a mighty puissance[8] about him, encountered with such of the King's people as were sent against him into
Lochaber and, discomfiting them, by mere[9] force took their captain
Malcolm and after the end of the battle smote off his head. This
overthrow, being notified to the King, did put him in wonderful[1] fear
by reason of his small skill in warlike affairs. Calling therefore his
nobles to a council, he asked of them their best advice for the subduing of Macdowald and other the rebels. Here in sundry heads (as
ever it happeneth) were sundry opinions, which they uttered according to every man his skill. At length Macbeth, speaking much against
the King's softness and overmuch slackness in punishing offenders,
whereby they had such time to assemble together, he promised, notwithstanding, if the charge were committed unto him and unto Banquo, so to order the matter that the rebels should be shortly
vanquished and quite put down, and that not so much as one of
them should be found to make resistance within the country.[2]

*   *   *

Shortly after happened a strange and uncouth[3] wonder, which
afterward was the cause of much trouble in the realm of Scotland,
as ye shall after hear. It fortuned, as Macbeth and Banquo journeyed
toward Forres where the King then lay, they went sporting[4] by the
way together without other company save only themselves, passing

6. bunch.
7. light-armed Irish foot soldiers.
8. power.
9. sheer.
1. great.
2. Macbeth and Banquo put down the rebellion, then vanquish the invading Sueno, king of
   Norway, and an accompanying force from Denmark.
3. uncommon.
4. for amusement.

thorough the woods and fields, when suddenly, in the midst of a
laund,[5] there met them three women in strange and wild apparel,
resembling creatures of elder world,[6] whom when they attentively
beheld, wondering much at the sight, the first of them spake and
said, "All hail, Macbeth, Thane of Glamis!" (for he had lately entered
into that dignity and office by the death of his father Sinel). The
second of them said, "Hail, Macbeth, Thane of Cawdor!" But the
third said, "All hail, Macbeth, that hereafter shalt be King of Scotland!"

Then Banquo: "What manner of women," saith he, "are you, that
seem so little favorable unto me, whereas to my fellow here, besides
high offices, ye assign also the kingdom, appointing forth nothing
for me at all?" "Yes," saith the first of them, "we promise greater
benefits unto thee than unto him, for he shall reign indeed, but with
an unlucky end; neither shall he leave any issue behind him to succeed in his place. Where, contrarily, thou in deed shalt not reign at
all, but of thee those shall be born which shall govern the Scottish
kingdom by long order of continual descent." Herewith the foresaid
women vanished immediately out of their sight. This was reputed at
the first but some vain fantastical illusion by Macbeth and Banquo,
insomuch that Banquo would call Macbeth, in jest, King of Scotland,
and Macbeth again would call him in sport likewise the father of
many kings. But afterwards the common opinion was that these
women were either the Weird Sisters, that is (as ye would say), the
goddesses of destiny, or else some nymphs or fairies endued with
knowledge of prophecy by their necromantical science,[7] because
everything came to pass as they had spoken. For shortly after, the
Thane of Cawdor being condemned at Forres of treason against
the King committed, his lands, livings, and offices were given of[8] the
King's liberality to Macbeth.

The same night after at supper Banquo jested with him and said,
"Now Macbeth, thou hast obtained those things which the two former sisters prophesied; there remaineth only for thee to purchase[9]
that which the third said should come to pass." Whereupon Macbeth, revolving the thing in his mind, began even then to devise how
he might attain to the kingdom. But yet he thought with himself that
he must tarry a time which should advance him thereto by the divine
providence, as it had come to pass in his former preferment.[1] But
shortly after it chanced that King Duncan, having two sons by his
wife (which was the daughter of Siward, Earl of Northumberland),

5. glade, an open space in the woods.
6. ancient times.
7. occult knowledge, perhaps gained from communication with the dead.
8. through.
9. obtain.
1. appointment (as Thane of Cawdor).

he made the elder of them called Malcolm, Prince of Cumberland, as it were thereby to appoint him his successor in the kingdom immediately after his decease. Macbeth, sore troubled herewith for that he saw by this means his hope sore hindered (where, by the old laws of the realm, the ordinance was that if he that should succeed were not of able age to take the charge upon himself, he that was next of blood unto him should be admitted), he began to take counsel how he might usurp the kingdom by force, having a just quarrel so to do, as he took[2] the matter, for that Duncan did what in him lay[3] to defraud him of all manner of title and claim which he might in time to come pretend[4] unto the crown.

The words of the three Weird Sisters also (of whom before ye have heard) greatly encouraged him hereunto; but specially his wife lay sore upon him[5] to attempt the thing, as she that was very ambitious, burning in unquenchable desire to bear the name of a queen. At length, therefore, communicating his purposed intent with his trusty friends, amongst whom Banquo was the chiefest, upon confidence of their promised aid he slew the King at Inverness or (as some say) at Bothgowanan in the sixth year of his reign. Then, having a company about him of such as he had made privy to his enterprise, he caused himself to be proclaimed king and forthwith went unto Scone, where by common consent he received the investure[6] of the kingdom according to the accustomed manner. The body of Duncan was first conveyed unto Elgin and there buried in kingly wise; but afterwards it was removed and conveyed unto Colmekill and there laid in a sepulture amongst his predecessors in the year after the birth of our Saviour 1046.

Malcolm Cammore and Donald Bane, the sons of King Duncan, for fear of their lives (which they might well know that Macbeth would seek to bring to end for his more sure confirmation in the estate), fled into Cumberland, where Malcolm remained till time that Saint Edward, the son of Ethelred, recovered the dominion of England from the Danish power; the which Edward received Malcolm by way of most friendly entertainment. But Donald passed over into Ireland where he was tenderly cherished by the king of that land. Macbeth, after the departure thus of Duncan's sons, used great liberality towards the nobles of the realm, thereby to win their favor. And when he saw that no man went about to trouble him, he set his whole intention to maintain justice and to punish all enormities and abuses which had chanced through the feeble and slothful administration of Duncan. * * * Macbeth, showing himself thus a most

2. understood.
3. whatever he could.
4. present as a claim.
5. pressed him vigorously.
6. investiture, the reception of the ceremonial robes and symbols of rule.

diligent punisher of all injuries and wrongs attempted by any disordered persons within realm, was accounted the sure defense and buckler[7] of innocent people; and hereto he also applied his whole endeavor to cause young men to exercise themselves in virtuous manners, and men of the Church to attend their divine service according to their vocations.

He caused to be slain sundry thanes, as of Caithness, Sutherland, Stranaverne, and Ross, because through them and their seditious attempts much trouble daily rose in the realm. He appeased the troubled state of Galloway, and slew one Magill, a tyrant who had many years before passed nothing of[8] the regal authority or power. To be brief, such were the worthy doings and princely acts of this Macbeth in the administration of the realm that if he had attained thereunto by rightful means and continued in uprightness of justice, as he began, till the end of his reign, he might well have been numbered amongst the most noble princes that anywhere had reigned. He made many wholesome laws and statutes for the public weal of his subjects.[9]

* * *

These and the like commendable laws Macbeth caused to be put as then in use, governing the realm for the space of ten years in equal justice. But this was but a counterfeit zeal of equity[1] showed by him, partly against his natural inclination, to purchase thereby the favor of the people. Shortly after, he began to show what he was, instead of equity practicing cruelty. For the prick of conscience (as it chanceth[2] ever in tyrants and such as attain to any estate by unrighteous means) caused him ever to fear lest he should be served of the same cup as he had ministered to his predecessor. The words also of the three Weird Sisters would not out of his mind, which, as they promised him the kingdom, so likewise did they promise it at the same time unto the posterity of Banquo. He willed therefore the same Banquo, with his son named Fleance, to come to a supper that he had prepared for them; which was indeed, as he had devised, present[3] death at the hands of certain murderers whom he hired to execute that deed, appointing them to meet with the same Banquo and his son without[4] the palace as they returned to their lodgings

7. shield.
8. respected not.
9. There follows a list of laws made by Macbeth.
1. false enthusiasm for justice.
2. happens.
3. immediate.
4. outside.

and there to slay them, so that he would not have his house[5] slandered, but that in time to come he might clear himself if anything were laid to his charge upon any suspicion that might arise.

It chanced yet by the benefit of the dark night that though the father were slain, the son yet by the help of almighty God reserving him to better fortune, escaped that danger; and afterwards having some inkling, by the admonition of some friends which he had in the court, how his life was sought no less than his father's (who was slain not by chance-medley,[6] as by the handling of the matter Macbeth would have had it to appear) but even upon a prepensed device,[7] whereupon, to avoid further peril he fled into Wales.[8]

* * *

But to return unto Macbeth in continuing the history and to begin where I left, ye shall understand that after the contrived slaughter of Banquo, nothing prospered with the foresaid Macbeth. For in manner[9] every man began to doubt his own life and durst uneath[1] appear in the King's presence; and even as there were many that stood in fear of him, so likewise stood he in fear of many, in such sort that he began to make those away by one surmised cavillation[2] or other whom he thought most able to work him any displeasure.

At length he found such sweetness by putting his nobles thus to death that his earnest thirst after blood in this behalf might in no wise be satisfied. For ye must consider he won double profit (as he thought) hereby: for first they were rid out of the way whom he feared; and then again his coffers were enriched by their goods which were forfeited to his use, whereby he might better maintain a guard of armed men about him to defend his person from injury of them whom he had in any suspicion. Further, to the end he might the more cruelly oppress his subjects with all tyrantlike wrongs, he builded a strong castle on the top of an high hill called Dunsinane, situate in Gowrie, ten miles from Perth, on such a proud height that, standing there aloft, a man might behold well near all the countries of Angus, Fife, Stormont, and Earndale as it were lying underneath him. This castle, then, being founded on the top of that high hill, put the realm to great charges before it was finished, for all the stuff necessary to the building could not be brought up without much toil

5. royal house or lineage.
6. the accidental killing of a man though with some culpability for the murderer (a legal term).
7. premeditated plot.
8. Holinshed next traces the line of Scottish kings from Fleance to James VI of Scotland, i.e., James I of England (1603–25).
9. in some way.
1. dared only with difficulty.
2. phony technicality.

and business. But Macbeth, being once determined to have the work
go forward, caused the thanes of each shire within the realm to come
and help towards that building, each man his course about.[3]

At the last, when the turn fell unto Macduff, Thane of Fife, to
build his part, he sent workmen with all needful provision and commanded them to show such diligence in every behalf that no occasion
might be given for the King to find fault with him in that he came
not himself, as other had done, which he refused to do for doubt[4]
lest the King, bearing him (as he partly understood) no great good
will, would lay violent hands upon him as he had done upon divers
other. Shortly after, Macbeth coming to behold how the work went
forward and because he found not Macduff there, he was sore
offended and said, "I perceive this man will never obey my commandments till he be ridden with a snaffle,[5] but I shall provide well
enough for him." Neither could he afterwards abide to look upon
the said Macduff, either for that he thought his puissance overgreat,
either else for that he had learned of certain wizards in whose words
he put great confidence (for that the prophecy had happened so right
which the three fairies or Weird Sisters had declared unto him) how
that he ought to take heed of Macduff, who in time to come should
seek to destroy him.

And surely hereupon had he put Macduff to death but that a certain witch, whom he had in great trust, had told that he should never
be slain with man born of any woman nor vanquished till the wood
of Birnam came to the castle of Dunsinane. By this prophecy Macbeth put all fear out of his heart, supposing he might do what he
would, without any fear to be punished for the same; for by the one
prophecy he believed it was unpossible for any man to vanquish him,
and by the other unpossible to slay him. This vain hope caused him
to do many outrageous things, to the grievous oppression of his subjects. At length Macduff, to avoid peril of life, purposed with himself[6]
to pass into England to procure[7] Malcolm Cammore to claim the
crown of Scotland. But this was not so secretly devised by Macduff
but that Macbeth had knowledge given him thereof, for kings (as is
said) have sharp sight like unto Lynx[8] and long ears like unto Midas.[9]
For Macbeth had in every nobleman's house one sly fellow or other
in fee with him[1] to reveal all that was said or done within the same,

3. taking his turn.
4. fear.
5. bridle.
6. decided.
7. induce.
8. Lynceus, who could see through the earth.
9. a king who had ass's ears.
1. in his payment.

by which sleight he oppressed the most part of the nobles of his realm.

Immediately, then, being advertised[2] whereabout Macduff went, he came hastily with a great power into Fife and forthwith besieged the castle where Macduff dwelled, trusting to have found him therein. They that kept the house without any resistance opened the gates and suffered him to enter, mistrusting none evil. But, nevertheless, Macbeth most cruelly caused the wife and children of Macduff, with all other whom he found in that castle, to be slain. Also, he confiscated the goods of Macduff, proclaimed him traitor, and confined[3] him out of all the parts of his realm. But Macduff was already escaped out of danger and gotten into England unto Malcolm Cammore, to try what purchase[4] he might make by means of his support to revenge the slaughter so cruelly executed on his wife, his children, and other friends. At his coming unto Malcolm he declared into what great misery the estate of Scotland was brought by the detestable cruelties exercised by the tyrant Macbeth, having committed many horrible slaughters and murders both as well of the nobles as commons, for the which he was hated right mortally of all his liege people,[5] desiring nothing more than to be delivered of that intolerable and most heavy yoke of thralldom[6] which they sustained at such a caitiff's[7] hands.

Malcolm, hearing Macduff's words which he uttered in very lamentable sort, for mere compassion and very ruth[8] that pierced his sorrowful heart bewailing the miserable state of his country, he fetched a deep sigh, which Macduff, perceiving, began to fall most earnestly in hand with him to enterprise the delivering of the Scottish people out of the hands of so cruel and bloody a tyrant as Macbeth by too many plain experiments[9] did show himself to be. Which was an easy matter for him to bring to pass, considering not only the good title he had but also the earnest desire of the people to have some occasion ministered whereby they might be revenged of those notable injuries which they daily sustained by the outrageous cruelty of Macbeth's misgovernance. Though Malcolm was very sorrowful for the oppression of his countrymen, the Scots, in manner as Macduff had declared, yet doubting whether he were come as one that meant unfeignedly as he spake or else as sent from Macbeth to betray

2. informed.
3. banished.
4. gain.
5. subjects.
6. captivity.
7. villain's.
8. pity.
9. trials.

him, he thought to have some further trial. And thereupon dissembling his mind[1] at the first, he answered as followeth: "I am truly very sorry for the misery chanced to my country of Scotland, but though I have never so great affection to relieve the same, yet by reason of certain incurable vices which reign in me I am nothing meet thereto.[2] First, such immoderate lust and voluptuous sensuality (the abominable fountain of all vices) followeth me that, if I were made King of Scots, I should seek to deflower your maids and matrons in such wise that mine intemperancy should be more importable[3] unto you than the bloody tyranny of Macbeth now is." Hereunto Macduff answered, "This surely is a very evil fault, for many noble princes and kings have lost both lives and kingdoms for the same. Nevertheless there are women enough in Scotland, and therefore follow my counsel. Make thyself king, and I shall convey the matter so wisely that thou shalt be so satisfied at thy pleasure in such secret wise[4] that no man shall be aware thereof."

Then said Malcolm, "I am also the most avaricious creature on the earth, so that if I were king I should seek so many ways to get lands and goods that I would slay the most part of all the nobles of Scotland by surmised[5] accusations to the end I might enjoy their lands, goods, and possessions. And, therefore, to show you what mischief may ensue on you through mine unsatiable covetousness, I will rehearse unto you a fable. There was a fox having a sore place on h[er] overset with a swarm of flies that continually sucked out her blood. And when one that came by and saw this manner demanded whether she would have the flies driven before her, she answered: 'No, for if these flies that are already full and by reason thereof suck not very eagerly should be chased away, other that are empty and felly anhungered[6] should light in their places and suck out the residue of my blood far more to my grievance than these, which now being satisfied, do not much annoy me.' Therefore," saith Malcolm, "suffer me to remain where I am, lest if I attain to the regiment of your realm, mine unquenchable avarice may prove such that ye would think the displeasures which now grieve you should seem easy in respect of the unmeasurable outrage which might ensue through my coming amongst you."

Macduff to this made answer how it was a far worse fault than the other. "For avarice is the root of all mischief, and for that crime the most part of our kings have been slain and brought to their final end. Yet, notwithstanding, follow my counsel and take upon thee the

1. hiding his thoughts.
2. not at all fit for that.
3. unbearable.
4. manner.
5. false.
6. cruelly starving.

crown. There is gold and riches enough in Scotland to satisfy thy greedy desire." Then said Malcolm again, "I am, furthermore, inclined to dissimulation, telling of leasings,[7] and all other kinds of deceit, so that I naturally rejoice in nothing so much as to betray and deceive such as put any trust or confidence in my words. Then, sith there is nothing that more becometh a prince than constancy, verity, truth, and justice, with the other laudable fellowship of those fair and noble virtues which are comprehended only in soothfastness[8] and that lying utterly overthroweth the same, you see how unable I am to govern any province or region; and, therefore, sith you have remedies to cloak and hide all the rest of my other vices, I pray you find shift to cloak this vice amongst the residue."

Then said Macduff, "This yet is the worst of all and there I leave thee and therefore say: 'O ye unhappy and miserable Scottishmen, which are thus scourged with so many and sundry calamities, each one above other! Ye have one cursed and wicked tyrant that now reigneth over you without any right or title, oppressing you with his most bloody cruelty. This other that hath the right to the crown is so replete with the inconstant behavior and manifest vices of Englishmen that he is nothing worthy to enjoy it; for by his own confession he is not only avaricious and given to unsatiable lust but so false a traitor withal[9] that no trust is to be had unto any word he speaketh. Adieu, Scotland, for now I account myself a banished man forever, without comfort or consolation.' " And with those words the brackish tears trickled down his cheeks very abundantly.

At the last, when he was ready to depart, Malcolm took him by the sleeve and said, "Be of good comfort, Macduff, for I have none of these vices before remembered, but have jested with thee in this manner only to prove[1] thy mind, for divers times heretofore hath Macbeth sought by this manner of means to bring me into his hands; but the more slow I have showed myself to condescend to thy motion and request, the more diligence shall I use in accomplishing the same." Incontinently[2] hereupon they embraced each other and, promising to be faithful the one to the other, they fell in consultation how they might best provide for all their business to bring the same to good effect. Soon after, Macduff, repairing to the borders of Scotland, addressed his letters with secret dispatch unto the nobles of the realm, declaring how Malcolm was confederate with him to come hastily into Scotland to claim the crown; and therefore he required them, sith he was right inheritor thereto, to assist him with their powers to recover the same out of the hands of the wrongful usurper.

7. lies.
8. truthfulness.
9. in addition.
1. test.
2. immediately.

In the meantime, Malcolm purchased such favor at King Edward's hands that old Siward, Earl of Northumberland, was appointed with ten thousand men to go with him into Scotland to support him in this enterprise for recovery of his right. After these news were spread abroad in Scotland, the nobles drew into two several[3] factions, the one taking part with Macbeth and the other with Malcolm. Hereupon ensued oftentimes sundry bickerings and divers light skirmishes, for those that were of Malcolm's side would not jeopard[4] to join with their enemies in a pight field[5] till his coming out of England to their support. But after that Macbeth perceived his enemies' power to increase by such aid as came to them forth of England with his adversary Malcolm, he recoiled back into Fife, there purposing to abide in camp fortified at the castle of Dunsinane and to fight with his enemies if they meant to pursue him. Howbeit, some of his friends advised him that it should be best for him either to make some agreement with Malcolm or else to flee with all speed into the Isles, and to take his treasure with him, to the end he might wage[6] sundry great princes of the realm to take his part, and retain strangers in whom he might better trust than in his own subjects, which stole daily from him. But he had such confidence in his prophecies that he believed he should never be vanquished till Birnam Wood were brought to Dunsinane, nor yet to be slain with any man that should be or was born of any woman.

Malcolm, following hastily after Macbeth, came the night before the battle unto Birnam Wood; and when his army had rested awhile there to refresh them, he commanded every man to get a bough of some tree or other of that wood in his hand, as big as he might bear, and to march forth therewith in such wise that on the next morrow they might come closely and without sight in this manner within view of his enemies. On the morrow, when Macbeth beheld them coming in this sort, he first marveled what the matter meant, but in the end remembered himself that the prophecy which he had heard long before that time of the coming of Birnam Wood to Dunsinane Castle was likely to be now fulfilled. Nevertheless, he brought his men in order of battle and exhorted them to do valiantly. Howbeit, his enemies had scarcely cast from them their boughs when Macbeth, perceiving their numbers, betook him straight to flight; whom Macduff pursued with great hatred even till he came unto Lunfannaine, where Macbeth, perceiving that Macduff was hard at his back, leapt beside[7] his horse, saying, "Thou traitor, what meaneth it that thou shouldst thus in vain follow me that am not appointed to be

3. separate.
4. risk.
5. prepared battleground.
6. hire.
7. dismounted from.

slain by any creature that is born of a woman? Come on, therefore, and receive thy reward which thou hast deserved for thy pains!" And therewithal he lifted up his sword, thinking to have slain him.

But Macduff, quickly avoiding[8] from his horse ere he came at him, answered with his naked sword in his hand, saying, "It is true, Macbeth, and now shall thine insatiable cruelty have an end, for I am even he that thy wizards have told thee of, who was never born of my mother but ripped out of her womb." Therewithal he stepped unto him and slew him in the place. Then, cutting his head from his shoulders, he set it upon a pole and brought it unto Malcolm. This was the end of Macbeth, after he had reigned seventeen years over the Scottishmen. In the beginning of his reign he accomplished many worthy acts, very profitable to the commonwealth as ye have heard; but afterward, by illusion of the devil, he defamed[9] the same with most terrible cruelty. He was slain in the year of the Incarnation 1057, and in the sixteenth year of King Edward's reign over the Englishmen.

8. dismounting.
9. discredited.

Cultural Controversies

DEBATE ON FREE WILL AND PREDESTINATION

MARTIN LUTHER

[An Attack on Free Will]†

After sin free will exists in name only and when it does what in it lies it sins mortally.

Unhappy free will! When a just man does a good deed, he sins mortally, as we have seen, and free will boasts that before justification it is something and can do something. Oh, wretched are they who condemn my article, which rests on the first sentence of chapter 4 in Augustine's *Concerning the Spirit and the Letter*: 'Free will without grace can do nothing but sin.' I ask you, what sort of freedom is it that can choose only one alternative, and that the worse one? Does freedom mean to be able to do nothing but sin? But let us say I don't believe Augustine. Let us listen to Scripture. In John 15[:5] Christ says: 'Without me you can do nothing.' What is this 'nothing' which free will does without Christ? It prepares itself for grace, they say, by morally good works. But here Christ calls these nothing; therefore it prepares itself by nothing. A marvelous preparation that is accomplished by nothing!

But he goes on to explain what this 'nothing' is, saying: 'If anyone does not dwell in me, he will be thrown out like a branch and he

† From *Collected Works of Erasmus*, vol. 76: *Controversies*, ed. Charles Trinkaus *et al.* Selection trans. Charles H. Miller (Toronto: University of Toronto Press, 1999), 301–10. Reprinted by permission of University of Toronto Press. All bracketed material in the text is Miller's. Footnotes are by the editor of this Norton Critical Edition, unless otherwise indicated. Martin Luther (protested against perceived abuses in the church and initiated the Protestant Reformation. In response Pope Leo X's bull, *Exsurge, Domine* (15 June 1520), condemned Luther for error and heresy in forty-one articles. Luther replied in his *Assertio omnium articulorum* (1520 / 21), from which this section affirms the doctrine of predestination and denies free will. Luther argues that the human will is enslaved to sin and that justification, the freeing from sin, occurs solely by God's election and grace. His argument and Erasmus's defense of free will (see the excerpt on pp. 123–31 in this edition) provide one theological context for the choices, actions, and consequences portrayed in *Macbeth*.

withers and they gather him up and throw him on the fire and he burns' [John 16:6]. I beg you, most holy Vicar of Christ, how can you have the meretricious effrontery to dare to contradict your Lord in this way? You say that free will can prepare itself to proceed to grace. On the other hand, Christ says that it is thrown out, so that it is further away from grace. How beautifully your bull harmonizes with the gospel! Let us listen, then, to Christ, who posits five steps in the perdition of the pruned branch, showing that it can not only not prepare itself for doing good but necessarily grows worse. The first is that it is thrown out and therefore not brought in; it is given over to the power of Satan, who does not allow it to attempt anything good. For what else can it mean to be thrown out? Secondly, it withers; that is, left to itself, it grows worse every day, and these are the two works of free will: namely, to sin and to persevere and grow worse in sinning, to be thrown out and to wither. For if free will can do anything else, Christ is certainly a liar. There are three punishments after that: they gather it up, that is, for judgment, so that it may be convicted together with the others. Then, when the sentence has been handed down, they throw it into eternal fire, where it finally does nothing but burn, that is, suffers eternal punishment. Therefore, that free will can do nothing does not mean, as they pretend, that it can do nothing meritorious, but that it is thrown out and withers. The pruned branch does not prepare itself for the vine, nor can it do so, but it becomes more removed from the vine and comes closer and closer to perishing: so too free will or a wicked person.

Genesis 6[:5] and 8[:21]: 'The understanding and every thought of the human heart is inclined to evil at all times.' I beg you, if someone says that every thought of the heart is evil, and is so at all times, what good thought does he leave which can prepare for grace? Does evil dispose someone to good? Nor can anyone escape from this authority by saying that a person can sometimes repress his evil thought. For a thought which does this, actively or passively, is good in either case, but it will not be included among those which are said to be all thoughts. If a single good thought can be there, Moses is a liar because he affirms that they are all evil. Moreover, we may represent the Hebrew text as follows: 'Because whatever the human heart desires and thinks is only evil every day'; to 'evil' it adds an exclusive particle which our translation did not render. It also did not render 'desires,' and the translation 'thought' does not fully render 'thinks.' For Moses intended to include not only idle and spontaneous thoughts but also thoughts conceived by the mind and thoughts by which a person deliberately intends to do something, and he also says that they are evil without exception, so that these

Pelagians[1] have no way of attributing to free will the power to do something good, if it works hard enough at it.

Again Genesis 6[:3]: 'My spirit does not remain in mankind, because it is flesh.' If mankind is flesh, what progress can it make towards good? Do we not know the works proper to the flesh in Galatians 5[:19–20], which are fornication, impurity, lewdness, anger, envy, murder, etc.? These are the things free will does when it does what in it lies; and these are all mortal sins. For Romans 8[:7] says: 'For the prudence of the flesh is death and an enemy to God.' How can death lead to life? How does enmity dispose itself to grace? For if the Spirit is not in mankind, it is dead before God. But a dead person necessarily does the works of death, not of life, and the work of death does not dispose to life. Therefore everything that has been treated in so many books about the preparation of free will for grace is mere fiction.

*   *   *

Isaiah says the same thing in the same place:[2] 'All flesh is grass and all its glory is like the flower of the grass. The grass is withered and the flower has fallen, because the Spirit of the Lord has blown upon it. But the word of the Lord remains forever' [Isaiah 40: 6–8]. Explain the grass and the flower. Is it not the flesh, man, or free will and whatever man has? Its flower and glory, is that not the power, wisdom, and justice of free will, which enable it to glory in the fact that it is something and can do something. What is the reason, then, that when the Spirit blows it is withered and falls and perishes, whereas the word remains? Is the Spirit not grace, by which you said free will is assisted and its preparation fulfilled? Why then does he say here that even the best parts of the flesh are withered and fall? Do you not see that the Spirit and free will are opposed to one another? For when the one blows the other falls and does not remain with the word. And it would not have fallen and perished if it had been fit and prepared for the breath of the Spirit and of the word.

Also Jeremiah in chapter 10 [verse 23] says as follows: 'I know, Lord, that a person's path is not his own and that a man does not have the power to direct his own steps.' What statement could be clearer? If a person's path and his steps are not in his power, how can God's path and God's steps be in his power? A person's path is what they call the natural power of doing what in him lies. See now that this is not in man's choice or free will. What, then, is free will

---

1. followers of Pelagius, fifth-century heretic who denied the Catholic doctrine of original sin and asserted that the human will is capable of good without the benefit of divine grace.
2. The 'same place' is Isaiah 40:2, 'She has received at the Lord's hand double measure for all her sins'; Luther glosses this verse with the explanation that 'grace is not given by the Lord except for sins, that is, for evil deeds.'

but a thing in name only? How can it prepare itself for the good when it does not even have the power to make its own paths evil? For God does even bad deeds in the wicked, as Proverbs 16[:4] says: 'The Lord made everything for his own sake, even the wicked for the evil day.' And Rom 1[:28]: 'God gave them up to their own depraved perception so that they do what is not fitting.' And in chapter 9 [verse 18]: 'He hardens as he wishes; he has mercy as he wishes.' Just as Exodus 9[:16] says about Pharaoh: 'For this very purpose I aroused you, that I might show my power in you.' For that is why God is terrible in his judgments and his deeds.

Again, Proverbs 16[:1] says this: 'It is man's part to prepare his heart, but it is the Lord's to govern his tongue.' That is, a man usually proposes many things, when in fact his deeds are so little in his control that he does not even have within his power the words for this deed of his but rather is forced by the marvelous providence of God both to speak and to act differently from what he had in mind, as was shown in Balaam (Numbers 24[:5–27])[3]. And Psalm 138[:4]: 'My tongue has no speech.' And even more clearly further on in Proverbs 16[:9]: 'The heart of a man thinks of his own path and the Lord directs his steps.' See, the path of a man does not proceed as he thinks, but as the Lord ordains. For that reason chapter 21[:1] says: 'Like water divided into channels, so the heart of the king is in the hand of the Lord; he will turn it wherever he wishes.' Where, then, is free will? It is completely fictitious.

And if Scripture did not show this, we would have abundant evidence of its truth from all histories, and everyone would see it from his own life. For who is there who always carried out everything he wanted to? Indeed, who is there who has not often had it in mind to do something and then suddenly changed his mind so as to do something else, not knowing how he changed it? Who would dare to deny that even in evil works he has been forced to do something different from what he had in mind? Don't you think the authors of this bull applied the sum total of their power of free will to the task of speaking in their favour and against Luther? And see how this thought and its execution did not lie in their choice! For they did everything against themselves and brought it all down on their own heads, so that I have never read of any persons who disgraced themselves more foully and more abominably, and out of blindness and ignorance they cast themselves quite openly into the shameful depths of error, heresy, and malice—so little control of himself does a person have, even when he conceives and executes evil deeds. And Paul spoke the truth in Ephesians 1[:11]: 'God works all things in all persons.'[4]

3. Balaam blesses instead of curses Israel.
4. 1 Cor 12:6, actually. [Miller's note.]

Here, then, that 'general influence'[5] disappears by which, according to their babble, we have it in our power to perform natural operations. The experience of everyone shows that this is not the case. And see how stupid we are: we know that the root of our works, namely our life, which is the source of all our works, is never for a single moment under our control, and do we dare to say that any intention is under our control? Could we say anything more absurd than that? Did God, who kept our life under his control, place our motions and works under our control? Far from it. Hence there can be no doubt that the teaching of Satan brought this phrase 'free will' into the church in order to seduce men away from God's path into his own paths. The brothers of Joseph fully intended to kill him, and lo and behold! they had so little choice about that very intention that they even changed it immediately to something entirely different, as he said, 'You intended to do me harm, but God changed it to something good' [Gen 50:20].

Have you got anything, miserable pope, to snarl against this? Hence it is also necessary to revoke this article. For I misspoke when I said that free will before grace exists in name only; rather I should have simply said 'free will is a fiction among real things, a name with no reality.' For no one has it within his control to intend anything, good or evil, but rather, as was rightly taught by the article of Wyclif[6] which was condemned at Constance, all things occur by absolute necessity. That was what the poet meant when he said, 'All things are settled by a fixed law' [Vergil, *Aeneid* 2:324]. And Christ in Matt 10[:29–30]: 'The leaf of a tree does not fall to the earth apart from the will of your Father who is in heaven, and the hairs of your head are all numbered.'[7] And Isaiah 41[:23] taunts them: 'Do good also or evil, if you can!'

Hence, as Elijah exhorted the prophets of Baal [3 Kings 18:25–27], I egg on these proponents of free will: 'Come on, be men, do what in you lies, at least for once put to the test what you teach, prepare yourselves for grace, and obtain what you want, since you say God does not deny anything if you do what free will can do. It is a dreadful disgrace that you cannot bring forward a single example of your teaching and you yourselves cannot provide a single work so that your wisdom consists merely in words.' But these efforts of theirs are a pretext for supporting Pelagius. For what does it matter if you deny that grace comes from our works if you nevertheless teach that it is given through our works? The meaning remains equally

---

5. *Influentia generalis*, a technical term, denoting the cooperation of first cause (God) with the second cause (the creature). Luther denies the existence of such cooperation.
6. Proposition of John Wyclif (fourteenth century), whom Catholics considered a heretic, Protestants, an early reformer.
7. Luther adapts this verse, substituting 'leaf' for 'sparrow.' [Miller's note.]

impious, since grace is believed to be given not gratuitously but because of our works. For the works which the Pelagians taught and performed and because of which they held that grace is given are not different from the ones you teach and perform. They are works of the same free will and of the same bodily members, but you gave them one name and they gave them another: fasting, prayer, alms-giving were the same things, but you said they are fitting for grace and they claimed they are worthy of grace, but everywhere the same Pelagius carried on triumphantly.

These miserable people are deceived by the inconstancy or (as they call it) the contingency of human affairs. They fix their stupid eyes on things in themselves and the actions of things and never lift them up to the sight of God so that they might recognize in God the things above things. For when we look at things here below they seem to be fortuitous and subject to choice but when we look upward all things are necessary, because we all live, act, and suffer everything not as we wish but as he wills. The free will which seems to bear on us and temporal things has no bearing on God, for in him, as James says, there is no variation or shadow of change [James 1:17], but here all things change and vary. And we are so stupid we measure the divine by the temporal, so that we presume to get ahead of God by free will and to wrest grace from him while he is asleep, as it were, whenever we please, as if he were able to change together with us and as if he willed something that at one time he did not will, and all by the working and willing of our free choice. Oh, monstrous madness beyond all madness!

And Paul in Ephesians 2[:3] says: 'We too were by nature sons of wrath like the rest.' If everyone apart from grace is a son of wrath by his very nature, then free will is also a son of wrath by its very nature; if it is so by its very nature, it is much more so by all its works. And how can someone be a son of wrath by his nature except because everything he does is evil, preparing not for grace but for wrath, indeed meriting wrath? Go on now, you Pelagians, and prepare your-selves for grace by your works, since Paul says here that by them no one merits anything except wrath. It would have been milder if he had said only 'We were sons of wrath,' but by adding 'by nature' he wanted it to be understood that everything we are and do by our nature merits wrath and not at all grace. You could hardly find a briefer, clearer, or more emphatic statement against free will in Scripture.

Why should we go on at length? From what has been said above, it is abundantly clear to us that even the just struggle mightily against their flesh in order to do good and that free will and the prudence of the flesh resist them; the flesh yearns with all its power against the spirit, despising whatever belongs to the Spirit and the law of

God. And how could it be possible that by its own nature and without the Spirit it could yearn for the Spirit or prepare itself for the Spirit by doing what in it lies? While it was in a state of grace, its nature was such that it fought fiercely against grace, and apart from grace can its nature be such that it assists the spirit? Could you imagine anything crazier than that? For such an unheard-of monstrosity would be as if someone who could not control an untamed wild animal while it was tied up should be mad enough to boast that before it was tied up or without being tied up it is so tame and gentle that it willingly tames itself or makes an effort to be tame. Stop being so crazy, I beg you, you miserable Pelagians! If free will in a state of grace sins and rages against grace, as we are all forced to recognize and as the Apostle and all the saints complain, certainly it goes against all common sense that it should be upright apart from grace or prepare itself for grace when it is absent, since it hates and persecutes grace when it is present.

It follows necessarily, then, that whatever is taught and done before grace in order to obtain grace is sheer fabrication and hypocrisy, for it is necessary that we should be preceded by the mercy of God even to wish for it, just as Augustine, writing against the epistles of Pelagius, says that God converts the reluctant and unwilling, as he demonstrated in the case of Paul, whom he converted when he was set against grace and at the height of his burning rage to persecute; and Peter did not look back at the Lord, so as to remember the words Jesus had said to him, but rather Jesus looked back at Peter, in the midst and at the very height of the business, and so Peter remembered the words and wept bitterly.

And so we see in the meaning of this article how deceptively Satan works in teaching this error. For since they cannot deny that we must be saved through the grace of God and cannot avoid this truth, impiety takes another path to avoid it, pretending that if our role is not to save ourselves, nevertheless it is our role to be prepared to be saved by the grace of God. What glory, I beg you, is left for God if we can do so much to be saved by his grace? Is such power a small thing if someone who does not have grace has enough power to be able to have grace whenever he wishes? What difference does it make if you do [not][8] say that we are saved without grace, as the Pelagians do, since you place the grace of God within the choice of men? You seem to me worse than Pelagius when you place the necessary grace of God, which he completely denied was necessary, within the power of men. It seems less impious, I say, to deny grace completely than to say it is prepared by our effort and work and to give us, as it were, control over it. And nevertheless the working of this error has

---

8. Miller adds a 'not' here, as Luther argues that his opponents are worse than Pelagians.

prevailed because it is specious and pleasing to nature and free will, so that it is difficult to confute it, especially when dealing with ignorant and crude minds.

We could put up with the frivolity and stupidity of the pope and his minions in the other articles about the papacy, councils, indulgences, and other unnecessary nonsense, but in this article, which is the best of all and the sum and substance of my case, we must deplore and lament that these wretches are so insane. For I believe the heavens will fall down before the pope and his disciples will ever understand a single jot about this mystery of God's grace. The truth of this article cannot coexist with the church of the pope, no more than Belial with Christ or light with darkness. For if the church of the pope had not taught and sold good works or had sincerely taught that we are justified by grace alone, it would not have grown so full of pompous display and, if by some chance it had done so, it would not have remained that way for a single hour. For this theology which condemns whatever the pope approves of and makes martyrs is based on the cross. That is why the best part of the church and almost all of it flourished when the period of the martyrs came to an end. Soon pleasure took the place of the cross, poverty was replaced by opulence, ignominy by glory, until what is now called the church has become more worldly than the world, so to speak, and more fleshly than the flesh itself. And I have no more powerful argument against the reign of the pope than that he reigns without the cross. His whole aim is not to suffer at all but rather to abound and to exult in all things, and he has not been cheated of his desire. He has what he wanted, and the faithful city has become a whore and truly the kingdom of the true Antichrist.

In this section my prolixity was necessitated by the subject itself, which has been repressed and extinguished not only by this bull (which I consider to be not worth the paper it's written on) but also by almost all teachers in the schools for more than thirteen hundred years. For on this point everyone writes against grace, not for it, so that no point needs to be handled as much as this one, and I have often wished to handle it, leaving aside that trivial papistical nonsense and matters which do not pertain to the church at all except to destroy it; but by length of time and widespread prevalence, the working of Satan has fixed itself so firmly in men's hearts and has used this error to blunt their minds so badly that I do not see anyone who is fit to understand it or even to dispute with me about it. Scripture is abundant on this subject but it has been so ravaged by our Nebuchadnezzar[9] that the very form and knowledge of the letters is

9. powerful Babylonian king.

gone, and we need some new Esdras[1] who will discover new letters
and recover the Bible for us once more, which I hope is now being
done as the Hebrew and Greek languages are flourishing all over the
world. Amen.

DESIDERIUS ERASMUS

[A Defense of Free Will]†

By 'free will' here we understand a power of the human will by
which man be able to direct himself towards, or turn away from,
what leads to eternal salvation.

* * *

[*Scriptural exhortations are meaningless if we have no power to comply.*]

But what point is there in quoting a few passages of this kind when
all Holy Scripture is full of exhortations like this: 'Turn back to me
with all your heart' [Joel 2:12]; 'Let every man turn from his evil way'
[John 3:8]; 'Come back to your senses, you transgressors' [Isa 46:8];
'Let everyone turn from his evil way, and I will repent the ill that I
have thought to do them on account of the evil of their endeavours';
and 'If you will not listen to me, to walk in my law' [Jer 26:3 4].
Nearly the whole of Scripture speaks of nothing but conversion,
endeavour, and striving to improve. All this would become meaningless once it was accepted that doing good or evil was a matter of
necessity; and so too would all the promises, threats, complaints,
reproaches, entreaties, blessings, and curses directed towards those
who have amended their ways, or those who have refused to change:
'As soon as a sinner groans at his sin' [Ezek 18:21; Isa 30:15]; 'I have
seen that this is a stubborn people' [Exod 32:9]; 'Oh my people, what
have I done to you?' [Mic 6:3]; and 'They have rejected my laws'

---

1. Esdras or Ezra, famous Hebrew scribe and priest, edited and corrected the Hebrew Scriptures and wrote the books of Chronicles, Ezra, Nehemiah, and perhaps others.
† From *Collected Works of Erasmus*, vol. 76: *Controversies*, ed. Charles Trinkaus et al. Selection trans. Peter Macardle, (Toronto: University of Toronto Press, 1999), 21, 36–38, 59–
   62, 75–80. Reprinted by permission of University of Toronto Press. All bracketed material
   in the text is Macardle's. Footnotes are by the editor of this Norton Critical Edition, unless
   otherwise indicated. Learned Dutch humanist, biblical and Patristics scholar, Desiderius
   Erasmus (1466?–1536) refuted Luther (see the excerpt on pp. 115–23 in this edition) in
   De Libero Arbitrio (1524). Erasmus argues that the doctrine of predestination makes Scriptural exhortation meaningless and that human will (a secondary cause) cooperates with
   divine grace (the primary cause) in acts of virtue or vice.

[Ezek 20:13]; 'Oh, that my people had listened to me, that Israel had walked in my ways!' [Ps 80:14]; 'He who wishes to see good days, let him keep his tongue from evil' [Ps 33:13–14] The phrase 'he who wishes to see' speaks of free will.

Since such phrases are frequently encountered, does it not immediately occur to the reader to ask, 'why promise conditionally what is entirely dependent on your will? Why complain of my behaviour, when all my actions, good or bad, are performed by you in me regardless of my will? Why reproach me, when I have no power to preserve the good you have given me, or keep out the evil you put into me? Why entreat me, when everything depends on you, and happens as it pleases you? Why bless me, as though I had done my duty, when whatever happens is your work? Why curse me, when I sinned through necessity?' What is the purpose of such a vast number of commandments if not a single person has it at all in his power to do what is commanded? For there are some who believe that man, albeit justified by the gift of faith and charity, cannot fulfill any of God's commandments, but rather that all good works, because they are done 'in the flesh,' would lead to damnation were not God in his mercy to pardon them on account of the merit of our faith.

Yet the word spoken by God through Moses in Deuteronomy, chapter 30[:11–14], shows that what he commands is not merely within our power, but that it demands little effort. He says: 'The commandment that I lay upon you this day is not beyond you, nor is it far away. It is not in heaven, that you might say, "Which one of us is strong enough to go up to heaven and bring it back to us, that we may hear and fulfill it?" Neither is it beyond the sea, that you should make excuses, and say, "Who among us can cross the sea and bring it back to us, that we may hear what is commanded?" No, the word is very near to you, on your lips and in your heart, that you may do it.'

Yet here he is speaking of the greatest commandment of all: 'that you turn back to the Lord your God with all your heart and with all your soul.' And what is the meaning of 'but if you will listen,' 'if you will keep the commandments,' 'if you will turn back' [Deut 30:10], if none of this is in our power at all? I will not attempt to quote an extensive selection of such texts, for the books of both testaments are so full of them wherever you look that anyone attempting to search them out would simply be 'looking for water in the sea,' as the saying goes. And so, as I said, a considerable amount of Holy Scripture will obviously become meaningless if you accept the last opinion discussed above, or the previous one.

*   *   *

[Passages from the New Testament supporting free will; Gospel exhortations are meaningless if we have no power to comply.]

The quotations so far have come from the Old Testament; this might be cause for objection, had they not been of the kind which the light of the Gospel not only fails to efface, but actually endows with new force. And so let us turn to the books of the New Testament. First we come across that place in the Gospel where Christ, weeping over the destruction of the city of Jerusalem, says: 'Jerusalem, Jerusalem, city that murders the prophets and stones those who are sent to you, how often I have wanted to gather you together, as a hen gathers her chicks under her wings, and you refused!' [Matt 22:37]. If everything happens by necessity, could Jerusalem not rightly reply to the Lord's lament, 'Why torment yourself with pointless weeping? If it was your will that we should not listen to the prophets, why did you send them? Why blame us for something that you did voluntarily, and we by necessity? You wanted to gather us together, and yet in us you did not want to: for in us you brought it about that we refused. Yet in our Lord's words, it is not necessity working in the Jews that is blamed, but their wicked, rebellious will: 'I wanted to gather you together; you refused.'

Again, elsewhere we find, 'If you want to enter into life, keep the commandments' [Matt 19:7]. How on earth could one say 'if you want to' to someone whose will was not free? Or, 'If you want to be perfect, go and sell what you have' [Matt 19:21] or Luke 9[:23], 'If anyone wants to come after me, let him deny himself, and take up his cross, and follow me.' Though the commandment is very difficult, our will is nevertheless mentioned. And shortly afterwards we find, 'Whoever wants to save his life shall lose it' [Luke 9:24]. Are not all Christ's excellent commandments emptied of their meaning if nothing is attributed to human will? 'But I tell you, but I tell you etc.' [Matt 5:22, 28]; and 'If you love me, keep my commandments' [John 14:15]. How greatly John stresses the commandments! How poorly the conjunction 'if' agrees with absolute necessity: 'If you remain in me, and my words remain in you' [John 15:7]; 'If you want to be perfect' [Matt 19:21].

Now, when good and bad deeds are mentioned so frequently, as is reward, I fail to see how there can be any room at all for absolute necessity: nature and necessity deserve no reward. And yet in Matthew 5[:12] our Lord Jesus says, 'rejoice and be glad, for your reward is great in heaven.' What is the sense of the parable of the hired labourers in the vineyard [Matt 20:1–16]? Can they be labourers, if their labour achieves nothing? As agreed, they receive one penny as reward for their labour. Someone will say that it is called a reward because it is in some sense owed by God, who has given his word to man if he will believe in God's promises. But this very act of believing is one in which free will plays some part, turning itself towards, or away from, faith. Why is the servant who increased his master's fortune by his own efforts praised, and why is the lazy good-for-nothing condemned [Matt 25: 14–30], unless we have some responsibility in such a case? And again, in Matthew, chapter 25, when Christ invites everyone to a share in his eternal kingdom, he refers not to necessity but to people's charitable deeds: 'You gave food and drink'; 'you took in the stranger'; 'you clothed the naked, etc.' [Matt 25: 35–36]; speaking to the goats on his left he reproaches not necessity, but their voluntary failures to perform good works: 'You saw the hungry, you were given an opportunity to do good, but you gave no food, etc.' [Matt 25:42]. Are not all the gospel writings in fact full of exhortations?

*   *   *

[*Passages cited by Luther to deny the existence of free will; limited application of Genesis 6:3 and 8:21 and Isaiah 40:6–8.*]

Now let us try the strength of the scriptural proofs which Martin Luther quotes to undermine the power of free will. He cites verses from Genesis 6[:3] and 8[:21]. 'My spirit will not remain in man forever, for he is flesh.' In this verse Scripture does not use 'flesh' simply in the sense of 'a wicked desire,' as Paul sometimes does, when he orders us to 'mortify the works of the flesh' [Rom 8:13], but in the sense of the weakness of our nature with its tendency to sinning, as Paul calls the Corinthians 'fleshly' because they were not yet ready to receive teaching in the form of solid food, being still (as it were) babes in Christ [1 Cor 3:1–2]. And in *Questions about the Hebrew* Jerome says that the Hebrew text reads differently from ours, namely, 'My spirit will not pass judgment on those men eternally, for they are flesh.' These words speak not of God's severity, but of his clemency: for by 'flesh' he means men naturally weak, prone to evil, and by 'spirit' he means wrath; and so he is saying that he will not save these people up for eternal punishment, but in his mercy will exact punishment from them in this life. And these words do not even apply to the entire human race, but only to the men of that age, whose heinous vices had utterly corrupted them; and so he says, 'those men.' And it does not even apply to all the men of that time, given that Noah is praised as a righteous man, pleasing to God [Gen 6:8–9].

In the same way it is possible to dismiss his quotations from chapter 8[:21] of the same book, 'For the thought and imagination of man's heart are inclined to evil from his youth on', and from chapter 6[:5], 'The heart's every thought is directed towards evil at all times.'

Even if the tendency to evil in most men cannot be overcome without the help of God's grace, it does not remove the freedom of the will completely, for if no aspect of repentance depends on the will, but everything is controlled by God through a kind of necessity, then why are men given time for repentance in this very passage: 'His days will be one hundred and twenty years' [Gen 6:3]? For in *Questions about the Hebrew,* Jerome considers that this verse refers not to the length of human life, but to the interval before the Flood; a time conceded to humans during which to change their ways if they wish, and if not, to be shown to deserve divine condemnation for having disdained God's leniency.

*   *   *

As for his quotation of Isaiah 40[:6–8]—'All flesh is grass, and all its glory is as the flower of the grass. The grass is withered and the flower has fallen because the Spirit of the Lord has blown upon it, but the word of the Lord abides for ever'—Luther, I feel, twists this somewhat violently to apply to grace and free will. For here Jerome understands 'spirit' as meaning divine wrath, 'flesh' as man's natural weakness, which is powerless against God, and 'flower' as the vainglory aroused by material good fortune. The Jews gloried in the temple, in circumcision, in sacrifices; the Greeks gloried in their wisdom: but now that the wrath of God has been revealed from heaven by the gospel, all that glory has withered.

Yet not every human inclination is 'flesh': there is 'soul' and there is 'spirit,' by which we strive towards goodness. This part of the psyche is called reason or the ruling principle—or was there not a single one of the pagan philosophers who strove for goodness, though they taught that we should a thousand times more readily go to our death than commit an evil action, even if we knew that it would be unknown to men and pardoned by God? Corrupt reason, it is true, often has poor judgment. 'You do not know,' said the Lord, 'to what spirit you belong': the disciples were mistakenly seeking vengeance, referring to the time long before when fire had come down from heaven in answer to Elijah's prayers and burned up the captains with their companies of fifty men [Luke 9:54–55]. In Romans 8[:16] Paul states that even in good people the human spirit is distinct from the spirit of God: 'for that spirit [of God] witnesses to our spirit that we are children of God.' And so, if anyone maintains that the highest powers of human nature are nothing but flesh, that is, evil inclinations, I will gladly agree—if he can demonstrate his assertion with proofs from Holy Scripture!

'What is born of the flesh is flesh, and what is born of the spirit is spirit' [John 3:6]. John further teaches that those who believe in the gospel are born of God and become children of God and even gods

[John 1:12, 10:34–36]; and Paul distinguishes the fleshly man, who does not understand the things that are of God, from the spiritual man, who can judge all things, and elsewhere he calls him a new creation in Christ [1 Cor 2:14–15]. If the whole man, even though reborn through faith, is still nothing but flesh, where is the 'spirit born of the spirit'? Where is the 'child of God'? Where is the 'new creation'? I would like instruction on these points; until then I will take full advantage of the authority of the ancients, who teach that there are certain seeds of goodness planted in men's minds,[1] with the help of which they can to some extent see and strive after the good, though there are also baser tendencies which tug them in the opposite direction. Furthermore, choice means the ability of the will to turn in either direction; and although the will is perhaps more inclined to evil than to good, on account of the tendency to sin left in us, yet no one is compelled to sin unless he actually wills it.

* * *

[*To assert necessity to the exclusion of free will makes God cruel and unjust.*]

First, how can you constantly read that holy people, full of good works, 'did justice' [2 Kings 8:15], 'walked righteously in the sight of God' [1 Kings 2:4], 'turned neither to the left nor to the right' [Deut 5:32], if everything that even the godliest do is a sin, and such a sin that without the intervention of God's mercy someone for whom Christ died would be cast into hell? How can you constantly read of a 'reward' where there is absolutely no merit? How can the obedience of those who complied with God's commandments conceivably be praised, and the disobedience of those who did not be condemned? Why is judgment constantly mentioned in the Scriptures if merits are not weighed at all? Why are we made to appear before the judgment-seat if we have done nothing through our own will, but everything has been done in us by absolute necessity?

There is the further objection: what need is there of the many admonitions, commands, threats, exhortations, and remonstrances in the Scriptures if we do nothing, but God works everything in us, the deed as well as the will, in accordance with his immutable will? God requires us to pray without ceasing, to stay vigilant, to struggle, to contend for the prize of eternal life. Why does he want to be constantly asked for something which he has already decided whether or not to give, seeing that his decisions cannot be changed,

---

1. Erasmus is here alluding to a central idea of the Stoics, which he encountered in the Fathers, especially Jerome. [Macardle's note.] The Stoics were ancient Greek and Roman philosophers who advocated the rule of reason, the following of nature in moderation, indifference to fortune, and resistance to all passions.

since he himself is unchangeable? Why does he tell us to labour to obtain what he has decided to bestow on us as a free gift? We suffer affliction, rejection, ridicule, torture, and death; thus God's grace fights, wins, and triumphs in us. A martyr undergoes such torments, yet no merit is credited to him for doing so—indeed he is said to have sinned in having exposed his body to suffering in the hope of heavenly life. But why did the all-merciful God wish to work in the martyrs in this way? A man would seem cruel if he had decided to make a friend a free gift of something, but would not give it to him until he had been tortured to the point of despair.

*   *   *

[Faith must not be exalted to the exclusion of free will: free will cooperates with grace.]

We listen with equanimity, however, to our opponents' boundlessly exalting faith in, and love of, God, for we are of the opinion that the corruption of Christian life everywhere by so many sins has no other cause than the coldness and drowsiness of our faith, which gives us a merest verbal belief in God: a faith on the lips only, whereas according to Paul 'man is justified by believing from the heart' [Rom 10:10]. Nor will I particularly take issue with those who refer all things to faith as their ultimate source, even though I believe that faith is born from and nurtured by charity, and charity in turn born from and nurtured by faith. Charity certainly feeds faith, just as the light in a lantern is fed by oil, for we more readily trust the person we ardently love: and there is no dearth of people who contend that faith is the beginning, rather than the completion, of salvation. But our argument does not concern these matters.[2]

Yet here we should beware of being so absorbed in enlarging on the praises of faith that we subvert the freedom of the will; and once it has been denied I do not see how the problem of the justice and mercy of God can be resolved. When the ancient authors found they could not extricate themselves from these difficulties, some were forced to posit two Gods: one of the Old Testament who they argued was only just, not good; and one of the New Testament who they argued was only good, not just. Tertullian[3] adequately refuted their wicked fabrication. Manichaeus,[4] as we said, dreamed up the notion of two natures in man, one which could not avoid sinning and one

2. Tangentially and briefly Erasmus expresses his reservations about Luther's doctrine of salvation *ex fide sola*, by faith alone. [Macardle's note.]
3. Tertullian (ca. 155–220), an important early Christian theologian and polemicist, refuted this heresy in *Adversus Marcionem*.
4. actually Mani (216–277), whose followers were Manicheans. He taught that two opposing principles, one of light and goodness, the other of darkness and evil, struggled against each other in the universe and in human life.

which could not avoid doing good. Pelagius,[5] concerned for God's
justice, attributed too much to free will. There is little difference
between him and those who attribute so much to human will as to
say that through our natural powers, by morally good works, it can
merit the supreme grace by which we are justified. They seem to me
to have wanted to urge man to moral effort by holding out a good
hope of obtaining salvation, just as Cornelius, because of his prayers
and almsgiving, deserved to be taught by Peter, and the eunuch by
Philip [Acts 10:1–43; 8:26–38], and Saint Augustine, who assidu-
ously sought Christ in Paul's letters, deserved to find him. Here we
can placate those who believe that man cannot do any good deed
which he does not owe to God by saying that the whole work is no
less due to God, without whom we could achieve nothing; that the
contribution of free will is very small indeed; and that our very ability
to direct our mind to the things that pertain to salvation, or to coop-
erate with grace, is itself a gift of God. As a result of the controversy
with Pelagius, Augustine reached a less favourable view of free will
than he had previously held. In the opposite way Luther, who previously attributed something to free will, has been carried so far by
the heat of his defence as to remove it altogether. Yet I believe that
among the Greeks Lycurgus is blamed for having had the vines cut
down because he hated drunkenness, whereas by bringing the
sources of water closer he could have prevented drunkenness without abolishing wine-drinking.

  In my opinion free will could have been established in such a way
as to avoid that trust in our own merits and the other harmful consequences which Luther avoids, as well as those which we mentioned above, yet so as not to destroy the benefits which Luther
admires. This I believe is achieved by the opinion of those who
ascribe entirely to grace the impetus by which the mind is first
aroused, and only in the succeeding process attribute something to
human will in that it does not resist the grace of God. Since there
are three parts to everything—beginning, continuation, and completion—they ascribe the first and last to grace and allow that free will
has an effect only in the continuation, in so far as in a single, indi-
visible act there are two causes, divine grace and human will, working together. However, grace is the principal cause and will the
secondary cause, unable to do anything without the principal cause,
whereas the principal cause is sufficient in itself. Just so the power
inherent in fire burns, yet the principal cause is God acting at the
same time through the fire, a cause which would be sufficient in
itself, and without which fire would have no effect if that cause were
to withdraw itself.

5. fifth-century heretic who denied the Catholic doctrine of original sin and asserted that
   the human will is capable of good without the benefit of divine grace.

On this moderate view man must ascribe his salvation entirely to the grace of God; for what free will accomplishes in this is very insignificant indeed, and what it can accomplish is itself due to divine grace, which first created free will, then freed and healed it. And this will appease (if they can be appeased) those who believe that there is no good in man which he does not owe to God. Owe it he does, but in a different way and for a different reason, as an inheritance falling to children in equal shares is not called benevolence, since it comes to them all in the ordinary course of law. (It is called liberality if one or other of them has been given something over and above his legal due.) Yet children are indebted to their parents even on account of an inheritance.

DEBATE ON WITCHCRAFT

REGINALD SCOT

The Discovery of Witchcraft†

Book 1, Chapter 1: *An impeachment of witches' power in meteors and elementary bodies, tending to the rebuke of such as attribute too much unto them.*

The fables of witchcraft have taken so fast hold and deep root in the heart of man that few or none can nowadays with patience endure the hand and correction of God. For if any adversity, grief, sickness, loss of children, corn, cattle, or liberty happen unto them, by and by they exclaim upon witches. As though there were no God in Israel that ordereth all things according to his will, punishing both just and unjust with grief, plagues, and afflictions in manner and form as he thinketh good, but that certain old women here on earth, called witches, must needs be the contrivers of all men's calamities, and as though they themselves were innocents and had deserved no such punishments. Insomuch as they stick[1] not to ride and go to such as either are injuriously termed witches, or else are willing so to be accounted, seeking at their hands comfort and remedy in time

---

† From Reginald Scot, *The Dicouerie of Witchcraft* (London, 1584), sigs. ci–cviv. Footnotes are by the editor of this Norton Critical Edition. Spelling and punctuation have been modernized by the editor. Attacking Jacob Sprenger and Heinrich Krämer's seminal treatise on witchcraft, *Malleus Maleficarum* (1486), Reginald Scot (1538–1599) argued that God ruled the world and, therefore, that current beliefs in witchcraft resulted merely from ignorance, superstition, and deceit. Scot associated belief in witchcraft with Catholic practices and idolatry. King James I, a firm believer in devils and witches, responded (see the excerpts on pp. 138–48 in this edition) and their debate provides an interesting context for the witches of *Macbeth*.
1. hesitate.

of their tribulation, contrary to God's will and commandment in that behalf, who bids us resort to Him in all our necessities.

Such faithless people, I say, are also persuaded that neither hail nor snow, thunder nor lightning, rain nor tempestuous winds come from the heavens at the commandment of God, but are raised by the cunning and power of witches and conjurers. Insomuch as a clap of thunder, or a gale of wind is no sooner heard, but either they run to ring bells, or cry out to burn witches, or else burn consecrated things, hoping by the smoke thereof to drive the devil out of the air, as though spirits could be frayed[2] away with such external toys, howbeit these are right enchantments,[3] as Brentius[4] affirmeth.

But certainly it is neither a witch, nor devil, but a glorious God that maketh the thunder. I have read in the scriptures that God maketh the blustering tempests and whirlwinds, and I find that it is the Lord that altogether dealeth with them, and that they blow according to his will. But let me see any of them all rebuke and still the sea in time of tempest, as Christ did, or raise the stormy wind as God did with his word, and I will believe in them. Hath any witch or conjurer or any creature entered into "the treasures of the snow, or seen the secret places of the hail" (Job 38:22), which God hath prepared against the day of trouble, battle, and war? I, for my part, also think with Jesus Sirach[5] that at God's only commandment the snow falleth, and that the wind bloweth according to his will who only maketh all storms to cease and who, if we keep his ordinances, will send us rain in due season, and make the land to bring forth her increase, and the trees of the field to give their fruit (Sirach 43).

But little think our witchmongers that the Lord commandeth the clouds above or openeth the doors of heaven, as David (Psalms 78: 23) affirmeth, or that the Lord goeth forth in the tempests and storms, as the Prophet Nahum (Nahum 3) reporteth, but rather that witches and conjurers are then about their business.

The Marcionists[6] acknowledged one God the author of good things, and another the ordainer of evil; but these make the devil a whole god, to create things of nothing, to know men's cogitations, and to do that which God never did, as to transubstantiate men into beasts, etc. Which thing if devils could do, yet followeth it not that witches have such power. But if all the devils in hell were dead and all the witches in England burnt or hanged, I warrant you we should not fail to have rain, hail, and tempests, as now we have, according to the appointment and will of God, and according to the constitu-

---

2. frightened.
3. proper rituals.
4. Johann Brenz (1499–1570), Lutheran minister and author.
5. author of *Sirach* (also know as *Ecclesiasticus*), a book of the Bible.
6. followers of the second-century heretic Marcion.

tion of the elements and the course of the planets, wherein God hath set a perfect and perpetual order.

I am also well assured that if all the old women in the world were witches and all the priests conjurers, we should not have a drop of rain, nor a blast of wind the more or the less for them. For the Lord hath bound the waters in the clouds and hath set bounds about the waters until the day and night come to an end. Yea, it is God that raiseth the winds and stilleth them, and he saith to the rain and snow "Be upon the earth," and it falleth. The wind of the Lord and not the wind of witches shall destroy the treasures of their pleasant vessels and dry up the fountains, saith Hosea (Hosea 13:15). Let us also learn and confess with the prophet David (Psalms 39) that we ourselves are the causes of our afflictions, and not exclaim upon witches when we should call upon God for mercy.

* * *

Finally, if witches could accomplish these things, what needed it seem so strange to the people when Christ by miracle commanded both seas and winds, etc. For it is written, "Who is this, for both wind and sea obey him?" (Mark 4:41).

Book I, Chapter 3: *Who they be that are called witches, with a manifest declaration of the cause that moveth men so commonly to think, and witches themselves to believe, that they can hurt children, cattle, etc., with words and imaginations; and of cozening*[7] *witches.*

One sort of such as are said to be witches are women which be commonly old, lame, blear-eyed, pale, foul, and full of wrinkles, poor, sullen, superstitious, and papists, or such as know no religion, in whose drowsy minds the devil hath gotten a fine seat; so as what mischief, mischance, calamity, or slaughter is brought to pass, they are easily persuaded the same is done by themselves, imprinting in their minds an earnest and constant imagination hereof. They are lean and deformed, showing melancholy in their faces to the horror of all that see them. They are doting, scolds, mad, devilish, and not much differing from them that are thought to be possessed with spirits, so firm and steadfast in their opinions, as whosoever shall only have respect to the constancy of their words uttered would easily believe they were true indeed.

These miserable wretches are so odious unto all their neighbors and so feared, as few dare offend them or deny them anything they ask; whereby they take upon them, yea, and sometimes think that they can do such things as are beyond the ability of human nature. These go from house to house and from door to door for a pot full

---

7. deceiving.

of milk, yeast, drink, pottage,[8] or some such relief, without the which they could hardly live, neither obtaining for their service and pains, nor by their art, nor yet at the devil's hands (with whom they are said to make a perfect and visible bargain) either beauty, money, promotion, wealth, worship, pleasure, honor, knowledge, learning, or any other benefit whatsoever.

It falleth out many times that neither their necessities nor their expectation is answered or served in those places where they beg or borrow, but rather their lewdness is by their neighbors reproved. And, further, in tract of time the witch waxeth odious and tedious to her neighbors and they again are despised and despited[9] of her, so as sometimes she curseth one, and sometimes another, and that from the master of the house, his wife, children, cattle, etc., to the little pig that lieth in the sty. Thus in process of time they have all displeased her, and she hath wished evil luck unto them all, perhaps with curses and imprecations made in form. Doubtless, at length, some of her neighbors die or fall sick, or some of their children are visited with diseases that vex them strangely, as apoplexies, epilepsies, convulsions, hot fevers, worms, etc., which by ignorant parents are supposed to be the vengeance of witches. Yea, and their opinions and conceits are confirmed and maintained by unskillful physicians according to the common saying, *Inscitiae pallium maleficium et incantatio,* "Witchcraft and enchantment is the cloak of ignorance"; whereas, indeed, evil humors[1] and not strange words, witches, or spirits are the causes of such diseases. Also some of their cattle perish either by disease or mischance. Then they, upon whom such adversities fall, weighing the fame that goeth upon this woman (her words, displeasure, and curses meeting so justly with their misfortune) do not only conceive but also are resolved that all their mishaps are brought to pass by her only means.

The witch, on the other side, expecting her neighbors' mischances and seeing things sometimes come to pass according to her wishes, curses, and incantations (for Bodin[2] himself confesseth that not above two in a hundred of their witchings or wishings take effect), being called before a Justice, by due examination of the circumstances is driven to see her imprecations and desires and her neighbors' harms and losses to concur and, as it were, to take effect, and so confesseth that she (as a goddess) hath brought such things to pass. Wherein not only she but the accuser and also the Justice are

---

8. stew or soup.
9. held in contempt.
1. Ancient and medieval medical theory held that bodies consisted of four fluids (blood, phlegm, choler or bile, and melancholy or black bile), called humors, and that an excess or deficiency of any one caused ill health.
2. Jean Bodin, an important Catholic political thinker, urged severe punishments for witches in *De la demonologie* (1580).

foully deceived and abused, as being through her confession and other circumstances persuaded (to the injury of God's glory) that she hath done or can do that which is proper only to God Himself.

Another sort of witches there are which be absolutely cozeners. These take upon them either for glory, fame, or gain, to do anything which God or the devil can do, either for foretelling of things to come, bewraying[3] of secrets, curing of maladies, or working of miracles. But of these I will talk more at large hereafter.

Book 1, Chapter 4: *What miraculous actions are imputed to witches by witchmongers, papists, and poets.*

Although it be quite against the hair,[4] and contrary to the devil's will, contrary to the witches' oath, promise, and homage, and contrary to all reason that witches should help anything that is bewitched, but rather set forward their master's businesses, yet we read in *Malleus Maleficarum* of three sorts of witches, and the same is affirmed by all the writers hereupon, new and old. One sort, they say, can hurt and not help; the second can help and not hurt; the third can both help and hurt. And among the hurtful witches he saith there is one sort more beastly than any kind of beasts saving wolves, for these usually devour and eat young children and infants of their own kind. These be they, saith he, that raise hail, tempests, and hurtful weather, as lightning, thunder, etc. These be they that procure barrenness in man, woman, and beast. These can throw children into waters as they walk with their mothers, and not be seen. These can make horses kick till they cast the riders. These can pass from place to place in the air invisible. These can so alter the mind of judges that they can have no power to hurt them. These can procure to themselves and to others taciturnity and insensibility in their torments. These can bring trembling to the hands and strike terror into the minds of them that apprehend them. These can manifest unto others things hidden and lost, and foreshow things to come, and see them as though they were present. These can alter men's minds to inordinate love or hate. These can kill whom they list with lightning and thunder. These can take away man's courage and the power of generation. These can make a woman miscarry in childbirth and destroy the child in the mother's womb, without any sensible means either inwardly or outwardly applied. These can with their looks kill either man or beast.

*   *   *

And first Ovid (*Met.* 7) affirmeth that they can raise and suppress lightning and thunder, rain and hail, clouds and winds, tempests and

---

3. revealing.
4. contrary to the natural inclination, against the grain.

earthquakes. Others do write that they can pull down the moon and the stars. Some write that with wishing they can send needles into the livers of their enemies; some, that they can transfer corn in the blade from one place to another; some, that they can cure diseases supernaturally, fly in the air, and dance with devils. Some write that they can play the part of succubus, and contract themselves to incubus,[5] and so young prophets are upon them begotten, etc. Some say they can transubstantiate themselves and others, and take the forms and shapes of asses, wolves, ferrets, cows, apes, horses, dogs, etc. Some say they can keep devils and spirits in the likeness of toads and cats.

They can raise spirits, as others affirm, dry up springs, turn the course of running waters, inhibit the sun, and stay both day and night, changing the one into the other. They can go in and out at auger-holes,[6] and sail in an eggshell, a cockle,[7] or mussel shell, through and under the tempestuous seas. They can go invisible, and deprive men of their privities,[8] and otherwise of the act and use of venery.[9] They can bring souls out of the graves. They can tear snakes in pieces with words, and with looks kill lambs. But in this case a man may say, that *miranda canunt sed non credenda poetae*, ["poets sing of marvelous, but not credible, things"].[1] They can also bring to pass that churn as long as you list, your butter will not come; especially, if either the maids have eaten up the cream or the goodwife have sold the butter before in the market. Whereof I have had some trial, although there may be true and natural causes to hinder the common course thereof; as for example, put a little soap or sugar into your churn of cream, and there will never come any butter, churn as long as you list. But *Malleus Maleficarum* saith, that there is not so little a village where many women are not that bewitch, infect, and kill kine,[2] and dry up the milk, alleging for the strengthening of that assertion the saying of the apostle, *numquid deo cura est de bobus?* "Doth God take any care of oxen?" (1 Cor. 9:9).

Book I, Chapter 5: *A confutation of the common conceived opinion of witches and witchcraft, and how detestable a sin it is to repair to them for counsel or help in time of affliction.*

But whatsoever is reported or conceived of such manner of witchcrafts I dare avow to be false and fabulous, cozenage, dotage,[3] and

---

5. A succubus is a demon believed to have carnal intercourse with men during sleep; an incubus, with women.
6. holes made by an auger, or carpenter's manual drill.
7. sea shell.
8. genitals.
9. sexual intercourse.
1. a proverb attributed to Dionysius Cato, Latin moralist.
2. cows.
3. senility.

poisoning excepted; neither is there any mention made of these kinds of witches in the Bible. If Christ had known them, he would not have pretermitted[4] to inveigh against their presumption in taking upon them his office, as to heal and cure diseases, and to work such miraculous and supernatural things as whereby he himself was specially known, believed, and published to be God, his actions and cures consisting (in order and effect) according to the power by our witchmongers imputed to witches. Howbeit, if there be any in these days afflicted in such strange sort as Christ's cures and patients are described in the New Testament to have been, we fly from trusting in God to trusting in witches, who do not only in their cozening art take on them the office of Christ in this behalf, but use his very phrase of speech to such idolaters as come to seek divine assistance at their hands, saying, "Go thy ways, thy son or thy daughter, etc., shall do well, and be whole" (Mark 5:34).

It will not suffice to dissuade a witchmonger from his credulity that he seeth the sequel and event to fall out many times contrary to their assertion; but in such case to his greater condemnation he seeketh further to witches of greater fame. If all fail, he will rather think he came an hour too late than that he went a mile too far. Truly, I for my part cannot perceive what is to go a-whoring after strange gods, if this be not. He that looketh upon his neighbor's wife and lusteth after her hath committed adultery. And, truly, he that in heart and by argument maintaineth the sacrifice of the mass to be propitiatory for the quick and the dead is an idolater; as also he that alloweth and commendeth creeping to the cross[5] and such like idolatrous actions, although he bend not his corporal knees.

In like manner, I say, he that attributeth to a witch such divine power as duly and only appertaineth unto God (which all witchmongers do) is in heart a blasphemer, an idolater, and full of gross impiety, although he neither go nor send to her for assistance.

Book 8, Chapter 2: *That the gift of prophecy is ceased.*

That witches, nor the woman of Endor,[6] nor yet her familiar or devil, can tell what is to come, may plainly appear by the words of the prophet who saith, "Show what things are to come, and we will say you are gods, indeed" (Isaiah 41:23). According to that which Solomon saith, "Who can tell a man what shall happen him under the sun?" "Marry, that can I," saith the witch of Endor to Saul (1 Samuel 28). But I will rather believe Paul and Peter, which say that

4. omitted.
5. Catholic practice of advancing to the cross on knees and with bare feet on Good Friday; the act was a frequent target of Protestant ridicule.
6. In 1 Samuel 28, Saul in disguise has the witch of Endor raise the spirit of the prophet Samuel, who angrily predicts his defeat.

prophecy is the gift of God, and no worldly thing (1 Cor. 12:10; 2 Peter 1:21).

*   *   *

Indeed, we read that Samuel could tell where things lost were strayed, etc.; but we see that gift also ceased by the coming of Christ, according to the saying of Paul: "At sundry times and in divers manners God spoke in the old times by our fathers the prophets; in these last days he hath spoken unto us by his son," etc. (Hebrews 1:1–2). And, therefore, I say that gift of prophecy, wherewith God in times past endued[7] his people, is also ceased, and counterfeits and cozeners are come in their place according to this saying of Peter: "There were false prophets among the people even as there shall be false teachers among you," etc. (2 Peter 2:1). And think not that so notable a gift should be taken from the beloved and elect people of God, and committed to Mother Bungie,[8] and such like of her profession.

KING JAMES I OF ENGLAND
(JAMES VI OF SCOTLAND)

News from Scotland [1591]†

God by his omnipotent power hath at all times and daily doth take such care, and is so vigilant for the weal[1] and preservation of his own, that thereby He disappointeth the wicked practices and evil intents of all such as by any means whatsoever seek indirectly to conspire any thing contrary to his holy will. Yea, and by the same power He hath lately overthrown and hindered the intentions and wicked dealings of a great number of ungodly creatures, no better than devils, who, suffering themselves to be allured and enticed by the Devil whom they served and to whom they were privately sworn, entered into the detestable art of witchcraft. Which they studied and practiced so long time that in the end they had seduced by their sorcery a number of others to be as bad as themselves, dwelling in the bounds of Lothian, which is a principal shire or part of Scotland,

---

7. endowed.
8. a legendary witch.
† From *Newes from Scotland*, (London, 1592; 2nd ed.), sigs. Aiv–Ci(v), Diii. Footnotes are by the editor of this Norton Critical Edition. Spelling and punctuation have been modernized by the editor. In *News from Scotland* (1591), James VI of Scotland (1566–1625), later James I of England from 1603 to 1625, relates his own experiences with witchcraft, both as a potential victim and as a judicial examiner. The excerpts illustrate the lurid mix of black magic, superstition, eroticism, and sensational crime that characterizes the witch literature of the day.
1. welfare.

where the King's Majesty useth to make his chiefest residence or abode. And to the end that their detestable wickedness, which they privily[2] had pretended against the King's Majesty, the commonweal of that country, with the nobility and subjects of the same, should come to light, God of his unspeakable goodness did reveal and lay it open in very strange sort,[3] thereby to make known unto the world that their actions were contrary to the law of God and the natural affection which we ought generally to bear one to another; the manner of the revealing whereof was as followeth:

Within the town of Tranent in the kingdom of Scotland there dwelleth one David Seaton, who, being deputy bailiff[4] in the said town, had a maidservant called Gillis Duncan, who used secretly to be absent and to lie forth of her master's house every other night. This Gillis Duncan took in hand to help all such as were troubled or grieved with any kind of sickness or infirmity, and in short space did perform many matters most miraculous; which things, forasmuch as she began to do them upon a sudden, having never done the like before, made her master and others to be in great admiration,[5] and wondered thereat. By means whereof the said David Seaton had his maid in some great suspicion that she did not those things by natural and lawful ways, but rather supposed it to be done by some extraordinary and unlawful means.

Whereupon her Master began to grow very inquisitive and examined her which way and by what means she were able to perform matters of so great importance; whereat she gave him no answer. Nevertheless, her master, to the intent that he might the better try and find out the truth of the same, did with the help of others torment her with the torture of the pilliwinks[6] upon her fingers, which is a grievous torture, and binding or wrenching her head with a cord or rope, which is a most cruel torment also. Yet would she not confess anything. Whereupon they, suspecting that she had been marked by the Devil (as commonly witches are), made diligent search about her, and found the enemy's mark to be in her forecrag, or forepart of her throat; which being found, she confessed that all her doings was done by the wicked allurements and enticements of the Devil and that she did them by witchcraft.

After this her confession, she was committed to prison, where she continued for a season, where immediately she accused these persons following to be notorious witches, and caused them forthwith to be apprehended one after another, viz., Agnes Sampson, the eldest witch of them all, dwelling in Haddington; Agnes Tompson of Edin-

2. privately.
3. manner.
4. an officer under a sheriff, who executes writs and processes.
5. astonishment.
6. a device for crushing fingers.

burgh; Doctor Fian, alias John Cunningham, master of the school at Saltpans in Lothian, of whose life and strange acts you shall hear more largely in the end of this discourse. These were by the said Gillis Duncan accused, as also George Mott's wife dwelling in Saltpans, Robert Grierson, skipper, and Janet Bandilandis, with the porter's wife of Seaton, the smith at the Bridge Halls, with innumerable others in that parts, and dwelling in those bounds aforesaid. Of whom some are already executed; the rest remain in prison to receive the doom of judgment at the King's Majesty's will and pleasure.

The said Gillis Duncan also caused Euphemia MacCalrean to be apprehended, who conspired and performed the death of her godfather, and who used her art upon a gentleman, being one of the lords and justices of the Session,[7] for bearing good will to her daughter. She also caused to be apprehended one Barbara Napier, for bewitching to death Archibald, last Earl of Angus, who languished to death by witchcraft and yet the same was not suspected, but that he died of so strange a disease as the physician knew not how to cure or remedy the same. But of all, other the said witches these two last before recited[8] were reputed for as civil honest women as any that dwelled within the city of Edinburgh, before they were apprehended. Many other besides were taken dwelling in Leith, who are detained in prison until His Majesty's further will and pleasure be known, of whose wicked doings you shall particularly hear, which was as followeth:

This aforesaid Agnes Sampson, which was the elder witch, was taken and brought to Holyrood House[9] before the King's Majesty and sundry other of the nobility of Scotland, where she was straitly[1] examined. But all the persuasions which the King's Majesty used to her with the rest of his Council might not provoke or induce her to confess anything, but stood stiffly in the denial of all that was laid to her charge. Whereupon they caused her to be conveyed away to prison, there to receive such torture as hath been lately provided for witches in that country. And forasmuch as by due examination of witchcraft and witches in Scotland, it hath lately been found that the Devil doth generally mark them with a privy mark, by reason the witches have confessed themselves that the Devil doth lick them with his tongue in some privy part of their body before he doth receive them to be his servants; which mark commonly is given them under the hair in some part of their body, whereby it may not easily be found out or seen, although they be searched. And generally so long as the mark is not seen to those which search them, so long the

---

7. the Scottish law court. An illustration (sig. Bi[v]) shows two magistrates watching a man raise a stick over four kneeling women.
8. the other witches noted before these last two (MacCalrean and Napier).
9. the royal palace in Edinburgh.
1. strictly.

parties that hath the mark will never confess anything. Therefore, by special commandment this Agnes Sampson had all her hair shaven off, in each part of her body, and her head thrawen[2] with a rope according to the custom of that country, being a pain most grievous, which she continued almost an hour, during which time she would not confess anything until the Devil's mark was found upon her privities.[3] Then she immediately confessed whatsoever was demanded of her, and justifying those persons aforesaid to be notorious witches.

Item,[4] the said Agnes Tompson was after brought again before the King's Majesty and his council, and being examined of the meetings and detestable dealings of those witches, she confessed that upon the night of All Hallow's Even[5] last, she was accompanied as well with the persons aforesaid, as also with a great many other witches to the number of two hundred, and that all they together went by sea, each one in a riddle or sieve,[6] and went in the same very substantially with flagons[7] of wine, making merry and drinking by the way in the same riddles or sieves to the kirk[8] of North Berwick in Lothian, and that after they had landed, took hands on the land and danced this reel[9] or short dance, singing all with one voice:

Comer,[1] go ye before, comer, go ye,
If ye will not go before, comer, let me.

At which time she confessed that this Gillis Duncan did go before them playing this reel or dance upon a small trump, called a Jew's trump,[2] until they entered into the Kirk of North Berwick.

These confessions made the King in a wonderful admiration, and sent for the said Gillis Duncan, who upon the like trump did play the said dance before the King's Majesty, who in respect of the strangeness of these matters took great delight to be present at their examinations.

Item, the said Agnes Tompson confessed that the Devil, being then at North Berwick Kirk attending their coming in the habit or likeness of a man, and seeing that they tarried over long, he at their coming enjoined them all to a penance, which was that they should kiss his buttocks in sign of duty to him; which, being put over the pulpit bare, everyone did as he had enjoined them. And having made

2. twisted.
3. genitals.
4. likewise.
5. Halloween (October 31).
6. A riddle is a coarse-meshed sieve. Sailing in a sieve was a traditional means of travel for witches.
7. in substance (i.e., corporeally) with large bottles.
8. church.
9. lively Scottish dance, usually performed by facing couples.
1. one who comes or arrives.
2. a Jew's harp, an instrument held between the teeth, consisting of a frame and a projecting tongue that is struck with the finger.

his ungodly exhortations, wherein he did greatly inveigh against the King of Scotland, he received their oaths for their good and true service towards him and departed; which done, they returned to sea and so home again.

At which time the witches demanded of the Devil why he did bear such hatred to the King, who answered, by reason the King is the greatest enemy he hath in the world; all which their confessions and depositions are still extant upon record.

Item, the said Agnes Sampson confessed before the King's Majesty sundry things which were so miraculous and strange, as that His Majesty said they were all extreme liars; whereat she answered, she would not wish His Majesty to suppose her words to be false, but rather to believe them, in that she would discover such matter unto him as His Majesty should not any way doubt of.

And thereupon taking His Majesty a little aside, she declared unto him the very words which passed between the King's Majesty and his Queen at Oslo in Norway the first night of their marriage, with their answer each to other; whereat the King's Majesty wondered greatly, and swore by the living God that he believed that all the devils in hell could not have discovered the same, acknowledging her words to be most true and, therefore, gave the more credit to the rest which is before declared.

Touching this Agnes Tompson, she is the only woman who by the Devil's persuasion should have intended and put in execution the King's Majesty's death in this manner:

She confessed that she took a black toad, and did hang the same up by the heels three days, and collected and gathered the venom as it dropped and fell from it in an oyster shell, and kept the same venom close covered, until she should obtain any part or piece of foul linen cloth that had appertained to the King's Majesty, as shirt, handkercher, napkin or any other thing; which she practiced[3] to obtain by means of one John Kers, who being attendant in His Majesty's chamber, desired him for old acquaintance between them to help her to one or a piece of such a cloth as is aforesaid; which thing the said John Kers denied to help her to, saying he could not help her to it.

And the said Agnes Tompson by her depositions since her apprehension saith that if she had obtained any one piece of linen cloth which the King had worn and fouled, she had bewitched him to death, and put him to such extraordinary pains, as if he had been lying upon sharp thorns and ends of needles.

Moreover she confessed that at the time when His Majesty was in Denmark, she being accompanied with the parties before specially

3. contrived.

named, took a cat and christened it, and afterward bound to each
part of that cat the chiefest parts of a dead man and several joints
of his body, and that in the night following the said cat was conveyed
into the midst of the sea by all these witches sailing in their riddles
or sieves, as is aforesaid, and so left the said cat right before the town
of Leith in Scotland. This done, there did arise such a tempest in
the sea, as a greater hath not been seen. Which tempest was the
cause of the perishing of a boat or vessel coming over from the town
of Brunt Island to the town of Leith, wherein was sundry jewels and
rich gifts, which should have been presented to the now Queen of
Scotland at Her Majesty's coming to Leith.

Again it is confessed that the said christened cat was the cause
that the King's Majesty's ship at his coming forth of Denmark had a
contrary wind to the rest of his ships then being in his company;
which thing was most strange and true, as the King's Majesty ack-
nowledgeth, for when the rest of the ships had a fair and good wind,
then was the wind contrary and altogether against His Majesty. And
further the said witch declared that His Majesty had never come
safely from the sea if his faith had not prevailed above their intentions.

Moreover, the said witches being demanded how the Devil would
use them when he was in their company, they confessed that when
the Devil did receive them for his servants, and that they had vowed
themselves unto him, then he would carnally use them, albeit to their
little pleasure in respect of his cold nature, and would do the like at
sundry other times.

*   *   *

This strange discourse before recited may perhaps give some occasion of doubt to such as shall happen to read the same, and thereby
conjecture that the King's Majesty would not hazard himself in the
presence of such notorious witches, lest thereby might have ensued
great danger to his person and the general state of the land, which
thing in truth might well have been feared. But to answer generally
to such, let this suffice: that first it is well known that the King is
the child and servant of God, and they but servants to the Devil; he
is the Lord's anointed, and they but vessels of God's wrath; he is a
true Christian and trusteth in God, they worse than infidels, for they
only trust in the Devil, who daily serve[s] them till he have brought
them to utter destruction. But hereby it seemeth that His Highness
carried a magnanimous and undaunted mind, not feared with their
enchantments, but resolute in this: that so long as God is with him,
he feareth not who is against him. And truly the whole scope of this
treatise doth so plainly lay open the wonderful providence of the
Almighty, that if he had not been defended by his omnipotence and

power, His Highness had never returned alive in his voyage from
Denmark; so that there is no doubt but God would as well defend
him on the land as on the sea, where they pretended[4] their damnable
practice.

Daemonology [1597]†

Philomathes: These witches, on the other part, being enticed
either for the desire of revenge or of worldly riches, their whole
practices are either to hurt men and their goods or what they
possess, for satisfying of their cruel minds in the former, or else
by the wrack in whatsoever sort of any whom God will permit
them to have power of, to satisfy their greedy desire in the last
point.

Epistemon: In two parts their actions may be divided: the
actions of their own persons, and the actions proceeding from
them towards any other. And this division being well understood
will easily resolve you what is possible to them to do. For
although all that they confess is no lie upon their part, yet,
doubtlessly, in my opinion a part of it is not, indeed, according
as they take it to be; and in this I mean by the actions of their
own persons. For as I said before, speaking of magi,[1] that the
Devil illudes[2] the senses of these scholars of his in many things,
so say I the like of these witches.

Philomathes: Then I pray you first to speak of that part of
their own persons, and syne[3] ye may come next to their actions
towards others.

Epistemon: To the effect that they may perform such services
of their false master, as he employs them in, the Devil as God's
ape[4] counterfeits in his servants this service and form of adoration that God prescribed and made his servants to practice.
For as the servants of God publicly use to convene for serving
of him, so makes he them in great numbers to convene (though
publicly they dare not) for his service. As none convenes to the
adoration and worshipping of God except they be marked with
his seal, the sacrament of baptism, so none serves Satan and
convenes to the adoring of him that are not marked with that
mark whereof I already spake. As the minister sent by God

---

4. presented.
† From *Daemonologie* (Edinburgh, 1597), sigs. F2–3, G2–3, G4–H1. James I wrote *Daemonologie* against Reginald Scot and Johann Weyer to prove that witchcraft existed and
 that it originated in Satan.
1. practitioners of forbidden, occult arts.
2. deceives.
3. next (Scottish).
4. God's clumsy imitator.

teacheth plainly at the time of their public conventions how to serve him in spirit and truth, so that unclean spirit in his own person teacheth his disciples at the time of their convening how to work all kind of mischief and craves 'count[5] of all their horrible and detestable proceedings passed for advancement of his service. Yea, that he may the more vilely counterfeit and scorn God he oft times makes his slaves to convene in these very places which are destinate[6] and ordained for the convening of the servants of God (I mean by churches). But this far, which I have yet said, I not only take it to be true in their opinions, but even so to be indeed. For the form that he used in counterfeiting God amongst the Gentiles makes me so to think: as God spake by his oracles, spake he not so by his? As God had as well bloody sacrifices as others without blood, had not he the like? As God had churches sanctified to his service with altars, priests, sacrifices, ceremonies, and prayers, had he not the like polluted to his service? As God gave responses by Urim and Thummim,[7] gave he not his responses by the entrails of beasts, by the singing of fowls, and by their actions in the air? As God by visions, dreams, and ecstasies revealed what was to come and what was his will unto his servants, used he not the like means to forewarn his slaves of things to come? Yea, even as God loved cleanness, hated vice and impurity, and appointed punishments therefore, used he not the like (though falsely, I grant, and but in eschewing the less inconvenient to draw them upon a greater) yet dissimuled[8] he not, I say, so far as to appoint his priests to keep their bodies clean and undefiled before their asking responses of him? And feigned he not God to be a protector of every virtue and a just revenger of the contrary?

* * *

Epistemon: In their [witches'] actions used towards others three things ought to be considered: first, the manner of their consulting thereupon; next, their part as instruments; and last, their master's part, who puts the same in execution. As to their consultations thereupon, they use them oftest[9] in the churches where they convene for adoring; at what time their master, inquiring at them what they would be at, every one of them propones[1] unto him what wicked turn they would have done either for obtaining of riches, or for revenging them upon any whom they have malice at. Who, granting their demand, as no

---

5. account.
6. destined.
7. the sacred rite by which Hebrews discovered God's will.
8. dissembled.
9. most often.
1. proposes.

doubt willingly he will since it is to do evil he teacheth them the means whereby they may do the same. As for little trifling turns that women have ado with, he causeth them to joint[2] dead corpses and to make powders thereof, mixing such other things there amongst as he gives unto them.

Philomathes: But before ye go further, permit me, I pray you, to interrupt you one word, which ye have put me in memory of by speaking of women. What can be the cause that there are twenty women given to that craft, where there is one man?

Epistemon: The reason is easy for as that sex is frailer than man is so is it easier to be entrapped in these gross snares of the Devil, as was over well proved to be true by the serpent's deceiving of Eva at the beginning, which makes him the homelier with that sex sensine.[3]

Philomathes: Return now where ye left.

Epistemon: To some others at these times he teacheth how to make pictures of wax or clay, that by the roasting thereof the persons that they bear the name of may be continually melted or dried away by continual sickness. To some he give such stones or powders as will help to cure or cast on[4] diseases. And to some he teacheth kinds of uncouth poisons which mediciners[5] understands not (for he is far cunninger than man in the knowledge of all the occult properties of nature) not that any of these means which he teacheth them (except the poisons which are composed of things natural) can of themselves help anything to these turns that they are employed in, but only being God's ape as well in that as in all other things. Even as God by his sacraments, which are earthly of themselves, works a heavenly effect, though no ways by any cooperation in them. And as Christ by clay and spittle wrought together opened the eyes of the blind man (John, 9), suppose there was no virtue in that which he outwardly applied; so the Devil will have his outward means to be shows, as it were, of his doing, which hath no part of cooperation in his turns with him, how far that ever the ignorants[6] be abused in the contrary. And as to the effects of these two former parts, to wit, the consultations and the outward means, they are so wonderful as I dare not allege any of them without joining a sufficient reason of the possibility thereof. For leaving all the small trifles among wives and to speak of the principal points of their craft, for the common trifles thereof they can do without converting well enough by themselves; these principal points, I say, are these: they can make men or

2. dismember.
3. the more familiar with that sex since then.
4. inflict.
5. apothecaries (i.e., pharmacists) or physicians.
6. ignorant persons.

women to love or hate other, which may be very possible to the Devil to effectuate, seeing he being a subtle spirit, knows well enough how to persuade the corrupted affection of them whom God will permit him so to deal with. They can lay the sickness of one upon another, which likewise is very possible unto him. For since by God's permission he laid sickness upon Job, why may he not far easier lay it upon any other. For as an old practition[7] he knows well enough what humor domines[8] most in any of us, and as a spirit he can subtly waken up the same, making it peccant or to abound,[9] as he thinks meet for troubling of us, when God will so permit him.

*   *   *

Philomathes: But will God permit these wicked instruments by the power of the Devil their master to trouble by any of these means any that believes in him?

Epistemon: No doubt, for there are three kinds of folks whom God will permit so to be tempted or troubled: the wicked for their horrible sins, to punish them in the like measure; the godly that are sleeping in any great sins or infirmities and weakness in faith, to waken them up the faster by such an uncouth form; and even some of the best, that their patience may be tried before the world as Job's was. For why may not God use any kind of extraordinary punishment when it pleases him, as well as the ordinary rods of sickness or other adversities?

Philomathes: Who then may be free from these devilish practices?

Epistemon: No man ought to presume so far as to promise any impunity to himself, for God hath before all beginnings preordinated as well the particular sorts of plagues as of benefits for every man, which in the own time he ordains them to be visited with. And yet ought we not to be the more afraid for that of anything that the Devil and his wicked instruments can do against us. For we daily fight against the Devil in a hundred other ways. And, therefore, as a valiant captain, affrays[1] no more being at the combat, nor stays from his purpose for the rummishing shot of a cannon nor the small clack of a pistolet,[2] suppose he be not certain what may light upon him. Even so ought we boldly to go forward in fighting against the Devil without any greater terror for these his rarest weapons nor for the ordinary whereof we have daily the proof.

7. deceiver.
8. which essential body fluid (**humor**) dominates.
9. corrupt (**peccant**) or excessive (thus causing disease).
1. fears.
2. the roaring shot of a cannon or the noise of a small pistol.

Philomathes: Is it not lawful then by the help of some other witch to cure the disease that is casten[3] on by that craft?

Epistemon: No ways lawful, for I gave you the reason thereof in that axiom of theology[4] which was the last words I spoke of magi.

Philomathes: How then may these diseases be lawfully cured?

Epistemon: Only by earnest prayer to God, by amendment of their lives, and by sharp pursuing every one, according to his calling, of these instruments of Satan, whose punishment to the death will be a salutary sacrifice for the patient. And this is not only the lawful way but likewise the most sure. For by the Devil's means can never the Devil be casten out (Mark 3), as Christ saith. And when such a cure is used, it may well serve for a short time, but at the last it will doubtlessly tend to the utter perdition of the patient both in body and soul.

DEBATE ON TYRANNICIDE

CHURCH OF ENGLAND

An Homily against Disobedience and Willful Rebellion†

As God, the creator and Lord of all things, appointed his angels and heavenly creatures in all obedience to serve and to honor his majesty, so was it his will that man, his chief creature upon the earth, should live under the obedience of his creator and Lord. And for that cause, God, as soon as he had created man, gave unto him a certain precept and law, which he, being yet in the state of innocency and remaining in paradise, should observe as a pledge and token of his due and bounden[1] obedience, with denunciation of death if he did transgress and break the said law and commandment. And as God would have man to be his obedient subject, so did he make all earthly

3. cast.
4. *Numquam faciendum est malum ut bonum inde eveniat* (sig. Ei[v]), "Evil must never be done so that good may result."
† From *An Homilie agaynst disobedience and wylful rebellion* (London, 1570), sigs. Ai–Ai(v), Bii–Biv, Cii(v)–Di, Fi–Fi(v). Footnotes are by the editor of this Norton Critical Edition. Spelling and punctuation have been modernized by the editor. This homily, commissioned by Elizabeth in response to the Northern Rebellion of Catholics (1568), condemns all rebellion and urges instead humble obedience and patient endurance. Those who raise a hand against the Lord's anointed, the preacher argues, re-enact the Fall as well as Lucifer's rebellion and deserve eternal damnation. The arguments from Roman history and from the biblical story of King Saul and David directly oppose Juan de Mariana's reading of the classical and scriptural precedents. Together, this homily and Mariana's treatise (see the excerpt on pp. 154–59 in this edition) provide a polemical context for the killings of both Duncan and Macbeth.
1. obligated.

creatures subject unto man, who kept their due obedience unto man so long as man remained in his obedience unto God. In the which obedience if man had continued still, there had been no poverty, no diseases, no sickness, no death, nor other miseries wherewith mankind is now infinitely and most miserably afflicted and oppressed. So here appeareth the original kingdom of God over angels and man and universally over all things, and of man over earthly creatures which God had made subject unto him, and withal[2] the felicity and blessed state which angels, man, and all creatures had remained in, had they continued in due obedience unto God their king. For as long as in this first kingdom the subjects continued in due obedience to God their king, so long did God embrace all his subjects with his love, favor, and grace, which to enjoy is perfect felicity. Whereby it is evident that obedience is the principal virtue of all virtues and indeed the very root of all virtues and the cause of all felicity. But as all felicity and blessedness should have continued with the continuance of obedience, so with the breach of obedience and breaking in of rebellion, all vices and miseries did withal break in and overwhelm the world. The first author of which rebellion, the root of all vices and mother of all mischiefs was Lucifer, first God's most excellent creature and most bounden subject, who, by rebelling against the majesty of God, of the brightest and most glorious angel is become the blackest and most foulest fiend and devil, and from the height of heaven is fallen into the pit and bottom of hell.

* * *

But what if the prince be undiscreet[3] and evil in deed, and it also evident to all men's eyes that he so is? I ask again, what if it belong of the wickedness of the subjects that the prince is undiscreet or evil? Shall the subjects both by their wickedness provoke God for their deserved punishment to give them an undiscreet or evil prince, and also rebel against him and withal against God, who for the punishment of their sins did give them such a prince? Will you hear the Scriptures concerning this point? God (say the Holy Scriptures) maketh a wicked man to reign for the sins of the people. Again, God giveth a prince in his anger (meaning an evil one) and taketh away a prince in his displeasure (meaning specially when he taketh away a good prince for the sins of the people); as in our memory he took away our good Josias, King Edward, in his young and good years for our wickedness.[4] And, contrarily, the Scriptures do teach that God giveth wisdom unto princes, and maketh a wise and good king to

2. in addition.
3. without sound judgment.
4. Protestants often compared King Edward VI (1537–1553) to the youthful reformer Josias (2 Kings 22–3; 2 Chron. 34–5).

reign over that people whom he loveth and who loveth him. Again, "If the people obey God, both they and their king shall prosper and be safe, else both shall perish," saith God by the mouth of Samuel (1 Sam. 12:14–15, 25).

Here you see that God placeth as well evil princes as good, and for what cause he doth both. If we, therefore, will have a good prince either to be given us or to continue now we have such a one, let us by our obedience to God and to our prince move God thereunto. If we will have an evil prince (when God shall send such a one) taken away, and a good in his place, let us take away our wickedness, which provoketh God to place such a one over us, and God will either displace him or of an evil prince make him a good prince, so that we first will change our evil into good. For will you hear the Scriptures? "The heart of the prince is in God's hand; which way soever it shall please him, he turneth it" (Prov. 21:1). Thus say the Scriptures. Wherefore let us turn from our sins unto the Lord with all our hearts, and he will turn the heart of the prince unto our quiet and wealth. Else for subjects to deserve through their sins to have an evil prince, and then to rebel against him, were double and treble evil by provoking God more to plague them. Nay, let us either deserve to have a good prince, or let us patiently suffer and obey such as we deserve.

And whether the prince be good or evil, let us, according to the counsel of the Holy Scriptures pray for the prince—for his continuance and increase in goodness if he be good, and for his amendment if he be evil. Will you hear the Scriptures concerning this most necessary point? "I exhort, therefore," saith Saint Paul, "that above all things prayers, supplications, intercessions, and giving of thanks be had for all men, for kings, and all that are in authority, that we may live a quiet and peaceable life with all godliness, for that is good and acceptable in the sight of God our Saviour, etc." (1 Tim. 2:1–3). This is Saint Paul's counsel. And who, I pray you, was prince over the most part of Christians when God's holy spirit by Saint Paul's pen gave them this lesson? Forsooth, Caligula, Claudius, or Nero, who were not only no Christians, but pagans, and also either foolish rulers or most cruel tyrants. Will you yet hear the word of God to the Jews when they were prisoners under Nebuchadnezzar, King of Babylon, after he had slain their king, nobles, parents, children and kinfolks, burned their country, cities, yea, Jerusalem itself, and the holy temple, and had carried the residue remaining alive captives with him unto Babylon? Will you hear yet what the prophet Baruch saith unto God's people being in this captivity? "Pray you," saith the prophet, "for the life of Nebuchadnezzar, King of Babylon, and for the life of Balthasar, his son, that their days may be as the days of heaven upon the earth, that God also may give us strength and lighten our eyes that we may live under the defense of Nebuchadnezzar, King of

Babylon, and under the protection of Balthasar, his son, that we may long do them service and find favor in their sight. Pray for us also unto the Lord our God, for we have sinned against the Lord our God" (1 Bar. 1:11–13). Thus far the prophet Baruch his words, which are spoken by him unto the people of God of that king who was a heathen, a tyrant, and cruel oppressor of them, and had been a murderer of many thousands of their nation and a destroyer of their country, with a confession that their sins had deserved such a prince to reign over them.

And shall the old Christians, by Saint Paul's exhortation, pray for Caligula, Claudius or Nero, shall the Jews pray for Nebuchadnezzar—these emperors and kings being strangers unto them, being pagans and infidels, being murderers, tyrants, and cruel oppressors of them, and the destroyers of their country, countrymen, and kinsmen, the burners of their villages, towns, cities and temples? And shall not we pray for the long, prosperous, and godly reign of our natural prince, no stranger (which is observed as a great blessing in the Scriptures), of our Christian, our most gracious Sovereign, no heathen, nor pagan prince?

* * *

As in the first part of this treaty[5] of obedience of subjects to their princes and against disobedience and rebellion I have alleged divers sentences out of the Holy Scriptures for proof, so shall it be good for the better both declaration and confirmation of the said wholesome doctrine to allege one example or two out of the same Holy Scriptures of the obedience of subjects, not only unto their good and gracious governors, but also unto their evil and unkind princes.

As King Saul was not of the best, but rather of the worst sort of princes, as being out of God's favor for his disobedience against God in sparing (in a wrong pity) the King Agag, whom almighty God commanded to be slain, according to the justice of God against his sworn enemy.[6] And although Saul of a devotion meant to sacrifice such things as he spared of the Amalekites to the honor and service of God, yet Saul was reproved for his wrong mercy and devotion, and was told that obedience would have more pleased Him than such lenity, which sinful humanity (saith holy Chrysostom) is more cruel before God than any murder or shedding of blood when it is commanded of God. But yet, how evil soever Saul the King was and out of God's favor, yet was he obeyed of his subject David, the very best of all subjects and most valiant in the service of his prince and country in the wars, the most obedient and loving in peace, and always

5. treatise.
6. The story of King Saul, the Amalekites, and King Agag appears in 1 Samuel 15; the story of Saul and David follows, chapters 16–31, and 2 Samuel 1.

most true and faithful to his sovereign and lord, and furthest off from all manner rebellion. For the which his most painful, true, and faithful service, King Saul yet rewarded him not only with great unkindness, but also sought his destruction and death by all means possible, so that David was fain[7] to save his life, not by rebellion, nor any resistance, but by flight and hiding himself from the King's sight. Which, notwithstanding, when King Saul upon a time came alone into the cave where David was, so that David might easily have slain him, yet would he neither hurt him himself, neither suffer any of his men to lay hands upon him. Another time also David, entering by night with one Abisai, a valiant and a fierce man, into the tent where King Saul did lie asleep, where also he might yet more easily have slain him, yet would he neither hurt him himself nor suffer Abisai, who was willing and ready to slay King Saul, once to touch him. Thus did David deal with Saul, his prince, notwithstanding that King Saul continually sought his death and destruction. It shall not be amiss unto these deeds of David to add his words, and to show you what he spake unto such as encouraged him to take his opportunity and advantage to slay King Saul as his mortal enemy when he might: "The Lord keep me," saith David, "from doing that thing and from laying hands upon my lord, God's anointed. For who can lay his hand upon the Lord's anointed and be guiltless? As truly as the Lord liveth, except that the Lord do smite him, or his days shall come to die, or that he go down to war and be slain in battle, the Lord be merciful unto me that I lay not my hand upon the Lord's anointed" (1 Sam. 24:6, 26:9–11).

These be David's words spoken at sundry times to divers his servants, provoking him to slay King Saul when opportunity served him thereunto. Neither is it to be omitted and left out how, when an Amalekite had slain King Saul even at Saul's own bidding and commandment (for he would live no longer now for that he had lost the field against his enemies, the Philistines), the said Amalekite, making great haste to bring first word and news thereof unto David as joyous unto him for the death of his mortal enemy, bringing withal the crown that was upon King Saul's head and the bracelet that was upon his arm, both as a proof of the truth of his news and also as fit and pleasant presents unto David, being by God appointed to be King Saul his successor in the kingdom. Yet was that faithful and godly David so far from rejoicing at these news that he rent his clothes, wept, and mourned, and fasted; and so far off from thanksgiving to the messenger, either for his deed in killing the King, though his deadly enemy, or for his message and news, or for his presents that he brought, that he said unto him, "How happened it that thou was

7. obliged.

not afraid to lay thy hands upon the Lord's anointed to slay him?" Whereupon immediately he commanded one of his servants to kill the messenger, and said, "Thy blood be upon thine own head, for thine own mouth hath witnessed against thyself in confessing that thou hast slain the Lord's anointed" (2 Sam 1:13–16).

This example, dearly beloved, is notable, and the circumstances thereof are well to be considered, for the better instruction of all subjects in their bounden duty of obedience, and perpetual fearing[8] of them from attempting of any rebellion or hurt against their prince. On the one part, David was not only a good and true subject, but also such a subject as both in peace and war had served and saved his prince's honor and life and delivered his country and countrymen from great dangers of infidels, foreign and most cruel enemies, horribly invading the king and his country; for the which David was in singular favor with all the people, so that he might have had great numbers of them at his commandment if he would have attempted anything. Besides this, David was no common or absolute[9] subject, but heir apparent to the crown and kingdom, by God appointed to reign after Saul, which, as it increased the favor of the people that knew it towards David, so did it make David's cause and case much differing from the case of common and absolute subjects. And, which is most of all, David was highly and singularly in the favor of God. On the contrary part, King Saul was out of God's favor for that cause which is before rehearsed, and he, as it were, God's enemy, and therefore like in war and peace to be hurtful and pernicious unto the commonwealth; and that was known to many of his subjects, for that he was openly rebuked of Samuel for his disobedience unto God, which might make the people the less to esteem him. King Saul was also unto David a mortal and deadly enemy, though without David's deserving, who by his faithful, painful, profitable, yea, most necessary service had well deserved as of his country, so of his prince. But King Saul far otherwise: the more was his unkindness, hatred, and cruelty towards such a good subject both odious and detestable. Yet would David neither himself slay nor hurt such an enemy for that he was his prince and lord, nor would suffer any other to kill, hurt, or lay hand upon him when he might have been slain without any stir, tumult, or danger of any man's life.

* * *

In foreign wars our countrymen in obtaining the victory win the praise of valiantness. Yea, and though they were overcome and slain, yet win they an honest commendation in this world and die in a good

8. frightening.
9. pure and simple.

conscience for serving God, their prince, and their country, and be children of eternal salvation. But in rebellion, how desperate and strong soever they be, yet win they shame here in fighting against God, their prince, and country, and, therefore, justly do fall headlong into hell if they die, and live in shame and fearful conscience, though they escape. But commonly they be rewarded with shameful deaths, their heads and carcasses set upon poles, or hanged in chains, eaten with kites and crows, judged unworthy the honor of burial, and so their souls, if they repent not (as commonly they do not), the devil harrieth[1] them into hell in the midst of their mischief. For which dreadful execution Saint Paul (Rom. 13) showeth the cause of obedience, not only for fear of death but also in conscience to Godward[2] for fear of eternal damnation in the world to come.

Wherefore, good people, let us as the children of obedience fear the dreadful execution of God and live in quiet obedience to be the children of everlasting salvation. For as heaven is the place of good, obedient subjects, and hell the prison and dungeon of rebels against God and their prince, so is that realm happy where most obedience of subjects doth appear, being the very figure of heaven; and contrariwise, where most rebellions and rebels be, there is the express similitude of hell, and the rebels themselves are the very figures of fiends and devils, and their captain the ungracious pattern of Lucifer and Satan, the prince of darkness, of whose rebellion as they be followers, so shall they of his damnation in hell undoubtedly be partakers; and as undoubtedly children of peace the inheritors of heaven with God the Father, God the Son, and God the Holy Ghost, to whom be all honor and glory forever and ever, Amen.

JUAN DE MARIANA

[A Defense of Disobedience and Tyrannicide]†

Whether It Is Right to Destroy a Tyrant.

These are the defenses of each side, and after they have been carefully considered, it will not be difficult to set forth what must be decided about the proposed question. For certainly I see that the

---

1. carries off.
2. toward God.
† From Juan de Mariana, *De Rege et Regis Institutione* (Toledo, 1599), 74–82. Translation and footnotes by the editor of this Norton Critical Edition. Juan de Mariana (1536–1624), a Spanish Jesuit, argues that kings who act as tyrants forfeit their right to rule and that anyone may depose or kill them if there is no other remedy and if the will of the people so mandates. Mariana's work was widely condemned for instigating the assassination of Henri IV of France in 1610, about the time of *Macbeth*.

philosophers and theologians agree in this matter, that the prince who has taken possession of a republic by force and arms and, moreover, with no right and no public consent of the citizens can be killed by anyone and be deprived of his life and dominion.[1] Because he is a public enemy and oppresses his country with all evils, and because he truly and properly puts on the name and nature of a tyrant, he may be removed by any method and he may put off his power as violently as he took possession of it. (With this merit, then, Ehud, having insinuated himself into the graces of Eglon, King of the Moabites, slew him with a dagger plunged into the stomach; he snatched his people from the hard servitude which had oppressed them for eighteen years.)[2]

For if the prince holds power by the consent of the people or by hereditary right, his vices and lusts must be borne until he neglects those laws of honor and virtue by which he is bound. For princes must not be changed easily lest the republic fall into greater evils and serious disturbances arise, as was set down in the beginning of this disputation. But if, in truth, he destroys the republic, considers public and private fortunes as his own booty, holds public laws and sacred religion in contempt, and if he makes a virtue out of pride, brazenness, and impiety against heaven—this cannot be dissembled. One must consider carefully, however, what method of rejecting his prince should be taken, lest evil be piled upon evil and crime be avenged with crime.

And the readiest and safest way is to debate what must be decided by common consent, if the opportunity for a public meeting may be given, and to ratify and validate what has been decided by the common opinion. In which matter one may proceed by these steps: first, the prince will have to be warned and summoned back to sanity; if he regulates his conduct, makes satisfaction to the republic, and corrects the faults of his past life, the process must be halted, I think, and no harsher remedies attempted. If he spits out the medicine, however, and no hope of sanity is left, it will be permissible for the republic by a declared sentence first to reject his sovereignty. And since war necessarily will be provoked, it will then be permissible to make plans for driving him out, to bring forth arms, to raise money from the people for the costs of war, and if the matter requires and if the republic cannot be protected otherwise, by its same right of defense and in truth by its better and proper authority, to declare the prince a public enemy and to slay him with a sword. Let there be the same opportunity to any private citizen whatsoever who, with

1. Mariana describes the tyrant in entrance (*ex defectu tituli*, "from defect of title"), the ruler who unlawfully seizes power; below, he will describe the tyrant in practice (*ex parte exercitii*, "from the part of practice"), the ruler who abuses his power.
2. For the Old Testament story of Ehud, Eglon, and the freeing of the Israelites, see Judges 3:12–4:1.

all hope of impunity tossed aside and his own safety ignored, wishes to step forward in the attempt to help the republic.

You may ask what must be done if the opportunity to hold a public meeting will have been taken away, as often can happen. The same, certainly, in my opinion, will be the judgment when the republic is oppressed by the tyranny of a prince, when the capacity for public meeting has been taken away from the citizens, when the will is not lacking to destroy the tyranny, to avenge manifest and intolerable crimes of the prince, and to crush his destructive efforts, so that if the sacred fatherland should fall into ruins and attract public enemies into the province, I shall think that the man who, heeding the people's prayers, tries to kill the tyrant, has in no way acted as an enemy. And this is sufficiently confirmed by those arguments which are placed against the tyrant later in this disputation.

So the question of fact in this controversy is, "Who is properly considered to be a tyrant?" The question of law is clear, that it will be right to kill a tyrant. There is no danger that many by this example will rage against the life of princes as though they were tyrants; for we place the matter in the private will neither of any one citizen, nor of many, unless the public voice of the people is present and serious and learned men are brought together in council. Things would turn out very well in human affairs if many men of strong heart were found for the liberty of their country to be contemptuous of life and health; but the contrary desire for safety often holds back many in great endeavors. So, from such a great number of tyrants as have existed in ancient times, it is possible to reckon that only a few perished by the sword of their own people. In Spain scarcely one or two, although one should attribute this to the loyalty of the subjects and the clemency of princes, who received sovereignty with the best right and exercised it modestly and humanely.[3] Nevertheless, it is a salutary reflection that it may be impressed upon princes, if they oppress the republic and are intolerable because of their vices and foulness, that they live in such a condition that they may be killed, not only by right but also with praise and glory. Perhaps this fear will hinder someone, lest he allow himself to be deeply corrupted by vices and praises; it will put reins on madness. This is the main point, that it be impressed upon the prince that the authority of the whole republic is greater than that of one man; and that he not believe the worst men affirming something different in their desire to please him, which is a great wickedness.

There was not sufficient cause for David to kill King Saul,[4] it used

---

3. Mariana wrote a popular history of Spain, *Historiae de rebus Hispaniae* (1592), which he revised several times and translated into Spanish (1601).
4. The story of King Saul and David appears in 1 Samuel 16–2 Samuel 1; for a different interpretation, see the *Homily*, pp. 151–53 in this Norton Critical Edition.

to be objected, since David was able to reach safety by flight. If he, using this logic to save himself, were to slay a king especially established by God, it would have been impiety, not love of the republic. For Saul was not so depraved in morals that he was oppressing his subjects in tyranny, that he was overturning divine and human laws, that he was treating the citizens as spoil. The rights of rule certainly were transferred to David so that he might succeed the dead king, not, however, so that he might seize the life and power from the living one. Moreover, Augustine (*Contra Adimantus*, ch. 17) says this, namely that David did not wish to kill Saul, but that it would have been permissible.[5] It is not necessary to go on about the Roman emperors: by the blood and suffering of the pious the foundations of the church's greatness were laid out precisely to the very ends of the earth. And it was the greater miracle that the oppressed church was growing and, diminished in number, was gaining greater increments day by day. And in truth, the church was not free according to its doctrines in that time, nor even in this time, to do all the things which had been granted to it by right and laws. Thus, the famous historian Sozomen (Book 6, chapter 2) says that if a soldier happened to have killed the Emperor Julian,[6] since at that time they were actually accusing him specifically, he would have done so by right and with honor.

Finally, we think that upheavals in the republic must be avoided. Care must be taken lest joy from the expulsion of tyrants run wild in a brief moment and turn out to be empty; and all remedies for restoring a prince to health must be tried before it comes to this last and most serious measure. But if it is the case that every hope has been taken away and the public safety and the holiness of religions are called into danger, who will be so poor in counsel as not to avow that it is allowable to strike at the tyrant by right, by law, and by arms? One, perhaps, would move to this extreme position of denial because the following proposal was rejected by the Fathers at the Council of Constance[7] in the 15th session, "A tyrant can and ought to be killed by any subject, not only by open force but also through plotting and deceit." But, in truth, I do not find that conciliar decree approved by the Roman Pope Martin V, nor by Pope Eugene or his successors, by whose consent the holiness of ecclesiastical councils stands.

* * *

5. not merely for self-preservation, that is, but under certain circumstances.
6. Julian the Apostate was a Roman emperor from 361–63 and an enemy of Christianity; Christian lawyer in Constantinople, Sozomen (400–450) compiled a church history for the period 324–439.
7. The sixteenth ecumenical council of the Church (1414–18), the Council of Constance settled rival claims to the papacy, combated heresy, and initiated some reforms.

It is pleasing to conclude this disputation with the words of the Tribune Flavius, who, convicted of conspiracy against Domitius Nero,[8] in the midst of the questions about why he had acted oblivious to his oath of allegiance: "I hated you," he said, "but no soldier was more faithful to you while you deserved to be loved; I began to hate you after you became the murderer of your own mother and wife, a charioteer and actor, and an arsonist." A spirit soldierly and brave, according to Tacitus, Book 15.

Whether it is licit to kill a tyrant with poison.[9]

A wicked mind has unfathomable internal torments and the conscience of a tyrant is his own executioner. So even if no external adversary approaches, depravity of life and morals makes every joy and liberty of life bitter. For what condition of life, and how miserable, is it to singe off the beard and hair with burning coals for fear of the barber, as Dionysius the Tyrant[1] used to do? What pleasure was there to him who hid himself in the citadel like a snake in the time of quiet and sleep, as Clearchus, the Pontic tyrant,[2] was accustomed to do? What fruit of rule enjoyed Argive Aristodemus,[3] who used to conceal himself in a garret by means of a hanging door with a ladder added and removed? Or could there be greater unhappiness than to trust no one, not even friends and family? To quake at any noise and shadow as if rebellion had broken out and the spirits of all were enraged against him? He clearly lives a miserable life whose life is such that the one who slays him will have great gratitude and praise.

It is a glorious thing to exterminate all of this pestilent and deadly species from the human community. For in truth certain limbs are cut off if they are rotten lest they infect the rest of the body; so the monstrosity of a beast in this likeness of a man ought to be removed from the republic as from a body and cut out with a blade. Certainly the tyrant who spreads terror ought to fear; but the terror he arouses is not greater than the fear he endures. There is not so much protection in military strength, arms, and troops as there is danger in the people's hatred, whence destruction threatens. All orders busy themselves to remove a monster conspicuous for his abominations of villainy and his sordid deeds of cowardice. After hatreds have grown daily, either insurrection breaks out and there is a rush to

---

8. fifth Roman emperor (54–68), infamous for debauchery and the persecution of Christians.
9. Mariana will answer the title question in the negative, arguing, remarkably, that such a method of assassination puts the victim's soul at risk by forcing him to commit a kind of suicide.
1. ruthless tyrant of Syracuse, ruling from 405–367 B.C.E.
2. severe Spartan governor of Byzantium, 411–401 B.C.E.
3. tyrant of Cumae, early sixth century C.E.

open force when the people have taken up arms (which admirable spirit of nature we ought to restore to our country, by which means not a few tyrants have perished by open force!), or else with greater caution, by fraud and plotting, tyrants perish by one or a few individuals gathering secretly and working to regain safety for the republic at their own peril. But if they succeed, they are regarded in every station of life as great heroes; if it should fall out otherwise, they fall as sacrifices pleasing to heaven and pleasing to men, famous to all posterity for their noble attempt.

DEBATE ON EQUIVOCATION

HENRY GARNET

A Treatise of Equivocation [before 1606]†

And we may say with the logicians that there be four kinds of propositions. The first is a mental position, only conceived in the mind, and not uttered by any exterior signification; as when I think with myself these words, "God is not unjust." The second is a vocal proposition, as when I utter those words with my mouth. The third is a written proposition, as if I should set the same down in writing. The last of all is a mixed proposition, when we mingle some of these positions (or parts of them) together, as in our purpose, when being demanded whether John at Style be in such a place, I, knowing that he is there indeed, do say nevertheless "I know not"—reserving or understanding within myself these other words "to th'end for to tell you."[1] Here is a mixed proposition containing all this, "I know not to th'end for to tell you." And yet part of it is expressed, part reserved in the mind.

Now unto all these propositions it is common that then they are true when they are conformable to the thing itself; that is, when they so affirm or deny as the matter itself in very deed doth stand. Whereof we infer that this last sort of proposition, which partly consisteth in voice and partly is reserved in the mind, is then to be adjudged true, not when that part only which is expressed or the

---

† From Henry Garnet, *A Treatise of Equivocation*, ed. David Jardine (London, 1851), 8–11. Spelling and punctuation have been modernized by the editor of this Norton Critical Edition. Henry Garnet, SJ (1553/4–1606) was Jesuit Superior in England from 1587 until his execution for complicity in the Gunpowder Plot, allegedly a scheme by Catholics to blow up Parliament. Garnet propounded a theory of equivocation, which enabled Catholics to tell partial truths or to deceive interrogators and thereby survive persecution. Condemning equivocation, the Porter in *Macbeth* (2.3.1–8) alludes to Garnet, who sometimes adopted the alias of "Farmer."

1. for the purpose of telling you [*Editor's note*].

other only which is reserved is true, but when both together do contain a truth. For as it were a perverse thing in that vocal proposition, "God is not unjust," to say that position is false because if we leave out the last word the other three contain a manifest heresy (as if we affirmed God were not at all), the truth of every vocal proposition being to be measured not according to some parts but according to all together; even so that other proposition of which we spake, being a mixed proposition, is not to be examined according to the variety of the part expressed alone, but according to the part reserved also, they both together compounding one entire proposition.

Herein, therefore, consisteth the difficulty and this will we endeavor to prove: that whosoever frameth a true position in his mind and uttereth some part thereof in words, which of themselves being taken several from the other part reserved, were false, does not say false or lie before God, howsoever he may be thought to lie before men or otherwise commit therein some other sin. For yet we will not clear this party of sin herein, whereof we will speak hereafter, but only at this present we defend him not to have lied.

Adaptations

WILLIAM DAVENANT

Macbeth†

[1.5]

Enter LADY MACBETH *and* LADY MACDUFF, *Lady Macbeth having a letter in her hand.*

LADY MACBETH   Madam, I have observed since you came hither,
You have been still disconsolate. Pray tell me,
Are you in perfect health?

LADY MACDUFF   Alas, how can I?
My lord, when honor called him to the war,
Took with him half of my divided soul,
Which, lodging in his bosom, liked so well
The place that 'tis not yet returned.

LADY MACBETH   Methinks
That should not disorder you, for no doubt
The brave Macduff left half his soul behind him
To make up the defect[1] of yours.

LADY MACDUFF   Alas,
The part transplanted from his breast to mine,
As 'twere by sympathy, still bore a share

† From William Davenant, *Macbeth, A Tragedy with All the Alterations, Amendments, Additions, and New Songs* (London, 1674), sigs. B1v–B2, B3v–B4, D1–D2v, D4v–F1 [no sig. E], F4–F4v, G1v–G2, G2v–G3, H2–H3v, K1. Footnotes are by the editor of this Norton Critical Edition. Spelling and punctuation have also been modernized by the editor. William Davenant (1606–1668), an accomplished poet, dramatist, and manager of the Drury Lane Theatre, produced several adaptations of Shakespeare. His *Macbeth* tinkered with phrasing, expanded spectacle, especially the witches' parts, developed Lady Macduff into a foil for Lady Macbeth, omitted the Porter scene, and flattened the tragedy into a tale of ambition.
1. deficiency. The conversation turns on the conception of marriage as a state in which two souls become one.

In all the hazards which the other half
Incurred, and filled my bosom up with fears.

LADY MACBETH Those fears, methinks, should cease now he is
safe.

LADY MACDUFF Ah, madam, dangers which have long prevailed
Upon the fancy, even when they are dead,
Live in the memory awhile.

LADY MACBETH Although his safety has not power enough to
put
Your doubts to flight, yet the bright glories which
He gained in battle might dispel those clouds.

LADY MACDUFF The world mistakes the glories gained in war,
Thinking their luster true. Alas, they are
But comets, vapors by some men exhaled
From others' blood,[2] and kindled in the region
Of popular applause, in which they live
Awhile then vanish; and the very breath
Which first inflamed them blows them out again.

LADY MACBETH [*Aside*] I willingly would read this letter but
Her presence hinders me; I must divert her.
—If you are ill, repose may do you good;
You'd best retire and try if you can sleep.

LADY MACDUFF My doubtful thoughts too long have kept me
waking,
Madam. I'll take your counsel.   *Exit Lady Macduff.*

[1.7]

Enter MACBETH.

MACBETH If it were well when done, then it were well
It were done quickly; if his death might be
Without the death of nature in myself,
And killing my own rest, it would suffice.
But deeds of this complexion[3] still return
To plague the doer and destroy his peace.
Yet, let me think: he's here in double trust.
First, as I am his kinsman and his subject,
Strong both against the deed; then, as his host,
Who should against his murderer shut the door,
Not bear the sword myself. Besides, this Duncan

2. Glory is a brief flash like a comet or an insubstantial vapor drawn forth (**exhaled**) from
bloodshed.
3. kind.

Has born his faculties[4] so meek, and been
So clear in his great office that his virtues
Like angels plead against so black a deed.
Vaulting Ambition! Thou o'erleapst thyself
To fall upon another.

[2.5] *An heath.*

Enter LADY MACDUFF, MAID, *and* SERVANT.

LADY MACDUFF   Art sure this is the place my lord appointed
  Us to meet him?
SERVANT   This is the entrance o'th'heath; and here
  He ordered me to attend him with the chariot.
LADY MACDUFF   How fondly[5] did my lord conceive that we
  Should shun the place of danger by our flight
  From Inverness! The darkness of the day
  Makes the heath seem the gloomy walks of death.
  We are in danger still; they who dare here
  Trust Providence may trust it anywhere.
MAID   But this place, madam, is more free from terror.
  Last night methoughts I heard a dismal noise
  Of shrieks and groanings in the air.
LADY MACDUFF   'Tis true, this is a place of greater silence,
  Not so much troubled with the groans of those
  That die, nor with the outcries of the living.
MAID   Yes, I have heard stories how some men
  Have in such lonely places been affrighted
  With dreadful shapes and noises.   *Macduff* [*within*] *hollows.*[6]
LADY MACDUFF   But hark, my lord sure hollows!
  'Tis he; answer him quickly.
SERVANT [*Shouting*]   Illo, ho, ho, ho!

Enter MACDUFF.

LADY MACDUFF   Now I begin to see him. Are you afoot,
  My lord?
MACDUFF   Knowing the way to be both short and easy,
  And that the chariot did attend me here,
  I have adventured. Where are our children?
LADY MACDUFF   They are securely sleeping in the chariot.

[*Enter* WITCHES.] *First Song by Witches.*

4. powers.
5. foolishly.
6. cries out a greeting.

FIRST WITCH   Speak, sister, speak; is the deed done?
SECOND WITCH   Long ago, long ago—
  Above twelve glasses[7] since have run.
THIRD WITCH   Ill deeds are seldom slow
  Nor single. Following crimes on former wait.
  The worst of creatures fastest propagate.
  Many more murders must this one ensue,
  As if in death were propagation[8] too.
SECOND WITCH   He will—
FIRST WITCH   He shall—
THIRD WITCH   He must spill much more
    blood
  And become worse to make his title good.
FIRST WITCH   Now let's dance.
SECOND WITCH   Agreed.
THIRD WITCH   Agreed.
FOURTH WITCH   Agreed.
CHORUS[9] [*Singing and dancing*]   We should rejoice when good
    kings bleed.
  When cattle die, about we go,
  What then, when monarchs perish, should we do?
MACDUFF   What can this be?
LADY MACDUFF   This is most strange, but why seem you afraid?
  Can you be capable of fears, who have
  So often caused it in your enemies?
MACDUFF   It was a hellish song. I cannot dread
  Aught that is mortal, but this is something more.

Second Song.

  Let's have a dance upon the heath;
  We gain more life by Duncan's death.
  Sometimes like brinded[1] cats we show,
  Having no music but our mew.
  Sometimes we dance in some old mill,
  Upon the hopper,[2] stones, and wheel,
  To some old saw or bardish rhyme,
  Where still the mill-clack[3] does keep time.
  Sometimes about a hollow tree,
  Around, around, around dance we.
  Thither the chirping cricket comes,

7. hourglasses.
8. birth and increase.
9. all the witches.
1. streaked or spotted.
2. container for feeding grain into the grinding machines.
3. instrument that strikes the hopper (a funnel-shaped receptacle) to pour out the grain.

And beetle, singing, drowsy hums.
Sometimes we dance o'er fens and furze,[4]
To howls of wolves and barks of curs.
And when with none of those we meet,
We dance to th'echoes of our feet.
At the night-raven's dismal voice,
Whilst others tremble, we rejoice;
And nimbly, nimbly dance we still
To th'echoes from an hollow hill.

MACDUFF   I am glad you are not afraid.
LADY MACDUFF   I would not willingly to fear submit;
None can fear ill but those that merit it.
MACDUFF [*Aside*]   Am I made bold by her? How strong a guard
Is innocence!—If anyone would be
Reputed valiant, let him learn of you.
Virtue both courage is, and safety too.

> *A dance of witches. Enter two* WITCHES.

MACDUFF   These seem foul spirits; I'll speak to 'em.
—If you can anything by more than nature know,
You may in those prodigious times foretell
Some ill we may avoid.
FIRST WITCH   Saving thy blood will cause it to be shed.
SECOND WITCH   He'll bleed by thee, by whom thou first hast
bled.
THIRD WITCH   Thy wife shall, shunning danger, dangers find,
And fatal be to whom she most is kind.   *Exeunt Witches.*
LADY MACDUFF   Why are you altered, sir? Be not so thoughtful.
The messengers of darkness never spake
To men but to deceive them.
MACDUFF   Their words seem to foretell some dire predictions.
LADY MACDUFF   He that believes ill news from such as these,
Deserves to find it true. Their words are like
Their shape—nothing but fiction. Let's hasten to our journey.
MACDUFF   I'll take your counsel; for to permit
Such thoughts upon our memories to dwell,
Will make our minds the registers of hell.   *Exeunt all.*

---

4. marshes and spiny shrubs.

[3.2]

Enter MACDUFF *and* LADY MACDUFF.

MACDUFF   It must be so. Great Duncan's bloody death
     Can have no other author but Macbeth.
     His dagger now is to a scepter grown;
     From Duncan's grave he has derived his throne.
LADY MACDUFF   Ambition urged him to that bloody deed.
     May you be never by ambition led.
     Forbid it, heav'n, that in revenge you should
     Follow a copy that is writ in blood.
MACDUFF   From Duncan's grave methinks I hear a groan
     That calls aloud for justice.
LADY MACDUFF   If the throne
     Was by Macbeth ill gained, heavens may
     Without your sword sufficient vengeance pay.
     Usurpers' lives have but a short extent;
     Nothing lives long in a strange element.
MACDUFF   My country's dangers call for my defense
     Against the bloody tyrant's violence.
LADY MACDUFF   I am afraid you have some other end,
     Than merely Scotland's freedom to defend.
     You'd raise yourself, whilst you would him dethrone,
     And shake his greatness to confirm your own.
     That purpose will appear, when rightly scanned,
     But usurpation at the second hand.
     Good sir, recall your thoughts.
MACDUFF   What if I should
     Assume the scepter for my country's good?
     Is that an usurpation? Can it be
     Ambition to procure the liberty
     Of this sad realm, which does by treason bleed?
     That which provokes will justify the deed.
LADY MACDUFF   If the design should prosper, the event
     May make us safe, but not you innocent;
     For whilst to set our fellow subjects free
     From present death or future slavery,
     You wear a crown not by your title due,
     Defense in them is an offense in you.
     That deed's unlawful though it cost no blood,
     In which you'll be at best unjustly good.
     You, by your pity which for us you plead,
     Weave but ambition of a finer thread.

MACDUFF   Ambition does the height of power affect;[5]
My aim is not to govern but protect.
And he is not ambitious that declares,
He nothing seeks of scepters but their cares.
LADY MACDUFF   Can you so patiently yourself molest,
And lose your own, to give your country rest?
In plagues what sound physician would endure
To be infected for another's cure?
MACDUFF   If by my troubles I could yours release,
My love would turn those torments to my ease;
I should at once be sick and healthy too,
Though sickly in myself, yet well in you.
LADY MACDUFF   But, then, reflect upon the danger, sir,
Which you by your aspiring would incur:
From fortune's pinnacle you will too late
Look down, when you are giddy with your height.
Whilst you with fortune play to win a crown,
The people's stakes are greater than your own.
MACDUFF   In hopes to have the common ills redressed,
Who would not venture single interest?[6]

[3.6]

Enter MACDUFF *and* LADY MACDUFF.

LADY MACDUFF   Are you resolved then to be gone?
MACDUFF   I am.
I know my answer cannot but inflame
The tyrant's fury to pronounce my death;
My life will soon be blasted by his breath.
LADY MACDUFF   But why so far as England must you fly?
MACDUFF   The farthest part of Scotland is too nigh.
LADY MACDUFF   Can you leave me, your daughter, and young son,
To perish by that tempest which you shun?
When birds of stronger wing are fled away,
The ravenous kite[7] does on the weaker prey.
MACDUFF   He will not injure you; he cannot be
Possessed with such unmanly cruelty.
You will your safety to your weakness owe,
As grass escapes the scythe by being low.
Together we shall be too slow to fly;

5. desire.
6. private gain or advantage.
7. bird of prey.

Single, we may outride the enemy.
I'll from the English King such succors[8] crave,
As shall revenge the dead, and living save.
My greatest misery is to remove,
With all the wings of haste from what I love.
LADY MACDUFF   If to be gone seems misery to you,
Good sir, let us be miserable too.
MACDUFF   Your sex, which here is your security,
Will by the toils of flight your danger be.

Enter MESSENGER.

What fatal news does bring thee out of breath?
MESSENGER   Sir, Banquo's killed.
MACDUFF   Then I am warned of death.
Farewell. Our safety us awhile must sever.
LADY MACDUFF   Fly, fly, or we may bid farewell for ever.
MACDUFF   Flying from death, I am to life unkind,
For leaving you, I leave my life behind.   *Exit.*
LADY MACDUFF   Oh, my dear lord, I find now thou art gone,
I am more valiant when unsafe alone.
My heart feels manhood; it does death despise,
[*Weeps*] Yet I am still a woman in my eyes.
And of my tears thy absence is the cause;
So falls the dew when the bright sun withdraws.   *Exeunt.*

[3.8]

[*Enter* HECATE *and three* WITCHES.] *Music and Song.*[9]

[SPIRITS *within*] Hecate, Hecate, Hecate, oh, come away!
[HECATE]   Hark, I am called. My little spirit, see,
Sits in a foggy cloud and stays for me.
[SPIRITS *within*] Come away, Hecate, Hecate, oh, come away!

Machine descends [*carrying* SPIRITS.][1]

HECATE   I come, I come, with all the speed I may.
With all the speed I may. Where's Stadling?

---

8. supports.
9. The song "Come away, come away" is sung off-stage in Shakespeare's play (3.5.35 S.D.),
   as is the song following, "Black spirits" (4.1.43 S.D.). Both songs occur in Thomas Middleton's play *The Witch* (1610–15, pub. 1778), and suggest that Middleton had a hand in
   composing or revising *Macbeth*. William Davenant's versions of the songs may derive from
   the King's Men's performing text of *Macbeth*, to which he had acquired the rights, and so
   may present the verses as sung in Shakespeare's play.
1. A mechanical contrivance that is used to lower the spirits and other characters increases
   the spectacle of the scene. The ensuing lines identify Hecate's companions as spirits, who
   may or may not differ in production from the witches.

SECOND SPIRIT   Here.

HECATE   Where's Puckle?

THIRD SPIRIT   Here, and Hopper too, and Hellway too.

FIRST SPIRIT   We want[2] but you, we want but you!
   Come away, make up the count.

HECATE   I will but 'noint,[3] and then I mount;
   I will but 'noint, and then I mount.

FIRST SPIRIT   Here comes down one to fetch his due,
   A kiss, a coll,[4] a sip of blood;
   And why thou stayst so long I muse,[5]
   Since the air's so sweet and good.

[HECATE]   Oh, art thou come? What news?

SECOND SPIRIT   All goes fair for our delight.
   Either come, or else refuse.

[HECATE]   Now I'm furnished for the flight;
   Now I go, and now I fly,
   Malkin,[6] my sweet spirit, and I.

THIRD SPIRIT   Oh, what a dainty pleasure's this,
   To sail i'th'air while the moon shines fair,
   To sing, to toy, to dance, and kiss.
   Over woods, high rocks, and mountains,
   Over hills and misty fountains,
   Over steeples, towers, and turrets,
   We fly by night 'mongst troops of spirits!
   No ring of bells to our ears sounds,
   No howls of wolves nor yelps of hounds,
   No, nor the noise of water's breach,
   Nor cannons' throats our height can reach.
                                    [*Exeunt Hecate and the spirits.*]

FIRST WITCH   Come, let's make haste; she'll soon be back again.

SECOND WITCH   But whilst she moves through the foggy air,
   Let's to the cave and our dire charms prepare.   [*Exeunt all.*]

2. lack.
3. anoint (myself).
4. hug.
5. wonder.
6. a name for a familiar, i.e., attendant spirit, often in the shape of a cat.

[4.3]

Enter HECATE *and the other three* WITCHES [*to the three witches*].[7]

HECATE   Oh, well done; I commend your pains.
  And everyone shall share the gains.
  And now about the cauldron sing,
  Like elves and fairies in a ring.

Music and song.

  Black spirits and white,
  Red spirits and gray,
  Mingle, mingle, mingle,[8]
  You that mingle may.
FIRST WITCH   Tiffin, Tiffin, keep it stiff in.
  Firedrake[9] Pucky, make it lucky.
  Liar Robin, you must bob in.
CHORUS   Around, around, about, about,
  All ill come running in, all good keep out.
FIRST WITCH   Here's the blood of a bat!
HECATE   Oh, put in that, put in that!
SECOND WITCH   Here's lizard's brain!
HECATE   Put in a grain!
FIRST WITCH   Here's juice of toad, here's oil of adder,
  That will make the charm grow madder.
SECOND WITCH   Put in all these; 'twill raise the stench.
HECATE   Nay, here's three ounces of a red-haired wench.
CHORUS   Around, around, about, about,
  All ill come running in, all good keep out.
SECOND WITCH   I, by the pricking of my thumbs,
  Know something wicked this way comes.
  Open locks, whoever knocks.

Enter MACBETH.

---

7. i.e., to those already onstage.
8. mix together (also, have sexual intercourse).
9. a mythological dragon.

[4.4]

Enter MACBETH *and* SEYTON.

MACBETH   Seyton, go bid the army march.
SEYTON   The posture of affairs requires your presence.
MACBETH   But the indisposition of my wife
   Detains me here.
SEYTON   Th'enemy is upon our borders; Scotland's in danger.
MACBETH   So is my wife, and I am doubly so.
   I am sick in her and in my kingdom too.
   Seyton!
SEYTON   Sir?
MACBETH   The spur of my ambition prompts me to go
   And make my kingdom safe, but love, which softens
   Me to pity her in her distress, curbs my resolves.
SEYTON [*Aside*]   He's strangely disorder'd.
MACBETH   Yet why should love, since confined, desire
   To control ambition, for whose spreading hopes
   The world's too narrow. It shall not; great fires
   Put out the less. Seyton, go bid my grooms
   Make ready; I'll not delay my going.
SEYTON   I go.
MACBETH   Stay, Seyton, stay; compassion calls me back.
SEYTON [*Aside*]   He looks and moves disorderly.
MACBETH   I'll not go yet.
SEYTON   Well, sir.

Enter a SERVANT, *who whispers* [*to*] *Macbeth.*

MACBETH [*To the Servant*]   Is the Queen asleep?
SEYTON [*Aside*]   What makes 'em whisper and his countenance
      change?
   Perhaps some new design has had ill success.
MACBETH   Seyton, go see what posture our affairs are in.
SEYTON   I shall, and give you notice, sir.   *Exit Seyton.*

Enter LADY MACBETH.

MACBETH   How does my gentle love?
LADY MACBETH   Duncan is dead.
MACBETH   No words of that.
LADY MACBETH   And yet to me he lives.
   His fatal ghost is now my shadow, and pursues me
   Where e'er I go.
MACBETH   It cannot be, my dear;
   Your fears have misinformed your eyes.

[*Enter* DUNCAN'S GHOST.]

LADY MACBETH   See there! Believe your own!
[*To the Ghost*] Why do you follow me? I did not do it.
MACBETH   Methinks there's nothing.
LADY MACBETH   If you have valor, force him hence!

[*Exit Ghost.*]

Hold, hold, he's gone. Now you look strangely.
MACBETH   'Tis the strange error of your eyes.
LADY MACBETH   But the strange error of my eyes
Proceeds from the strange action of your hands.
Distraction does by fits possess my head
Because a crown unjustly covers it.
I stand so high that I am giddy grown.
A mist does cover me, as clouds the tops
Of hills. Let us get down apace.
MACBETH   If by your high ascent you giddy grow,
'Tis when you cast your eyes on things below.
LADY MACBETH   You may in peace resign the ill-gained crown.
Why should you labor still to be unjust?
There has been too much blood already spilt.
Make not the subjects victims to your guilt.
MACBETH   Can you think that a crime, which you did once
Provoke me to commit? Had not your breath
Blown my ambition up into a flame,
Duncan had yet been living.
LADY MACBETH   You were a man.
And by the charter of your sex you should
Have governed me; there was more crime in you
When you obeyed my counsels than I contracted
By my giving it. Resign your kingdom now,
And with your crown put off your guilt.
MACBETH   Resign the crown, and with it both our lives.
I must have better counselors.
LADY MACBETH   What, your witches?
Curse on your messengers of hell! Their breath
Infected first my breast. See me no more.
As king your crown sits heavy on your head,
But heavier on my heart. I have had too much
Of kings already.

[DUNCAN'S] GHOST *appears.*

See, the ghost again!
MACBETH   Now she relapses.
LADY MACBETH [*To Macbeth*]   Speak to him if thou canst.

[*To the Ghost*] Thou lookst on me, and showst thy wounded
    breast.
  Show it the murderer!   [*Exit Ghost.*]
MACBETH [*Calling*]   Within there, ho!

                              Enter WOMEN.

LADY MACBETH   Am I ta'en prisoner? Then the battle's lost.

              Exit Lady Macbeth, led out by women.

MACBETH   She does from Duncan's death to sickness grieve,
And shall from Malcolm's death her health receive.
When by a viper bitten, nothing's good
To cure the venom but a viper's blood.

[5.8]

MACBETH   I scorn to yield! I will in spite of enchantment
Fight with thee, though Birnam Wood be come to Dunsinane,
And thou art of no woman born; I'll try
If by a man it be thy fate to die.

        They fight. Macbeth falls. They shout within.

MACDUFF   This for my royal master, Duncan,
  This for my dearest friend, my wife,
  This for those pledges of our loves, my children.
                    (*Shout within.*)

  Hark, I hear a noise. Sure, there are more
  Reserves to conquer. I'll as a trophy bear
  Away his sword to witness my revenge.
             Exit Macduff [*with Macbeth's sword.*]

MACBETH   Farewell vain world, and what's most vain in it,
    ambition. *Dies.*

174

MACBETH TRAVESTIES†

[1.1, By Francis Talfourd, 1850]

A blasted heath, rain, thunder, and lightning.

Enter MACBETH *and* BANQUO, *under an umbrella.* (*L.*)

The three WITCHES *discovered crouching, one smoking a short pipe.* (*R.*)

BANQUO   So foul and fair a day I never saw.
MACBETH   No! You don't say so—well, I never—Lor'.
BANQUO   I think so, really. Macbeth, my fine feller,
  Confess 'twas well I brought the umberella.
MACBETH   You'll just allow me to observe, my pippin,[1]
  You get its shelter, and give me the dripping.
  But who (*Seeing witches*) are these abominable hags?
  Why, Banquo, did you ever see such scrags?[2]
  What ugly brutes! How rough and wild in dress!
  —Who and what are ye? Answer.
WITCHES   Can't you guess?
MACBETH   You should be women, but I never heard
  Of women wearing whiskers, and a beard!
  Speak, if you can, and if you can't, why don't;
  Come, speak out plainly—won't you—oh, you won't?
                              (*Menaces them.*)
FIRST WITCH   Hail! Thane of Glamis!
SECOND WITCH   Thane of Cawdor, hail!
THIRD WITCH   Macbeth, by perseverance, shall not fail
  To be the king of Scotland
ALL   Hail! Hail! Hail!
MACBETH   What mean these salutations, noble Thane?
BANQUO   These showers of "hail!" prognosticate your "reign"!
MACBETH   (*To Witches*)   Young women, do you see aught in my
    eye,
  That smacks at all of verdure, that you try

---

† From Rush Moore, *Macbeth Travestie, in Three Acts* (Calcutta, 1820); W. K. Northall, *Macbeth Travestie* (New York, 1847); Francis Talfourd, *Macbeth Travestie: A Burlesque* (Oxford, 1850; 3rd ed.); and *Macbeth, A Burlesque* (Nottingham, 1866). Poking irreverent fun, the travesties ridicule perceived excesses, puncture pretensions, and, in Francis Talfourd's rewriting, cheerfully reverse the irreversible forces of evil and doom. The Norton editor has excerpted scenes from these four plays to provide a parodic version of *Macbeth*. Act and scene numbers in brackets refer to Shakespeare's play; the abbreviations *L.* and *R.* indicate stage left and right, respectively. Footnotes are by the editor of this Norton Critical Edition. Spelling and punctuation have also been modernized by the editor.
1. fine fellow (slang).
2. lean, wretched people.

To gammon me?[3] I'm far too old a bird
Thus to be caught with chaff—it's too absurd.
In what the first fair creature says no harm is,
By Sinel's death I know I'm Thane of Glamis.
But this fact is in my digestion sticking:
The Thane of Cawdor is alive—and kicking—
A jolly sort of cove[4]—and to be a king!
Oh, gemini, who'd dream of such a thing?
No more than to be Cawdor (*Aside*) —yet, good gracious,
To be a king would really be splendacious!

BANQUO (*To Witches*) Really, young ladies, you are rather going
    it,
  For my lot I don't care much for the knowing it;
  But since you are in a prophesying vein,
  Just tell us what you think of me. Again,
  I say, with nonsense don't attempt to cram one,
  And, as you'd save your bacon, spare your gammon.[5]

WITCHES   Thou shalt get kings, though thou thyself be none!

BANQUO   Oh, stuff and nonsense!

MACBETH   I am diddled—done!
  Don't go, young women, till you've said from whence
  You owe this very strange intelligence:
  D'ye think that we don't know the time o' day,
  That on this blasted heath you stop our way?
  Stay—none of that. If you don't quickly speak,
  I'll send you on a visit to next week.   (*Witches vanish. R.*)
  They've vanished!

BANQUO   I am sorry this you troubles;
  The earth, sir, like the water, has its bubbles.

[1.7, By W. K. Northall, 1847]

Enter MACBETH, *thoughtfully R.*

MACBETH   If it were done when 'tis done, there's no doubt
  'Twere quite as well 'twere quickly set about.
  If the same knife which cuts poor Duncan's life supporters
  Could only cut the throats of common news reporters,
  And thus make dumb the press—it's pretty clear
  This cut would be the be-all and the end-all here.

---

3. Do you see anything green (from inexperience) in my eye that you try to trick (**gammon**) me?
4. fellow.
5. And as you'd save yourselves, spare us your tricks.

But this even-handed justice is a sorry jade,[1]
And may commend to my own throat the self-same blade.
He's here in double trust, but then he's had long credit,
And yet I'm called upon to write more debit.
But still I am his kinsman, and his subject too;
In either case, the bloody work is hard to do.
I think I'll hire a man to do the deed:
I shouldn't murder when I ought to feed.
And who can bear to be the common scoff,
For "the deep damnation of his taking off"?
I have no spur to prick me on—full well I know it—
So, vaulting ambition, I say, prithee, go it!
Don't overleap yourself, and then come tumbling down
With dislocated neck or broken crown.

Enter LADY MACBETH, *R.*

How now, Mrs. M., did he eat those oysters that you stewed?
LADY MACBETH   He supped on nothing else—your leaving us
    was rude.
MACBETH   I will not do this deed; he has honoured me of late,
    And bought me golden pippins,[2] which I ate.   (*Walks L.*)
LADY MACBETH   Coward! You much desire to be a king,
    But tremble at the means which do the thing.
MACBETH   I dare do all that becomes a man, so do not vex me,
    If more you want, why, damn it, ma'am, unsex me.

[1.7 *continued*, By Francis Talfourd, 1850]

LADY MACBETH   The old boy's abed, and now's your time to do it.
MACBETH   I'm out of sorts—I feel a kind of dizziness,
    And won't proceed no farther in this business.
LADY MACBETH   Pooh! you're a spoon.[3]
MACBETH   To tell the truth, I'm loath
    To stop the old man's wizen.[4]
LADY MACBETH   But your oath!
    You're bold enough when there's no danger nigh—
    When once it comes then you're for "fighting shy."
MACBETH   I dare do all that may a man become.

1. horse.
2. apples.
3. fool.
4. throat.

LADY MACBETH   To an oath once made you should stick fast—
    by Gum!
  If 'tis not from cowardice you keep aloof,
  Strike off the prince, and let me have a proof.
MACBETH   Suppose the king disposed of—yet, my dear,
  It seems my next course isn't over clear—
  Malcolm, my cousin, nine times removed, or so!
  I'm in a fix—I fear it is no go.
LADY MACBETH   Nine times removed already! Then it's plain
  It can't hurt to remove him once again!
  Macbeth, pluck up a little courage, do, man!
MACBETH   Who would believe you were a female woman?
  We shall be sorry for it!
LADY MACBETH   For a warrior
  I may say that I never saw a sorrier!
  Say, who hast sought in battle undismayed
  The hot affray,[5] of what thou art afraid!
MACBETH   Egad—I'll do it!
LADY MACBETH   Why do you turn so pale?
MACBETH   An awkward thought's just struck me—should we
  fail!
LADY MACBETH   Fail! Stuff and nonsense—Fail! Your courage
  screw
  But to the sticking-place, and we shall do.
  Come, "if you['d] die a pantile, be a brick!"[6]
MACBETH   The sticking-place is exactly where I stick!
LADY MACBETH   Duncan's attendants are so full of beer,
  They'll be quite muddled, that is very clear;
  When they're asleep, bedaub their faces o'er—
MACBETH   With blood? I understand. O my! O Lor!
  Is this a clasp-knife,[7] such as plough-boys use
  For cutting bread-and-cheese? You'll me excuse,
  —Perhaps you are but a clasp-knife of the brain.
                               (*Snatches at it.*)

  Egad, I missed it—there it is again!
  And o[n]'ts blade gouts[8] of—No—the maker's name,
  Which was not there before—it's all a sham!   (*Bell rings.*)
LADY MACBETH   Of course it is! Now go, d'ye hear the bell?
MACBETH   Hear it not, Duncan, for it is a knell
  That tolls you into heaven, or to— never mind,
  Which of the two it is, you'll too soon find.   (*Exit R.*)

5. fray.
6. If you want to amount to something, be strong now. A pantile is a roofing tile; brick refers
  literally to the construction element of clay and figuratively to strength.
7. a knife that folds its blade into the handle.
8. on its blade drops.

Lady Macbeth sings. Air "Lucy Neal."

Softly slip your shoes off,
Soft to the chamber steal;
When Duncan finds you by his side,
How happy he will feel.

Oh, poor King Duncan!
When he finds the steel
In his bread-basket,[9] I should guess,
Will wriggle a great deal!

But soft, he is about it,
I thought I heard a squeal;
When Duncan has it in his side,
How happy he will feel.

Re-enter MACBETH, *with daggers.*

LADY MACBETH   Is't done, my husband? What's the matter now?
MACBETH   I've done the deed; didn't you hear the row?[1]
   I stumbled (where I hadn't seen them standing)
   Over the old boy's bluchers[2] on the landing;
   You heard it?
LADY MACBETH   No one else did.
MACBETH   That's all right,
   But just look here—this is a sorry sight.
                              (*Looking at his hands*)
LADY MACBETH   Pshaw! Stuff!
MACBETH   One sung out in his sleep—how soon,
   I fear he'll sing to quite another tune!
   They were both beery—one declared outright
   He'd no intention to go home that night.
   The other in no high state of sobriety,
   Heedless of manners, sung out—*"Tulla-li-ety"*;
   I couldn't echo it—What was amiss?
LADY MACBETH   Oh! nonsense, now, you mustn't think of this.
MACBETH   How much more need of joyousness had I, yet he
   Sung, and I couldn't echo *"Tulla-li-ety."*
LADY MACBETH   Why did you bring those daggers from their
      places?
   Go, take them back, and smear the sleepers' faces
   With blood.

9. stomach.
1. commotion.
2. boots.

MACBETH (*Doggedly*)   No, come you know, I've done one
   murder;
  That's quite enough, and I sha'nt go no furder.
LADY MACBETH   Don't leave the job unfinished, come now, don't;
   Go!
MACBETH   If I do I'm—, never mind, I won't!
LADY MACBETH   Be mine the task, since you the courage lack;
  Give me the daggers, I shall soon be back.   (*Exit R.*)
MACBETH (*Alone*)   Were all the waters of the Serpentine,
  With those of the New River to combine—
  Were e'en the potent Thames to lend its aid,
  And Regent Park's canal, I am afraid,
  Failing to wash from off my hands this gore,
  They'd make red what mud-coloured was before.

Re-enter LADY MACBETH.

LADY MACBETH   My hands are like yours, p'raps a little redder.
(*Loud knocking*)
  I thought I heard a knock; we'd best to bed.
MACBETH   Ah!
  And not to lose the public's good opinion—
LADY MACBETH   We'll red our eyebrows with a Spanish onion!
(*Knocking repeated*)

Air—"Who's dat knocking at the door?"

MACBETH   Who's that knocking at the door?   (*Knock*)
LADY MACBETH   Who's that knocking at the door?   (*Knock*)
MACBETH   I don't care a pin,
  He sha'nt come in.
LADY MACBETH   Our hands are not clean,
  So he can't come in!
BOTH   Whoever is a-knocking at the door, at the door?
  Whoever is a-knocking at the door?   (*Loud knocking*)

[1.7 *continued*, From *Macbeth, A Burlesque,* 1866][1]

*Macbeth and Lady M. perform "Duncan Gray," Lady
Macbeth singing and beating time.*

---

1. In this burlesque Duncan eats a pie with twenty-four blackbirds baked in it, according to
  the nursery rhyme; they wake inside him and escape, causing his death.

DUNCAN, *dressed in night-gown and night-cap, puts his head in at the door.*

Music continues for some time after he has begun to speak.

DUNCAN Oh, murder! Oh, stop there! Oh, stop, I say. I command you to stop that excruciating duet! 'Tis passing horrible. I can't sleep, upon my soul, I can't. Macbeth doth murder sleep. My noble hosts, you forget the supper and the repose needed after such a feast. I haven't had a wink, and the sun is already beginning to shine in the east. Your pie, fair hostess, I mean the blackbird pie, was so uncommonly good, that I thought I'd *like* to eat it, and I thought I *could* eat it, and I thought I *would*. So the whole four-and-twenty blackbirds disappeared one after the other down the red lane, not omitting the crust; and I feel just now, craving your pardon, as the American showman would say, "kinder like to bust." Besides, the worst remains to be told. When you your music begin, all the four-and-twenty birds flutter about and begin to sing; isn't that a pretty comfortable state of things for the home affairs of a constitutional king?[2] Here take this crown for your music (*flings to him a crown-piece*), and once more, good night.   (*Retires.*)

[4.1, By Rush Moore, 1820]

A dark cave. In the middle a cauldron boiling.

Enter HECATE *and three* WITCHES.

HECATE By the itching of my noddle,[1]
Some great rogue does this way toddle.

Enter MACBETH.

The thumb of my left hand too itches.
MACBETH How now, ye sacred midnight bitches!
What's the rig,[2] I'm going to task[3] you,
And beg you'll answer what I ask you.
Though you untie the winds and let,
Eunuchs twins of maidens get,[4]
Who shall upon the throne be set,

2. "Isn't that a dainty dish to set before the king?" says the nursery rhyme.
1. head.
2. swindle.
3. test.
4. eunuchs beget twins from maidens.

Though St. Paul's steeple should be bent,
Until it meet the monument,
Or though a mare at Drury Lane,
Should tread the boards as Crazy Jane?[5]
HECATE   Speak, we'll answer all your queries.
FIRST WITCH   With us there sure no cause for fear is.
HECATE   Will you from us instruction gather,
    Or from our masters had you rather?

*   *   *

Thunder. The APPARITION *of an armed head rises.*

Song: Tune: "Moll in the Wad."

APPARITION   Macbeth, Macbeth, be up to snuff.
    Beware of that thundering rogue, Macduff.
    For well I know the Thane of Fife,
    Has whetted for you a shear[6] steel knife.
MACBETH   The which I suppose he does intend,
    Unto my ribs to recommend:
    But he shall lose his aim for once,
    And find his friend Macbeth no dunce.   *Apparition vanishes.*

Thunder. An APPARITION *of a bloody child rises.*

APPARITION   Macbeth!
MACBETH   Go on, I'll hear thee through't.
APPARITION   Be bloody, bold, and resolute,
    Laugh the power of man to scorn,
    Fear none that are of woman born.
MACBETH   Tip us your daddle,[7] old two shoes,
    I thank ye kindly for your news.
    I'd grind[8] my sword, my shield I'll brighten,
    You've put me in a mood for fighting!   *Apparition descends.*

Thunder. An APPARITION *of a child crowned rises.*

APPARITION   None shall vanquish thee, bold Thane,
    Till Birnam Wood to Dunsinane,
    Shall its respects, obsequious pay,
    And 'fore its walls, its branches lay.
MACBETH   My thanks that you'll accept, I beg;
    I'm now all right as my left leg.

5. Macbeth imagines St. Paul's steeple bending over and then another impossible eventuality,
   a horse playing the role of Crazy Jane, a mad woman, at Drury Lane Theatre.
6. strengthened.
7. shake our hands.
8. sharpen.

Yet much I wish to know one thing.
Shall Banquo's line produce a king?   *Apparition descends.*
Deny me this and by Saint Paul,
I'll kick you soundly one and all.
FIRST WITCH   Show.
SECOND WITCH   Show.
ALL   Show his eyes,
    Sights that would Old Nick[9] surprise.

        Eight KINGS *pass over the stage,* BANQUO *following.*

MACBETH   Down, Banquo, to thy hell go down,
    What the deuce brought you to town?
    The sight of thee doth make me blind;
    I, therefore, hope you'll be so kind,
    As to be off, sans hesitation,
    And with you take this generation
    Of unsubstantial looking things,
    Who are rigged out[1] in the garb of kings,
    And which that horrid smile of thine,
    Doth seem to say shall reign ere mine.
HECATE   Now that your wishes are fulfilled,
    You seem as though you had been drilled,
    By something which has made a hole,
    Through your pure, majestic soul.
    But we must all now elsewhere fly.
    Farewell, Macbeth, Mac'mind your eye.
                        Hecate and witches vanish.
MACBETH   Where the devil are they gone?
    I wonder what they ride upon.
    This day of all my life the worst,
    Shall stand i'th' calendar accurst.
    [*He orders offstage.*] Without there, ho! Pray, walk within,
    And with thee some kind cordial bring.

        Enter ROSS, *holding a glass of gin, which Macbeth drinks.*

MACBETH   Oh, the virtue that lays in
    A simple glass of English gin!
    It gives one's vitals such relief,
    As really is beyond belief.
    But, Ross, what I should first have asked you,
    Is which way those damned witches passed you?

9. name for the devil.
1. dressed up.

[5.5, By W. K. Northall, 1847]

MACBETH   Wherefore was that cry?
SEYTON   The Queen, my lord, is dead, and I—
MACBETH   She should have died hereafter, but she'll keep;
And perhaps tomorrow I shall have time to weep.
Tomorrow—and tomorrow—and tomorrow—
Ay, that's well thought of—I've a note to pay,
And the last recorded dollar to me lent,
Was yesterday in whiskey-punches[1] spent!
Out, out, short candle! For burn brightly as you may,
You cannot burn much longer anyway.
Life's but a walking shadow—or a poor player at most—
Who murders Hamlet once, and then is cast the ghost.

Enter OFFICER, *with bill, R.*

MACBETH   How now, thy message? Let not thy tongue stand still.
OFFICER   As I stood looking at my watch upon the hill,
   A cartman bade me give you this little bill,
   For a load that he brought you of Birnam's wood.
MACBETH   Liar! Slave!
OFFICER [*Kneels.*]   I could not have misunderstood;
   And if it be not so, why, take my head and thump it—
   I'll swear I saw him at your door but just now dump it.
MACBETH   If that thou liest and deceivest me,
   I'll have thee hung alive upon a tree,
   A thing for rooks and daws[2] to pick at,
   And men and women to turn sick at.   *Exit Officer. R.*

[5.8, By Francis Talfourd, 1850]

MACDUFF   Then yield, beast, and to badger ye
   We'll have you in a traveling menagerie,
   Stirred up between the bars with heartless poles,
   Or poked at by the ladies' parasols!
   And o'er it thus inscribe, for want of betterer,
   "Here may you see the live"—you know—*et cetera,*
   Adding moreover, "He's put here because

1. mixed drinks containing whiskey.
2. large and small crows.

He led a life he *didn't ought to was!*"

MACBETH Have you been draining cups of whiskey toddy,
That thus you boast? No, no, before my body
I throw my shield!

MACDUFF Hallo! That's not a bad one!

MACBETH I mean I should have thrown it, if I had one,
At it like one o'clock.[1] Lay on, Macduff,
Perhaps you'll sing out when you've had enough.

They fight in the extreme of melodrama; a pause.

MACDUFF Why, you're sewn up. (*To audience*) I'll into him now pitch.

MACBETH No, not sewn up, I've only got one stitch.

They fight as before. Macbeth falls.

MACBETH Oh, lor! Will someone a physician run for?
For I've a strange suspicion that I'm done for! (*Dies.*)

MACDUFF Ha! Ha! My boy, hurrah! His neck I'll wring,
Cut off his head, then cut off to the king.

Enter MALCOLM, LORDS, ARMY, ATTENDANTS, *etc.*

MALCOLM There is no need for, see, the King is here!
—Refresh our soldier with a pint of beer.

*A pint of beer is brought to Macduff; he drinks and
passes it on to the army, etc.*

MACDUFF The tyrant's dead! You now the kingdom claim;
Receive the crown. (*Presenting it*)

DUNCAN *enters, comes between them, nods and winks at
them, takes the crown and places it on his own head.
They fall back in astonishment.*

DUNCAN Thank you! If it's all the same
To you, I'll wear it! (*Puts it on.*)

MALCOLM Well, this is a balker![2]
I thought you were spifflicated.[3]

DUNCAN Walker![4]
I'm not the cove,[5] my boy, so soon to die.

MACDUFF Well, well, I never!

MACBETH (*Rising to a sitting posture, and looking round.*)

1. vigorously.
2. stopper, disappointment.
3. utterly destroyed.
4. no way!
5. chap.

No more did I!
If that old cock can jest and sport his squibs[6]
After those several one-ers in the ribs,
I don't see why I shouldn't live as well,
And so here goes. (*Rises.*)
MACDUFF   I say, hallo, my swell![7]
You're an ex-Monarch, but it don't appear;
If treble-ex you'd think yourself small beer![8]
MACBETH (*To Duncan*)   I tender, sir, of course, my resignation,
                            (*They appear satisfied.*)
Since all's in train[9] for me to leave my station.
So at your feet I lay my regal diadem
Without regret, nor wish again that I had 'em.

     Enter at back BANQUO *and* LADY MACBETH, *arm-in-arm,*
     the latter with an extravagant bonnet, parasol, and shawl.
     They make their way through the army to the front.

My wife and Banquo too! This is a treat.
BANQUO   You don't down there get half enough to eat;
I didn't like it; and so, with your wife,
Gave up the ghost.
MACBETH   Died?
LADY MACBETH   No, we came to life.
MACBETH   We live at present, but how long depends
Upon the kind indulgence of our friends;
Let me entreat them but their favour give,
And kind applause, and we shall truly live!

WELCOME MSOMI

uMabatha†

Characters

MABATHA, *later* Chief Mbathazeli (Macbeth), the King's cousin
KAMADONSELA (Lady Macbeth), his wife

6. show off his sarcasms and satires.
7. fine fellow.
8. Three x's, apparently, marked a current brand of beer; **small beer**: i.e., insignificant.
9. ready, with puns on **train** and **station**.
† From Welcome Msomi, *uMabatha: An Adaptation of Shakespeare's "Macbeth"* (Praetoria: Johannesburg: Via Afrika / Skotaville Publishers, 1996). Reprinted by permission of Welcome Msomi. Copyright © by Welcome Msomi. (The "u" before Mabatha is an honorific Zulu prefix, roughly equivalent to "Mr.") Footnotes are by the editor of this Norton Critical

DANGANE / MDANGAZELI (Duncan), King
DONEBANE (Donalbain), Prince
MAKHIWANE (Malcolm), Prince
ISANGOMA 1, 2 & 3 (3 Witches), witchdoctors[1]
BHANGANE (Banquo), the King's Induna[2]
FOLOSE (Fleance), Bhangane's son
MAFUDU (Macduff), King's cousin
KAMAKHAWULANA (Lady Macduff), Mafudu's wife
INDODANA (Boy), Mafudu's son
IMBONGI the King's praise singer
HOSHWENI (Captain)
LINOLO (Lennox), attendant
ANGANO (Angus), attendant
INYANGA (Doctor), herbal doctor
ISALUKAZI (Gentlewoman), nurse
MSIMBITHI (Messenger), a messenger
3 MURDERERS
SPIRITS
WARRIORS
SWAZI IMPI[3]
WOMEN

1.3

Thunder and strong winds. Enter SANGOMA I, II & III.

SANGOMA I　Where have you been, Mngoma?[4]
SANGOMA II　I have been spitting strange spells.
SANGOMA III　What spells have you been spitting, Mngoma?
SANGOMA II　I have been spitting my venom
　To the spirits of darkness and misfortune.
SANGOMA II　Spit them Mngoma, spit so that we can hear.
SANGOMA III　Yes, spit, Mngoma, spit so that we can hear.
SANGOMA I　Elele! Elele! Elele![5]
SANGOMA II & III　Spread your venom!
SANGOMA I　I spit to the moon.
SANGOMA II & III　Spit them!
SANGOMA I　I spit to the sun so that the world becomes dark.

Edition. Welcome Msomi adapts Shakespeare's *Macbeth* into *uMabatha*, a tale of Zulu
ambition, murder, greed, and fear. *uMabatha* is based on the story of Shaka (1787–1828),
a legendary, brutal Zulu warrior who built a formidable army and created an empire in
South Africa before being murdered.
1. (I)Sangoma, usually female, are witchdoctors with powers of healing and divination.
2. chief counselor.
3. Impi(s) are warriors organized into a regiment; these come from Swaziland in South Africa.
4. diviner.
5. a cry of joy.

SANGOMA II & III   Spit them!

SANGOMA I   I spit to the sun,
So that the world becomes dark.

SANGOMA II & III   Spit! Spit! Spit your venom!

SANGOMA II   I! I will spit to the spirits of misfortune,
And spread the shadow of my venom
Between the sun and the new day.

SANGOMA III   I will spit to the wind;
My venom will cloud the clear water with blood.

(*Slow drumbeat*)

SANGOMA I   That is the sign
Mabatha is near.

ALL THREE (*Sing and dance*)   We miss the wisdom of the stones
When we shake and throw our bones.

Enter MABATHA *and* BHANGANE.

MABATHA   This day's battle
Will beat in my veins
Until my life runs out.

BHANGANE   The night is at our heels;
If we linger
Its shadow will reach Umfolosi before we do.
Hawu![6] Spirit of my father! What are these!
By the heavens above!—What are you doing here?
Speak! What are you doing?
You just stare at me, dumb as the stones,
Hissing like angry mambas.[7]

MABATHA   Speak! Who are you?

SANGOMA I (*Throwing bones*)   Mabatha! Chief of Dlamasi!

SANGOMA II (*Throwing bones*)   Mabatha! Chief of
Mkhawundeni![8]

SANGOMA III   Mabatha! The bones rattle for a mighty chief.

ALL THREE   Elele! Elele! Elele!

BHANGANE   Hawu, my friend! What is it? You shake
Like an old tree, struck by lightning,
Whose roots have lost their hold.
Why do you let the breath of these Sangomas
Blow through your branches
Like truth?
Listen to me, you serpents!
You tell my friend all that will befall him hereafter,

6. an exclamation of surprise or shock.
7. venomous African snakes.
8. The Dlamasi are the people of Macbeth's village; the Mkhawundeni are the people of
Khondo's (Cawdor's) village.

Hailing him as a chief,
But to me you are dumb.
Throw your bones for me, too, if you can.
But I want you to know
I do not beg for food like an old hungry dog.
In my eyes you are the beggars,
You are less than dirt.
Do you hear what I say?

ALL THREE   Oh, Great One!

SANGOMA I (*Throwing bones*)   You who seem so very small,
Like an ant in Mabatha's shadow,
You have your own power.

SANGOMA II (*Throwing bones*)   Your life is like an empty pool,
But soon the water will overflow.

SANGOMA III (*Throwing bones*)   Your seeds will grow to be the
tallest trees of the forest,
But your leaves will never see the light.

ALL THREE   Mabatha! Bhangane! Mabatha! Bhangane!

MABATHA   Stay, you serpents, I say, stay!
After my father's death
I know that I will be chief of Dlamasi,
But when you talk of Mkhawundeni
Your tongues are forked
Because I know Khondo is still alive.
No, these Sangomas prick our ears with thorns.
Tell me,
From which bad egg did you suck your wisdom?
Answer me!

ALL THREE   Elele! Elele! Elele!   *The Sangomas disappear.*

2.1 *Mvanencane, Mabatha's kraal.*[9]

Enter KAMADONSELA *with four* WOMEN *bearing pots on
their heads and singing. They busy themselves with
stamping corn and preparing tshwala.*[1] *Distant drumbeat.*

KAMADONSELA (*Listening*)   On the day of our victory
Came three Sangomas out of the earth
And spoke strange truths.
(*Drumbeat*) When we challenged them
With taunts, they became shadows of the night.
(*Drumbeat*) As we stood wrapped in wonder,
Mdangazeli's word was brought,

9. Mvanencane is the name of Macbeth's kraal, or enclosed village, comprised of huts.
1. traditional beer.

Hailing me as Chief of Mkhawundeni.
This title these Sangomas' bones foretold,
And further, greatest of all chiefs.
(*Drumbeat*) Let this drumbeat echo in your heart
Till I return.
—Chief of Dlamasi, when you went hence.
When you return, I welcome Khondo,
Chief of Mkhawundeni.
And more shall befall as they foretold.
But yet I fear
The gentle dove that nestles in your heart,
Where I would have the wind-swift hawk
That falls like lightning on his prey.
What can you grasp
Without the strong claws of the hawk,
And what advantage take
Without his sharp eye and his swift flight?
Yes, my Khondo,
The prey that lies in wait was meant for you.
And therefore I have called
On all the spirits of my ancestors
To breathe fire in your heart
And burn away your fears.

Enter MSIMBITHI.

What has happened?
MSIMBITHI   Mother of the Great Kraal!
KAMADONSELA   What is it? Speak, what is your news?
MISIMBITHI   Oh, Great One, I bring word
   That King Mdangazeli will visit Mvanencane today.
KAMADONSELA   What! Do you speak the truth?
MISIMBITHI   I swear this is the truth.
   My Prince Mabatha
   Follows close behind me
   To tell the news again.
   Oh, pardon me, I gasp for breath.
   This news gave my feet wings
   For they hardly touched the ground.
KAMADONSELA [*To women*]   Drown his thirst with tshwala;
   He has brought good news this day.
                    Exeunt women singing, with Msimbithi.
This messenger rolls his eyes
And gasps the name of Dangane in our kraal;
Even so will Dangane gasp his life away,
The skies crash down on him.

I call again
On all the spirits of my ancestors:
Let my heart be like the devil's thorn,
My blood of mamba's poison,
That where I strike no life returns;
Dry up my woman's tears,
And let my breasts shrivel with serpent's milk.
I call on you
To shade my eyes
And fill my ears with earth,
So none can see or hear
Iklwa,
The assegai's clean path.[2]

Enter MABATHA.

Khondo! Greatest of all warriors!
I heard your message carried on the wind.
Although the sky is red tonight,
Our tomorrow will be clear and bright.

MABATHA   Dangane, our Chief, comes here today.

KAMADONSELA   And when will he depart?

MABATHA   With the rising of the sun.

KAMADONSELA   Never will he rise again!
Khondo, I see your face
As in a still pool,
Starting from the waters.
Look and see yourself.
Walk bravely, laugh,
And welcome our great guest,
While in your hand a hissing mamba waits.
Dangane comes like a tame bull
To the slaughter-block.
Sharpen your spear,
Be ready for the sacrifice.

MABATHA   Let us think about this further.

KAMADONSELA   Yes, my Khondo,
The fruit is ripe and must be plucked,
Or else waste on the branch.

Exeunt all.

---

2. **Assegai** is a slender iron-tipped spear; **Iklwa** is a short spear.

2.4

Enter KAMADONSELA.

KAMADONSELA   The guards robbed of their senses give me
strength.   (*A dog howls.*)
Khondo is busy now. The guards
Are snoring deep in their last sleep.

(*A muffled shout from the hut*)

KAMADONSELA   I am afraid they have awakened before his work
is done.
Then this attempt will mean our death.
I left the assegai where he could not miss it.

Enter MABATHA [*with bloody hands and knife*].

MABATHA   It is done. Did you hear any sound?

KAMADONSELA   I heard the dog howl.

MABATHA   Did you cry out?

KAMADONSELA   When? Now?

MABATHA   As I left the hut.

KAMADONSELA   Who, me?

MABATHA   Wait! Who sleeps in the next hut?

KAMADONSELA   Donebane.

MABATHA   Donebane! These hands smell of death.

KAMADONSELA   It is foolish to nurse these thoughts.

MABATHA   I heard the sound of weeping in the dark,
Then someone cried, "The earth is gaping!"

KAMADONSELA   The King's sons are both asleep.

MABATHA   They called upon the spirits of their ancestors for
help;
I thought they had seen my hands, stained with blood.

KAMADONSELA   Khondo, pluck this thorn out of your mind.

MABATHA   I, too, wanted to summon the spirits of my
ancestors.

KAMADONSELA   When the rains come we cannot hold back the
flood.
If you let this dark stream rush into your mind,
It will lead to madness.

MABATHA   My eyes were blind,
The blood in my ears drummed out the watchman's cry:
"Awake! Mabatha comes to steal your life away."
A warrior's life should not end with this slow horror.

KAMADONSELA   What do you mean?

MABATHA   A voice was singing in my head,
"All your days, Mabatha,
Men will hunt you like the cowardly jackal."

KAMADONSELA   What voice did you hear?
   You make me wonder, Khondo; are you not a warrior,
   And does a warrior shake when a shadow crosses his path?
   Khondo! Khondo, why did you bring the assegai?
   It must lie with the drunken guards.
MABATHA   No! The darkness smothers me.
   I cannot go back to that foul place.
KAMADONSELA   Give me the assegai!
   The sleeping guards are harmless as their King.
   I will smear them with his blood.   *Kamadonsela exits.*

Calls from within: "Mabatha!"

MABATHA   What voice is that?
   Why do I shake like a fevered child?
   See how the sun's wound stains the sky;
   Even so this blood will stain my hands forever.

Re-enter KAMADONSELA.

KAMADONSELA   Khondo, my hands are like yours
   But my heart is firm.   (*Calls from within*)
   There is someone calling at the gate!
   Let us wash this blood from our hands.
   Come, Khondo, let us return to our hut
   And be found sleeping.   *Exit.*
MABATHA   There is no hole deep enough to hide my fear.
                   (*Calls from within*)
   All your breath cannot wake Mdangazeli now.   *Exit.*

3.3 *Mvanencane, Mabatha's kraal.*

*Sounds of feasting and rejoicing. Warriors and maidens
perform a dance, and sing the song of welcome:
"Mbathazeli has come!"
Enter* MABATHA (*as the Chief Mbathazeli*), KAMADONSELA,
HOSHWENI, LINOLO *and* ATTENDANTS.

ALL   Mbathazeli!
MABATHA   Sit now. Let our chiefs and counselors be near me.
   Let the tshwala flow;
   Attend to all their needs, my wife.

MURDERER I *appears.*

   Your face is streaked with blood!
MURDERER I   It is Bhangane's
MABATHA   You should not then come here

Where every eye can see your deed.

MURDERER I   Yes, my Chief, his breath is stopped.

MABATHA   That is well. You are, indeed, brave warriors.
And Folose lies with his father?

MURDERER I   No, Mbathazeli, Folose escaped.

MABATHA   Hawu! You have failed me. Folose still lives?

MURDERER I   It was not our aim, my Chief,
But the night's dark hand that was at fault.

MABATHA   Do you swear that Bhangane is no more?

MURDERER I   As I stand here, my Chief,
The vultures will enjoy his flesh.

MABATHA   I thank you for what you have done.
Go now, we will meet tomorrow.   *Exit Murderer I.*

KAMADONSELA   Khondo, the feast is cold
When the Chief does not drink with his guests.

MABATHA   I have not forgotten, my wife;
A pressing matter held me back.

> *The* SPIRIT OF BHANGANE *enters.*

LINOLO   Here is your place, Mbathazeli.

MABATHA   Where?

LINOLO   Here, my Chief. What is it? Why does Mbathazeli
shake?

MABATHA   All! Who did this?

ALL   What, Mbathazeli?

MABATHA [*To the Spirit*]   Do not look at me! My hands are
clean.

HOSHWENI   I think it would be wise to bid the guests farewell.
Mbathazeli is not well.

KAMADONSELA   Stay, friends. This sickness is like a cloud
That soon will pass and show the sun again.
He is often thus. If you depart
You will do him wrong. Sit and drink.

> [*Kamadonsela and Mabatha converse apart.*]

Khondo! What foolishness is this?

MABATHA   You do not know what witchcraft is practised here!

KAMADONSELA   You disappoint me, Khondo.
When all our plans have reached this height,
And all men hail you as their King,
You show your weakness and your fears to every eye.
What is it now? Why do you stare so wildly?

MABATHA   What do you say? Look! Look there!
This is witchcraft when those we know are dead
Appear once more.

The Spirit disappears.

KAMADONSELA   What do you mean?

MABATHA   I saw him sitting there!

KAMADONSELA   Khondo, there is no such thing.

MABATHA   I have killed many men in battle.
When they fell by my assegai, the earth swallowed them,
Their bones were food for ants.
Now they rise and follow us.

KAMADONSELA   Khondo, you have alarmed our guests.

MABATHA   I do forget, my wife.
—Friends and warriors,
I ask you all
To pardon me. This is a sickness.
Which means nothing to those that know me.
Come, let us drink and enjoy the feast.
Give me some tshwala. There is only one small cloud
That darkens our feast, my brother
Bhangane's absence.
Drink, my friends.

ALL   Mbathazeli!

Re-enter the SPIRIT OF BANGHANE.

MABATHA   Keep away! Keep away from me!
Why do you follow me and glare
With your dead eyes. Keep away, evil spirit!

KAMADONSELA   Khondo! Khondo, what is the matter?
Why do you disrupt our feast
With these wild words?

MABATHA   This is witchcraft!
The spirits of the dead have risen,
And you ask why I stare.
This horror turns my blood to water.

HOSHWENI   What horror, Mbathazeli?

KAMADONSELA   I beg you not to question him,
His sickness grows. I entreat you now
To leave and return to your homes.

LINOLO   Stay in peace, Great Lady.
We hope Mbathazeli soon shakes off this sickness
And is himself again.

Exeunt all except Mabatha and Kamadonsela.

KAMADONSELA   Khondo, what poisonous beetles feed on your
mind?

MABATHA   I swear by my ancestors I saw him standing there.

KAMADONSELA   It is almost day; come, Khondo,

Sleep is your only medicine.

MABATHA   Tomorrow when the sun sets
I will visit the three Sangomas.
They will make all things known to me,
Uncover all dark secrets with their bones.
I cannot now turn back;
The path behind is washed with blood
And I must climb, whatever dangers lie ahead.

KAMADONSELA   Khondo, sleep and rest will cool the fever of
your thoughts.

MABATHA   Leave me! Keep away!
You cannot see or feel
This horror that follows me.

Exit Mabatha followed by Kamadonsela.

4.1 *In the veld.*[3]

Enter SANGOMA I, II, & III [*with a pot*].

SANGOMA I   The jackal howls three times.

SANGOMA II   Three times the Tokoloshe[4] screams.

SANGOMA III   The evil bird cries three times.

SANGOMA I   Yes, Bangoma, that means it is time
To prepare our medicine in the pot.

ALL THREE (*Dancing and singing*)   It boils and boils here in the
pot,
The fire burns, the juice is hot.

SANGOMA II   Into the pot I throw the skin of
An old horned snake, a horse, and beetles,
Strong medicine to call up the spirits of our ancestors.

ALL THREE   It boils and boils here in the pot,
The fire burns, the juice is hot.

SANGOMA III   A sheep's ear and the eye of an ox,
Cow-dung mixed with the hoof of a goat,
All boil together in the pot.

ALL THREE   It boils and boils here in the pot,
The fire burns, the juice is hot.

SANGOMA I   And now the blood of an old baboon,
Slaughtered when the moon was full.

The three Sangomas sneeze.[5] *Slow beating of a drum.*

---

3. the open plain.
4. a mischievous, lascivious hairy dwarf in South African folklore.
5. a sign of divine inspiration.

I smell out a stranger approaching our circle.
ALL THREE (*Softly*)   It boils and boils here in the pot,
  The fire burns, the juice is hot.

                                          Enter MABATHA.

MABATHA   Yes, evil ones, what are you doing?
ALL THREE   Work we perform in the dark.
MABATHA   Where did you learn this wisdom?
  Answer me! You may hiss with the serpent,
  And listen to the whisper of the wind,
  But listen now to me.
SANGOMA I   Speak!
SANGOMA II   Ask!
SANGOMA III   We will answer!
SANGOMA I   Do not forget, the voices that speak through us are
    the spirits of the dead.
MABATHA   Let me hear them speak for your tongues are forked.
SANGOMA I   We will call them, they will appear.
ALL THREE   Rise! Rise from the earth!
  Awake and rise, spirits of the dead.

              Drumbeats and cries. The Sangomas perform a frenzied
                          dance and fall exhausted.
                        The FIRST SPIRIT *appears.*

FIRST SPIRIT   Mabatha! Mabatha! Mabatha!
  Beware of someone. I warn you,
  Beware of someone
  Who is of unnatural birth.
  That is all.   *Exit.*
MABATHA   I thank you for this warning. Wait
  There is more—
SANGOMAS   He will not stay. Here is another
  Greater than the first.

                            [SECOND SPIRIT] *appearing.*

SECOND SPIRIT   Mabatha! Mabatha!
  Be great as the lion who scorns
  The assegai of men.
  No ordinary warrior can match your strength.   *Exit.*
MABATHA   These are words that gladden my heart.

              Thunder and drumbeats. THIRD SPIRIT *appears.*

  What is this that rises like a mighty chief?
SANGOMAS   Be still! Listen to his words!

THIRD SPIRIT   The lionhearted Mbathazeli will be the only chief
    to reign
Until the leaves of the forest become impis and approach his
    kraal.   *Exit.*
MABATHA   Hah! These are wonders that only children dream of.
How can the leaves of Mdansane[6] grow legs and become impis?
You have poured cool water on the fire in my head.
But the thorn that pricks me still is this:
Will the sons of Bhangane
Ever grow to be chiefs?
SANGOMAS   Do not question more!
MABATHA   If you disobey
My warriors will tear out your hearts
And leave your flesh for jackal meat.
Tell me what witchcraft this is!
Which spirits do you summon now?

The Sangomas sway and chant over the pot.

SANGOMAS   Appear! Appear! Appear!
Show! Show! Show!
Shadows of the night, destroy his sight.

A ROW OF SPIRITS with identical masks appears.
The last one is the SPIRIT OF BANGHANE.

MABATHA   Who are these that appear
In number like the fingers of my hands,
One like the other,
And all like Bhangane?
Out of my sight! Be gone, evil spirits!
They all point and stare at me.
What does this mean?
And last of all is Bhangane,
Who laughs at me and mocks me.
Are these all the seeds of Bhangane
Grown to be mighty chiefs?
Answer me!

The Sangomas dance and then disappear.

MABATHA   Where are they?
Their words still echo in my ears.
Who is there?

6. a jungle region (equivalent to Birnam Wood).

Enter LINOLO.

LINOLO How can I serve you, my King?

MABATHA Did you see the three Sangomas?

LINOLO No, Mbathazeli.

MABATHA Did they not pass near you?
  Let any man who sees them kill them.
  Their breath is like the rotten smell
  That rises from the still, green pool,
  And brings a sickness with it.
  Do you bring me any news?

LINOLO Your messengers, my King, came to report.
  Mafudu has fled to Swaziland.

MABATHA Swaziland!

LINOLO Yes, great King.

MABATHA Fool, not to listen to the message of my blood!
  My thoughts were children, tortoise-slow,
  But now I will strike
  Swifter than the crouching lion
  Who smells the terror of his prey.
  I will destroy Mafudu's kraal,
  His wife, his children, all, and waste no time.
  Lead me to these warriors.   *Exeunt.*

5.1 *At Mvanencane.*

Enter INYANGA *and* ISALUKAZI.

INYANGA The moon's eye has closed
  Since first you summoned me.
  When did you last see this madness seize her?

ISALUKAZI I have attended her since
  Mbathazeli climbed his high mountain,
  And thrice have I heard her sing so strangely,
  Seen her seize the hide around her loins
  And tear it with hands and teeth
  Like some wild animal.

INYANGA No, old woman,
  My gums are too soft to chew this bone.
  We are like two old dogs
  Shivering as we guard the kraal,
  When we should be sleeping by the fireside.

Enter KAMADONSELA, *singing and playing the*
makhweyana.[7]

7. a wooden musical bow with a single string that is struck by a grass stalk.

Hush! Here she comes!
Hawu, what grief can make her wail
And sway so wildly?

ISALUKAZI   She is sick. It seems
There is a poison within her
That she must vomit out.

Kamadonsela kneels and drops the makhweyana.

INYANGA   No, this woman is not sick.
There is some animal caged within her
That fights to be free.

ISALUKAZI   That is true, my son.

KAMADONSELA   Here is blood! Here is blood!

INYANGA   What is she doing now?
Why does she rub her hands?

ISALUKAZI   She is often seen clasping her hands
And rubbing them thus.

KAMADONSELA   Khondo! It is time.
Be brave and fearless.
Why do you shake with fear
When no eyes can see your deed?
Mafudu has fled to Swaziland,
Where is his wife, where is she?
Khondo! Your weakness is an open pit
That will swallow us both.

INYANGA   Let us go! What she has spoken
Should not be uttered or heard.

ISALUKAZI   She has opened the sore,
And we have seen the poison.

INYANGA   Her guilt is a load too heavy to bear.

ISALUKAZI   It is a sorrowful sight.

INYANGA   I have not the skill to cure her sickness.

KAMADONSELA   The smell of the blood follows me.

She picks up the makhweyana and caresses it.

INYANGA   What is she doing now?

ISALUKAZI   I cannot tell. This madness is like a fever.

KAMADONSELA   Go, wash your hands;
Be not afraid. Bhangane is with his ancestors;
He cannot trouble us.   *She moves off, singing.*

INYANGA   Will she sleep now?

ISALUKAZI   Yes, the fit has left her weak.

KAMADONSELA   Someone is calling! Someone is calling!   *Exit.*

INYANGA   Strange things have happened,
But my old eyes have never seen such nights before.

Go now, old man, go and rest,
And do not speak what you have seen this night.
ISALUKAZI   I am a dumb beast. Farewell.
INYANGA   No, my father, he must find another Inyanga.
I cannot cure her sickness.
I must seek some way to leave this evil place.

5·4

Drums and chanting. The WARRIORS *at Bhanganoma near
Mvanencane perform a war dance.*
Enter MAKHIWANE, DONEBANE, MAFUDU, HOSHWENI, *and
the* SWAZI IMPI. *The two Impis engage in battle, and*
MABATHA'S *warriors are driven off. Mabatha fights
Donebane and slays him.*
MAFUDU *enters and challenges Mabatha.*

MAFUDU   I have returned! Turn and face me, murdering dog!
MABATHA   Mafudu, there is no hatred in my heart
For you. Come not near
Lest I be forced to spill your blood.
MAFUDU   You talk of spilling blood!
What about the blood of my children?
The blood of my wife?
The blood of all those dear to me.
You are not a man, Mabatha,
But a stinking dog.
MABATHA   Mafudu, to see you die
For a cause that is not your own—
MAFUDU   What do you mean?
MABATHA   Even your children died because of your ill thinking,
Fighting a battle of Mdangazeli.
Donebane, the son of Mdangazeli,
Is now food for the vultures;
His death is justified.
Only the sons of Mdangazeli
Must fight this battle—not you!
MAFUDU   Mabatha, your hands are steeped in blood
Of thousands of our people of KwaZulu[8]
That you have sent to our ancestors.
Your calabash[9] of greed
Has left thousands without kraals,
Without food, without hope.

8. name of the province in South Africa that (with Natal) is home to the Zulu nation.
9. gourd or pumpkin, the shells of which function as a vessel.

MABATHA   Stop hiding behind words;
  Fight like a man.
MAFUDU   You, Mabatha, have destroyed
  The spirit of tranquility;
  The bones of the innocent speak to me.
  They say that the vicious dog must die.
  Your time has come, Mabatha!
MABATHA   You cannot tell me anything.
  The Sangomas prophesied that Bhangane's sons
  Shall be kings, but they are all dead.
  Mafudu, you will bend like a reed
  Before my blows.
  The only warrior I fear in my life
  Is the one who came into this world
  Like a spirit from the dead.
MAFUDU   Then turn and fight.
  Mabatha! I am the one who came
  Into this world in a way unnatural,
  Like a spirit from the dead.
MABATHA   If that is so, I will not fight you, Mafudu.

> *Mabatha runs to stage right. Warriors push him down to
> stage right, and he tries to escape through other exits,
> finally being surrounded by more warriors.*

MAFUDU   You have nowhere to go, Mabatha.
MABATHA   I know now, the Sangomas' words have confirmed
  the truth.
MAFUDU   This is your day to meet your ancestors.

> *Mabatha and Mafudu fight until Mabatha is slain.*
> MAKHIWANE, *who enters with a group of* WARRIORS,
> *rejoices at the death of Mabatha.*
> *Makhiwane congratulates Mafudu.*

MAKHIWANE   Warriors! Brave warriors!
  What you have done this day
  Will always make you honoured
  In my father's land,
ALL   Mntwana![1]
MAKHIWANE   The dog who snarled and showed his teeth
  Is dead. And the evil one, his wife,
  Has taken her own life.
ALL   Mntwana!
MAKHIWANE   All those loyal warriors who fled
  From the tyrant's cruel hand

1. Prince.

Can return and live in peace.
The spear has broken.

> *He throws the spear into the ground. Makhiwane is crowned the new king.*

ALL   Mntwana!
Makhiwane, son of Mdangazeli,
Makhiwane, son of Mdangazeli,
Makhiwane, son of Mdangazeli,

> *Drums and chanting. Warriors exeunt, led by Makhiwane.*

CRITICISM

SIMON FORMAN

[Eyewitness Account of *Macbeth*, 1611]†

In *Macbeth* at the Globe, 1610,[1] the 20 of April, Saturday, there was to be observed first how Macbeth and Banquo, two noblemen of Scotland, riding through a wood,[2] there stood before them three women fairies or nymphs,[3] and saluted Macbeth, saying three times unto him, "Hail Macbeth, King of Codon,[4] for thou shalt be a king, but shall beget no kings, etc" [1.3.50ff.]. Then said Banquo, "What, all to Macbeth and nothing to me?" "Yes," said the nymphs, "Hail to thee, Banquo, thou shalt beget kings, yet be no king" [1.3.68]. And so they departed and came to the court of Scotland, to Duncan, King of Scots, and it was in the days of Edward the Confessor. And Duncan bade them both kindly welcome, and made Macbeth forthwith Prince of Northumberland, and sent him home to his own castle,[5] and appointed Macbeth to provide for him,[6] for he would sup with him the next day at night, and did so. And Macbeth contrived to kill Duncan, and through the persuasion of his wife did that night murder the King in his own castle, being his guest. And there were many prodigies[7] seen that night and the day before. And when Macbeth had murdered the King, the blood on his hands could not be washed off by any means, nor from his wife's hands, which handled the bloody daggers in hiding them, by which means they became both much amazed and affronted.[8] The murder being known, Duncan's two sons fled, the one to England, the [other to] Wales, to save

† From Forman's *Booke of Plaies* (1611), which is at Oxford University (MS Ashmole 208). Reprinted by permission of Oxford University Press. The NCE editor has modernized the transcription by E. K. Chambers, *William Shakespeare: A Study of Facts and Problems*, (Oxford: Clarendon Press, 1930; rpt. 1951), 2: 337–38. Footnotes are by the editor of this Norton Critical Edition. References to act, scene, and line numbers in this Norton Critical Edition have been added in brackets. The earliest eyewitness account of the play belongs to Simon Forman, a doctor and astrologer, who made notes on four Shakespeare plays he saw at the Globe in the spring of 1611. Forman's reminiscence, demonstrably faulty in parts, nevertheless raises intriguing questions about the original performance, particularly its staging.

1. An error for 1611 (April 20 was a Saturday in 1611, not 1610).
2. Did Banquo and Macbeth ride horses onto a stage imagined as a wood rather than a heath? Probably not; Forman may be remembering an illustration in Holinshed's 1577 edition of the *Chronicles*, which shows Macbeth and Banquo on horseback meeting the witches in front of a tree.
3. The description possibly conflicts with the "black and midnight hags" (4.1.48) of Shakespeare's play.
4. Thane of Cawdor (another error).
5. Forman misrecalls the naming of Malcolm Prince of Cumberland (1.4.38–40). Malcolm does not return to his own castle in the play but accompanies the King to Macbeth's castle at Inverness.
6. Duncan.
7. marvels, portents.
8. ashamed. Forman recalls unwashable blood on the hands, a striking stage effect in apparent contradiction to the surviving text.

themselves. They being fled, they were supposed guilty of the murder of their father, which was nothing so. Then was Macbeth crowned king, and then he for fear of Banquo, his old companion, that he should beget kings but be no king himself, he contrived the death of Banquo, and caused him to be murdered on the way as he rode. The next night, being at supper with his noblemen whom he had bid to a feast to the which also Banquo should have come, he began to speak of noble Banquo and to wish that he were there. And as he thus did, standing up to drink a carouse to him, the ghost of Banquo came and sat down in his chair behind him.[9] And he, turning about to sit down again, saw the ghost of Banquo, which fronted[1] him so, that he fell into a great passion of fear and fury, uttering many words about his murder, by which, when they heard that Banquo was murdered, they suspected Macbeth.

Then Macduff fled to England to the King's son, and so they raised an army and came into Scotland and at Dunsinane overthrew Macbeth. In the meantime, while Macduff was in England, Macbeth slew Macduff's wife and children, and after in the battle Macduff slew Macbeth.

Observe also how Macbeth's queen did rise in the night in her sleep, and walk, and talked and confessed all, and the Doctor noted her words.

SAMUEL JOHNSON

Miscellaneous Observations on the Tragedy of Macbeth†

Act 1, Scene 1: Enter three Witches.

In order to make a true estimate of the abilities and merit of a writer it is always necessary to examine the genius of his age and the opinions of his contemporaries. A poet who should now make the whole action of his tragedy depend upon enchantment and produce the chief events by the assistance of supernatural agents would be censured as transgressing the bounds of probability. He would be banished from the theatre to the nursery and condemned to write fairy tales instead of tragedies. But a survey of the notions that prevailed at the time when this play was written will prove that Shake-

9. A possible indication of the original staging and its powerful dramatic effect.
1. confronted.
† From Samuel Johnson, *Miscellaneous Observations on the Tragedy of Macbeth* (London, 1745), 1–2, 4–6, 22–23, 44–47, 58–59. Footnotes are by the editor of this Norton Critical Edition. Spelling and punctuation have also been modernized by the editor. References to act scene, and line numbers in this Norton Critical Edition have been added in brackets.

speare was in no danger of such censures, since he only turned the system that was then universally admitted to his advantage, and was far from overburdening the credulity of his audience.

The reality of witchcraft or enchantment—which, though not strictly the same, are confounded in this play—has in all ages and countries been credited by the common people, and in most by the learned themselves. These phantoms have indeed appeared more frequently in proportion as the darkness of ignorance has been more gross; but it cannot be shown that the brightest gleams of knowledge have at any time been sufficient to drive them out of the world. The time in which this kind of credulity was at its height seems to have been that of the Holy War,[1] in which the Christians imputed all their defeats to enchantments or diabolical opposition, as they ascribed their success to the assistance of their military saints.

* * *

The Reformation did not immediately arrive at its meridian,[2] and though day was gradually increasing upon us, the goblins of witchcraft still continued to hover in the twilight. In the time of Queen Elizabeth was the remarkable trial of the witches of Warbois, whose conviction is still commemorated in an annual sermon at Huntingdon.[3] But in the reign of King James, in which this tragedy was written, many circumstances concurred to propagate and confirm this opinion. The King, who was much celebrated for his knowledge, had before his arrival in England not only examined in person a woman accused of witchcraft, but had given a very formal account of the practices and illusions of evil spirits, the compacts of witches, the ceremonies used by them, the manner of detecting them, and the justice of punishing them, in his dialogues of *Daemonologie*, written in the Scottish dialect and published at Edinburgh.[4] This book was soon after his accession reprinted at London, and as the ready way to gain K. James's favor was to flatter his speculations, the system of *Daemonologie* was immediately adopted by all who desired either to gain preferment or not to lose it. Thus the doctrine of witchcraft was very powerfully inculcated, and as the greatest part of mankind have no other reason for their opinions than that they are in fashion, it cannot be doubted but this persuasion made a rapid progress, since vanity and credulity cooperated in its favor and it had a

1. The Crusades (1095–1281), a series of expeditions from Western Christendom to reclaim Eastern holy lands from Islamic rule.
2. midday position, highest point.
3. Hysterical girls in the Throgmorton family of Warbois in the country of Huntingdon accused an old woman, evidently ugly and half-witted, of bewitching them. On 7 April 1593, the woman, Alice Samuels, her husband, and their daughter were executed.
4. *Daemonologie* first appeared in 1597 (see the excerpt on pp. 144–48 in this edition); two publishers in London brought out editions of the book in 1603.

tendency to free cowardice from reproach. The infection soon reached the Parliament, who in the first year of King James made a law by which it was enacted (Ch. XII): That (1) "if any person shall use any invocation or conjuration of any evil or wicked spirit; (2) or shall consult, covenant with, entertain, employ, feed or reward any evil or cursed spirit to or for any intent or purpose; (3) or take up any dead man, woman or child out of the grave, or the skin, bone, or any part of the dead person, to be employed or used in any manner of witchcraft, sorcery, charm, or enchantment; (4) or shall use, practice or exercise any sort of witchcraft, sorcery, charm, or enchantment; (5) whereby any person shall be destroyed, killed, wasted, consumed, pined, or lamed in any part of the body; (6) that every such person being convicted shall suffer death."[5]

Thus, in the time of Shakespeare was the doctrine of witchcraft at once established by law and by the fashion, and it became not only unpolite but criminal to doubt it; and as prodigies are always seen in proportion as they are expected, witches were every day discovered, and multiplied so fast in some places that Bishop Hall mentions a village in Lancashire where their number was greater than that of the houses. The Jesuits and sectaries took advantage of this universal error and endeavoured to promote the interest of their parties by pretended cures of persons afflicted by evil spirits, but they were detected and exposed by the clergy of the established Church.[6]

Upon this general infatuation Shakespeare might be easily allowed to found a play, especially since he has followed with great exactness such histories as were then thought true; nor can it be doubted that the scenes of enchantment, however they may now be ridiculed, were both by himself and his audience thought awful and affecting.

[Act 1, Scene 7]

The arguments by which Lady Macbeth persuades her husband to commit the murder afford a proof of Shakespeare's knowledge of human nature. She urges the excellence and dignity of courage, a glittering idea which has dazzled mankind from age to age, and animated sometimes the housebreaker and sometimes the conqueror; but this sophism Macbeth has forever destroyed by distinguishing true from false fortitude in a line and a half, of which it may almost be said that they ought to bestow immortality on the author, though all his other productions had been lost:

> I dare do all that may become a man,
> Who dares do more is none. [1.7.46–47]

---

5. Johnson cites "A.. Act against Conjuration, Witchcraft, and Dealing with Evil and Wicked Spirits," 1604.
6. Johnson here articulates the standard anti-Catholic position, also evident in James I's *Daemonologie*.

This topic, which has been always employed with too much success, is used in this scene with peculiar propriety, to a soldier by a woman. Courage is the distinguishing virtue of a soldier, and the reproach of cowardice cannot be borne by any man from a woman without great impatience.

She then urges the oaths by which he had bound himself to murder Duncan, another art of sophistry by which men have sometimes deluded their consciences and persuaded themselves that what would be criminal in others is virtuous in them. This argument Shakespeare, whose plan obliged him to make Macbeth yield, has not confuted, though he might easily have shown that a former obligation could not be vacated by a latter.

Act 4, Scene 1

As this is the chief scene of enchantment in the play, it is proper in this place to observe with how much judgment Shakespeare has selected all the circumstances of his infernal ceremonies, and how exactly he has conformed to common opinions and traditions.

> Thrice the brinded cat hath mew'd. [4.1.1]

The usual form in which familiar spirits are reported to converse with witches is that of a cat. A witch who was tried about half a century before the time of Shakespeare had a cat named Rutterkin, as the spirit of one of those witches was Grimalkin; and when any mischief was to be done she used to bid Rutterkin, "go and fly!" But once, when she would have sent Rutterkin to torment a daughter of the Countess of Rutland, instead of going or flying he only cried "Mew," from which she discovered that the lady was out of his power—the power of witches being not universal but limited, as Shakespeare has taken care to inculcate.

> Though his bark cannot be lost,
> Yet it shall be tempest tost. [1.3.25–26]

The common afflictions which the malice of witches produced was melancholy, fits, and loss of flesh, which are threatened by one of Shakespeare's witches.

> Weary sev'nnights nine times nine
> Shall he dwindle, peak, and pine. [1.3.24–25]

It was likewise their practice to destroy the cattle of their neighbors, and the farmers have to this day many ceremonies to secure their cows and other cattle from witchcraft; but they seem to have been most suspected of malice against swine. Shakespeare has accordingly made one of his witches declare that she has been "killing swine," and Dr Harsnett[7] observes that about that time a sow could not be ill of the measles, nor a girl of the sullens,[8] but some old woman was charged with witchcraft.

> Toad, that under the cold stone
> Days and nights has forty-one
> Swelter'd venom sleeping got,
> Boil thou first i'th'charmed pot. [4.1.6–9]

Toads have likewise long lain under the reproach of being by some means accessory to witchcraft, for which reason Shakespeare in the first scene of this play calls one of the spirits "Paddock" or toad, and now takes care to put a toad first into the pot. When Vaninus[9] was seized at Toulouse there was found at his lodgings *ingens bufo vitro inclusus*, "a great toad shut in a vial," upon which those that prosecuted him, *Veneficium exprobrabant* ["they were exuding venom"], charged him, I suppose, with witchcraft

> Fillet of a fenny snake
> In the cauldron boil and bake;
> Eye of newt and toe of frog
> . . . .
> For a charm, etc. [4.1.12ff.]

The propriety of these ingredients may be known by consulting the books *De Viribus Animalium* and *De Mirabilibus Mundi,* ascribed to Albertus Magnus,[1] in which the reader who has time and credulity may discover very wonderful secrets.

> Finger of birth-strangled babe,
> Ditch-deliver'd by a drab. [4.1.30–31]

It has been already mentioned in the law against witches that they are supposed to take up dead bodies to use in enchantments, which was confessed by the woman whom King James examined, and who had of a dead body that was divided in one of their assemblies two fingers for her share. It is observable that Shakespeare, on this great occasion which involves the fate of a king, multiplies all the circumstances of horror. The babe whose finger is used must be strangled in its birth; the grease must not only be human, but must have dropped from a gibbet,[2] the gibbet of a murderer; and even the sow

7. Archbishop Samuel Harsnett (1561–1631) wrote several works exposing fraudulent possessions and exorcisms, including *A Declaration of Egregious Popish Impostures* (1603), which Shakespeare drew upon for *King Lear.*
8. fits of melancholy.
9. A pantheist, Giulio Cesare (or Lucilio Vanini), was convicted as an atheist and burned at the stake in 1619 in Toulouse, in southern France.
1. Albert the Great (1206–1280), scientist, philosopher, theologian, and Dominican priest.
2. gallows, structure for hanging.

whose blood is used must have offended nature by devouring her own farrow.[3] These are touches of judgment and genius.

[Act 5, Scene 5]

She should have died hereafter,
There would have been a time for such a word. [5.5.17–18]

This passage has very justly been suspected of being corrupt. It is not apparent for what "word" there would have been a "time," and that there would or would not be a "time" for any "word" seems not a consideration of importance sufficient to transport Macbeth into the following exclamation. I read, therefore:

She should have died hereafter.
There would have been a time for—such a world!—
Tomorrow, etc.

It is a broken speech in which only part of the thought is expressed and may be paraphrased thus: "The Queen is dead." Macbeth: "Her death should have been deferred to some more peaceful hour; had she lived longer, there would at length have been a time for the honours due to her as a queen, and that respect which I owe her for her fidelity and love. Such is the world—such is the condition of human life, that we always think tomorrow will be happier than today, but tomorrow and tomorrow steals over us unenjoyed and unregarded, and we still linger in the same expectation to the moment appointed for our end. All these days which have thus passed away have sent multitudes of fools to the grave, who were engrossed by the same dream of future felicity, and, when life was departing from them, they were like me reckoning on tomorrow."

ELIZABETH MONTAGU

The Genius of Shakespeare†

This piece is perhaps one of the greatest exertions of the tragic and poetic powers that any age or any country has produced. Here are opened new sources of terror, new creations of fancy. The agency

3. offspring.
† From Elizabeth Montagu, *An Essay on the Writings and Genius of Shakespeare* (London, 1769), 173–74, 177–79, 183–86, 188–89, 194–95, 200–03. Spelling and punctuation have been modernized by the Norton editor. References to act, scene, and line numbers in this Norton Critical Edition have been added in brackets.

of witches and spirits excites a species of terror that cannot be affected by the operation of human agency or by any form or disposition of human things. For the known limits of their powers and capacities set certain bounds to our apprehensions; mysterious horrors, undefined terrors, are raised by the intervention of beings whose nature we do not understand, whose actions we cannot control, and whose influence we know not how to escape. Here we feel through all the faculties of the soul and to the utmost extent of her capacity. The apprehension of the interposition of such agents is the most salutary of all fears. It keeps up in our minds a sense of our connection with awful and invisible spirits to whom our most secret actions are apparent, and from whose chastisement innocence alone can defend us.

*　*　*

If the mind is to be medicated by the operations of pity and terror, surely no means are so well adapted to that end as a strong and lively representation of the agonizing struggles that precede, and the terrible horrors that follow, wicked actions. Other poets thought they had sufficiently attended to the moral purpose of the drama in making the furies pursue the perpetrated crime. Our author waives their bloody daggers in the road to guilt, and demonstrates that as soon as a man begins to hearken to ill suggestions terrors environ and fears distract him. Tenderness and conjugal love combat in the breasts of a Medea and a Herod in their purposed vengeance. Personal affection often weeps [i]n the theater while jealousy or revenge whet the bloody knife; but Macbeth's emotions are the struggles of conscience; his agonies are the agonies of remorse. They are lessons of justice and warnings to innocence. I do not know that any dramatic writer except Shakespeare has set forth the pangs of guilt separate from the fear of punishment. Clytemnestra is represented by Euripides[1] as under great terrors on account of the murder of Agamemnon, but they arise from fear not repentance. It is not the memory of the assassinated husband which haunts and terrifies her but an apprehension of vengeance from his surviving son; when she is told Orestes is dead her mind is again at ease. It must be allowed that on the Grecian stage it is the office of the chorus to moralize, and to point out on every occasion the advantages of virtue over vice. But how much less affecting are their animadversions than the testimony of the person concerned!

*　*　*

1. Greek playwright, fifth century B.C.E. [Editor's note].

Our author has so tempered the constitutional character of Macbeth by infusing into it the milk of human kindness and a strong tincture of honor, as to make the most violent perturbation and pungent remorse naturally attend on those steps to which he is led by the force of temptation. Here we must commend the poet's judgment and his invariable attention to consistency of character. But more amazing is the art with which he exhibits the movement of the human mind and renders audible the silent march of thought, traces its modes of operation in the course of deliberating—the pauses of hesitation and the final act of decision, shows how reason checks and how the passions impel, and displays to us the trepidations that precede and the horrors that pursue acts of blood. No species of dialogue but that which a man holds with himself could effect this. The soliloquy has been permitted to all dramatic writers, but its true use has been understood only by our author, who alone has attained to a just imitation of nature in this kind of self-conference.

It is certain men do not tell themselves who they are and whence they came; they neither narrate nor declaim in the solitude of the closet, as Greek and French writers represent. Here then is added to the drama an imitation of the most difficult and delicate kind, that of representing the internal process of the mind in reasoning and reflecting. And it is not only a difficult but a very useful art, as it best assists the poet to expose the anguish of remorse, to repeat every whisper of the internal monitor, conscience, and upon occasion to lend her a voice "to amaze the guilty and appall the free." As a man is averse to expose his crimes and discover the turpitude of his actions even to the faithful friend and trusty confidant, it is more natural for him to breathe in soliloquy the dark and heavy secrets of the soul than to utter them to the most intimate associate. The conflicts in the bosom of Macbeth before he committed the murder could not by any other means have been so well exposed. He entertains the prophecy of his future greatness with complacency, but the very idea of the means by which he is to attain it shocks him to the highest degree.

> This supernatural soliciting
> Cannot be ill; cannot be good. If ill,
> Why hath it giv'n me the earnest of success,
> Commencing in a truth? I'm Thane of Cawdor.
> If good, why do I yield to that suggestion,
> Whose horrid image doth unfix my hair,
> And make my seated heart knock at my ribs
> Against the use of nature? [1.3.133–40]

There is an obscurity and stiffness in part of these soliloquies, which I wish I could charge entirely to the confusion of Macbeth's mind

from the horror he feels at the thought of the murder; but our author
is too much addicted to the obscure bombast much affected by all
sorts of writers in that age.

* * *

Macbeth, in debating with himself, chiefly dwells upon the guilt,
and touches something on the danger of assassinating the King.
When he argues with Lady Macbeth, knowing her too wicked to be
affected by the one and too daring to be deterred by the other, he
urges with great propriety what he thinks may have more weight with
one of her disposition, the favor he is in with the king and the esteem
he has lately acquired of the people. In answer to her charge of
cowardice he finely distinguishes between manly courage and brutal
ferocity.

> I dare do all that may become a man;
> Who dares do more is none. [1.7.46–47]

At length, overcome rather than persuaded, he determines on the
bloody deed.

> I am settled, and bend up
> Each corp'ral agent to this terrible feat. [1.7.79–80]

How terrible to him, how repugnant to his nature, we plainly perceive when, even in the moment that he summons up the resolution
needful to perform it, horrid phantasms present themselves; murder
alarumed by his sentinel, the wolf stealing towards his design, witchcraft celebrating pale Hecate's offerings, the midnight ravisher
invading sleeping innocence seem his associates, and bloody daggers
lead him to the very chamber of the king.

* * *

The alacrity with which he attacks young Siward and his reluc-
tance to engage with Macduff, of whose blood he says he has already
had too much, complete a character which is uniformly preserved
from the opening of the fable to its conclusion. We find him ever
answering to the first idea we were made to conceive of him.

The man of honor pierces through the traitor and the assassin.
His mind loses its tranquility by guilt, but never its fortitude in danger. His crimes presented to him, even in the unreal mockery of a
vision or the harmless form of sleeping innocence, terrify him more
than all his foes in arms.

* * *

The difference between a mind naturally prone to evil and a frail one warped by force of temptations is delicately distinguished in Macbeth and his wife. There are also some touches of the pencil that mark the male and female character. When they deliberate on the murder of the King the duties of host and subject strongly plead with him against the deed. She passes over these considerations, goes to Duncan's chamber resolved to kill him, but could not do it because, she says, he resembled her father while he slept. There is something feminine in this and perfectly agreeable to the nature of the sex who, even when void of principle, are seldom entirely divested of sentiment. And thus the poet who, to use his own phrase, had overstepped the modesty of nature in the exaggerated fierceness of her character, returns back to the line and limits of humanity, and that very judiciously, by a sudden impression which has only an instantaneous effect. Thus she may relapse into her former wickedness and from the same susceptibility, by the force of other impressions, be afterwards driven to distraction. As her character was not composed of those gentle elements out of which regular repentance could be formed, it was well judged to throw her mind into the chaos of madness; and as she had exhibited wickedness in its highest degree of ferocity and atrociousness, she should be an example of the wildest agonies of remorse. As Shakespeare could most exactly delineate the human mind in its regular state of reason, so no one ever so happily caught its varying forms in the wanderings of delirium.

* * *

This piece may certainly be deemed one of the best of Shakespeare's compositions, and though it contains some faulty speeches and one whole scene [the Porter scene, 2.3.1–36] entirely absurd and improper, which art might have corrected or lopped away, yet genius, powerful genius only (wild nature's vigor working at the root!), could have produced such strong and original beauties and adapted both to the general temper and taste of the age in which it appeared.

THOMAS DAVIES

[On David Garrick's and Hannah Pritchard's Eighteenth-Century Performances]†

Is this a dagger which I see before me! [2.1.33]

Many stage critics suppose this to be one of the most difficult situations in acting. The sudden start on seeing the dagger in the air, the endeavour of the actor to seize it, the disappointment, the suggestion of its being only a vision of the disturbed fancy, the seeing it still in form most palpable, with the reasoning upon it—these are difficulties which the mind of Garrick was capable of encountering and subduing. So happy did he think himself in the exhibition of this scene [2.1], that, when he was in Italy, and requested by the Duke of Parma to give a proof of his skill in action,[1] to the admiration of that prince, he at once threw himself into the attitude of Macbeth's seeing the air-drawn dagger. The Duke desired no farther proof of Garrick's great excellence in his profession, being perfectly convinced by this specimen that he was an absolute master of it.

* * *

To know my deed 'twere best not know myself. [2.2.76]

"Whilst I am conscious of having committed this murder, I cannot but be miserable; I have no remedy but in the total forgetfulness of the deed, or, to speak more plainly, in the loss of my senses."

The merit of this scene [2.2] transcends all panegyric. Amongst the many discourses which from the earliest time to the present hour have been composed on the subject of murder, it will be difficult to find so powerful a dissuasive or dehortation[2] from that dreadful crime as the tragedy of *Macbeth* exhibits. In drawing the principal character of the play, the author has deviated somewhat from history, but by abating the fierceness of Macbeth's disposition he has rendered him a fitter subject for the drama. The rational and severe delight which the spectator feels from the representation of this piece proceeds in a great measure from the sensibility of the murderer, from his remorse and agonies, and from the torments he suffers in the midst of his successful villainy.

---

† From Thomas Davies, *Dramatic Miscellanies*, 3 vols. (London, 1783–84), 2: 140–41, 147–49, 166–67. Footnotes are by the editor of this Norton Critical Edition. Spelling and punctuation have been modernized by the editor. References to act, scene, and line numbers in this Norton Critical Edition have been added in brackets.
1. acting.
2. argument against.

The representation of this terrible part of the play by Garrick and Mrs. Pritchard can no more be described than I believe it can be equalled. I will not separate these performers for the merits of both were transcendent. His distraction of mind and agonizing horrors were finely contrasted by her seeming apathy, tranquility, and confidence. The beginning of the scene after the murder was conducted in terrifying whispers. Their looks and action supplied the place of words. You heard what they spoke, but you learned more from the agitation of mind displayed in their action and deportment. The poet here gives only an outline to the consummate actor. "I have done the deed!—Didst thou not hear a noise?—When?—Did you not speak" [2.214ff.]? The dark colouring given by the actor to these abrupt speeches makes the scene awful and tremendous to the auditors! The wonderful expression of heartful horror which Garrick felt when he showed his bloody hands can only be conceived and described by those who saw him!

* * *

This admirable scene [3.4] was greatly supported by the speaking terrors of Garrick's look and action. Mrs. Pritchard showed admirable art in endeavouring to hide Macbeth's frenzy from the observation of the guests by drawing their attention to conviviality. She smiled on one, whispered to another, and distantly saluted a third; in short, she practiced every possible artifice to hide the transaction that passed between her husband and the vision his disturbed imagination had raised. Her reproving and angry looks which glanced toward Macbeth at the same time were mixed with marks of inward vexation and uneasiness. When, at last, as if unable to support her feelings any longer, she rose from her feet and seized his arm and with a half-whisper of terror said, "Are you a man!" [3.4.59], she assumed a look of such anger, indignation, and contempt as cannot be surpassed.

SAMUEL TAYLOR COLERIDGE

[On *Macbeth*, 1808–19]†

Macbeth stands in contrast throughout with *Hamlet*, in the manner of opening more especially. In the latter there is a gradual ascent

---

† From *The Literary Remains of Samuel Taylor Coleridge*, ed. Henry Nelson Coleridge, vol. 2 (London: William Pickering, 1836), 235–50. Spelling and punctuation have been modernized by the Norton editor. References to act, scene, and line numbers in this Norton Critical Edition have been added in brackets.

from the simplest forms of conversation to the language of impassioned intellect—yet the intellect still remaining the seat of passion. In the former the invocation is at once made to the imagination and the emotions connected therewith. Hence the movement throughout is the most rapid of all Shakespeare's plays; and hence also, with the exception of the disgusting passage of the Porter (2.3), which I dare pledge myself to demonstrate to be an interpolation of the actors, there is not, to the best of my remembrance, a single pun or play on words in the whole drama. I have previously given an answer to the thousand times repeated charge against Shakespeare upon the subject of his punning, and I here merely mention the fact of the absence of any puns in *Macbeth* as justifying a candid doubt, at least, whether even in these figures of speech and fanciful modifications of language, Shakespeare may not have followed rules and principles that merit and would stand the test of philosophic examination. And hence, also, there is an entire absence of comedy, nay, even of irony and philosophic contemplation in *Macbeth*—the play being wholly and purely tragic.

For the same cause, there are no reasonings of equivocal morality, which would have required a more leisurely state and a consequently greater activity of mind; no sophistry of self-delusion except only that previously to the dreadful act, Macbeth mistranslates the recoilings and ominous whispers of conscience into prudential and selfish reasonings, and, after the deed done, the terrors of remorse into fear from external dangers, like delirious men who run away from the phantoms of their own brains, or, raised by terror to rage, stab the real object that is within their reach—whilst Lady Macbeth merely endeavours to reconcile his and her own sinkings of heart by anticipations of the worst and an affected bravado in confronting them. In all the rest Macbeth's language is the grave utterance of the very heart, conscience-sick, even to the last faintings of moral death. It is the same in all the other characters. The variety arises from rage, caused ever and anon by disruption of anxious thought and the quick transition of fear into it.

In *Hamlet* and *Macbeth* the scene opens with superstition, but in each it is not merely different but opposite. In the first it is connected with the best and holiest feelings; in the second, with the shadowy, turbulent, and unsanctified cravings of the individual will. Nor is the purpose the same: in the one the object is to excite, whilst in the other it is to mark a mind already excited. Superstition of one sort or another is natural to victorious generals; the instances are too notorious to need mentioning. There is so much of chance in warfare, and such vast events are connected with the acts of a single individual—the representative, in truth, of the efforts of myriads, and yet to the public, and doubtless to his own feelings, the aggregate of all—that the proper temperament for generating or receiving superstitious impressions is naturally produced. Hope, the master element of a commanding genius, meeting with an active and combining intellect, and an imagination of just that degree of vividness which disquiets and impels the soul to try to realize its images, greatly increases the creative power of the mind, and hence the images become a satisfying world of themselves, as is the case of every poet and original philosopher. But hope fully gratified, and yet the elementary basis of the passion remaining, becomes fear; and, indeed, the general, who must often feel, even though he may hide it from his own consciousness, how large a share chance had in his successes, may very naturally be irresolute in a new scene, where he knows that all will depend on his own act and election.

The Weird Sisters are as true a creation of Shakespeare's as his Ariel and Caliban, fates, furies, and materializing witches being the elements. They are wholly different from any representation of witches in the contemporary writers and yet presented a sufficient external resemblance to the creatures of vulgar prejudice to act immediately on the audience. Their characters consist in the imaginative disconnected from the good; they are the shadowy, obscure and, fearfully anomalous of physical nature, the lawless of human nature, elemental avengers without sex or kin.

*   *   *

The true reason for the first appearance of the witches is to strike the key-note of the character of the whole drama, as is proved by their reappearance in the third scene, after such an order as the King's as establishes their supernatural power of information.

*   *   *

[1.5]. Macbeth is described by Lady Macbeth so as at the same time to reveal her own character. Could he have everything he wanted, he would rather have it innocently—ignorant, as, alas, how many of us are, that he who wishes a temporal end for itself does in truth will the means, and hence the danger of indulging fancies. Lady Macbeth, like all in Shakespeare, is a class individualized; of high rank, left much alone, and feeding herself with day-dreams of ambition, she mistakes the courage of fantasy for the power of bearing the consequences of the realities of guilt. Hers is the mock fortitude of a mind deluded by ambition; she shames her husband with a superhuman audacity of fancy which she cannot support, but sinks in the season of remorse, and dies in suicidal agony. Her speech, "Come, all you spirits / That tend on mortal thoughts, unsex me here" [1.5.38ff.], etc., is that of one who had habitually familiarized her

imagination to dreadful conceptions, and was trying to do so still
more. Her invocations and requisitions are all the false efforts of a
mind accustomed only hitherto to the shadows of the imagination,
vivid enough to throw the everyday substances of life into shadow,
but never as yet brought into direct contact with their own corre-
spondent realities. She evinces no womanly life, no wifely joy, at the
return of her husband, no pleased terror at the thought of his past
dangers. Whilst Macbeth bursts forth naturally, "My dearest love"
[1.5.56], and shrinks from the boldness with which she presents his
own thoughts to him. With consummate art she at first uses as incen-
tives the very circumstances, Duncan's coming to their house, etc.,
which Macbeth's conscience would most probably have adduced to
her as motives of abhorrence or repulsion. Yet Macbeth is not prepared: "We will speak further" [1.5.69].

   [1.6] The lyrical movement with which this scene opens, and the
free and unengaged mind of Banquo, loving nature and rewarded in
the love itself, form a highly dramatic contrast with the laboured
rhythm and hypocritical over-much of Lady Macbeth's welcome, in
which you cannot detect a ray of personal feeling, but all is thrown
upon the "dignities," the general duty.

WILLIAM HAZLITT

[Characters in *Macbeth*]†

   Macbeth and *Lear, Othello* and *Hamlet,* are usually reckoned
Shakespeare's four principal tragedies. *Lear* stands first for the profound intensity of the passion; *Macbeth* for the wildness of the imagination and the rapidity of the action; *Othello* for the progressive
interest and powerful alternations of feeling; *Hamlet* for the refined
development of thought and sentiment. If the force of genius shown
in each of these works is astonishing, their variety is not less so. They
are like different creations of the same mind, not one of which has
the slightest reference to the rest. This distinctness and originality
is indeed the necessary consequence of truth and nature. Shakespeare's genius alone appeared to possess the resources of nature.
He is "your only *tragedy-maker*." His plays have the force of things
upon the mind. What he represents is brought home to the bosom

---

† From William Hazlitt, *Characters of Shakespear's Plays* (London, 1817), 15–32. Footnotes
  are by the editor of this Norton Critical Edition. Spelling and punctuation have been
  modernized by the editor. References to act, scene, and line numbers in this Norton
  Critical Edition have been added in brackets.

as a part of our experience, implanted in the memory as if we had known the places, persons, and things of which he treats. *Macbeth* is like a record of a preternatural and tragical event. It has the rugged severity of an old chronicle with all that the imagination of the poet can engraft upon traditional belief. The castle of Macbeth, round which "the air smells wooingly," and where "the temple-haunting martlet" builds [1.6.4ff.] has a real subsistence in the mind; the Weïrd Sisters meet us in person on "the blasted heath" [1.3.78]; the "air-drawn dagger"[3.4.63] moves slowly before our eyes; the "gracious Duncan" [3.6.3], the "blood-boultered Banquo" [4.1.123] stand before us; all that passed through the mind of Macbeth passes, without the loss of a tittle, through ours. All that could actually take place, and all that is only possible to be conceived, what was said and what was done, the workings of passion, the spells of magic, are brought before us with the same absolute truth and vividness.

Shakespeare excelled in the openings of his plays; that of *Macbeth* is the most striking of any. The wildness of the scenery, the sudden shifting of the situations and characters, the bustle, the expectations excited, are equally extraordinary. From the first entrance of the Witches and the description of them when they meet Macbeth,

> What are these
> So wither'd and so wild in their attire,
> That look not like the inhabitants of th'earth
> And yet are on't? [1.3.40–43]

the mind is prepared for all that follows.

This tragedy is alike distinguished for the lofty imagination it displays and for the tumultuous vehemence of the action, and the one is made the moving principle of the other. The overwhelming pressure of preternatural agency urges on the tide of human passion with redoubled force. Macbeth himself appears driven along by the violence of his fate like a vessel drifting before a storm; he reels to and fro like a drunken man; he staggers under the weight of his own purposes and the suggestions of others; he stands at bay with his situation, and from the superstitious awe and breathless suspense into which the communications of the Weïrd Sisters throw him, is hurried on with daring impatience to verify their predictions, and with impious and bloody hand to tear aside the veil which hides the uncertainty of the future. He is not equal to the struggle with fate and conscience. He now "bends up each corporal instrument to the terrible feat" [1.7.79–80]; at other times his heart misgives him, and he is cowed and abashed by his success. "The deed, no less than the attempt, confounds him" [2.2.10–11]. His mind is assailed by the stings of remorse, and full of "preternatural solicitings" [1.3.133]. His speeches and soliloquies are dark riddles on human life, baffling solution, and entangling him in their labyrinths. In thought he is absent and perplexed, sudden and desperate in act, from a distrust of his own resolution. His energy springs from the anxiety and agitation of his mind. His blindly rushing forward on the objects of his ambition and revenge, or his recoiling from them, equally betrays the harassed state of his feelings.

This part of his character is admirably set off by being brought in connection with that of Lady Macbeth, whose obdurate strength of will and masculine firmness give her the ascendancy over her husband's faltering virtue. She at once seizes on the opportunity that offers for the accomplishment of all their wished-for greatness, and never flinches from her object till all is over. The magnitude of her resolution almost covers the magnitude of her guilt. She is a great bad woman whom we hate, but whom we fear more than we hate. She does not excite our loathing and abhorrence like Regan and Goneril.[1] She is only wicked to gain a great end; and is perhaps more distinguished by her commanding presence of mind and inexorable self-will, which do not suffer her to be diverted from a bad purpose, when once formed, by weak and womanly regrets, than by the hardness of her heart or want of natural affections. The impression which her lofty determination of character makes on the mind of Macbeth is well described where he exclaims,

> Bring forth men children only;
> For thy undaunted mettle should compose
> Nothing but males! [1.7.72–74]

Nor do the pains she is at to "screw his courage to the sticking-place" [1.7.60], the reproach to him not to be "lost so poorly in himself" [2.2.74–5], the assurance that "a little water clears them of this deed" [2.2.70], show anything but her greater consistency in depravity. Her strong-nerved ambition furnishes ribs of steel to "the sides of his intent" [1.7.26], and she is herself wound up to the execution of her baneful project with the same unshrinking fortitude in crime that in other circumstances she would probably have shown patience in suffering. The deliberate sacrifice of all other considerations to the gaining "for their future days and nights sole sovereign sway and masterdom" [1.5.67–68] by the murder of Duncan is gorgeously expressed in her invocation on hearing of "his fatal entrance under her battlements" [1.5.37–38]:

> Come all you spirits
> That tend on mortal thoughts, unsex me here:
> And fill me, from the crown to th'toe, top-full

1. wicked daughters of Shakespeare's King Lear.

Of direst cruelty; make thick my blood,
Stop up the access and passage to remorse,
That no compunctious visitings of nature
Shake my fell purpose, nor keep peace between
The effect and it. Come to my woman's breasts,
And take my milk for gall, you murthering ministers,
Wherever in your sightless substances
You wait on nature's mischief. Come, thick night!
And pall thee in the dunnest smoke of hell,
That my keen knife see not the wound it makes,
Nor heav'n peep through the blanket of the dark,
To cry, hold, hold! [1.5.38–52]

When she first hears that "Duncan comes there to sleep" she is so overcome by the news, which is beyond her utmost expectations, that she answers the messenger, "Thou'rt mad to say it" [1.5.29]; and on receiving her husband's account of the predictions of the Witches, conscious of his instability of purpose, and that her presence is necessary to goad him on to the consummation of his promised greatness, she exclaims,

Hie thee hither,
That I may pour my spirits in thine ear,
And chastise with the valour of my tongue
All that impedes thee from the golden round,
Which fate and metaphysical aid doth seem
To have thee crowned withal. [1.5.23–28]

This swelling exultation and keen spirit of triumph, this uncontrollable eagerness of anticipation, which seems to dilate her form and take possession of all her faculties, this solid, substantial, flesh-and-blood display of passion, exhibit a striking contrast to the cold, abstracted, gratuitous, servile malignity of the Witches, who are equally instrumental in urging Macbeth to his fate for the mere love of mischief, and from a disinterested delight in deformity and cruelty. They are hags of mischief, obscene panders to iniquity, malicious from their impotence of enjoyment, enamoured of destruction, because they are themselves unreal, abortive, half-existences, and who become sublime from their exemption from all human sympathies and contempt for all human affairs, as Lady Macbeth does by the force of passion! Her fault seems to have been an excess of that strong principle of self-interest and family aggrandizement, not amenable to the common feelings of compassion and justice, which is so marked a feature in barbarous nations and times. A passing reflection of this kind, on the resemblance of the sleeping king to her father, alone prevents her from slaying Duncan with her own hand.

In speaking of the character of Lady Macbeth, we ought not to pass over Mrs. Siddons's manner of acting that part.[2] We can conceive of nothing grander. It was something above nature. It seemed almost as if a being of a superior order had dropped from a higher sphere to awe the world with the majesty of her appearance. Power was seated on her brow, passion emanated from her breast as from a shrine; she was tragedy personified. In coming on in the sleeping-scene, her eyes were open but their sense was shut. She was like a person bewildered and unconscious of what she did. Her lips moved involuntarily, all her gestures were involuntary and mechanical. She glided on and off the stage like an apparition. To have seen her in that character was an event in everyone's life, not to be forgotten.

The dramatic beauty of the character of Duncan, which excites the respect and pity even of his murderers, has been often pointed out. It forms a picture of itself. An instance of the author's power of giving a striking effect to a common reflection by the manner of introducing it occurs in a speech of Duncan, complaining of his having been deceived in his opinion of the Thane of Cawdor, at the very moment that he is expressing the most unbounded confidence in the loyalty and services of Macbeth.

> There is no art
> To find the mind's construction in the face;
> He was a gentleman, on whom I built
> An absolute trust.
> O worthiest cousin, (*addressing himself to Macbeth.*)
> The sin of my ingratitude e'en now
> Was great upon me, etc. [1.4.12–17]

Another passage to show that Shakespeare lost sight of nothing that could in any way give relief or heightening to his subject, is the conversation which takes place between Banquo and Fleance immediately before the murder-scene of Duncan.

> *Banquo.* How goes the night, boy?
> *Fleance.* The moon is down: I have not heard the clock.
> *Banquo.* And she goes down at twelve.
> *Fleance.* I take't, 'tis later, sir.
> *Banquo.* Hold, take my sword. There's husbandry in heav'n,
> Their candles are all out.—
> A heavy summons lies like lead upon me,
> And yet I would not sleep; merciful powers,
> Restrain in me the cursed thoughts that nature
> Gives way to in repose. [2.1.1–9]

2. Hazlitt here pays tribute to Sarah Siddons's celebrated portrayal of Lady Macbeth; see Siddon's own reflections, reprinted on pp. 232–37 in this edition.

In like manner, a fine idea is given of the gloomy coming on of evening, just as Banquo is going to be assassinated.

> Light thickens and the crow
> Makes wing to the rocky wood. [3.2.53–54]
> ....
> Now spurs the lated traveller apace
> To gain the timely inn. [3.3.6–7]

Macbeth (generally speaking) is done upon a stronger and more systematic principle of contrast than any other of Shakespeare's plays. It moves upon the verge of an abyss, and is a constant struggle between life and death. The action is desperate and the reaction is dreadful. It is a huddling together of fierce extremes, a war of opposite natures which of them shall destroy the other. There is nothing but what has a violent end or violent beginnings. The lights and shades are laid on with a determined hand; the transitions from triumph to despair, from the height of terror to the repose of death, are sudden and startling; every passion brings in its fellow-contrary, and the thoughts pitch and jostle against each other as in the dark. The whole play is an unruly chaos of strange and forbidden things, where the ground rocks under our feet. Shakespeare's genius here took its full swing, and trod upon the farthest bounds of nature and passion. This circumstance will account for the abruptness and violent antitheses of the style, the throes and labour which run through the expression, and from defects will turn them into beauties. "So fair and foul a day I have not seen" [1.3.39], etc. "Such welcome and unwelcome news together" [4.3.139]. "Men's lives are like the flowers in their caps, dying or ere they sicken" [4.3.172–4]. "Look like the innocent flower, but be the serpent under it" [1.5.63–64]. The scene before the castle-gate follows the appearance of the Witches on the heath, and is followed by a midnight murder. Duncan is cut off betimes by treason leagued with witchcraft, and Macduff is ripped untimely from his mother's womb to avenge his death. Macbeth, after the death of Banquo, wishes for his presence in extravagant terms, "To him and all we thirst" [3.4.93], and when his ghost appears, cries out, "Avaunt and quit my sight" [3.4.95], and being gone, he is "himself again" [3.4.110]. Macbeth resolves to get rid of Macduff, that "he may sleep in spite of thunder" [4.1.86]; and cheers his wife on the doubtful intelligence of Banquo's taking off with the encouragement, "Then be thou jocund: ere the bat has flown his cloistered flight; ere to black Hecate's summons the shard-born beetle has rung night's yawning peal, there shall be done—a deed of dreadful note" [3.2.43–47]. In Lady Macbeth's speech "Had he not resembled my father as he slept, I had done't" [2.2.12–13], there is murder and filial piety together; and in urging him to fulfill his vengeance against the defenseless king, her thoughts spare the blood neither of infants nor old age. The description of the Witches is full of the same contradictory principle; they "rejoice when good kings bleed"; they are neither of the earth nor the air but both; "they should be women, but their beards forbid it" [1.3.46–48]; they take all the pains possible to lead Macbeth on to the height of his ambition, only to betray him "in deeper consequence" [1.3.128], and after showing him all the pomp of their art, discover their malignant delight in his disappointed hopes by that bitter taunt, "Why stands Macbeth thus amazedly" [4.1.125–126]? We might multiply such instances everywhere.

The leading features in the character of Macbeth are striking enough, and they form what may be thought at first only a bold, rude, Gothic outline. By comparing it with other characters of the same author we shall perceive the absolute truth and identity which is observed in the midst of the giddy whirl and rapid career of events. Macbeth in Shakespeare no more loses his identity of character in the fluctuations of fortune or the storm of passion than Macbeth in himself would have lost the identity of his person. Thus he is as distinct a being from Richard III as it is possible to imagine, though these two characters in common hands, and indeed in the hands of any other poet, would have been a repetition of the same general idea, more or less exaggerated.[3] For both are tyrants, usurpers, murderers, both aspiring and ambitious, both courageous, cruel, treacherous. But Richard is cruel from nature and constitution. Macbeth becomes so from accidental circumstances. Richard is from his birth deformed in body and mind and naturally incapable of good. Macbeth is full of "the milk of human kindness" [1.5.15], is frank, sociable, generous. He is tempted to the commission of guilt by golden opportunities, by the instigations of his wife, and by prophetic warnings. Fate and metaphysical aid conspire against his virtue and his loyalty. Richard on the contrary needs no prompter, but wades through a series of crimes to the height of his ambition from the ungovernable violence of his temper and a reckless love of mischief. He is never gay but in the prospect or in the success of his villainies: Macbeth is full of horror at the thoughts of the murder of Duncan, which he is with difficulty prevailed on to commit, and of remorse after its perpetration. Richard has no mixture of common humanity in his composition, no regard to kindred or posterity; he owns no fellowship with others, he is "himself alone" [3.1.44–45]. Macbeth is not destitute of feelings of sympathy, is accessible to pity, is even

---

3. The comparison of Shakespeare's two tyrants, *Richard III* and *Macbeth*, is an important critical exercise, perhaps beginning with Richard Whately, *Remarks on Some of the Characters of Shakespeare* (1785); see Brian Vickers, ed. *Shakespeare: The Critical Heritage*, 6 vols. (London; Boston: Routledge & Kegan Paul, 1974–81), 6: 407–29.

made in some measure the dupe of his uxoriousness, ranks the loss of friends, of the cordial love of his followers, and of his good name, among the causes which have made him weary of life, and regrets that he has ever seized the crown by unjust means, since he cannot transmit it to his posterity,

> For Banquo's issue have I fil'd my mind—
> For them the gracious Duncan have I murther'd,
> ....
> To make them kings, the seed of Banquo kings. [3.1.67–68, 72]

In the agitation of his mind, he envies those whom he has sent to peace. "Duncan is in his grave; after life's fitful fever he sleeps well" [3.2.24–25].

It is true he becomes more callous as he plunges deeper in guilt, "direness is thus rendered familiar to his slaughterous thoughts" [5.5.14], and he in the end anticipates his wife in the boldness and bloodiness of his enterprises, while she for want of the same stimulus of action, "is troubled with thick-coming fancies that rob her of her rest" [5.3.39–40], goes mad and dies. Macbeth endeavors to escape from reflection on his crimes by repelling their consequences, and banishes remorse for the past by the meditation of future mischief. This is not the principle of Richard's cruelty, which displays the wanton malice of a fiend as much as the frailty of human passion. Macbeth is goaded on to acts of violence and retaliation by necessity; to Richard, blood is a pastime.

There are other decisive differences inherent in the two characters. Richard may be regarded as a man of the world, a plotting, hardened knave, wholly regardless of everything but his own ends and the means to secure them. Not so Macbeth. The superstitions of the age, the rude state of society, the local scenery and customs, all give a wildness and imaginary grandeur to his character. From the strangeness of the events that surround him, he is full of amazement and fear, and stands in doubt between the world of reality and the world of fancy. He sees sights not shown to mortal eye, and hears unearthly music. All is tumult and disorder within and without his mind; his purposes recoil upon himself, are broken and disjointed; he is the double thrall of his passions and his evil destiny. Richard is not a character either of imagination or pathos, but of pure self-will. There is no conflict of opposite feelings in his breast. The apparitions which he sees only haunt him in his sleep; nor does he live like Macbeth in a waking dream. Macbeth has considerable energy and manliness of character, but then he is "subject to all the skyey influences." He is sure of nothing but the present moment. Richard in the busy turbulence of his projects never loses his self-possession, and makes use of every circumstance that happens as an instrument of his long-reaching designs. In his last extremity we can only regard him as a wild beast taken in the toils: while we never entirely lose our concern for Macbeth; and he calls back all our sympathy by that fine close of thoughtful melancholy—

> My way of life is fallen into the sear,
> The yellow leaf; and that which should accompany old age,
> As honor, troops of friends, I must not look to have;
> But in their stead, curses not loud but deep,
> Mouth-honor, breath, which the poor heart
> Would fain deny, and dare not. [5.3.22–28]

We can conceive a common actor to play Richard tolerably well; we can conceive no one to play Macbeth properly, or to look like a man that had encountered the Weïrd Sisters. All the actors that we have ever seen, appear as if they had encountered them on the boards of Covent Garden or Drury Lane, but not on the heath at Forres, and as if they did not believe what they had seen. The Witches of *Macbeth* indeed are ridiculous on the modern stage, and we doubt if the Furies of Aeschylus would be more respected. The progress of manners and knowledge has an influence on the stage, and will in time perhaps destroy both tragedy and comedy. Filch's picking pockets in the *Beggar's Opera* is not so good a jest as it used to be; by the force of the police and of philosophy, Lillo's murders and the ghosts in Shakespeare will become obsolete. At last, there will be nothing left, good nor bad, to be desired or dreaded, on the theatre or in real life.

A question has been started with respect to the originality of Shakespeare's Witches, which has been well answered by Mr. Lamb in his notes to the *Specimens of Early Dramatic Poetry*.[4]

> Though some resemblance may be traced between the charms in *Macbeth,* and the incantations in this play (*The Witch* of Middleton), which is supposed to have preceded it, this coincidence will not detract much from the originality of Shakespeare. His witches are distinguished from the witches of Middleton by essential differences. These are creatures to whom man or woman plotting some dire mischief might resort for occasional consultation. Those originate deeds of blood and begin bad impulses to men. From the moment that their eyes first meet with Macbeth's, he is spell-bound. That meeting sways his destiny. He can never break the fascination. These witches can hurt the body; those have power over the soul. Hecate in Middleton has a son, a low buffoon; the hags of Shake-

4. Charles Lamb (1775–1834), essayist and literary critic, first published *Specimens of English Dramatic Poets in* 1808 (Hazlitt misremembers the title).

speare have neither child of their own, nor seem to be descended from any parent. They are foul anomalies, of whom we know not whence they are sprung, nor whether they have beginning or ending. As they are without human passions, so they seem to be without human relations. They come with thunder and lightning, and vanish to airy music. This is all we know of them. Except Hecate, they have no names, which heightens their mysteriousness. The names, and some of the properties which Middleton has given to his hags, excite smiles. The Weïrd Sisters are serious things. Their presence cannot co-exist with mirth. But, in a lesser degree, the witches of Middleton are fine creations. Their power too is, in some measure, over the mind. They raise jars, jealousies, strifes, "like a thick scurf o'er life."

THOMAS DE QUINCEY

On the Knocking at the Gate in *Macbeth* [1823]†

From my boyish days I had always felt a great perplexity on one point in *Macbeth*. It was this: the knocking at the gate which succeeds to the murder of Duncan produced to my feelings an effect for which I never could account. The effect was that it reflected back upon the murder[1] a peculiar awfulness and a depth of solemnity; yet, however obstinately I endeavoured with my understanding to comprehend this, for many years I never could see *why* it should produce such an effect.

* * *

My solution is this: Murder, in ordinary cases, where the sympathy is wholly directed to the case of the murdered person, is an incident of coarse and vulgar horror; and for this reason—that it flings the interest exclusively upon the natural but ignoble instinct by which we cleave to life, an instinct which, as being indispensable to the primal law of self-preservation, is the same in kind (though different in degree) amongst all living creatures. This instinct, therefore, because it annihilates all distinctions, and degrades the greatest of men to the level of "the poor beetle that we tread on," exhibits human nature in its most abject and humiliating attitude. Such an attitude

---

† From Thomas De Quincey, *Confessions of an English Opium-Eater* (London: Walter Scott, 1886), 142–48. Footnotes are by the editor of this Norton Critical Edition. Spelling and punctuation have been modernized by the editor. References to act, scene, and line numbers in this Norton Critical Edition have been added in brackets.
1. De Quincey originally published this article in *London Magazine* (1823). *London Magazine* reads "murder" here; some later collections read "murderer."

would little suit the purposes of the poet. What then must he do? He must throw the interest on the murderer; our sympathy must be with *him* (of course, I mean a sympathy of comprehension, a sympathy by which we enter into his feelings and are made to understand them—not a sympathy[2] of pity or approbation). In the murdered person, all strife of thought, all flux and reflux of passion and of purpose, are crushed by one overwhelming panic; the fear of instant death smites him "with its petrific mace." But in the murderer, such a murderer as a poet will condescend to, there must be raging some great storm of passion—jealousy, ambition, vengeance, hatred—which will create a hell within him, and into this hell we are to look.

In *Macbeth,* for the sake of gratifying his own enormous and teeming faculty of creation, Shakespeare has introduced two murderers; and, as usual in his hands, they are remarkably discriminated. But—though in Macbeth the strife of mind is greater than in his wife, the tiger spirit not so awake, and his feelings caught chiefly by contagion from her—yet, as both were finally involved in the guilt of murder, the murderous mind of necessity is finally to be presumed in both. This was to be expressed; and on its own account, as well as to make it a more proportionable antagonist to the unoffending nature of their victim, "the gracious Duncan" [3.1.68], and adequately to expound "the deep damnation of his taking off" [1.7.20], this was to be expressed with peculiar energy. We were to be made to feel that the human nature—i.e., the divine nature of love and mercy, spread through the hearts of all creatures and seldom utterly withdrawn from man—was gone, vanished, extinct, and that the fiendish nature had taken its place. And as this effect is marvellously accomplished in the dialogues and soliloquies themselves, so it is finally consummated by the expedient under consideration; and it is to this that I now solicit the reader's attention.

If the reader has ever witnessed a wife, daughter, or sister in a fainting fit, he may chance to have observed that the most affecting moment in such a spectacle is *that* in which a sigh and a stirring announce the recommencement of suspended life. Or if the reader has ever been present in a vast metropolis on the day when some great national idol was carried in funeral pomp to his grave, and, chancing to walk near the course through which it passed, has felt powerfully, in the silence and desertion of the streets, and in the stagnation of ordinary business, the deep interest which at that moment was possessing the heart of man—if all at once he should hear the death-like stillness broken up by the sound of wheels rat-

---

2. In a note De Quincey argues against "the unscholar-like use of the word sympathy, at present so general, by which, instead of taking it in its proper sense as the act of reproducing in our minds the feelings of another, whether for hatred, indignation, love, pity, or approbation, it is made a mere synonym of the word *pity*."

tling away from the scene, and making known that the transitory vision was dissolved, he will be aware that at no moment was his sense of the complete suspension and pause in ordinary human concerns so full and affecting as at that moment when the suspension ceases and the goings-on of human life are suddenly resumed. All action in any direction is best expounded, measured, and made apprehensible by reaction. Now, apply this to the case in *Macbeth*. Here, as I have said, the retiring of the human heart and the entrance of the fiendish heart was to be expressed and made sensible. Another world has stepped in; and the murderers are taken out of the region of human things, human purposes, human desires. They are transfigured: Lady Macbeth is "unsexed"; Macbeth has forgot that he was born of woman; both are conformed to the image of devils; and the world of devils is suddenly revealed. But how shall this be conveyed and made palpable? In order that a new world may step in, this world must for a time disappear. The murderers and the murder must be insulated—cut off by an immeasurable gulf from the ordinary tide and succession of human affairs—locked up and sequestered in some deep recess; we must be made sensible that the world of ordinary life is suddenly arrested, laid asleep, tranced, racked into a dread armistice; time must be annihilated, relation to things without abolished, and all must pass self-withdrawn into a deep syncope[3] and suspension of earthly passion. Hence it is that, when the deed is done, when the work of darkness is perfect, then the world of darkness passes away like a pageantry in the clouds: the knocking at the gate is heard, and it makes known audibly that the reaction has commenced; the human has made its reflux upon the fiendish; the pulses of life are beginning to beat again; and the reestablishment of the goings-on of the world in which we live first makes up profoundly sensible of the awful parenthesis that had suspended them.

O mighty poet! Thy works are not as those of other men, simply and merely great works of art, but are also like the phenomena of nature, like the sun and the sea, the stars and the flowers, like frost and snow, rain and dew, hailstorm and thunder, which are to be studied with entire submission of our own faculties, and in the perfect faith that in them there can be no too much or too little, nothing useless or inert, but that, the farther we press in our discoveries, the more we shall see proofs of design and self-supporting arrangement where the careless eye had seen nothing but accident![4]

---

3. fainting spell.
4. The last paragraph provides an example of the Shakespeare-worship that usually disables, rather than enables, critical judgment.

SARAH SIDDONS

[On Playing Lady Macbeth]†

It was my custom to study my characters at night, when all the domestic cares and business of the day were over. On the night preceding that in which I was to appear in this part for the first time, I shut myself up, as usual, when all the family were retired, and commenced my study of Lady Macbeth. As the character is very short, I thought I should soon accomplish it. Being then only twenty years of age, I believed, as many others do believe, that little more was necessary than to get the words into my head; for the necessity of discrimination and the development of character at that time of my life had scarcely entered into my imagination. But, to proceed. I went on with tolerable composure, in the silence of the night (a night I never can forget) till I came to the assassination scene, when the horrors of the scene rose to a degree that made it impossible for me to get farther. I snatched up my candle and hurried out of the room in a paroxysm of terror. My dress was of silk and the rustling of it as I ascended the stairs to go to bed seemed to my panic-struck fancy like the movement of a spectre pursuing me. At last I reached my chamber, where I found my husband fast asleep. I clapt my candlestick down upon the table, without the power of putting the candle out, and I threw myself on my bed, without daring to stay even to take off my clothes. At peep of day I rose to resume my task; but so little did I know of my part when I appeared in it at night that my shame and confusion cured me of procrastinating my business for the remainder of my life.

About six years afterwards I was called upon to act the same character in London. By this time I had perceived the difficulty of assuming a personage with whom no one feeling of common general nature was congenial or assistant. One's own heart could prompt one to express with some degree of truth the sentiments of a mother, a daughter, a wife, a lover, a sister, etc., but, to adopt this character must be an effort of the judgment alone.

Therefore it was with the utmost diffidence, nay terror, that I undertook it, and with the additional fear of Mrs. Pritchard's[1] rep-

---

† From Thomas Campbell, *Life of Mrs. Siddons*, 2 vols. (London: Effingham Wilson, 1834), 2: 35–39, 10–12, 15–16, 20–21, 30–33. Footnotes are by the editor of this Norton Critical Edition. Spelling and punctuation have been modernized by the editor. References to act, scene, and line numbers in this Norton Critical Edition have been added in brackets. Perhaps the most celebrated Lady Macbeth, the graceful and statuesque Sarah Siddons (1755–1831) acted the role from 1781 to 1817.

1. Hannah Pritchard (1711–1768), whose angry and imposing Lady Macbeth won great admiration previously (see Davies' account, reprinted on pp. 216–17 in this edition).

utation in it before my eyes. The dreaded first night at length arrived, when, just as I had finished my toilette, and was pondering with fearfulness my first appearance in the grand fiendish part, comes Mr. Sheridan,[2] knocking at my door and insisting, in spite of all my entreaties not to be interrupted at this to me tremendous moment, to be admitted. He would not be denied admittance, for he protested he must speak to me on a circumstance which so deeply concerned my own interest that it was of the most serious nature. Well, after much squabbling, I was compelled to admit him that I might dismiss him the sooner, and compose myself before the play began. But, what was my distress and astonishment when I found that he wanted me, even at this moment of anxiety and terror, to adopt another mode of acting the sleeping scene. He told me he had heard with the greatest surprise and concern that I meant to act it without holding the candle in my hand; and when I urged the impracticability of washing out that 'damned spot' with the vehemence that was certainly implied by both her own words and by those of her gentlewoman, he insisted that if I did put the candle out of my hand, it would be thought a presumptuous innovation, as Mrs. Pritchard had always retained it in hers. My mind, however, was made up, and it was then too late to make me alter it; for I was too agitated to adopt another method. My deference for Mr. Sheridan's taste and judgment was, however, so great that, had he proposed the alteration whilst it was possible for me to change my own plan, I should have yielded to his suggestion; though, even then, it would have been against my own opinion and my observation of the accuracy with which somnambulists perform all the acts of waking persons. The scene, of course, was acted as I had myself conceived it, and the innovation, as Mr. Sheridan called it, was received with approbation.[3] Mr. Sheridan himself came to me after the play and most ingenuously congratulated me on my obstinacy. When he was gone out of the room I began to undress, and, while standing up before my glass, and taking off my mantle, a diverting circumstance occurred, to chase away the feelings of this anxious night; for while I was repeating and endeavouring to call to mind the appropriate tone and action to the following words, 'Here's the smell of blood still!' [5.1.42], my dresser innocently exclaimed, 'Dear me, ma'am, how very hysterical you are tonight; I protest and vow, ma'am, it was not blood but rose-pink[4] and water, for I saw the property-man mix it up with my own eyes.'

2. Richard Brinsley Sheridan (1751–1816), actor, statesman, dramatist (*The Rivals, The School for Scandal*) and manager of Drury Lane Theatre.
3. Siddons's portrayal of Lady Macbeth in this scene has influenced many other actresses.
4. pink or red pigment used for stage effects.

Remarks on the Character of Lady Macbeth

In this astonishing creature one sees a woman in whose bosom the passion of ambition has almost obliterated all the characteristics of human nature; in whose composition are associated all the sub-jugating powers of intellect and all the charms and graces of personal beauty. You will probably not agree with me as to the character of that beauty; yet, perhaps, this difference of opinion will be entirely attributable to the difficulty of your imagination disengaging itself from that idea of the person of her representative which you have been so long accustomed to contemplate.[5] According to my notion, it is of that character which I believe is generally allowed to be most captivating to the other sex—fair, feminine, nay, perhaps, even frag-ile—

> Fair as the forms that, wove in Fancy's loom,
> Float in light visions round the poet's head.

Such a combination only, respectable in energy and strength of mind, and captivating in feminine loveliness, could have composed a charm of such potency as to fascinate the mind of a hero so daunt-less, a character so amiable, so honourable as Macbeth, to seduce him to brave all the dangers of the present and all the terrors of a future world; and we are constrained, even whilst we abhor his crimes, to pity the infatuated victim of such a thralldom. His letters, which have informed her of the predictions of those preternatural beings which accosted him on the heath, have lighted up into daring and desperate determinations all those pernicious slumbering fires which the enemy of man is ever watchful to awaken in the bosoms of his unwary victims. To his direful suggestions she is so far from offering the least opposition, as not only to yield up her soul to them, but moreover to invoke the sightless ministers of remorseless cruelty to extinguish in her breast all those compunctious visitings of nature which otherwise might have been mercifully interposed to counter-act, and perhaps eventually to overcome, their unholy instigations. But having impiously delivered herself up to the excitements of hell, the pitifulness of heaven itself is withdrawn from her, and she is abandoned to the guidance of the demons whom she has invoked.

* * *

It is very remarkable that Macbeth is frequent in expressions of tenderness to his wife, while she never betrays one symptom of affec-tion towards him, till, in the fiery furnace of affliction her iron heart is melted down to softness. For the present she flies to welcome the

5. Pritchard, whom Siddons purposefully plays against.

venerable gracious Duncan with such a show of eagerness as if allegiance in her bosom sat crowned with devotion and gratitude.

* * *

In the tremendous suspense of these moments [2.2], while she recollects her habitual humanity, one trait of tender feeling is expressed, 'Had he not resembled my father as he slept, I had done it' [12–13]. Her humanity vanishes, however, in the same instant; for when she observes that Macbeth, in the terror and confusion of his faculties, has brought the daggers from the place where they had agreed they should remain for the crimination of the grooms, she exhorts him to return with them to that place and to smear those attendants of the sovereign with blood. He, shuddering, exclaims, 'I'll go no more! I am affear'd to think of what I have done. Look on't again I dare not' [53–55].

Then instantaneously the solitary particle of her human feeling is swallowed up in her remorseless ambition, and, wrenching the daggers from the feeble grasp of her husband, she finishes the act which the infirm of purpose had not courage to complete, and calmly and steadily returns to her accomplice with the fiend-like boast,

> My hands are of your colour;
> But I would scorn to wear a heart so white. [67–68]

A knocking at the gate interrupts this terrific[6] dialogue; and all that now occupies her mind is urging him to wash his hands and put on his nightgown, 'lest occasion call,' says she, 'and show us to be the watchers' [73–74]. In a deplorable depravation of all rational knowledge, and lost to every recollection except that of his enormous guilt, she hurries him away to their own chamber.

* * *

Now, it is not possible that she should hear all these ambiguous hints about Banquo [3.2.39–58] without being too well aware that a sudden, lamentable fate awaits him. Yet, so far from offering any opposition to Macbeth's murderous designs, she even hints, I think, at the facility, if not the expediency, of destroying both Banquo and his equally unoffending child, when she observes that, 'in them Nature's copy is not eterne' [41]. Having, therefore, now filled the measure of her crimes, I have imagined that the last appearance of Banquo's ghost became no less visible to her eyes than it became to those of her husband. Yes, the spirit of the noble Banquo has smilingly filled up, even to overflowing, and now commends to her own lips the ingredients of her poisoned chalice.

6. terrifying.

The Fifth Act

Behold her now, with wasted form, with wan and haggard countenance, her starry eyes glazed with the ever-burning fever of remorse, and on their lids the shadows of death. Her ever-restless spirit wanders in troubled dreams about her dismal apartment; and, whether waking or asleep, the smell of innocent blood incessantly haunts her imagination:

> Here's the smell of the blood still.
> All the perfumes of Arabia will not sweeten
> This little hand. [5.1.42–44]

How beautifully contrasted is this exclamation with the bolder image of Macbeth in expressing the same feeling!

> Will all great Neptune's ocean wash the blood
> Clean from this hand? [2.2.63–64]

And how appropriately either sex illustrates the same idea!

During this appalling scene [5.1], which, to my sense, is the most so of them all, the wretched creature, in imagination, acts over again the accumulated horrors of her whole conduct. These dreadful images, accompanied with the agitations they have induced, have obviously accelerated her untimely end; for in a few moments the tidings of her death are brought to her unhappy husband. It is conjectured that she died by her own hand. Too certain it is that she dies and makes no sign. I have now to account to you for the weakness which I have, a few lines back, ascribed to Macbeth; and I am not quite without hope that the following observations will bear me out in my opinion. Please to observe, that he (I must think pusillanimously, when I compare his conduct to her forbearance) has been continually pouring out his miseries to his wife. His heart has therefore been eased from time to time by unloading its weight of woe, while she, on the contrary, has perseveringly endured in silence the uttermost anguish of a wounded spirit.

> The grief that does not speak
> Whispers the o'erfraught heart, and bids it break. [4.3.210–211]

Her feminine nature, her delicate structure, it is too evident, are soon overwhelmed by the enormous pressure of her crimes. Yet it will be granted that she gives proofs of a naturally higher toned mind than that of Macbeth. The different physical powers of the two sexes are finely delineated in the different effects which their mutual crimes produce. Her frailer frame and keener feelings have now sunk under the struggle—his robust and less sensitive constitution has not only resisted it, but bears him on to deeper wickedness, and to experience the fatal fecundity of crime.

A. C. BRADLEY

[The Tragedy of *Macbeth*]†

Macbeth, it is probable, was the last-written of the four great tragedies, and immediately preceded *Antony and Cleopatra.* In that play Shakespeare's final style appears for the first time completely formed, and the transition to this style is much more decidedly visible in *Macbeth* than in *King Lear.* Yet in certain respects *Macbeth* recalls *Hamlet* rather than *Othello* or *King Lear.* In the heroes of both plays the passage from thought to a critical resolution and action is difficult, and excites the keenest interest. In neither play, as in *Othello* and *King Lear,* is painful pathos one of the main effects. Evil, again, though it shows in *Macbeth* a prodigious energy, is not the icy or stony inhumanity of Iago or Goneril; and, as in *Hamlet,* it is pursued by remorse. Finally, Shakespeare no longer restricts the action to purely human agencies, as in the two preceding tragedies; portents once more fill the heavens, ghosts rise from their graves, an unearthly light flickers about the head of the doomed man. The special popularity of *Hamlet* and *Macbeth* is due in part to some of these common characteristics, notably to the fascination of the supernatural, the absence of the spectacle of extreme undeserved suffering, the absence of characters which horrify and repel and yet are destitute of grandeur. The reader who looks unwillingly at Iago gazes at Lady Macbeth in awe, because though she is dreadful she is also sublime. The whole tragedy is sublime.

In this, however, and in other respects, *Macbeth* makes an impression quite different from that of *Hamlet.* The dimensions of the principal characters, the rate of movement in the action, the supernatural effect, the style, the versification, are all changed; and they are all changed in much the same manner. In many parts of *Macbeth* there is in the language a peculiar compression, pregnancy, energy, even violence; the harmonious grace and even flow, often conspicuous in *Hamlet,* have almost disappeared. The chief characters, built on a scale at least as large as that of *Othello,* seem to attain at times an almost superhuman stature. The diction has in

---

† From A. C. Bradley, *Shakespearean Tragedy: Lectures on* Hamlet, Othello, King Lear, Macbeth (London: Macmillan & Co., 1904), 331–40, 349–65. All footnotes are Bradley's, unless otherwise indicated. Not all of Bradley's footnotes have been retained for this edition. References to act, scene, and line numbers in this Norton Critical Edition have been added in brackets.

places a huge and rugged grandeur, which degenerates here and there into tumidity. The solemn majesty of the royal Ghost in *Hamlet*, appearing in armour and standing silent in the moonlight, is exchanged for shapes of horror, dimly seen in the murky air or revealed by the glare of the caldron fire in a dark cavern, or for the ghastly face of Banquo badged with blood and staring with blank eyes. The other three tragedies all open with conversations which lead into the action: here the action bursts into wild life amidst the sounds of a thunderstorm and the echoes of a distant battle. It hurries through seven very brief scenes of mounting suspense to a terrible crisis, which is reached, in the murder of Duncan, at the beginning of the Second Act. Pausing a moment and changing its shape, it hastes again with scarcely diminished speed to fresh horrors. And even when the speed of the outward action is slackened, the same effect is continued in another form: we are shown a soul tortured by an agony which admits not a moment's repose, and rushing in frenzy towards its doom. *Macbeth* is very much shorter than the other three tragedies, but our experience in traversing it is so crowded and intense that it leaves an impression not of brevity but of speed. It is the most vehement, the most concentrated, perhaps we may say the most tremendous, of the tragedies.

I

A Shakespearean tragedy, as a rule, has a special tone or atmosphere of its own, quite perceptible, however difficult to describe. The effect of this atmosphere is marked with unusual strength in *Macbeth*. It is due to a variety of influences which combine with those just noticed, so that, acting and reacting, they form a whole; and the desolation of the blasted heath, the design of the Witches, the guilt in the hero's soul, the darkness of the night, seem to emanate from one and the same source. This effect is strengthened by a multitude of small touches, which at the moment may be little noticed but still leave their mark on the imagination. We may approach the consideration of the characters and the action by distinguishing some of the ingredients of this general effect.

Darkness, we may even say blackness, broods over this tragedy. It is remarkable that almost all the scenes which at once recur to memory take place either at night or in some dark spot. The vision of the dagger, the murder of Duncan, the murder of Banquo, the sleepwalking of Lady Macbeth, all come in night-scenes. The Witches dance in the thick air of a storm, or, 'black and midnight hags' [4.1.48] receive Macbeth in a cavern. The blackness of night is to the hero a thing of fear, even of horror; and that which he feels becomes the spirit of the play. The faint glimmerings of the western sky at twilight are here menacing: it is the hour when the traveller hastens to reach safety in his inn, and when Banquo rides homeward to meet his assassins; the hour when 'light thickens' when 'night's black agents to their prey do rouse' [3.2.53, 56], when the wolf begins to howl, and the owl to scream, and withered murder steals forth to his work. Macbeth bids the stars hide their fires that his 'black' desires may be concealed; Lady Macbeth calls on thick night to come, palled in the dunnest smoke of hell. The moon is down and no stars shine when Banquo, dreading the dreams of the coming night, goes unwillingly to bed, and leaves Macbeth to wait for the summons of the little bell. When the next day should dawn, its light is 'strangled,' and 'darkness does the face of earth entomb' [2.4.9]. In the whole drama the sun seems to shine only twice; first, in the beautiful but ironical passage where Duncan sees the swallows flitting round the castle of death; and, afterwards, when at the close the avenging army gathers to rid the earth of its shame. Of the many slighter touches which deepen this effect I notice only one. The failure of nature in Lady Macbeth is marked by her fear of darkness; 'she has light by her continually' [5.1.19–20]. And in the one phrase of fear that escapes her lips even in sleep, it is of the darkness of the place of torment that she speaks.[1]

The atmosphere of *Macbeth*, however, is not that of unrelieved blackness. On the contrary, as compared with *King Lear* and its cold dim gloom, *Macbeth* leaves a decided impression of colour; it is really the impression of a black night broken by flashes of light and colour, sometimes vivid and even glaring. They are the lights and colours of the thunder-storm in the first scene; of the dagger hanging before Macbeth's eyes and glittering alone in the midnight air; of the torch borne by the servant when he and his lord come upon Banquo crossing the castle-court to his room; of the torch, again, which Fleance carried to light his father to death, and which was dashed out by one of the murderers; of the torches that flared in the hall on the face of the Ghost and the blanched cheeks of Macbeth; of the flames beneath the boiling cauldron from which the apparitions in the cavern rose; of the taper which showed to the Doctor and Gentlewoman the wasted face and blank eyes of Lady Macbeth. And, above all, the colour is the colour of blood. It cannot be an accident that the image of blood is forced upon us continually, not merely by the events themselves, but by full descriptions, and even by reiteration of the word in unlikely parts of the dialogue. The Witches, after their first wild appearance, have hardly quitted the stage when there staggers onto it a 'bloody man' [1.2.1], gashed with wounds. His tale is of a

---

1. 'Hell is murky' [5.1.31]. This, surely, is not meant for a scornful repetition of something said long ago by Macbeth. He would hardly in those days have used an argument or expressed a fear that could provoke nothing but contempt.

hero whose 'brandished steel smoked with bloody execution,' 'carved out a passage' to his enemy, and 'unseam'd him from the nave to the chaps' [1.2.17ff.]. And then he tells of a second battle so bloody that the combatants seemed as if they 'meant to bathe in reeking wounds' [1.2.39]. What metaphors! What a dreadful image is that with which Lady Macbeth greets us almost as she enters, when she prays the spirits of cruelty so to thicken her blood that pity cannot flow along her veins! What pictures are those of the murderer appearing at the door of the banquet-room with Banquo's 'blood upon his face' [3.4.14]; of Banquo himself 'with twenty trenched gashes on his head' [3.4.28], or 'blood-bolter'd' [4.1.123] and smiling in derision at his murderer; of Macbeth, gazing at his hand, and watching it dye the whole green ocean red; of Lady Macbeth, gazing at hers, and stretching it away from her face to escape the smell of blood that all the perfumes of Arabia will not subdue! The most horrible lines in the whole tragedy are those of her shuddering cry, 'Yet who would have thought the old man to have had so much blood in him' [5.1.33–34]? And it is not only at such moments that these images occur. Even in the quiet conversation of Malcolm and Macduff, Macbeth is imagined as holding a bloody sceptre, and Scotland as a country bleeding and receiving every day a new gash added to her wounds. It is as if the poet saw the whole story through an ensanguined mist, and as if it stained the very blackness of the night. When Macbeth, before Banquo's murder, invokes night to scarf up the tender eye of pitiful day, and to tear in pieces the great bond that keeps him pale, even the invisible hand that is to tear the bond is imagined as covered with blood.

Let us observe another point. The vividness, magnitude, and violence of the imagery in some of these passages are characteristic of Macbeth almost throughout; and their influence contributes to form its atmosphere. Images like those of the babe torn smiling from the breast and dashed to death; of pouring the sweet milk of concord into hell; of the earth shaking in fever; of the frame of things disjointed; of sorrows striking heaven on the face, so that it resounds and yells out like syllables of dolour; of the mind lying in restless ecstasy on a rack; of the mind full of scorpions; of the tale told by an idiot, full of sound and fury;—all keep the imagination moving on a 'wild and violent sea' [4.2.21], while it is scarcely for a moment permitted to dwell on thoughts of peace and beauty. In its language, as in its action, the drama is full of tumult and storm. Whenever the Witches are present we see and hear a thunder-storm: when they are absent we hear of ship-wrecking storms and direful thunders; of tempests that blow down trees and churches, castles, palaces and pyramids; of the frightful hurricane of the night when Duncan was murdered; of the blast on which pity rides like a new-born babe, or

on which Heaven's cherubim are horsed. There is thus something
magnificently appropriate in the cry 'Blow, wind! Come, wrack!'
[5.5.51] with which Macbeth, turning from the sight of the moving
wood of Birnam, bursts from his castle. He was borne to his throne
on a whirlwind, and the fate he goes to meet comes on the wings of
storm.

Now all these agencies—darkness, the lights and colours that illuminate it, the storm that rushes through it, the violent and gigantic
images—conspire with the appearances of the Witches and the
Ghost to awaken horror, and in some degree also a supernatural
dread. And to this effect other influences contribute. The pictures
called up by the mere words of the Witches stir the same feelings—
those, for example, of the spell-bound sailor driven tempest-tost for
nine times nine weary weeks, and never visited by sleep night or day;
of the drop of poisonous foam that forms on the moon, and, falling
to earth, is collected for pernicious ends; of the sweltering venom of
the toad, the finger of the babe killed at its birth by its own mother,
the tricklings from the murderer's gibbet. In Nature, again, something is felt to be at work, sympathetic with human guilt and supernatural malice. She labours with portents.

> Lamentings heard in the air, strange screams of death,
> And prophesying with accents terrible, [2.3.50–51]

burst from her. The owl clamours all through the night; Duncan's
horses devour each other in frenzy; the dawn comes, but no light
with it. Common sights and sounds, the crying of crickets, the croak
of the raven, the light thickening after sunset, the homecoming of
the rooks, are all ominous. Then, as if to deepen these impressions,
Shakespeare has concentrated attention on the obscurer regions of
man's being, on phenomena which make it seem that he is in the
power of secret forces lurking below, and independent of his consciousness and will: such as the relapse of Macbeth from conversation into a reverie, during which he gazes fascinated at the image of
murder drawing closer and closer; the writing on his face of strange
things he never meant to show; the pressure of imagination heightening into illusion, like the vision of a dagger in the air, at first bright,
then suddenly splashed with blood, or the sound of a voice that cried
"Sleep no more' [2.2.38] and would not be silenced. To these are
added other, and constant, allusions to sleep, man's strange half-
conscious life, to the misery of its withholding; to the terrible dreams
of remorse; to the cursed thoughts from which Banquo is free by
day, but which tempt him in his sleep: and again to abnormal disturbances of sleep; in the two men, of whom one during the murder
of Duncan laughed in his sleep, and the other raised a cry of murder;
and in Lady Macbeth, who rises to re-enact in somnambulism those

scenes the memory of which is pushing her on to madness or suicide. All this has one effect, to excite supernatural alarm and, even more, a dread of the presence of evil not only in its recognised seat but all through and around our mysterious nature. Perhaps there is no other work equal to *Macbeth* in the production of this effect.

It is enhanced—to take a last point—by the use of a literary expedient. Not even in *Richard III*, which in this, as in other respects, has resemblances to Macbeth, is there so much of Irony. I do not refer to irony in the ordinary sense; to speeches, for example, where the speaker is intentionally ironical, like that of Lennox in III.vi. I refer to irony on the part of the author himself, to ironical juxtapositions of persons and events, and especially to the 'Sophoclean irony' by which a speaker is made to use words bearing to the audience, in addition to his own meaning, a further and ominous sense, hidden from himself and, usually, from the other persons on the stage. The very first words uttered by Macbeth,

> So foul and fair a day I have not seen, [1.3.39]

are an example to which attention has often been drawn; for they startle the reader by recalling the words of the Witches in the first scene,

> Fair is foul, and foul is fair. [1.1.11]

When Macbeth, emerging from his murderous reverie, turns to the nobles saying, 'Let us toward the King' [1.3.156], his words are innocent, but to the reader have a double meaning. Duncan's comment on the treachery of Cawdor,

> There's no art
> To find the mind's construction in the face:
> He was a gentleman on whom I built
> An absolute trust, [1.4.12–15]

is interrupted[2] by the entrance of the traitor Macbeth, who is greeted with effusive gratitude and a like 'absolute trust.' I have already referred to the ironical effect of the beautiful lines in which Duncan and Banquo describe the castle they are about to enter. To the reader Lady Macbeth's light words,

> A little water clears us of this deed:
> How easy is it then, [2.2.70–71]

summon up the picture of the sleep-walking scene. The idea of the Porter's speech, in which he imagines himself the keeper of hell-gate, shows the same irony. So does the contrast between the obvious and the hidden meanings of the apparitions of the armed head, the

---

2. The line is a foot short.

bloody child, and the child with the tree in his hand. It would be easy to add further examples. Perhaps the most striking is the answer which Banquo, as he rides away, never to return alive, gives to Macbeth's reminder, 'Fail not our feast.' 'My lord, I will not' [3.1.29–30], he replies, and he keeps his promise. It cannot be by accident that Shakespeare so frequently in this play uses a device which contributes to excite the vague fear of hidden forces operating on minds unconscious of their influence.

3

From this murky background stand out the two great terrible figures, who dwarf all the remaining characters of the drama. Both are sublime, and both inspire, far more than the other tragic heroes, the feeling of awe. They are never detached in imagination from the atmosphere which surrounds them and adds to their grandeur and terror. It is, as it were, continued into their souls. For within them is all that we felt without—the darkness of night, lit with the flame of tempest and the hues of blood, and haunted by wild and direful shapes, 'murdering ministers' [1.5.46], spirits of remorse, and maddening visions of peace lost and judgment to come. The way to be untrue to Shakespeare here, as always, is to relax the tension of imagination, to conventionalise, to conceive Macbeth, for example, as a half-hearted cowardly criminal, and Lady Macbeth as a whole-hearted fiend.

These two characters are fired by one and the same passion of ambition; and to a considerable extent they are alike. The disposition of each is high, proud, and commanding. They are born to rule, if not to reign. They are peremptory or contemptuous to their inferiors. They are not children of light, like Brutus and Hamlet; they are of the world. We observe in them no love of country, and no interest in the welfare of anyone outside their family. Their habitual thoughts and aims are, and, we imagine, long have been, all of station and power. And though in both there is something, and in one much, of what is higher—honour, conscience, humanity—they do not live consciously in the light of these things or speak their language. Not that they are egoists, like Iago; or, if they are egoists, theirs is an *egoïsme à deux*.[3] They have no separate ambitions.[4] They support and love one another. They suffer together. And if, as time goes on, they drift a little apart, they are not vulgar souls, to be alienated and recriminate when they experience the fruitlessness of their ambition. They remain to the end tragic, even grand.

3. egoism shared by two [*Editor's note*].
4. The assertion that Lady Macbeth sought a crown for herself, or sought anything for herself, apart from her husband, is absolutely unjustified by anything in the play. It is based on a sentence of Holinshed's which Shakespeare did *not* use.

So far there is much likeness between them. Otherwise they are contrasted, and the action is built upon this contrast. Their attitudes towards the projected murder of Duncan are quite different; and it produces in them equally different effects. In consequence, they appear in the earlier part of the play as of equal importance, if indeed Lady Macbeth does not overshadow her husband; but afterwards she retires more and more into the background, and he becomes unmistakably the leading figure. His is indeed far the more complex character: and I will speak of it first.

Macbeth, the cousin of a King mild, just, and beloved, but now too old to lead his army, is introduced to us as a general of extraordinary prowess, who has covered himself with glory in putting down a rebellion and repelling the invasion of a foreign army. In these conflicts he showed great personal courage, a quality which he continues to display throughout the drama in regard to all plain dangers. It is difficult to be sure of his customary demeanour, for in the play we see him either in what appears to be an exceptional relation to his wife, or else in the throes of remorse and desperation; but from his behaviour during his journey home after the war, from his *later* conversations with Lady Macbeth, and from his language to the murderers of Banquo and to others, we imagine him as a great warrior, somewhat masterful, rough, and abrupt, a man to inspire some fear and much admiration. He was thought 'honest,' or honourable; he was trusted, apparently, by everyone; Macduff, a man of the highest integrity, 'loved him well' [4.3.13]. And there was, in fact, much good in him. We have no warrant, I think, for describing him, with many writers, as of a 'noble' nature, like Hamlet or Othello; but he had a keen sense both of honour and of the worth of a good name. The phrase, again, 'too much of the milk of human kindness' [1.5.15], is applied to him in impatience by his wife, who did not fully understand him; but certainly he was far from devoid of humanity and pity.

At the same time he was exceedingly ambitious. He must have been so by temper. The tendency must have been greatly strengthened by his marriage. When we see him, it has been further stimulated by his remarkable success and by the consciousness of exceptional powers and merit. It becomes a passion. The course of action suggested by it is extremely perilous: it sets his good name, his position, and even his life on the hazard. It is also abhorrent to his better feelings. Their defeat in the struggle with ambition leaves him utterly wretched, and would have kept him so, however complete had been his outward success and security. On the other hand, his passion for power and his instinct of self-assertion are so vehement that no inward misery could persuade him to relinquish the fruits of crime, or to advance from remorse to repentance.

In the character as so far sketched there is nothing very peculiar though the strength of the forces contending in it is unusual. But there is in Macbeth one marked peculiarity, the true apprehension of which is the key to Shakespeare's conception. This bold ambitious man of action has, within certain limits, the imagination of a poet—an imagination on the one hand extremely sensitive to impressions of a certain kind, and, on the other, productive of violent disturbance both of mind and body. Through it he is kept in contact with supernatural impressions and is liable to supernatural fears. And through it, especially, come to him the intimations of conscience and honour. Macbeth's better nature—to put the matter for clearness' sake too broadly—instead of speaking to him in the overt language of moral ideas, commands, and prohibitions, incorporates itself in images which alarm and horrify. His imagination is thus the best of him, something usually deeper and higher than his conscious thoughts; and if he had obeyed it he would have been safe. But his wife quite misunderstands it, and he himself understands it only in part. The terrifying images which deter him from crime and follow its commission, and which are really the protest of his deepest self, seem to his wife the creations of mere nervous fear, and are sometimes referred by himself to the dread of vengeance or the restlessness of insecurity. His conscious or reflective mind, that is, moves chiefly among considerations of outward success and failure, while his inner being is convulsed by conscience. And his inability to understand himself is repeated and exaggerated in the interpretations of actors and critics, who represent him as a coward, cold-blooded, calculating, and pitiless, who shrinks from crime simply because it is dangerous, and suffers afterwards simply because he is not safe. In reality his courage is frightful. He strides from crime to crime, though his soul never ceases to bar his advance with shapes of terror, or to clamour in his ears that he is murdering his peace and casting away his 'eternal jewel' [3.1.70].

It is of the first importance to realise the strength, and also (what has not been so clearly recognised) the limits, of Macbeth's imagination. It is not the universal meditative imagination of Hamlet. He came to see in man, as Hamlet sometimes did, the 'quintessence of dust'; but he must always have been incapable of Hamlet's reflections on man's noble reason and infinite faculty, or of seeing with Hamlet's eyes 'this brave o'erhanging firmament, this majestical roof fretted with golden fire' Nor could he feel, like Othello, the romance of war or the infinity of love. He shows no sign of any unusual sensitiveness to the glory or beauty in the world or the soul; and it is partly for this reason that we have no inclination to love him, and that we regard him with more of awe than of pity. His imagination is excitable and intense, but narrow. That which stimulates it is, almost solely, that which thrills with sudden, startling, and often supernatural fear. There is a famous passage late in the play which is here very significant, because it refers to a time before his conscience was burdened, and so shows his native disposition:

> The time has been, my senses would have cool'd
> To hear a night-shriek; and my fell of hair
> Would at a dismal treatise rise and stir
> As life were in't. [5.5.10–13]

This 'time' must have been in his youth, or at least before we see him. And, in the drama, everything which terrifies him is of this character, only it has now a deeper and a moral significance. Palpable dangers leave him unmoved or fill him with fire. He does himself mere justice when he asserts he 'dare do all that may become a man' [1.7.46], or when he exclaims to Banquo's ghost,

> What man dare, I dare:
> Approach thou like the rugged Russian bear,
> The arm'd rhinoceros, or the Hyrcan tiger;
> Take any shape but that, and my firm nerves
> Shall never tremble. [3.4.101–105]

What appals him is always the image of his own guilty heart or bloody deed, or some image which derives from them its terror or gloom. These, when they arise, hold him spell-bound and possess him wholly, like a hypnotic trance which is at the same time the ecstasy of a poet. As the first 'horrid image' [1.3.138] of Duncan's murder— of himself murdering Duncan—rises from unconsciousness and confronts him, his hair stands on end and the outward scene vanishes from his eyes. Why? For fear of 'consequences'? The idea is ridiculous. Or because the deed is bloody? The man who with his 'smoking' steel 'carved out his passage' to the rebel leader, and 'unseam'd him from the nave to the chaps' [1.2.17ff.], would hardly be frightened by blood. How could fear of consequences make the dagger he is to use hang suddenly glittering before him in the air, and then as suddenly dash it with gouts of blood? Even when he *talks* of consequences, and declares that if he were safe against them he would 'jump the life to come,' his imagination bears witness against him, and shows us that what really holds him back is the hideous vileness of the deed:

> He's here in double trust;
> First, as I am his kinsman and his subject,
> Strong both against the deed; then, as his host,
> Who should against his murderer shut the door,
> Not bear the knife myself. Besides, this Duncan
> Hath borne his faculties so meek, hath been

So clear in his great office, that his virtues
Will plead like angels, trumpet-tongued, against
The deep damnation of his taking-off;
And pity, like a naked new-born babe,
Striding the blast, or heaven's cherubim, horsed
Upon the sightless couriers of the air,
Shall blow the horrid deed in every eye,
That tears shall drown the wind. [1.7.12–25]

It may be said that he is here thinking of the horror that others will feel at the deed—thinking therefore of consequences. Yes, but could he realise thus how horrible the deed would look to others if it were not equally horrible to himself?

It is the same when the murder is done. He is well-nigh mad with horror, but it is not the horror of detection. It is not he who thinks of washing his hands or getting his nightgown on. He has brought away the daggers he should have left on the pillows of the grooms, but what does he care for that? What *he* thinks of is that, when he heard one of the men awaked from sleep say 'God bless us,' he could not say 'Amen' [2.2.31–32]; for his imagination presents to him the parching of his throat as an immediate judgment from heaven. His wife heard the owl scream and the crickets cry; but what *he* heard was the voice that first cried 'Macbeth doth murder sleep' [2.2.39], and then, a minute later, with a change of tense, denounced on him, as if his three names gave him three personalities to suffer in, the doom of sleeplessness:

Glamis hath murdered sleep, and therefore Cawdor
Shall sleep no more, Macbeth shall sleep no more. [2.2.45–
46]

There comes a sound of knocking. It should be perfectly familiar to him; but he knows not whence, or from what world, it comes. He looks down at his hands, and starts violently: 'What hands are here?' [2.2.62]. For they seem alive, they move, they mean to pluck out his eyes. He looks at one of them again; it does not move; but the blood upon it is enough to dye the whole ocean red. What has all this to do with fear of 'consequences'? It is his soul speaking in the only shape in which it can speak freely, that of imagination.

So long as Macbeth's imagination is active, we watch him fascinated; we feel suspense, horror, awe; in which are latent, also, admiration and sympathy. But so soon as it is quiescent these feelings vanish. He is no longer 'infirm of purpose' [2.2.55] he becomes domineering, even brutal, or he becomes a cool pitiless hypocrite. He is generally said to be a very bad actor, but this is not wholly true. Whenever his imagination stirs, he acts badly. It so possesses him, and is so much stronger than his reason, that his face betrays him,

and his voice utters the most improbable untruths or the most artificial rhetoric. But when it is asleep he is firm, self-controlled and
practical, as in the conversation where he skillfully elicits from Banquo that information about his movements which is required for the
successful arrangement of his murder. Here he is hateful; arid so he
is in the conversation with the murderers, who are not professional
cut-throats but old soldiers, and whom, without a vestige of remorse,
he beguiles with calumnies against Banquo and with such appeals
as his wife had used to him. On the other hand, we feel much pity
as well as anxiety in the scene [1.7] where she overcomes his opposition to the murder; and we feel it (though his imagination is not
specially active) because this scene shows us how little he understands himself. This is his great misfortune here. Not that he fails
to realise in reflection the baseness of the deed (the soliloquy with
which the scene opens shows that he does not). But he has never,
to put it pedantically, accepted as the principle of his conduct the
morality which takes shape in his imaginative fears. Had he done so,
and said plainly to his wife, 'The thing is vile, and, however much I
have sworn to do it, I will not,' she would have been helpless; for all
her arguments proceed on the assumption that there is for them no
such point of view. Macbeth does approach this position once, when,
resenting the accusation of cowardice, he answers,

> I dare do all that may become a man;
> Who dares do more is none. [1.7.46–47]

She feels in an instant that everything is at stake, and, ignoring the
point, overwhelms him with indignant and contemptuous personal
reproach. But he yields to it because he is himself half ashamed of
that answer of his, and because, for want of habit, the simple idea
which it expresses has no hold on him comparable to the force it
acquires when it becomes incarnate in visionary fears and warnings.

Yet these were so insistent, and they offered to his ambition a
resistance so strong, that it is impossible to regard him as falling
through the blindness or delusion of passion. On the contrary, he
himself feels with such intensity the enormity of his purpose that, it
seems clear, neither his ambition not yet the prophecy of the Witches
would ever without the aid of Lady Macbeth have overcome this
feeling. As it is, the deed is done in horror and without the faintest
desire or sense of glory—done, one may almost say, as if it were an
appalling duty; and, the instant it is finished, its futility is revealed
to Macbeth as clearly as its vileness had been revealed beforehand.
As he staggers from the scene he mutters in despair,

> Wake Duncan with thy knocking! I would thou could'st.
>   [1.7.77]

When, half an hour later, he returns with Lennox from the room of
the murder, he breaks out:

> Had I but died an hour before this chance,
> I had lived a blessed time; for from this instant
> There's nothing serious in mortality:
> All is but toys: renown and grace is dead;
> The wine of life is drawn, and the mere lees
> Is left this vault to brag of. [2.3.88–94]

This is no mere acting. The language here has none of the false
rhetoric of his merely hypocritical speeches. It is meant to deceive,
but it utters at the same time his profoundest feeling. And this he
can henceforth never hide from himself for long. However he may
try to drown it in further enormities, he hears it murmuring,

> Duncan is in his grave:
> After life's fitful fever he sleeps well: [3.2.24–25]

or,

> better be with the dead: [3.2.21]

or,

> I have lived long enough: [5.3.22]

and it speaks its last words on the last day of his life:

> Out, out, brief candle!
> Life's but a walking shadow, a poor player
> That struts and frets his hour upon the stage
> And then is heard no more: it is a tale
> Told by an idiot, full of sound and fury,
> Signifying nothing. [5.5.23–28]

How strange that this judgment on life, the despair of a man who
had knowingly made mortal war on his own soul, should be frequently quoted as Shakespeare's own judgment, and should even be
adduced, in serious criticism, as a proof of his pessimism!

It remains to look a little more fully at the history of Macbeth after
the murder of Duncan. Unlike his first struggle this history excites
little suspense or anxiety on his account: we have now no hope for
him. But it is an engrossing spectacle, and psychologically it is perhaps the most remarkable exhibition of the *development* of a character to be found in Shakespeare's tragedies.

That heart-sickness which comes from Macbeth's perception of
the futility of his crime, and which never leaves him for long, is not,
however, his habitual state. It could not be so, for two reasons. In
the first place the consciousness of guilt is stronger in him than the

consciousness of failure; and it keeps him in a perpetual agony of restlessness, and forbids him simply to droop and pine. His mind is 'full of scorpions' [3.2.39]. He cannot sleep. He 'keeps alone,' moody and savage. 'All that is within him does condemn itself for being there' [5.2.24–25]. There is a fever in his blood which urges him to ceaseless action in the search for oblivion. And, in the second place, ambition, the love of power, the instinct of self-assertion, are much too potent in Macbeth to permit him to resign, even in spirit, the prize for which he has put rancours in the vessel of his peace. The 'will to live' is mighty in him. The forces which impelled him to aim at the crown re-assert themselves. He faces the world, and his own conscience, desperate, but never dreaming of acknowledging defeat. He will see 'the frame of things disjoint' [3.2.18] first. He challenges fate into the lists.

The result is frightful. He speaks no more, as before [of] Duncan's murder, or honour or pity. That sleepless torture, he tells himself, is nothing but the sense of insecurity and the fear of retaliation. If only he were safe, it would vanish. And he looks about for the cause of his fear; and his eye falls on Banquo. Banquo, who cannot fail to suspect him, has not fled or turned against him: Banquo has become his chief counsellor. Why? Because, he answers, the kingdom was promised to Banquo's children. Banquo, then, is waiting to attack him, to make a way for them. The 'bloody instructions' [1.7.9] he himself taught when he murdered Duncan, are about to return, as he said they would, to plague the inventor. *This* then, he tells himself, is the fear that will not let him sleep; and it will die with Banquo. There is no hesitation now, and no remorse: he has nearly learned his lesson. He hastens feverishly, not to murder Banquo, but to procure his murder: some strange idea is in his mind that the thought of the dead man will not haunt him, like the memory of Duncan, if the deed is done by other hands.[5] The deed is done: but, instead of peace descending on him, from the depths of his nature his half-murdered conscience rises; his deed confronts him in the apparition of Banquo's Ghost, and the horror of the night of his first murder returns. But, alas, *it* has less power, and *he* has more will. Agonised and trembling, he still faces this rebel image, and it yields:

> Why, so: being gone,
> I am a man again. [3.4.109–110]

Yes, but his secret is in the hands of the assembled lords. And, worse, this deed is as futile as the first. For, though Banquo is dead and even his Ghost is conquered, that inner torture is unassuaged. But he will not bear it. His guests have hardly left him when he turns roughly to his wife:

5. See his first words to the Ghost: 'Thou canst not say I did it' [3.4.51].

How say'st thou, that Macduff denies his person
At our great bidding? [3.4.130–131]

Macduff it is that spoils his sleep. He shall perish—he and aught
else that bars the road to peace.

> For mine own good
> All causes shall give way: I am in blood
> Stepp'd in so far that, should I wade no more,
> Returning were as tedious as go o'er:
> Strange things I have in head that will to hand,
> Which must be acted ere they may be scann'd. [3.4.137–
> 142]

She answers, sick at heart,

> You lack the season of all natures, sleep. [143]

No doubt: but he has found the way to it now:

> Come, we'll to sleep. My strange and self abuse
> Is the initiate fear that wants hard use.
> We are yet but young in deed. [144–146]

What a change from the man who thought of Duncan's virtues, and
of pity like a naked new-born babe! What a frightful clearness of self-
consciousness in this descent to hell, and yet what a furious force
in the instinct of life and self-assertion that drives him on!

He goes to seek the Witches. He will know, by the worst means,
the worst. He has no longer any awe of them.

> How now, you secret, black and midnight hags! [4.1.48]

—so he greets them, and at once he demands and threatens. They
tell him he is right to fear Macduff. They tell him to fear nothing,
for none of woman born can harm him. He feels that the two statements are at variance; infatuated, suspects no double meaning; but,
that he may 'sleep in spite of thunder' [4.1.86], determines not to
spare Macduff. But his heart throbs to know one thing, and he forces
from the Witches the vision of Banquo's children crowned. The old
intolerable thought returns, 'for Banquo's issue have I filed my
mind' [3.1.67]; and with it, for all the absolute security apparently
promised him, there returns that inward fever. Will nothing quiet it?
Nothing but destruction. Macduff, one comes to tell him, has
escaped him; but that does not matter: he can still destroy:[6]

6. 'For only in destroying I find ease / To my relentless thoughts' [*Paradise Lost*, ix. 129].
Milton's portrait of Satan's misery here, and at the beginning of Book IV, might well have
been suggested by *Macbeth*. Coleridge, after quoting Duncan's speech [1.4.34ff.] says: 'It
is a fancy, but I can never read this, and the following speeches of Macbeth, without
involuntarily thinking of the Miltonic Messiah and Satan.' I doubt if it was a mere fancy.
(It will be remembered that Milton thought at one time of writing a tragedy on Macbeth.)

> And even now,
> To crown my thoughts with acts, be it thought and done:
> The castle of Macduff I will surprise;
> Seize upon Fife; give to the edge o' the sword
> His wife, his babes, and all unfortunate souls
> That trace him in's line. No boasting like a fool;
> This deed I'll do before this purpose cool.
> But no more sights! [4.1.148–155]

No, he need fear no more 'sights.' The Witches have done their work, and after this purposeless butchery his own imagination will trouble him no more. He has dealt his last blow at the conscience and pity which spoke through it.

The whole flood of evil in his nature is now let loose. He becomes an open tyrant, dreaded by everyone about him, and a terror to his country. She 'sinks beneath the yoke' [4.3.40].

> Each new morn
> New widows howl, new orphans cry, new sorrows
> Strike heaven on the face. [4.3.4–6]

She weeps, she bleeds, 'and each new day a gash is added to her wounds' [4.3.41–42]. She is not the mother of her children, but their grave;

> where nothing,
> But who knows nothing, is once seen to smile:
> Where sighs and groans and shrieks that rend the air
> Are made, not mark'd. [4.3.167–170]

For this wild rage and furious cruelty we are prepared; but vices of another kind start up as he plunges on his downward way.

> I grant him bloody,
> Luxurious, avaricious, false, deceitful,
> Sudden, malicious, [4.3.58–60]

says Malcolm; and two of these epithets surprise us. Who would have expected avarice or lechery in Macbeth? His ruin seems complete.

Yet it is never complete. To the end he never totally loses our sympathy; we never feel towards him as we do to those who appear the born children of darkness. There remains something sublime in the defiance with which, even when cheated of his last hope, he faces earth and hell and heaven. Nor would any soul to whom evil was congenial be capable of that heart-sickness which overcomes him when he thinks of the 'honour, love, obedience, troops of friends' which 'he must not look to have' [5.3.25–26] (and which Iago would never have cared to have), and contrasts with them

> Curses, not loud but deep, mouth-honour, breath,
> Which the poor heart would fain deny, and dare not, [27–
>   28]

(and which Iago would have accepted with indifference). Neither can I agree with those who find in his reception of the news of his wife's death proof of alienation or utter carelessness. There is no proof of these in the words,

> She should have died hereafter;
> There would have been a time for such a word, [5.5.17–18]

spoken as they are by a man already in some measure prepared for such news, and now transported by the frenzy of his last fight for life. He has no time now to feel. Only, as he thinks of the morrow when time to feel will come—if anything comes, the vanity of all hopes and forward-lookings sinks deep into his soul with an infinite weariness, and he murmurs,

> To-morrow, and to-morrow, and to-morrow,
> Creeps in this petty pace from day to day
> To the last syllable of recorded time,
> And all our yesterdays have lighted fools
> The way to dusty death. [19–23]

In the very depths a gleam of his native love of goodness, and with it a touch of tragic grandeur, rests upon him. The evil he has desperately embraced continues to madden or to wither his inmost heart. No experience in the world could bring him to glory in it or make his peace with it, or to forget what he once was and Iago and Goneril never were.

KENNETH MUIR

Image and Symbol in *Macbeth*†

A good deal has been written about the imagery of *Macbeth* since Caroline Spurgeon showed[1] that the iterative image was that of a man in ill-fitting garments. It has been pointed out, for example, that the image can be interpreted in more than one way and that we need not necessarily suppose that Shakespeare looked on his hero as a small man in garments too large for him: we may rather suppose that the point of the image is that the garments were stolen or that they symbolize the hypocrisy to which Macbeth is reluctantly committed when he embarks on his career of crime. It has also been pointed out[2] that this particular image should be considered in relation to a wider group of tailoring images, of which the imaginary tailor, admitted by the Porter of Hell-gate, may be regarded as a kind of patron.[3]

What is more important is that, since the publication of R. B. Heilman's books on *King Lear* and *Othello*,[4] W. H. Clemen's *The Development of Shakespeare's Imagery* and G. Wilson Knight's series of interpretations, Miss Spurgeon's concentration on a single iterative image, even though numerically predominant, is apt to be misleading. The total meaning of each play depends on a complex of interwoven patterns and the imagery must be considered in relation to character and structure.

One group of images to which Cleanth Brooks called attention was that concerned with babes.[5] It has been suggested[6] by Muriel C. Bradbrook that Shakespeare may have noticed in the general description of the manners of Scotland included in Holinshed's *Chronicles* that every Scotswoman 'would take intolerable pains to bring up and nourish her own children'; and H. N. Paul pointed out[7] that one of the topics selected for debate before James I, during his visit to Oxford in the summer of 1605, was whether a man's character was influenced by his nurse's milk. Whatever the origin of the

---

† From Kenneth Muir, "Image and Symbol in *Macbeth*," in *Shakespeare Survey* 19 (Cambridge: Cambridge University Press, 1966), 45–54. Reprinted with the permission of Cambridge University Press. References to act, scene, and line numbers in this Norton Critical Edition have been added in brackets.

1. C. F. E. Spurgeon, *Leading Motives in the Imagery of Shakespeare's Tragedies*.
2. K. Muir, ed., *Macbeth* (1951), pp. xxxiii, 7.
3. H. L. Rogers has recently argued (*R.E.S.* 1965, p. 44) that the tailor may refer to a man associated in the public mind with the Garnet trial; as Father Garnet went under the name of 'Mr Farmer', equivocator, tailor and farmer were all allusions to the Gunpowder Plot and its aftermath.
4. *This Great Stage* (1948); *Magic in the Web* (1956).
5. *The Well Wrought Urn* (1947), pp. 22–49.
6. *Shakespeare Survey* 4 (1951), p. 40.
7. *The Royal Play of 'Macbeth'* (1950), p. 388.

images in *Macbeth* relating to breast-feeding, Shakespeare uses them for a very dramatic purpose. Their first appearance is in Lady Macbeth's invocation of the evil spirits to take possession of her:

> Come to my woman's breasts,
> And take my milk for gall, you murd'ring ministers,
> Wherever in your sightless substances
> You wait on nature's mischief. [1.5.45–48]

They next appear in the scene where she incites Macbeth to the murder of Duncan:

> I have given suck, and know
> How tender 'tis to love the babe that milks me—
> I would, while it was smiling in my face,
> Have pluck'd my nipple from his boneless gums,
> And dash'd the brains out, had I so sworn as you
> Have done to this. [1.7.54–59]

In between these two passages, Macbeth himself, debating whether to do the deed, admits that

> Pity, like a naked new-born babe
> Striding the blast, [1.7.21–22]

would plead against it; and Lady Macbeth, when she first considers whether she can persuade her husband to kill Duncan, admits that she fears his nature:

> It is too full o' th' milk of human kindness
> To catch the nearest way. [1.5.14–15]

Later in the play, Malcolm, when he is pretending to be worse even than Macbeth, says that he loves crime:

> Nay, had I pow'r, I should
> Pour the sweet milk of concord into hell,
> Uproar the universal peace, confound
> All unity on earth. [4.3.98–101]

In these passages the babe symbolizes pity, and the necessity for pity, and milk symbolizes humanity, tenderness, sympathy, natural human feelings, the sense of kinship, all of which have been outraged by the murderers. Lady Macbeth can nerve herself to the deed only by denying her real nature; and she can overcome Macbeth's scruples only by making him ignore his feelings of human-kindness— his kinship with his fellow-men.

Cleanth Brooks suggests therefore that it is appropriate that one of the three apparitions should be a bloody child, since Macduff is converted into an avenger by the murder of his wife and babes. On one level, the bloody child stands for Macduff; on another level, it is the naked new-born babe whose pleadings Macbeth has ignored. Helen Gardner took Cleanth Brooks to task for considering these images in relation to one another.[8] She argued that in his comments on 'Pity, like a naked new-born babe' [1.7.21] he had sacrificed

> a Shakespearian depth of human feeling . . . by attempting to interpret an image by the aid of what associations it happens to arouse in him, and by being more interested in making symbols of babes fit each other than in listening to what Macbeth is saying. *Macbeth* is a tragedy and not a melodrama or a symbolic drama of retribution. The reappearance of 'the babe symbol' in the apparition scene and in Macduff's revelation of his birth has distracted the critic's attention from what deeply moves the imagination and the conscience in this vision of a whole world weeping at the inhumanity of helplessness betrayed and innocence and beauty destroyed. It is the judgment of the human heart that Macbeth fears here, and the punishment which the speech foreshadows is not that he will be cut down by Macduff, but that having murdered his own humanity he will enter a world of appalling loneliness, of meaningless activity, unloved himself, and unable to love.

Although this is both eloquent and true, it does not quite dispose of Brooks's interpretation of the imagery. Miss Gardner shows that, elsewhere in Shakespeare, 'a cherub is thought of as not only young, beautiful, and innocent, but as associated with the virtue of patience'; and that in the *Macbeth* passage the helpless babe and the innocent and beautiful cherub 'call out the pity and love by which Macbeth is judged. It is not terror of heaven's vengeance which makes him pause, but the terror of moral isolation.' Yet, earlier in the same speech Macbeth expresses fear of retribution in this life— fear that he himself will have to drink the ingredients of his own poisoned chalice—and his comparison of Duncan's virtues to 'angels, trumpet-tongued' [1.7.19] implies a fear of judgment in the life to come, notwithstanding his boast that he would 'jump' it. We may assume, perhaps, that the discrepancy between the argument of the speech and the imagery employed is deliberate. On the surface Macbeth appears to be giving merely prudential reasons for not murdering Duncan; but Shakespeare makes him reveal by the imagery he employs that he, or his unconscious mind, is horrified by the thought of the deed to which he is being driven.[9]

Miss Gardner does not refer to the breast-feeding images—even

8. *The Business of Criticism* (1959), p. 61. Cf. K. Muir, 'Shakespeare's Imagery—Then and Now', *Shakespeare Survey* 18 (1965), p. 55.
9. K. Muir, *Macbeth*, p. lviii, and 'Shakespeare's Soliloquies', *Ocidente*, LXVII (1964), p. 65.

Cleanth Brooks does not mention one of the most significant—yet all these images are impressive in their contexts and, taken together, they coalesce into a symbol of humanity, kinship and tenderness violated by Macbeth's crimes. Miss Gardner is right in demanding that the precise meaning and context of each image should be considered, but wrong, I believe, in refusing to see any significance in the group as a whole. *Macbeth,* of course, is a tragedy; but I know of no valid definition of tragedy which would prevent the play from being at the same time a symbolic drama of retribution.[1]

Another important group of images is concerned with sickness and medicine, and it is significant that they all appear in the last three acts of the play after Macbeth has ascended the throne; for Scotland is suffering from the disease of tyranny, which can be cured, as fever was thought to be cured, only by bleeding or purgation. The tyrant, indeed, uses sickness imagery of himself. He tells the First Murderer that so long as Banquo is alive he wears his health but sickly; when he hears of Fleance's escape he exclaims 'Then comes my fit again' [3.4.22]; and he envies Duncan in the grave, sleeping after life's fitful fever, since life itself is one long illness. In the last act of the play a doctor, called in to diagnose Lady Macbeth's illness, confesses that he cannot

> minister to a mind diseas'd,
> Pluck from the memory a rooted sorrow,
> Raze out the written troubles of the brain,
> And with some sweet oblivious antidote
> Cleanse the stuff'd bosom of that perilous stuff
> Which weighs upon the heart. [5.3.41–46]

Macbeth then professes to believe that what is amiss with Scotland is not his own evil tyranny but the English army of liberation:

> What rhubarb, cyme, or what purgative drug
> Would scour these English hence? [5.3.56–57]

On the other side, the victims of tyranny look forward to wholesome days when Scotland will be freed. Malcolm says that Macbeth's very name blisters their tongues and he laments that 'each new day a gash' is added to Scotland's wounds. In the last act Caithness refers to Malcolm as 'the medicine of the sickly weal' [5.2.27],

---

1. More questionably, Cleanth Brooks associates the babe images with the question, much debated in the play, of what constitutes manliness. See, especially, the discussion between Macbeth and his wife in I.vii and between Macbeth and the murderers in III.i. Macbeth, before he falls, declares: 'I dare do all that may become a man: / Who dares do more is none' [1.7.46–47]. He is humanized, it has been said, by his fears. When, at the end of the play, he can no longer feel fear, he dies like a hunted beast. This, in turn, links up with the animal imagery, which is of some importance in *Macbeth,* though less prevalent than in *King Lear* or *Othello.*

> And with him pour we in our country's purge
> Each drop of us. [28–29]

Lennox adds:

> Or so much as it needs
> To dew the sovereign flower and drown the weeds. [29–30]

Macbeth is the disease from which Scotland is suffering; Malcolm, the rightful king, is the sovereign flower, both royal and curative. Macbeth, it is said,

> Cannot buckle his distemper'd cause
> Within the belt of rule. [5.2.15–16]

James I, in *A Counter-blast to Tobacco*, referred to himself as 'the proper Phisician of his Politicke-bodie', whose duty it was 'to purge it of all those diseases, by Medicines meet for the same'. It is possible that Shakespeare had read this pamphlet,[2] although, of course, disease-imagery is to be found in most of the plays written about this time. In *Hamlet* and *Coriolanus* it is applied to the body politic, as indeed it was by many writers on political theory. Shakespeare may have introduced the King's Evil as an allusion to James I's reluctant use of his supposed healing powers; but even without this topical reference, the incident provides a contrast to the evil supernatural represented by the Weird Sisters and is therefore dramatically relevant.

The contrast between good and evil is brought out in a variety of ways. There is not merely the contrast between the good and bad kings, which becomes explicit in the scene where Malcolm falsely accuses himself of avarice, lechery, cruelty and all of Macbeth's vices, and disclaims the possession of the king-becoming graces:

> Justice, verity, temperance, stableness,
> Bounty, perseverance, mercy, lowliness,
> Devotion, patience, courage, fortitude. [4.3.93–95]

There is also a contrast throughout the play between the powers of light and darkness. It has often been observed that many scenes are set in darkness. Duncan arrives at Inverness as night falls; he is murdered during the night; Banquo returns from his last ride as night is again falling; Lady Macbeth has light by her continually; and even the daylight scenes during the first part of the play are mostly gloomy in their setting—a blasted heath, wrapped in mist, a dark cavern. The murder of Duncan is followed by darkness at noon— 'dark night strangles the travelling lamp' [2.4.7]. Before the murder

2. H. N. Paul, *op. cit.*, p. 391.

Macbeth prays to the stars to hide their fires and Lady Macbeth invokes the night to conceal their crime:

> Come, thick night,
> And pall thee in the dunnest smoke of hell,
> That my keen knife see not the wound it makes,
> Nor heaven peep through the blanket of the dark
> To cry 'Hold, hold'. [1.5.48–52]

Macbeth, as he goes towards the chamber of the sleeping Duncan, describes how

> o'er the one half-world
> Nature seems dead, and wicked dreams abuse
> The curtain'd sleep. [2.1.49–51]

The word 'night' echoes through the first two scenes of the third act; and Macbeth invokes night to conceal the murder of Banquo:

> Come, seeling night,
> Scarf up the tender eye of pitiful day . . .
>   Light thickens, and the crow
> Makes wing to th' rooky wood;
> Good things of day begin to droop and drowse,
> Whiles night's black agents to their preys do rouse.
>   [3.2.49ff.]

In the scene in England and in the last act of the play—except for the sleep-walking scene—the darkness is replaced by light.

The symbolism is obvious. In many of these contexts night and darkness are associated with evil, and day and light are linked with good. The 'good things of day' are contrasted with 'night's black agents'; and, in the last act, day stands for the victory of the forces of liberation [5.4.1; 5.7.29; 5.8.37]. The 'midnight hags' are 'the instruments of darkness'; and some editors believe that when Malcolm (at the end of Act IV) says that 'The Powers above / Put on their instruments' [4.3.242–243] he is referring to their human instruments—Malcolm, Macduff and their soldiers.

The opposition between the good and evil supernatural is paralleled by similar contrasts between angel and devil, heaven and hell, truth and falsehood—and the opposites are frequently juxtaposed:

> This supernatural soliciting
> Cannot be ill; cannot be good. [1.3.133–134]

> Merciful powers
> Restrain in me the cursed thoughts that nature
> Gives way to in repose! [2.1.7–9]

> It is a knell
> That summons thee to heaven or to hell. [2.1.63–64]

Several critics have pointed out the opposition in the play between night and day, life and death, grace and evil, a contrast which is reiterated more than four hundred times.[3]

The evidence for this has gone beyond imagery proper and most modern imagistic critics have extended their field to cover not merely metaphor and simile, but the visual symbols implied by the dialogue, which would be visible in performance, and even the iteration of key words. The Poet Laureate once remarked that *Macbeth* is about blood; and from the appearance of the bloody sergeant in the second scene of the play to the last scene of all, we have a continual vision of blood. Macbeth's sword in the battle 'smok'd with bloody execution' [1.2.18]; he and Banquo seemed to 'bathe in reeking wounds' [39]; the Sergeant's 'gashes cry for help' [42]. The Second Witch comes from the bloody task of killing swine. The visionary dagger is stained with 'gouts of blood' [2.1.46]. Macbeth, after the murder, declares that not all great Neptune's ocean will cleanse his hands:

> this my hand will rather
> The multitudinous seas incarnadine,
> Making the green one red. [2.2.64–66]

Duncan is spoken of as the fountain of his son's blood; his wounds

> look'd like a breach in nature
> For ruin's wasteful entrance. [2.3.110–111]

The world had become a 'bloody stage' [2.4.6]. Macbeth, before the murder of Banquo, invokes the 'bloody and invisible hand' [3.2.51] of night. We are told of the twenty trenched gashes on Banquo's body and his ghost shakes his 'gory locks' [3.4.52] at Macbeth, who is convinced that 'blood will have blood' [3.4.124]. At the end of the banquet scene, he confesses wearily that he is 'stepp'd so far' [3.4.139] in blood, that

> should I wade no more,
> Returning were as tedious as go o'er. [139–140]

The Second Apparition, a bloody child, advises Macbeth to be 'bloody, bold, and resolute' [4.1.79]. Malcolm declares that Scotland bleeds,

---

3. F. C. Kolbe, *Shakespeare's Way* (1930), pp. 21–22, Cf. also G. Wilson Knight, *The Imperial Theme* (1931); L. C. Knights, *Explorations* (1946); Roy Walker, *The Time Is Free* (1949).

> and each new day a gash
> Is added to her wounds. [4.3.41–42]

Lady Macbeth, sleep-walking, tries in vain to remove the 'damned spot' from her hands:

> Here's the smell of the blood still. All the perfumes of
> Arabia will not sweeten this little hand. [5.1.42–43]

In the final scene, Macbeth's severed head is displayed on a pole. As Kott has recently reminded us, the subject of the play is murder, and the prevalence of blood ensures that we shall never forget the physical realities in metaphysical overtones.

Equally important is the iteration of sleep. The first statement of the theme is when the First Witch curses the Master of the *Tiger*:

> Sleep shall neither night nor day
> Hang upon his penthouse lid. [1.3.20–21]

After the murder of Duncan, Macbeth and his wife

> sleep
> In the affliction of these terrible dreams
> That shake us nightly; [3.2.19–21]

while Duncan, 'after life's fitful fever . . . sleeps well' [3.2.25]. An anonymous lord looks forward to the overthrow of the tyrant, when they will be able to sleep in peace. Because of 'a great perturbation in nature' [5.1.8], Lady Macbeth

> is troubled with thick coming fancies
> That keep her from her rest. [5.3.39–40]

The key passage in the theme of sleeplessness, derived apparently from Holinshed and Seneca's *Hercules Furens,* occurs just after the murder of Duncan, when Macbeth hears a voice which cries 'Sleep no more!' [2.2.38] It is really the echo of his own conscience. As Bradley noted, the voice 'denounced on him, as if his three names [Glamis, Cawdor, Macbeth] gave him three personalities to suffer in, the doom of sleeplessness'; and, as Murry puts it:

> He has murdered Sleep, that is 'the death of each day's life'—
> that daily death of Time which makes Time human.

The murder of a sleeping quest, the murder of a sleeping king, the murder of a saintly old man, the murder, as it were, of sleep itself, carries with it the appropriate retribution of insomnia.[4]

---

4. Cf. J. M. Murry, *Shakespeare* (1935), p. 333.

As Murry's comment suggests, the theme of sleep is linked with that of time. Macbeth is promised by the Weird Sisters that he will be king 'hereafter' and Banquo wonders if they 'can look into the seeds of time' [1.3.59]. Macbeth, tempted by the thought of murder, declares that 'Present fears/Are less than horrible imaginings' [1.3.140–141] and decides that 'Time and the hour runs through the roughest day' [1.3.151]. Lady Macbeth says she feels 'The future in the instant' [1.5.54]. In his soliloquy in the last scene of Act 1, Macbeth speaks of himself as 'here upon this bank and shoal of time' [1.7.6], time being contrasted with the sea of eternity. He pretends that he would not worry about the future, or about the life to come, if he could be sure of success in the present; and his wife implies that the conjunction of time and place for the murder will never recur. Just before the murder, Macbeth reminds himself of the exact time and place, so that he can relegate (as Stephen Spender suggests)[5] 'the moment to the past from which it will never escape into the future'. Macbeth is troubled by his inability to say amen, because he dimly realizes he has forfeited the possibility of blessing and because he knows that he has become 'the deed's creature'. The nightmares of the guilty pair and the return of Banquo from the grave symbolize the haunting of the present by the past. When Macbeth is informed of his wife's death, he describes how life has become for him a succession of meaningless days, the futility he has brought upon himself by his crimes:

> To-morrow, and to-morrow, and to-morrow,
> Creeps in this petty pace from day to day
> To the last syllable of recorded time,
> And all our yesterdays have lighted fools
> The way to dusty death. [5.5.19–23]

At the very end of the play, Macduff announces that with the death of the tyrant 'The time is free' [5.8.55] and Malcolm promises, without 'a large expense of time' [5.8.60] to do what is necessary ('which would be planted newly with the time' [5.8.65]) and to bring back order from chaos 'in measure, time, and place' [5.8.73].

From one point of view *Macbeth* can be regarded as a play about the disruption of order through evil, and its final restoration.[6] The play begins with what the witches call a hurly-burly and ends with the restoration of order by Malcolm. Order is represented throughout by the bonds of loyalty; and chaos is represented by the powers of darkness with their upsetting of moral values ('Fair is foul and

---

5. *Penguin New Writing*, no. 3, pp. 115–126. I am indebted to this article for several points in this paragraph.
6. Cf. Robert Speaight, *Nature in Shakespearean Tragedy* (1955), L. C. Knights, *op. cit.*, and G. Wilson Knight, *op. cit.*

foul is fair'). The witches can raise winds to fight against the churches, to sink ships and destroy buildings: they are the enemies both of religion and of civilization. Lady Macbeth invokes the evil spirits to take possession of her; and, after the murder of Duncan, Macbeth's mind begins to dwell on universal destruction. He is willing to 'let the frame of things disjoint, both the worlds suffer' [3.2.18] merely to be freed from his nightmares. Again, in his conjuration of the witches in the cauldron scene, he is prepared to risk absolute chaos, 'even till destruction sicken' [4.1.60] through surfeit, rather than not obtain an answer. In his last days, Macbeth is 'aweary of the sun' and he wishes 'the estate of the world' [5.5.49–50] were undone. Order in Scotland, even the moral order in the universe, can be restored only by his death. G. R. Elliott contrasts[7] the three-fold hail with which Malcolm is greeted at the end of the play with the threefold hail of the witches on the blasted heath: they mark the destruction of order and its restoration.

All through the play ideas of order and chaos are juxtaposed. When Macbeth is first visited by temptation his 'single state of man' is shaken and 'nothing is but what is not' [1.3.143, 145]. In the next scene (1.4) Shakespeare presents ideas of loyalty, duty, and the reward of faithful service, in contrast both to the treachery of the dead Thane of Cawdor and to the treacherous thoughts of the new thane. Lady Macbeth prays to be spared 'compunctious visitings of nature' [1.5.43] and in the next scene, after the description of the 'pleasant seat' [1.6.1] of the castle with its images of natural beauty, she expresses her gratitude and loyalty to the king. Before the murder, Macbeth reminds himself of the threefold tie of loyalty which binds him to Duncan, as kinsman, subject and host. He is afraid that the very stones will cry out against the unnaturalness of the murder, which is, in fact, accompanied by strange portents:

> Lamentings heard i' th' air, strange screams of death,
> And prophesying, with accents terrible,
> Of dire combustion and confus'd events
> New hatch'd to th' woeful time. [2.3.50–53]

The frequent iteration of the word 'strange' is one of the ways by which Shakespeare underlines the disruption of the natural order.

Passages which older critics deplored, and which even H. N. Paul regarded[8] as flattery of King James, may be seen as part of the theme we have been discussing. Macbeth's curious discourse on dogs is one of these passages. It was inserted not mainly because of James's proclamation on the subject, but to stress the order of nature— *naturae benignitas*—'the diverse functions and variety within a single species

7. *Dramatic Providence in Macbeth* (1958), p. 228.
8. *Op. cit.*, pp. 367 ff., 392 ff., 359 ff.

testifying to an overruling harmony and design'; and it is used to persuade his tools to murder Banquo. In the scene in England, Malcolm's self-accusations—in particular his confession of wishing to uproar the universal peace and confound all unity on earth—are disorders contrasted with the virtues he pretends not to have and with the miraculous powers of the pious Edward.

Reference must be made to two other groups of images, which I have discussed elsewhere in some detail—those relating to equivocation and those which are concerned with the contrast between what the Porter calls desire and performance.[9] The theme of equivocation runs all through the play. It was suggested, no doubt, by the topicality of the subject at Father Garnet's trial, but this links up with 'the equivocation of the fiend / That lies like truth' [5.5.43–44], the juggling fiends 'That keep the word of promise to our ear / And break it to our hope' [5.8.21–22], and Macbeth's own equivocation after the murder of Duncan:

> Had I but died an hour before this chance,
> I had liv'd a blessed time; for, from this instant,
> There's nothing serious in mortality—
> All is but toys; renown and grace is dead;
> The wine of life is drawn, and the mere lees
> Is left this vault to brag of. [2.3.88–93]

Macbeth's intention is to avert suspicion from himself by following his wife's advice to make their 'griefs and clamour roar upon' [1.7.78–79] Duncan's death. But, as he speaks the words, the audience knows that he has unwittingly spoken the truth. Instead of lying like truth, he has told the truth while intending to deceive. As he expresses it later, when full realization has come to him, life has become meaningless, a succession of empty tomorrows, 'a tale told by an idiot' [5.5.26–27].

The gap between desire and performance, enunciated by the Porter, is expressed over and over again by Macbeth and his wife. It takes the form, most strikingly, in the numerous passages contrasting eye and hand, culminating in Macbeth's cry—

> What hands are here? Ha! They pluck out mine eyes—
>   [2.2.62]

and in the scene before the murder of Banquo when the bloodstained hand is no longer Macbeth's, but Night's:

> Come, seeling night,
> Scarf up the tender eye of pitiful day,
> And with thy bloody and invisible hand

9. *Macbeth*, pp. xxvii–xxxii.

>Cancel and tear to pieces that great bond
>Which keeps me pale. [3.2.49–53]

In the sleep-walking scene, Lady Macbeth's unavailing efforts to wash the smell of the blood from her hand symbolize the indelibility of guilt; and Angus in the next scene declares that Macbeth feels

>His secret murders sticking on his hands. [5.2.17]

The soul is damned for the deeds committed by the hand.

It has recently been argued[1] that the opposition between the hand and eye provides the clearest explanation of that division in Macbeth between his clear 'perception of evil and his rapt drift into evil.' Lawrence W. Hyman suggests that Macbeth is able to do the murder only because of the deep division between his head and his hand. The

>almost autonomous action of Macbeth's dagger, as if it had no connection with a human brain or a human heart, explains the peculiar mood that pervades the murder scene . . . As soon as he lays down the dagger, however, his 'eye' cannot help but see what the hand has done.

A study of the imagery and symbolism in *Macbeth* does not radically alter one's interpretation of the play. It would, indeed, be suspect if it did. In reading some modern criticisms of Shakespeare one has the feeling that the critic is reading between the lines and creating from the interstices a play rather different from the one which Shakespeare wrote and similar to a play the critic himself might have written. Such interpretations lead us away from Shakespeare; they drop a veil between us and the plays; and they substitute a formula for the living reality, a philosophy or a theology instead of a dramatic presentation of life. I have not attempted to reshape *Macbeth* to a particular ideological image, nor selected parts of the play to prove a thesis. Some selection had to be made for reasons of space, but I have tried to make the selection representative of the whole.

We must not imagine, of course, that *Macbeth* is merely an elaborate pattern of imagery. It is a play; and in the theatre we ought to recover, as best we may, a state of critical innocence. We should certainly not attempt to notice the images of clothing or breast-feeding or count the allusions to blood or sleep. But, just as Shakespeare conveys to us the unconscious minds of the characters by means of the imagery, so, in watching the play, we may be totally unconscious of the patterns of imagery and yet absorb them unconsciously by means of our imaginative response to the poetry. In this way they will be subsumed under the total experience of the play.

---

1. Lawrence W. Hyman, *Tennessee Studies* (1960), pp. 97–100.

And what of the producer? It would be quite fatal for him to get his actors to underline the key images—to make them, as it were, italicize them with a knowing wink at the professors in the stalls or the students in the gallery. All we should ask of the producer in this matter is that he should give us what Shakespeare wrote, and all that Shakespeare wrote, and that he should not try to improve on the script provided by the dramatist.

HARRY LEVIN

Two Scenes from *Macbeth*†

Hamlet without the Prince would still be more of a spectacle than *Macbeth* without the Thane of Glamis. Though the latter is not introspective by nature, his soliloquizing is central to the play, as he considers intentions, casts suspicions, registers hallucinations, coerces his conscience, balances hope against fear, and gives thought to the unspeakable—all this while sustaining the most energetic role in the most intense of Shakespeare's plays. *Macbeth* is the fastest of them, as Coleridge pointed out, while *Hamlet,* at almost twice its length, is the slowest. Thus the uncut *Hamlet* has plenty of room for other well-defined characters and for highly elaborated subplots. Whereas *Macbeth,* which has come down to us in a version stripped for action, concentrates more heavily upon the protagonist. He speaks over thirty per cent of the lines; an overwhelming proportion of the rest bear reference to him; and Lady Macbeth has about eleven per cent, all of them referring to him directly or indirectly. Most of the other parts get flattened in this process, so that his may stand out in bold relief. Otherwise, as Dr. Johnson commented, there is "no nice discrimination of character." As Macbeth successively murders Duncan, Banquo, and Lady Macduff with her children, a single line of antagonism builds up through Malcolm and Fleance to the effectual revenger, Macduff. There is evidence, in the original text and in the subsequent stage-history, to show that the grim spareness of the plot was eked out by additional grotesqueries on the part of the Witches.

I make this preliminary obeisance to the centrality of the hero-villain because it is not to him that I shall be calling your attention, though it should be evident already that he will be reflected upon by my sidelights. In skipping over the poetry of his speeches or the moral and psychological dimensions of character, I feel somewhat like the

† From *Shakespeare's Craft: Eight Lectures,* ed. Philip H. Highfill, Jr. (Carbondale: Southern Illinois University Press: 1982), 48–68. Reprinted by permission of Southern Illinois University Press.

visitor to a Gothic edifice whose exclusive focus is devoted to a gargoyle here and there. I should not be doing so if the monument as a whole were less memorably familiar than it is, or if the artistic coherence of a masterpiece did not so frequently reveal itself through the scrutiny of an incidental detail. My two short texts are quite unevenly matched, though not disconnected in the long run. One of them, the Porter's Scene, has been regarded more often than not as a mere excrescence or intrusion. The other, the Sleepwalking Scene, has become one of the high spots in the repertory as a set piece for distinguished actresses. The lowest common denominator between them is that both have been written in prose. Apart from more functional purposes, such as documents and announcements, Shakespeare makes use of prose to convey an effect of what Brian Vickers terms "otherness," a different mode of diction from the norm. To cite the clearest instance, Hamlet's normal personality is expressed in blank verse; he falls into prose when he puts on his "antic disposition." This combines, as do the fools' roles, the two major uses of Shakespeare's non-metrical speech: on the one hand, comedy, low life, oftentimes both; on the other, the language of psychic disturbance.

Our two scenes are enacted in these two modes respectively. But, before we turn to them, let us take a very brief glance at the outdoor stage of the Shakespearean playhouse. On that subject there has been an infinite deal of specific conjecture over a poor halfpennyworth of reliable documentation, and many of those conjectures have disagreed with one another. Over its most general features, however, there is rough agreement, and that is all we need here. We know that its large jutting platform had a roof supported by two pillars downstage; one of which might conveniently have served as the tree where Orlando hangs his verses in *As You Like It*. We are also aware of an acting space "aloft" at stage rear, whence Juliet or Prospero could have looked down. As for the curtained space beneath, that remains an area of veiled uncertainty. Yet the back wall of the tiring-house had to include an outside doorway big enough to accommodate the inflow and outflow of sizable properties, and possibly to present a more or less literal gate upon due occasion. Hence it is not difficult to conceive of the stage as the courtyard of a castle, into which outsiders would arrive, and off of which branched chambers for the guests, who might hurriedly rush out from them if aroused by some emergency. Moreover, the surrounding auditorium, open to the skies and rising in three tiers of galleries, might itself have presented a kind of courtyard. Not that this arrangement was representational. It was the stylization of the theatrical arena that made possible its scope and adaptability.

Much depended, of course, upon the convention of verbal scenery.

When the aged, gracious, and serene King Duncan appears at the gate of Glamis Castle, his introductory words sketch the setting and suggest the atmosphere:

> This castle hath a pleasant seat, the air
> Nimbly and sweetly recommends itself
> Unto our gentle senses. (1.6.1–3)

The description is amplified by Banquo with his mention of "the temple-haunting marlet" (4), the bird whose presence almost seems to consecrate a church, one of the succession of birds benign and malign whose auspices are continually invoked. The description of the marlet's "procreant cradle" (8)—and procreation is one of the points at issue throughout—assures us that "the heaven's breath / Smells wooingly here" (5, 6). And Banquo completes the stage-design:

> Where they most breed and haunt, I have observ'd
> The air is delicate. (9, 10)

Knowing what we have been informed with regard to Duncan's reception, and what he is so poignantly unaware of, we may well find it a delicate situation. Stressing its contrast to the episodes that precede and follow it, Sir Joshua Reynolds called it "a striking instance of what in painting is termed *repose*." Repose—or rather, the absence of it—is fated to become a major theme of the tragedy. It will mean not rest but restlessness for Macbeth, when Duncan all too soon is accorded his last repose. Are we not much nearer, at this point, to the fumes of hell than to the heaven's breath? Macbeth, as he will recognize in a soliloquy, "should gainst his murtherer shut the door," rather than hypocritically welcoming Duncan in order to murder him (1.7.15). Duncan has been a ruler who exemplified royalty, a guest who deserved hospitality, and a man of many virtues who has commanded respect, as Macbeth himself acknowledges. The scene is set for the crimes and their consequences by this two-faced welcome into the courtyard of Macbeth's castle.

By the end of the incident-crowded First Act, in spite of his hesitant asides and soliloquies, everything has fallen into place for the consummation of the Witches' cackling prophecies. The Second Act begins ominously with Banquo's muted misgivings; he supplicates the "merciful powers"—who seem less responsive than those darker spirits addressed by Lady Macbeth—to restrain in him "the cursed thoughts that nature / Gives way to in repose," and retires after Macbeth has wished him "Good repose" (2.1.7–9, 29). This exchange would seem to occur in the courtyard, which becomes the base of operations for the murder. The first scene culminates in the vision of the dagger, hypnotically drawing Macbeth to the door of Duncan's quarters. Leaving them after the deed, as he recounts to his wife in the second scene, he has experienced another hallucination: the voice that cried "Sleep no more!" (2.2.32). Meanwhile Lady Macbeth has soliloquized, fortified with drink, and he has cried out offstage at the fatal instant. One residual touch of humanity, the memory of her own father, has inhibited her from killing the king herself; but she is Amazonian enough, taking the bloody daggers from her badly shaken husband with a crude and cruel joke (the pun on "gild" and "guilt"), to reenter the death chamber and plant them upon the sleeping grooms (2.2.53–54). It is then that the tensely whispered colloquies between the guilty couple are suddenly interrupted by that most portentous of sound effects: the knocking at the gate.

This is the point of departure for a well-known essay by Thomas De Quincey, who argues, rather overingeniously, that the interruption helps to restore normality, calming the excited sensibilities of the spectator. "The reaction has commenced; the human has made its reflux upon the fiendish; the pulses of life are beginning to beat again," De Quincey concludes, "the reestablishment of the goings-on of the world in which we live makes us profoundly sensible of the awful parenthesis that had suspended them." Here De Quincey, who elsewhere styled himself "a connoisseur of murder," seems to have got his proportions wrong. Surely it is the Porter's Scene that forms a parenthesis in an increasingly awful train of events. "Every noise appalls me," Macbeth has said (2.2.55). For him—and for us as well—the knock reverberates with the menace of retribution, like the opening notes of Beethoven's Fifth Symphony. It heralds no resumption of diurnal business as usual. Let us bear in mind that the knocker is to be the avenger, the victim who will have suffered most from the tyrant's cruelty. Macduff's quarrel with Macbeth, according to Holinshed's chronicle, first arose because the Thane of Fife did not fully participate when commanded by the King of Scotland to help him build the new castle at Dunsinane. It is surprising that Shakespeare did not utilize that hint of motivation; possibly he did, and the scene was among those lost through the rigors of cutting. It would have added another turn of the screw to Macbeth's seizure of Macduff's castle at Fife and the domestic massacre therein.

As for Dunsinane Castle, it is ironic that Macbeth should count upon its strength and that it should be so easily surrendered, "gently rend'red," after a few alarums and excursions (5.7.24). It comes as a final reversal of the natural order that he, besieged and bound in, should be assaulted and overcome by what appears to be a walking forest. So, in the earlier scenes, the manifest presumption is that the pleasantly situated Glamis Castle would be a haven and a sanctuary, associated with temples by Macbeth as well as Banquo. Rapidly it proves to be the opposite for its guests, whereas those menacing thumps at the gateway announce the arrival not of a dangerous enemy but of their predestined ally. Despite his sacrifice and suffering, his quasi-miraculous birth, and his intervention on the side of the angels, I shall refrain from presenting Macduff as a Christ-figure. There are altogether too many of these in current literary criticism— many more, I fear, than exist in real life. Yet it is enlightening to consider the suggested analogy between this episode and that pageant in the mystery cycles which dramatizes the Harrowing of Hell. Some of those old guildplays were still being acted during Shakespeare's boyhood; nearby Coventry was a center for them; and we meet with occasional allusions to them in Shakespeare's plays, notably to Herod whose furious ranting had made him a popular byword. Without the Slaughter of the Innocents, over which he presided, the horrendous slaughter at Macduff's castle would have been unthinkable. Many later audiences, which might have flinched, have been spared it.

When Jesus stands before the gates of hell, in the Wakefield cycle, his way is barred by a gatekeeper suggestively named Rybald, who tells his fellow devil Beelzebub to tie up those souls which are about to be delivered: "how, belsabub! bynde thise boys, / sich harow was never hard in hell." The command of Jesus that the gates be opened takes the form of a Latin cadence from the liturgy, *Attollite portas* . . . This, in turn, is based upon the vulgate phrasing of the Twenty-fourth Psalm: "Lift up your heads, O ye gates; even lift them up, ye everlasting doors; and the King of glory shall come in." The liturgical Latin echoes the rite of Palm Sunday celebrating Christ's entrance into Jerusalem. It was also chanted before the portals of a church during the ceremonies of consecration. In the mystery, Jesus enters hell to debate with Satan and ends by rescuing therefrom various worthies out of the Old Testament. That is the typological situation which prefigured Shakespeare's comic gag. We must now turn back to his dilatory Porter, after having kept the visitor waiting outside longer than the Porter will. Obviously the action is continuous between Scenes Two and Three, with the repeated knocking to mark the continuity. "Wake Duncan with thy knocking! I would thou couldst!" is the exit line (2.2.71). Macbeth, unnerved, is guided to their chamber by his wife, as he will be again in the Banquet Scene, and as she will imagine in the Sleepwalking Scene. There should be a minute when the stage is bare, and the only drama is the knocking.

But it will take a longer interval for the couple to wash off the blood and change into night attire. This is the theatrical necessity that provides the Porter with his cue and one of the troupe's comedians with a small part. Shakespeare's clowns tend to be more stylized than his other characters, most specifically the fools created by

Robert Armin, and probably to reflect the personal style of certain actors. Will Kemp, who preceded Armin as principal comedian, seems to have specialized in voluble servants. It may well have been Kemp who created the rather similar roles of Launce in *The Two Gentlemen of Verona* and Launcelot Gobbo in *The Merchant of Venice*. Each of these has his characteristic routine: a monologue which becomes a dialogue as the speaker addresses himself to imagined interlocutors. Gobbo's is especially apropos, since it pits his conscience against the fiend. Shakespeare did not abandon that vein after Kemp left the company; indeed he brought it to its highest pitch of development in Falstaff's catechism on honor. The Porter's little act is pitched at a much lower level, yet it can be better understood in the light of such parallels. The sleepy Porter stumbles in, bearing the standard attributes of his office, a lantern and some keys. He is not drunk now; but, like others in the castle, he has been carousing late; and his fantasy may be inspired by the penitential mood of the morning after. "If a man were Porter of Hell Gate"—that is the hypothesis on which he is ready to act—"he should have old turning the key"—he should have to admit innumerable sinners (2.3.1–3).

An audience acquainted with Marlowe's *Doctor Faustus* would not have to be reminded that the hellmouth had figured in the mysteries. And the dramatist who had conceived the Brothel Scene in *Othello* had envisioned a character, namely Emilia, who could be accused of keeping—as the opposite number of Saint Peter—"the gate of hell" (4.2.92). The Porter assumes that stance by choice, asking himself: "Who's there, i' th' name of Belzebub?" (3–4). He answers himself by admitting three social offenders. It has been his plan, he then confides, to have passed in review "all professions," doubtless with an appropriately satirical comment on each (18). But, despite the histrionic pretence that hellfire is roaring away, the Porter's teeth are chattering in the chill of early morning: "this place is too cold for hell" (16–17). Neither the time-serving farmer nor the hose-stealing tailor seems as pertinent a wrongdoer as the equivocator, "who could not equivocate to heaven" (10–11). Here the editors digress to inform us about the trial and execution of Henry Garnet, Superior of the Jesuit Order, in 1606. The topical allusion is helpful, insofar as it indicates how the word came to be in the air; and Garnet's casuistry had to do with treason and attempted regicide, the notorious Gunpowder Plot. But *Macbeth* is not exactly a satire on the Jesuits. Maeterlinck, in his translation, renders "equivocator" by "*jésuite*" because there is no cognate French equivalent. The thematic significance of the Porter's speech lies in its anticipation of the oracles ("these juggling fiends"), which turn out to be true in an unanticipated sense: "th' equivocation of the fiend" (5.8.19; 5.5.42). The Porter, who has been parrying the knocks by echoing them, finally shuffles to the gate, lets in Macduff and Lenox, and stands by for his tip: "I pray you remember the porter" (20–21). Drink, which has inebriated the grooms and emboldened Lady Macbeth, is his poor excuse for tardiness. The after-effects of drinking are the subject of his vulgar and not very funny riddle: "nose-painting, sleep, and urine" (28). Then, licensed perhaps by the precedent of the devil-porter Rybald, he moves on to the equivocal subject of lechery. If drink provokes the desire but takes away the performance, it is a paradigm for Macbeth's ambition. For, as Lady Macbeth will realize: "Nought's had, all's spent, / Where our desire is got without content" (3.2.4–5). When liquor is declared to be "an equivocator with lechery," that equivocation is demonstrated by the give-and-take of the Porter's rhythms: "it makes him, and it mars him; it sets him on, and it takes him off; it persuades him, and disheartens him; makes him stand to, and not stand to; in conclusion, equivocates him in a sleep, and giving him the lie, leaves him" (2.3.32–36). Each of these paired clauses, here again, links a false promise with a defeated expectation, expiring into drunken slumber after a moment of disappointed potency. The see-saw of the cadencing is as much of a prophecy as the Witches' couplets, and it has the advantage of pointing unequivocally toward the dénouement. The repartee trails off, after a lame pun about lying, with the reentrance of Macbeth, for which the Porter has been gaining time by going through his turn.

That turn has regularly been an object of expurgation, both in the theater and in print. I am not digressive if I recall that, when I wrote the introduction to a school-edition several years ago, the publishers wanted to leave out the Porter's ribaldry. I insisted upon an unbowdlerized text; but their apprehensions were commercially warranted; the textbook, though it is in a well-known series, has hardly circulated at all. Thousands of adolescents have been saved from the hazards of contemplating alcoholism, sex, and micturition. On a higher critical plane—some would say the highest—Coleridge was so nauseated by the whole scene that he ruled it out of the canon, declaring that it had been "written for the mob by another hand." The sentence about "the primrose way to th' everlasting bonfire," Coleridge conceded, had a Shakespearean ring (2.3.19). Without pausing to wonder whether it might have been echoed from *Hamlet*, he characteristically assumed that Shakespeare himself had interpolated it within the interpolation of his unknown collaborator. This enabled him to beg the question with Coleridgean logic and to comment further on "the entire absence of comedy, nay, even of irony . . . in *Macbeth*." Wholly apart from the comedy or the authenticity of the Porter Scene, it must strike us as singularly obtuse to overlook the fundamental ironies of the play: its ambiguous predictions, its self-destructive misdeeds. It could be urged, in Coleridge's defense, that the concept of dramatic irony had not yet been formulated. Kierkegaard's thesis on it was published in 1840, having been anticipated by Connop Thirlwall just a few years before.

Coleridge's rejection is sustained by another high literary authority. In Schiller's German adaptation, the Porter is high-minded and cold sober. He has stayed awake to keep guard over the King, and therefore over all Scotland, as he tells Macbeth in an ambitious jest. Instead of masquerading as an infernal gatekeeper, he has sung a pious hymn to the sunrise and has ignored the knocking in order to finish his *Morgenlied*. Yet, for a century now, the current of opinion has run the other way; commentators have held, with J. W Hales, that Shakespeare's Porter was authentic and by no means inappropriate. Robert Browning heartily agreed, and Bishop Wordsworth even allowed that the scene could be read with edification. So it should be, given its eschatological overtones. We have long discarded the neo-classical inhibitions regarding the intermixture of tragic and comic elements. We have learned, above all from Lear's Fool, that the comic can intensify the tragic, rather than simply offer itself as relief. Those "secret, black, and midnight hags," the Witches, who for Holinshed were goddesses of destiny, come as close as anything in Shakespeare to the chorus of Greek tragedy (4.1.48). But their outlandish imminence seems elusive and amoral because of their mysterious connection with the machinery of fate. The Porter's role is grotesquely choric in another sense. Like the Gardener in *Richard II*, he stands there to point the moral, to act out the object-lesson. This castle, far from reaching up toward heaven, is located at the brink of hell. Even now its lord has damned himself eternally.

Damnation is portended by the curse of sleeplessness, which has been foreshadowed among the spells that the First Witch proposed to cast upon the sea-captain: "Sleep shall neither night nor day / Hang upon his penthouse lid" (1.3.19–20). No sooner has the King been murdered than Macbeth hears the voice crying "Sleep no more!" and begins to extoll the blessing he has forfeited. The word itself is sounded thirty-two times, more than in any other play of Shakespeare's. Repeatedly sleep is compared with death. Almost enviously, after complaining of the "terrible dreams" that afflict him nightly, Macbeth evokes the buried Duncan: "After life's fitful fever he sleeps well" (3.2.18, 23). When he breaks down at the Banquet Scene before the apparition of Banquo's ghost, it is Lady Macbeth who assumes command, discharges the guests, and leads her husband off to bed with the soothing words: "You lack the season of all natures, sleep" (3.4.140). It should be noted that she does not see the ghost or hear the voice, and that she skeptically dismisses the air-drawn dagger as a subjective phenomenon: "the very painting of your fear" (3.4.60). Unlike Macbeth, she has no intercourse with the supernatural forces. To be sure, she has called upon the spirits to unsex her, fearing lest she be deterred from murder by the milk—the feminine attribute—of human kindness. And from the outset it is he, not she, who feels and expresses that remorse she has steeled herself against, those "compunctious visitings of nature" (1.5.45). When they ultimately overtake her, his insomnia will have its counterpart in her somnambulism.

In keeping with her aloofness from supernaturalism, Shakespeare's treatment of her affliction seems so naturalistic, that it is now and then cited among the clinical cases in abnormal psychology. According to the seventeenth-century frame of reference, she may show the symptoms of melancholia or—to invoke theological concepts that still can grip the audiences of films—demonic possession. Psychoanalysis tends to diagnose her malady as a manifestation of hysteria, which compels her to dramatize her anxiety instead of dreaming about it, to reenact the pattern of behavior that she has tried so desperately to repress. Freud regarded this sleepwalker and her sleepless mate as "two disunited parts of a single psychical individuality," together subsuming the possibilities of reaction to the crime, and underlined the transference from his response to hers, from his hallucinations to her mental disorder. In more social terms, the closeness of their complementary relationship seems strongly reinforced by the sexual bond between them. Three of the exit-lines emphasize their going to bed together. Caroline Spurgeon and other interpreters of Shakespeare's imagery have noticed that the most recurrent metaphor in the play has to do with dressing and undressing, transposed sometimes into arming and disarming or crowning and uncrowning. The sense of intimacy is enhanced by the recollection that the nightgowns mentioned are dressing-gowns, that under the bedclothes no clothing of any sort was worn in that day; and nakedness exposed is one of the other themes (a recent film has welcomed the opportunity for presenting a heroine in the nude).[1] Lady Macbeth, as M. C. Bradbrook has observed, must have been a siren as well as a fury.

Inquiries into her motives have dwelt upon her childlessness, after having borne a child who evidently died, and that frustration seems to have kindled Macbeth's hostility toward the families of Banquo and Macduff. Deprived of happy motherhood, she takes a somewhat maternal attitude toward her spouse, and she seeks a vicarious fulfillment in her ruthless ambitions for his career. Holinshed had stressed her single-minded goading-on of her husband, "burning in unquenchable desire to bear the name of a queen." She may be a "fiend-like queen" to Malcolm and other enemies, but the charac-

---

1. Roman Polanski's *Macbeth* (1971) [*Editor's note*].

terization is highly nuanced when we contrast it with the termagant queens of Shakespeare's earliest histories (5.9.35). Criticism ranges all the way from Hazlitt ("a great bad woman whom we hate, but whom we fear more than we hate") to Coleridge ("a woman of a visionary and daydreaming turn of mind"). Coleridge had re-created Hamlet in his own image, after all, and his Lady Macbeth might pose as a model for Madame Bovary. The variance in interpretations extends from Lamartine's "perverted and passionate woman" to Tieck's emphasis on her conjugal tenderness, which provoked the mockery of Heine, who envisages her billing and cooing like a turtle dove. She may not be "such a dear" as Bernard Shaw discerned in Ellen Terry's portrayal; but she encompasses most of these images, inasmuch as Shakespeare clearly understood the ambivalence of aggression and sympathy in human beings. Her emotions and Macbeth's are timed to a different rhythm. As he hardens into a fighting posture, and his innate virility reasserts itself, she softens into fragile femininity, and her insecurities come to the surface of her breakdown.

Distraction of the mind is rendered by Shakespeare in a pithy, terse, staccato idiom which might not inappropriately be termed distracted prose. Madness, along with all the other moods of English tragedy, had originally been conveyed through blank verse, as when Titus Andronicus "runs lunatic." So it was in Kyd's operatic *Spanish Tragedy*, though the later and more sophisticated ragings of its hero would be added by another hand in prose. The innovation was Marlowe's:[2] in the First Part of *Tamburlaine* the captive queen Zabina goes mad over the death of her consort Bajazet, and before her suicide gives utterance to a short prose sequence of broken thoughts. Her farewell line, "Make ready my coach . . ." must have given Shakespeare a suggestion for Ophelia. He seized upon this technique and developed it to the point where it became, in the phrase of Laertes, "A document in madness, / Thoughts and remembrance fitted." Ophelia distributing flowers, like King Lear distributing weeds, obsessively renews the source of grief. Edgar in the guise of Tom o'Bedlam deliberately imitates such language as does Hamlet when he simulates insanity. Lear's Fool is exceptional, since he is both a jester and a natural; yet, in that dual role, he may be looked upon as a mediator between the comic and the distracted prose. And in *King Lear* as a whole, in the interrelationship between the Lear-Cordelia plot and the Gloucester-Edgar underplot, we have our most highly wrought example of the two plots running parallel. As a matter of dramaturgic tradition, that parallel tended in the direction of parody.

Thus, in the Second Shepherds' Play at Wakefield, the serious plot

---

2. Christopher Marlowe (1564–93), a London playwright [*Editor's note*].

about the nativity is parodied by the sheepstealing underplot, since
the lamb is an emblem of Jesus. In the oldest English secular comedy, *Fulgens and Lucres,* while two suitors court the mistress, their
respective servants court the maid—probably the most traditional of
all comic situations, harking back as far as Aristophanes' *Frogs.* In
Doctor Faustus the clowns burlesque the hero's conjurations by pur-
loining his magical book and conjuring up a demon. This has its
analogue in *The Tempest,* where the conspiracy against Prospero is
burlesqued by the clownish complot. Having defended the essential
seriousness of the Porter's Scene, I am not moving toward an argument that there is anything comic per se in the Sleepwalking Scene;
but there is something distinctly parodic about the virtual repetition
of a previous scene in such foreshortened and denatured form. Murder will out, as the old adage cautions; the modern detective story
operates on the assumption that the murderer returns to the locality
of the crime. Lady Macbeth, always brave and bold when her husband was present, must sleep alone when he departs for the battlefield. It is then that her suppressed compunction, her latent sense
of guilt, wells up from the depths of her subconscious anguish.
Under the cover of darkness and semi-consciousness, she must now
reenact her part, going through the motions of that scene in the
courtyard on the night of Duncan's assassination, and recapitulating
the crucial stages of the entire experience.

When the late Tyrone Guthrie staged his production at the Old
Vic, he directed his leading lady, Flora Robson, to reproduce the
exact gesticulation of the murder scene. Such an effect could not
have been achieved within the Piranesi-like setting designed by Gor-
don Craig, where the sleepwalking was supposed to take place on
the steps of a sweeping spiral staircase. One of the most theatrical
features of this episode, however it be played, lies in the choreo-
graphic opportunity that it offers to the actress and the director. At
the Globe Playhouse the principal problem in staging would have
been the glaring fact that plays were performed there in broad daylight. That was simply met by a convention, which has been uncov-
ered through the researches of W. J. Laurence. A special point was
made of bringing out lanterns, tapers, or other lights, paradoxically
enough, to indicate the darkness. But the lighting of the Sleepwalking Scene is not merely conventional. Lady Macbeth, we learn, can
no longer abide the dark. "She has light by her continually," her
Waiting Gentlewoman confides to the Doctor (5.1.22–23). It is the
candle she carries when she enters, no mere stage property either,
throwing its beams like a good deed in a naughty world. Banquo, on
a starless night, has referred metaphorically to the overclouded stars
as extinguished candles. Macbeth, when the news of his wife's
suicide is subsequently brought to him, will inveigh against the

autumnal prospect of meaninglessness ahead, and the yesterdays behind that have "lighted fools / The way to dusty death" (5.5.22–23). Life itself is the brief candle he would now blow out.

Lady Macbeth presumably carried her candle throughout the scene until the London appearance of Sarah Siddons in 1785. She was severely criticized for setting it down on a table, so that she could pantomime the gesture of rubbing her hands. Sheridan, then manager of the Drury Lane, told her: "It would be thought a presumptuous innovation." Man of the theater that he was, he congratulated her upon it afterwards. But many in the audience were put off by it, and even more by her costume. She was wearing white satin, traditionally reserved for mad scenes, and later on would shift to a shroudlike garment. Mrs. Siddons as Lady Macbeth became, by wide consent, the greatest English actress in her greatest role. Hence we have a fair amount of testimony about her performance. A statuesque figure whose rich voice ranged from melancholy to peevishness, subsiding at times into eager whispers, she was "tragedy personified" for Hazlitt, who reports that "all her gestures were involuntary and mechanical." More physically active than her candleburdened predecessors, who seem to have mainly glided, she excelled particularly at stage-business. The hand-rubbing was accompanied by a gesture of ladling water out of an imaginary ewer. When she held up one hand, she made a face at the smell—a bit of business which Leigh Hunt considered "unrefined." Yet, after she had made her exit stalking backwards, one witness testified: "I swear that I smelt blood!" She herself has attested that, when as a girl of twenty she began to study the part, she was overcome by a paroxysm of terror.

Turning more directly to "this slumb'ry agitation," we are prepared for it by the expository conversation between the Gentlewoman and the Doctor (5.1.11). Lady Macbeth's twenty lines will be punctuated by their whispering comments. It is clear that there have been earlier visitations, and that Lady Macbeth has engaged in writing during one of them; but what she spoke the Gentlewoman firmly refuses to disclose. The Doctor, who has been watching with her during the last two nights, has so far witnessed nothing. But, from the account, he knows what to expect: "A great perturbation in nature, to receive at once the benefit of sleep and do the effects of watching!" (9–11). Sleep seems scarcely a benefit under the circumstances, much as it may be longed for by the watchful, the ever-wakeful Macbeth; and, though Lady Macbeth is actually sleeping, she is not only reliving the guilty past but incriminating herself. When she appears, the antiphonal comment ("You see her eyes are open." / "Ay, but their sense is shut.") raises that same question of moral blindness which Shakespeare explored in *King Lear* (24–25). If she could feel that her hands were cleansed when she washed them, her compulsive gesture would be a ritual of purification. Yet Pilate, washing his hands before the multitude, has become an archetype of complicity. Her opening observation and exclamation ("Yet here's a spot" . . . "Out, damn'd spot!") is a confession that prolonged and repeated ablutions have failed to purge her sins (31, 35). She continues by imagining that she hears the clock strike two: it is time for the assassination. Her revulsion from it compresses into three words all the onus of the Porter's garrulous commentary: "Hell is murky" (36).

That sudden glimpse of the bottomless pit does not keep her from the sanguinary course she has been pursuing. But the grandiose iambic pentameter of her courtyard speeches, inspiriting and rebuking her reluctant partner, has been contracted into a spasmodic series of curt, stark interjections, most of them monosyllabic. "Yet who would have thought the old man to have had so much blood in him?" (39–40). She had thought at least of her father, and had momentarily recoiled. Macbeth had feared that the deed might not "trammel up the consequence," might open the way for retributive counteraction, and indeed Duncan's blood has clamored for a terrible augmentation of bloodshed, has set off the chain-reaction of blood-feuds involving Banquo's progeny and Macduff's. Hitherto we had not been aware of Lady Macbeth's awareness of the latter, much less of how she might respond to his catastrophe. Her allusion to Lady Macduff seems reduced to the miniature scale of a nursery rhyme ("The Thane of Fife / had a wife"), but it culminates in the universal lamentation of *ubi est*: "Where is she now?" Then, more hand-washing, more conjugal reproach. Her listeners are realizing, more and more painfully, that they should not be listening; what she says should not be heard, should not have been spoken, should never have happened. "Here's the smell of the blood still" (50). The olfactory metaphor has a scriptural sanction, as Leigh Hunt should have remembered: evil was a stench in righteous nostrils, and the offence of Claudius smelled to heaven. The heartcry comes with the recognition that the smell of blood will be there forever: "All the perfumes of Arabia will not sweeten this little hand" (50–51).

She had been clear-headed, tough-minded, and matter-of-fact in tidying up after the murder: "A little water clears us of this deed." It was Macbeth, exhausted and conscience-stricken after his monstrous exertion, who had envisioned its ethical consequences in a hyperbolic comparison:

> Will all great Neptune's ocean wash this blood
> Clean from my hand? No; this my hand will rather
> The multitudinous seas incarnadine,
> Making the green one red. (2.2.57–60)

Her hand is smaller than his, and so—relatively speaking—is her hyperbole. All the perfumes of Arabia, all the oilwells of Arabia, could not begin to fill the amplitude of the ocean, and the contrast is completed by the oceanic swell of his Latinate polysyllables. She has come to perceive, unwillingly and belatedly, that the stigmata are irremovable. He had perceived this at once and, moreover, reversed his magniloquent trope. Never can the bloodstain be cleansed away; on the contrary, it will pollute the world. No one can, as she advised in another context, "lave our honors" (3.2.33). The sound that voices this perception on her part ("O, O, O!") was more than a sign when Mrs. Siddons voiced it, we are told (5.1.52). It was "a convulsive shudder—very horrible." The one-sided marital dialogue goes on, reverting to the tone of matter-of-factness. "Wash your hands, put on your nightgown, look not so pale" (62–63). If Duncan is in his grave, as Macbeth has mused, is not Banquo in a similar condition? Where is he now? Reminiscence here reverberates from the Banquet Scene: "I tell you yet again, Banquo's buried; he cannot come out on's grave" (63–64). These internalized anxieties that will not be so coolly exorcized are far more harrowing than the externalized ghosts that beset Richard III on the eve of battle. Having resumed his soldierly occupation and been reassured by the Witches' auguries, Macbeth has put fear behind him, whatever the other cares that are crowding upon him. It is therefore through Lady Macbeth that we apprehend the approach of nemesis.

And then her terminal speech: "To bed, to bed; there's knocking at the gate" (66–67). It is imaginary knocking; what we hear again is silence, a silence powerful enough to resurrect the encounter between those harbingers of revenge and damnation, Macduff and the Porter. Her fantasy concludes by repeating what we have already watched in both the Murder Scene and the Banquet Scene, when she led her faltering husband offstage. "Come, come, come, come, give me your hand" (67). Her next and penultimate remark harks back to the concatenation of earlier events. The First Witch, in her premonitory resentment against the sailor's wife, had promised him a swarm of nameless mischiefs (future tense): "I'll do, I'll do, and I'll do" (1.3.10). Macbeth's own ruminations at the edge of action had started from the premise (present tense, conditional and indicative): "If it were done, when 'tis done, then 'twere well / It were done quickly" (1.7.1–2). It was done quickly, whereupon Lady Macbeth sought to arrest his mounting disquietude with the flat affirmation (past, transitive): "What's done, is done" (3.2.12). Similar as it sounds, it was a far cry from her concluding negation, her fatalistic valediction to life: "What's done cannot be undone" (5.1.68). This implies the wish that it had not been done, reinforces Macbeth's initial feeling that it need not be done, and equilibrates the play's dialectical movement between free will and inevitability. The appeal, "To bed," is uttered five times. She moves off to the bedchamber they will never share again, as if she still were guiding her absent husband's steps and his bloodstained hand were still in hers.

The doctor, who has been taking notes, confesses himself to be baffled. The case is beyond his practise, it requires a divine rather than a physician. In the following scene he discusses it with Macbeth on a more or less psychiatric basis. Lady Macbeth is "Not so sick . . . / As she is troubled with thick-coming fancies, / That keep her from her rest" (5.3.37–39). The Doctor is not a psychiatrist; he cannot minister to a mind diseas'd" (40). Nor has he a cure for Scotland's disease, when Macbeth rhetorically questions him. Here we catch the connection with the one scene that passes in England, where the dramatic values center on Macduff's reaction to his domestic tragedy. His interview with Malcolm is a test of loyalty, and the invented accusations that Malcolm levels against himself—that he would, for instance, "Pour the sweet milk of concord into hell"—are more applicable to Macbeth, whose milky nature has gone just that way (4.3.98). We are at the court of Edward the Confessor, the saintly English king whose virtues make him a foil for the Scottish hellhound. A passage which might seem to be a digression expatiates on how the royal touch can cure his ailing subjects of the scrofula, known accordingly as the King's Evil. Shakespeare is complimenting the new Stuart monarch, James I, descendant of the legendary Banquo, who had revived the ancient superstition. But the pertinence goes further; for the spokesman of the English king is another doctor; and the antithesis is brought home when we compare the sickness of the one country with that of the other. The King's Evil? Given the omens, the tidings, the disaffections, is it not Scotland which suffers from that disease?

A. C. Bradley asserted that Lady Macbeth is "the only one of Shakespeare's great tragic characters who on a last appearance is denied the dignity of verse." That comment discloses a curious insensitivity not only to the ways of the theater, which never interested Bradley very much, but to the insights of psychology, for which he claimed an especial concern. It could be maintained that distracted prose constitutes an intensive vein of poetry. Somnambulism, though fairly rare as a habit among adults (much rarer than sleep talking), is such a striking one that we might expect it to have had more impact upon the imagination. Yet there seems to be little or no folklore about it, if we may judge from its omission in Stith Thompson's comprehensive *Index*. It has suggested the rather silly libretto of Bellini's opera, *La Sonnambula* (based upon a vaudeville-ballet by Scribe), where the sleepwalking heroine compromises herself by walking into a man's room at an inn, and then redeems her reputation by singing a coloratura aria while perambulating asleep on a rooftop. Dissimilarly, Verdi's *Macbetto* avoids such pyrotechnical possibilities. The prima donna, in her sleepwalking *scena*, sticks fairly close to Shakespeare's disjointed interjections, though her voice mounts to a Verdian lilt at the high point:

> Arabia intera
> rimandar sí piccol mano
> co' suoi balsami non puó,
> no, no, non puó . . . [3]

The only serious dramatization that I can recall, apart from Shakespeare's, is Kleist's *Prinz Friedrich von Homburg*. In contradistinction to Lady Macbeth, Prince Friedrich has already made his promenade when the play opens; he is discovered at morning seated in a garden; and the garland he is unconsciously weaving adumbrates his dreams of future military glory. The title of Hermann Broch's fictional trilogy, *Die Schlafwandler*, is purely figurative. A melodrama made famous by Henry Irving, *The Bells*, culminates in the mesmerized reenactment of a crime. It is worth noting that the first *Macbeth* acted in German (1773), freely adapted by Gottlob Stefanie der Jüngere, replaced the sleepwalking scene by a mad scene in which Macbeth was stabbed to death by his lady. Shakespeare would seem to have been as unique in his choice of subject as in his handling of it.

There is nothing to prevent a mad scene from taking place in the daytime. But Lady Macbeth must be a noctambulist as well as a somnambulist, for her climactic episode brings out the nocturnal shading of the tragedy. *Macbeth*, from first to last, is deeply and darkly involved with the night-side of things. Both Macbeth and Lady Macbeth apostrophize the darkness, calling upon it to cover their malefactions. The timing of crucial scenes is conveyed, not merely by the convention of lighting candles, but by the recurring imagery of nightfall, overcast and dreamlike as in the dagger speech:

> Now o'er the one half world
> Nature seems dead, and wicked dreams abuse
> The curtain'd sleep. (2.1, 49–51)

Characters, habitually undressing or dressing, seem to be either going to bed or getting up, like the Porter when he is so loudly wakened. "Light thickens," and the mood can be summed up by the protagonist in a single couplet:

3. Italian: 'All the perfumes of Arabia will not sweeten this little hand. No, no, they cannot . . .' [*Editor's note*].

Good things of day begin to droop and drowse,
Whiles night's black agents to their preys do rouse. (3.2.52–
53)

Critical decisions are reached and fell designs are carried out at
hours when night is "Almost at odds with morning, which is which,"
when the atmosphere—like hell—is murky, and it is hard to distinguish fair from foul or foul from fair (3.4.126). The penalty for wil-
fulness is watchfulness, in the sense of staying awake against one's
will, of fitfully tossing and turning between bad dreams. Existence
has become a watching, a waking, a walking dream. Yet "night's predominance," as one of the Thanes describes it, cannot last forever
(2.4.8). Malcolm offers consolation by saying: "The night is long that
never finds the day" (4.3.240). Macduff is fated to bring in the head
of Macbeth on a pike, like the Thane of Cawdor's at the beginning,
and to announce the good word: "the time is free" (5.9.21). The
human makes its reflux over the fiendish at long last. After so painful
and protracted an agony, after a spell so oneiric and so insomniac
by turns, we welcome the daylight as if we were awakening from a
nightmare.

MARVIN ROSENBERG

Culture, Character, and Conscience in Shakespeare†

One of the marvels of Shakespeare's work is his compacting, in
single characters, of the best and worst of human qualities, of high
wisdom and low impulse, of noble purposes and ignoble means, of
love and hate, of hope and despair. A further marvel is the fluidity
of these character configurations, never fixed, insistently changing
and developing.

I have elsewhere proposed the metaphor "polyphony" to suggest
how the many, sometimes conflicting notes in the character-
structures flow or jerk into different combinations, harmonious and
dissonant.[1] I am interested here in how major forces, internal and
external, are made to form and malform these polyphonies.

Shakespeare seemed to be aware, long before Freud, of how the

† From *Shakespeare and the Triple Play: From Study to Stage to Classroom*, ed. Sidney
Homan (Cranbury, NJ: Associated University Presses, 1988), 138–49. Reprinted by permission of Associated University Presses. Footnotes are by the author of this article, unless
otherwise indicated.
1. See my *Masks of Macbeth* (Berkeley and Los Angeles: University of California Press, 1978),
p. 1. In that study I discuss the various commentators on *Macbeth* mentioned in the
present essay, as well as provide bibliographic citations.

human organism is impelled by erotic and aggressive drives. His plays demonstrate his understanding of how society and family construct a "superego" to restrict and tame these drives: we can call this control the "culture." Shakespeare saw it as very powerful; but he knew another at least equally powerful control, a private one: conscience.

Conscience is commonly regarded as an innate moral force. It has been called only another-directed, culturally installed phenomenon. But what if it has a biological base, fixed in the tissue as a kind of self-protective, society-protective reflex, an inbuilt corrective to the more destructive native human energies? Shakespeare evidently sensed such a humanizing force.

So I will here enlarge the implications of conscience to suggest what is humane in the human condition; that which, for instance, leavens aggressive ambition to rule with a care for the welfare of the ruled; which leavens the erotic impulses with the love and tenderness that can illuminate the interpersonal experience. This conscience sets value on giving as well as getting; on sacrifice as well as success. Even in our own very learned time we know that not simply a combination of heredity and environment makes a personality: now, as in Shakespeare, seemingly identical products of such combinations manifest widely different quotients of compassion and constructiveness, wildly different mixes of destructive energies and what is here called conscience.

Whatever we call it, we surely recognize in Shakespeare's world view such a humanizing component: and what results when the stupendous surge of his characters' aggressive and erotic energies beats against the constraints of this conscience as well as the culture. Frustrated, the current recoils; and under insistent, sometimes intolerable pressure, elements in the deeps rise toward the surface, and alter the texture of tragic personality. We will see that the ratio in Shakespeare's tragic characters of inner resistance, as well as outer, to violent impulse can be one measure of their complexities—and of the playwright's.

To go so deeply with them into the pain of human experience can be daunting. Some whole cultures have not been able to endure the full measure of Shakespeare's mirroring of what it is to be torn between impulse and culture-conscience. I would like to consider how this has happened in historic interpretations of Macbeth and his Lady, as one way of discerning the deep outlines of Shakespeare's character sculpture.

The first useful information we have is from the eighteenth century. Then both criticism and the theater refused to share Shakespeare's immense vision of the resistances in the two roles.

Early in the century Charles Gildon said of them:

the characters of Macbeth and his Lady are too monstrous for the stage.

As the years wore on, differences began to be seen. Lady Macbeth, in the theater, became a victim of the Restoration "improvement" of the play, which drained the characters of Shakespeare's complexity. When Davenant turned *Macbeth* into a semimusical, the witches were transformed from the dangerous, death-contriving sisters of Shakespeare's text into harmless, broomsticked girls of the chorus. But the plot structure of the play somehow survived: Macbeth still had to be tempted to murder. Only Lady Macbeth was left for his outer motivation: she had to shoulder virtually all responsibility. She would be seen as vile; Dr. Johnson would call her merely detestable; and Lord Kames:

> I hope there is no such wretch to be found as is here repre-
> sented.

In the theater, two actresses in particular became famous for justifying such critical strictures by the uninhibited power with which they made a killer out of Macbeth—and by the hollowness they made of his inner life.

Hannah Pritchard, David Garrick's famous Lady, was described in the role as having

> a mind insensible to compunction, bent inflexibly to gain her
> purpose.

She manifested "apathy"—that is conscienceless unfeeling, a "horrible force of implacable cruelty." When Macbeth, his aggressiveness diminished, offered his faint resistance to her urging to murder, she turned on him scornfully:

> Her whole ambitious soul came forth in fury to her face, and
> sat in terror there.

Cuts in Shakespeare's text accommodated this Lady's halved image: thus she did not "faint" in act 2 when Macbeth told of murdering the grooms—Garrick assumed that audiences would laugh at the evident "hypocrisy" of such a monster. She was remorseless.

After Pritchard came Sarah Siddons. Siddon's own comments, and her admirers', tell how, in her dark, majestic way, she played "the female fiend of Scotland." She wrote that she would have preferred, in corrupting the now brave, honorable Macbeth, to appear as an innocent-looking, fair-haired woman, with

> all the charms and graces of personal beauty . . . fair, feminine,
> nay, even fragile.

Siddons was not allowed her vision. Her audiences wanted, not the seeming dove, but, as her biographer said, the hawk:

> Her idea of a delicate and blonde beauty . . . the public would have ill-exchanged for her dark locks and eagle eyes.

Hazlitt described her unrelieved image:

> Her turbulent and inhuman strength of spirit, her unrelieved fierceness yielding no intercourse with human sensation or human weakness. Vice was never so solitary and so grand. The step, look, voice of the Royal Murdress forces our eye after them as if of a being from a darker world, full of evil, but full of power—unconnected with life, but come to do its deeds of darkness, and then pass away.

What had happened to these eighteenth century Ladies was an accentuation in them of aggressive impulses and images—id images—that Shakespeare had discerned deep in our—his—subconscious. Here was the incarnation of what society found fierce and frightening in the female: the first adored, terrible, powerful woman of childhood with whom the male child spends so much time, who can give or deny love, who can punish and—in nightmare imagination—destroy, even by smashing the brains out. Here was the figure of Medusa, the Amazon, Omphale, Medea,[2] the Bad Mother, the matriarchal monitor, who would wean the son from pity, and conspire with him to destroy the father, and assume all power. Norman Holland has suggested that this fantasy encloses the fearful, buried implication that for a man to submit to a woman is in itself dangerous.[3] This female will refuse the nourishing tenderness of woman that men have felt comfortable with, in lieu of the kind of fearless force that men—especially Shakespearean men—assumed belonged to man. In this the terrible Lady Macbeth would echo, but without Shakespeare's modulation, the sinister, tempting, destructive energy of the three male-featured Sisters.

In a century ostensibly restrained, this Lady loosed aggression unbridled, unconstrained by the social and moral inhibitions Shakespeare designed. She would ask to be unsexed, meaning relieved of all her intended nutritive conscience—though, as was observed of Pritchard, she seemed to have no sex to lose: the culture would indulge stage violence, but the erotic had to hide in it. This Terrible Woman had no compunction about invoking the spirits of darkness: she commanded them to her service. Nor was the inhumanity of her

---

2. A witch who slew her own children; Medusa was a snake-haired monster; Amazons were legendary women warriors; Omphale was the Lydian queen who enslaved Hercules [*Editor's note*].
3. Norman Holland, *Psychoanalysis and Shakespeare* (New York: McGraw Hill, 1964), pp. 219ff., 227.

femaleness ameliorated, as in Shakespeare, by the warm, familial aura radiated by Lady Macduff, whose appearance was cut. The Terrible image alone survived.

What kind of Macbeth could stand up to so terrible a Lady? The century had the answer: the bloody but conscience-troubled tyrant was transformed fashionably into an honorable murderer—Shakespeare's inner dialectic almost gone. Macbeth became a man of sensibility, who grieved to do wrong, did it almost in spite of himself, in handsome anguish, and died repenting.

Subdued by such a wife as Pritchard's, Garrick's Macbeth could hardly be blamed for submitting to her commands. His aggression was sharply modified: besides the social code which the text stipulates as inhibiting the murder of his king, his conscience was enlarged, his impulse to aggression weakened. Guilt and remorse hollowed him—so much so that he ended not as Shakespeare's giant, inwardly divided criminal, but as a craven.

Garrick was the century's greatest actor and hence a model for its enfeeblement of Macbeth. His own conception of the role is revealing:

> An experienced general crown'd with conquest, innately ambitious and religiously humane, spurr'd on by metaphysical prophecies and the unconquerable pride of his wife, to a deed horrible in itself, and repugnant to his nature.

Grief and shame—the outriders of conscience and culture—would harry this Macbeth through the play. One of Garrick's correspondents complained to the actor about his absence of inner aggression:

> You almost everywhere discovered dejectedness of mind . . . more grief than horror . . . heart heavings, melancholy countenance and slack carriage of body . . . The sorrowful face and lowly gestures of a penitent which have ever a wan and pitiful look . . . quite incompatible with the character.

But the characterization was popular; Garrick won praise for his Macbeth's "humane" side—his sensibility, his sufferings:

> His pensively preparatory attitudes . . . the propriety and gracefulness wherewith he touches the soft falls of sorrow, terror, and compassion.

Accommodating Garrick's "defence" of Macbeth went textual cuts, that softened his aggression while by contrast enlarging his conscience. In the crucial act 1, scene 7 speech ("If it were done when 'tis done . . ."), Garrick simply cut "If th'assassination could trammel up the consequence . . . ," to avoid speaking the murder thought.

Scenes were eliminated to prettify Macbeth: so goodbye Lady Macduff and her babes, and the killing of young Seyward. A mealy "poetic justice" was grafted onto Macbeth's death scene, transforming Macbeth's giant passion into puny self-pity:

> 'Tis done. The scene of life will quickly close. Ambition's vain, delusive dreams are fled, and now I wake to darkness, guilt and horror. I cannot bear it. Let me shake it off—'T wo' not be; my soul is clogg'd with blood—and cannot rise. I dare not ask for mercy. It is too late, hell drags me down. Forever . . . O, I sink . . . Oh! . . . my soul is lost forever . . . O!

Inevitably, by the end of the century, and the beginning of the nineteenth, the Garrick/Pritchard pattern slowly lost favor as actors and actresses searched further into the polyphony of the characters. Meanwhile the prototypes of the Terrible Lady and her driven Thane had also found homes elsewhere in Europe, especially in Germany; but before 1800 a German actress, Rosalie Nouseul, had begun to discover—generally to the dismay of the conventional German critics—two modulations by which Shakespeare countered Lady Macbeth's aggressiveness; first, her conscience; and second, her love for her husband. Thus a German journal, in 1779:

> In an ecstasy of mind—caused by flattering visions of royal grandeur, Nouseul tries to realize a plan from which normally she would have shrunk. Thus she was able to seize our sympathy as well as our interest.

An outraged conservative critic insisted that the actress pleased audiences so much because she played the Lady wrong:

> People ask, how could a spectator's heart have been moved, when the Lady had fallen into madness? How could such an abnormal villain, such a female image of Richard, acquire our sympathy? If the actress had performed the Lady's part according to Shakespeare's portrayal, she would unquestionably never have gained our sympathy. *That* Lady is a superhuman monster . . . Mrs. Nousuel humanized this character.

It would be many years before Shakespeare's multiple tones could be widely heard in Germany, in England, in America, or elsewhere in Europe. Still, a gradual admission of the erotic as well as the aggressive impulses in the Lady led to some interesting variation in actresses' methods of overcoming Macbeth. One such was by the Italian actress Adelaide Ristori. For the power Pritchard and Siddons had used to overwhelm Macbeth, Ristori used corruption. In her portrayal English observers discerned

> a bloody-minded virago, without heart, without sensibility . . . a Lucretia Borgia, an adept at crime . . . the most unscrupulous

of all our Lady Macbeths . . . an Italian intriguante, such a woman as Catherine Medici was . . . she enjoys her power over Macbeth more than English actresses.

The comments reflect a kind of English outrage that Ristori was so masked, so underhanded in her persuasion of Macbeth, that she drew the erotic into her attack, and used it to half-seduce Macbeth into murder, reflecting the archetype of Circe, of the sirens, la belle dame, who lured men to their doom. Similarly, she did not command the murdering ministers, as the fierce Ladies did. She armed herself with supernatural powers, she said, speaking as if a spirit herself, from out of some abyss: she was invoking her sisters.

Outwardly, Ristori's Lady was a very attractive woman, and her physical sensuality—what she called the Lady's "extraordinary personal fascination"—hypnotized her Macbeths. They yielded with little struggle, their compunctions visitings of conscience and constraints of culture offering little resistance.

Slowly in Europe a groundswell was building up to recognize a more complex polyphony in both Macbeth and his Lady. Actresses learned that she might only temporarily smother conscience because of erotic love for her husband, as well as by ambitious impulses for herself and for him. Actors would find that he had his own impulses to kill. Both would be dogged by deep-lying conscience.

Edmund Kean, the first English star after Kemble, found the murder in Macbeth that Shakespeare designed, and also the polyphony that restrained him, as his biographer observed:

A marvellous compound of daring and irresolution, ambition and submissiveness, treachery and affection.

Kean's half-murderous characterization made it easier for his Ladies to discover conscience. Reviewers at first were not pleased:

We have . . . but one Lady Macbeth [i.e., Siddons] . . . [Miss Campbell] had none of the dignity, none of the masculine energy, none of the unrelenting cruelty, none of the devouring ambition which belongs to the cool murderess. She seemed to coax and wheedle her husband to the commission of the crime, instead of pouring her bold spirit into his milky nature.

This womanly Lady was one of the first in England who had to be unsexed. Gradually, some of the romantic critics in Germany, perhaps influenced by Nouseul's conception of Lady Macbeth, began to champion the possibility that countering forces were meant by Shakespeare to complicate the character. Most notable was Tieck, who knew the theater as practitioner as well as observer. He would irritate colleagues like Goethe, now grown conservative, by his perceptions of the Lady:

It is an old custom to exaggerate this role and to present it as a fury. Many actresses have gained fame in this way; and thus the poet's quiet, subtle hints, which he often provides, have remained unnoticed. Basically Macbeth and his spouse are noble, wise characters . . . What happens is that both she and he are torn from their proper place . . . She has to mobilize all her greatness of heart, all the anger and mockery her eyes and face are capable of. Thus the audience perceives her metamorphosis into an enigmatic creature, which is the more deeply moving, the more the loving woman shows through at times.

Tieck's interpretation first puzzled and then angered Goethe, who, a great artist himself, might have been expected to share Shakespeare's creative vision. In 1826 he suggested that perhaps Tieck didn't really mean it, was being paradoxical. Two years later Goethe was sardonic:

We good Germans cannot rid ourselves of Shakespeare the conqueror . . . ; we happily attribute every value and depth to [his work] . . . Recently even we have been so retrograde as to allow ourselves to be misled into constituting Lady Macbeth a loving wife. We have become so sick and tired of the truth, it doesn't seem desirable any more, and we prefer to indulge in nonsense.

Soon after, when the actress Auguste Stich-Crelinger (1834), more in tune with the Shakespearean mirror, dared to mix her "demonic forces of passion" with the tender notes of an "honest and fervent love"; again audiences were pleased, again a critic scolded her and her mentor, Tieck, in Goethe's fashion:

It is a shocking phenomenon, that a very famous critic and dramaturg has revealed all sorts of new findings concerning this character, which can only be perceived with greatest surprise. One of these [is] that love and only love is the motive of all the activity of Lady Macbeth. Unfortunately even celebrated actresses accepted this interpretation, [and] this grandiose tragedy becomes crooked and foolish.

Another German actress of the later nineteenth century helped lead the way toward enlarging, with a ripe sensuality, the Lady's "loving" side, as implied in Shakespeare's text. Fanny Janauschek channeled much of her force into the warmth of her relationship with her husband. An observer noted:

She loved him passionately, and, in her own tigress fashion, tenderly.

She was pointing the way toward an emphasis on the physicality of erotic love between the Macbeths that would come slowly in the world's theaters, that were used almost until this century to polite hints of sexual desire; Janauschek's Lady foreshadowed a frankness that would lead to modern Lady Macbeths fusing their erotic and aggressive forces, even rolling on floor or bed with their husbands, to seduce them physically as well as psychically.

Meanwhile, critics in England, prompted perhaps by creative stage interpretations, began to discover the Lady's conscience. Thus Maginn:

> With the blindness of affection she persuades herself that he is full of the milk of human kindness, and that he would reject false and unholy ways of attaining the object of his desires. She deems it, therefore, her duty to spirit him to the task . . . Her sex, her woman's breasts, her very nature, oppose the task she has prescribed herself; but she prays to the ministers of murder . . . and she succeeds in mustering the desperate courage that bears her through.

The critic George Fletcher was evidently *directly* influenced by an actress. In his essay, he mentioned Helena Faucit. A transitional figure between the Siddons and post-Siddons characterizations, Faucit had injected the love of a wife into her portrayal, though she still insisted on Lady Macbeth's power as well, Even so she was too mild for *The Lady's Newspaper*:

> She expresses care, anguish, and a fiendish vindictiveness with force. This, however, does not accord with our notion of the character, which requires the subtle hardihood and terrible immobility that the greatest actresses have hitherto given . . . She is an odious as well as a criminal woman, who could hardly be personated by the most feminine and delicate of our actresses, and the effort to throw tenderness into the part seems to us absurd.

But Faucit continued to plumb Shakespeare's perception of the Lady's disabling subtextual conscience. Significantly, she would "faint" after Macbeth told of the dead grooms, without seeming hypocritical.

Fletcher partly vindicated Lady Macbeth's "femininity" by shifting the essential criminal intent to Macbeth—who became the killer, bloodthirsty, selfish and callous, "poetically whining," "morbidly irritable." Lady Macbeth only for him so desperately invoked the murdering ministers. She tried to suppress her "human and feminine conscience."

Kean had helped restore Macbeth's semiautonomy, by calling up not only the deep aggressiveness of the character, but also the antisocial impulses symbolized in the Weird Sisters: he eliminated their "broomstick rubbish" and added their sinister equivocation to Macbeth's inner capacity for violence. Macready's Macbeth, particularly, let the supernatural intervene between his conscience and his impulse. He seemed to

> reel through a visionary region where he must stumble on, urged by a mysterious power which he cannot resist and cannot fathom, through a dark, unriddled, portent-laden future.

So far had the pendulum swung by late in the century that Macbeth and his Lady had changed places. He was now the almost conscienceless murderer; she grew in feeling, fought her conscience, even forced herself to help kill. Among the remarkable new Ladies emerging was, in France, Sarah Bernhardt:

> We have for the first time a womanly Lady Macbeth, a terrible creature, but still a woman . . . She is usually remorseless and brutal, but Madame Bernhardt has changed all that. There is human nature in all its strength and weakness.

In Poland the actress Modrejewska (who would be called Modjeska in the West) similarly found a vulnerability in her Lady. She

> stressed that Lady Macbeth really faints. Of course that would weaken our repulsion for her. But besides that, there was no scene in which she did not emphasize that there was a trace of humanity inside that monster.

An American counterpart, Clara Morris, by turns coaxing and clever, wrote:

> There is something appalling in [Lady Macbeth's] ready faith and eager summoning of the spirits of evil to her aid; and right in the invocation I find my proof that [she] was naturally womanly, pitiful, capable of repentance for wrong done.

The most famous English exemplar of the new Lady, who led her husband astray partly because she loved him so, was Ellen Terry. Hers was a most "feminine" wife, loving and tender: but she learned to yield to a murderous potential when she joined in collusion with her husband. She could both coax and drive him:

> feminine [her characterization] is; wifely it is; powerful it is; [she] seizes Macbeth in a vice, and uses it and him by sheer force . . . We observe for the first time the stormy, dominant woman of the eleventh century equipped with the capricious emotional subtlety of a woman of the nineteenth century . . . We can readily accept this clinging, and cajoling enchantress, whose enkindled ambition affects her with a temporary paralysis of conscience.

Terry's Macbeth, Henry Irving, following Fletcher's interpretation, now portrayed Macbeth as the primary villain, nervous, fearful, plausible, murderous—and still incomplete. By his time, in the later nineteenth century, when Freud was beginning, psychologists were learning to perceive character formations that the artist-actors had intuited—as Freud said must be the case. The theater began to recognize the traumas that Shakespeare knew would come when conscience and culture resisted impulses, erotic and hostile, toward father figures, mother figures, sibling figures; from the alliances, holy and unholy, between sexuality and power; from the craving for magic omnipotence; from the images of horror and degradation that lie behind rationality. The Continental theater was beginning to externalize some of these phenomena of felt life in expressionist drama. In more traditional theater, some German actors of Macbeth particularly began personating him so shaken in his single state of man by forbidden thoughts and urgings as to appear what was then called "neurasthenic"—we would say neurotic.

Irving, almost conscienceless as a villain-Macbeth, overcorrected. But he had a share in leading the stage and criticism to a more balanced view of the complexity of Shakespeare's two great figures. The humanity of each was to be recognized, and the criminality: that the Lady, in the terrible act of summoning the murdering ministers, might fearfully as well as daringly be calling on the magic powers that the children in all of us imagine, in spite of the conscience that would surface later; and that Macbeth, moved to repress his conscience and resist cultural restraints, might try to abolish them once and for all—and fail. The two figures need not be locked into gender; each touched with the androgyne Shakespeare felt, is endowed with ambiguous "male" and "female" tones. And so they could be portrayed as recognizable individuals, transcending the archetypal images lying in them. Then their inward struggles could seem so nearly balanced that, until their first killing—the point of no return—conscience and culture might still stop them, and negotiate a sublimation. But of course most tragedy is, almost by definition, a failure of sublimation. Shakespeare made Macbeth and his Lady our surrogates—and his: they are doomed to kill—and die—for us all.

Every new staging of the play brings us an opportunity to search out, from the insights of the actor-artists, new tones, new chords, that Shakespeare heard within himself so long ago. In stagings, the depth, intensity, and interrelation of the tones must depend on the actor's sense of the inward struggles shaping the character structures: how the Lady is roused—and how much she needs to be—to her frightening, antisocial aggression; how inhibited by humane conscience—and by the strangers at the door; how her personality shifts under intensifying pressures of conscience—and by the strangers at her table. Macbeth's many notes will be composed in the furnace of his aggressive and erotic drives as modulated by the pressures

wrought on him by the Sisters, by a structured—but competitive—
society, and by a wife more or less obsessed, sensual, loving; and
ultimately by his conscience and the cultural forces that seek to
restrict him from within, and, as these are repressed, from without.
The more intense the resistances, the harsher, and sadder, and
deeper the range of tones, the closer do they bring us to the full
experience of the complexity and depth in Shakespeare's characters.

JANET ADELMAN

Escaping the Matrix: The Construction of Masculinity in *Macbeth*†

Just before Lear rushes out into the storm, he prays to the absent
gods to "touch [him] with noble anger, / And let not women's weapons, water-drops, / Stain [his] man's cheeks" (2.4.278–80): threatened by the "mother" within (2.4.56), he attempts to mobilize manly
anger against her. But Lear cannot sustain his anger; and in the end,
after his great rage has passed, he dissolves mercifully into relationship with the mother he has made of Cordelia. The drive toward
masculine autonomy diverted in him is in effect deflected onto
Edmund, who becomes the standard-bearer for masculinity as he
orders Cordelia's death; and it is resurrected in Macbeth and Coriolanus, each of whom similarly constructs his exaggerated and
blood-thirsty masculinity as an attempt to ward off vulnerability to
the mother.[1] For the cannibalistic witch-mothers Lear finds in

† From Janet Adelman, *Suffocating Mothers: Fantasies of Maternal Origin in Shakespeare's Plays,* Hamlet *to* The Tempest (London: Routledge, 1992), 130–47. Reprinted by permission of Taylor and Francis, Inc. Some of the author's footnotes have been omitted. Footnotes are by the author of this article, unless otherwise indicated.
1. This chapter largely replicates two essays published separately in 1978 and 1987, each of which deals with the construction of a rigid male identity as a defense against overwhelming maternal power (" 'Anger's My Meat': Feeding, Dependency, and Aggression in *Coriolanus,*" in *Shakespeare: Pattern of Excelling Nature,* ed. David Bevington and Jay L. Halio [Newark, NJ: University of Delaware Press, 1978], pp. 108–24, reprinted in slightly altered form in *Representing Shakespeare: New Psychoanalytic Essays,* ed. Murray M. Schwartz and Coppélia Kahn [Baltimore: Johns Hopkins University Press, 1980], pp. 129–49; " 'Born of Woman': Fantasies of Maternal Power in *Macbeth,*" in *Cannibals, Witches, and Divorce: Estranging the Renaissance* [Selected Papers from the English Institute, 1985], ed. Marjorie Garber [Baltimore: Johns Hopkins University Press], pp. 90–121). I have tinkered very slightly with the *Macbeth* essay but have left the bulk of the *Coriolanus* essay unchanged. Insofar as my formulations of the dilemmas of masculinity shifted between the two essays, the shift reflects what I have learned from feminist object-relations psychoanalysis, and from a group of critics engaged with its terms: especially Richard Wheeler, Madelon Gohlke (now Sprengnether), Coppélia Kahn, Carol Neely, Peter Erickson, and Murray Schwartz. For the specific connections between *Macbeth* and *Coriolanus,* see especially Gohlke (" 'I wooed thee with my sword': Shakespeare's Tragic Paradigms," in *Representing Shakespeare,* pp. 176–77), Kahn (*Man's Estate: Masculine Identity in Shakespeare* [Berkeley: University of California Press, 1981], pp. 151–92), and Wheeler

Goneril and Regan are resurrected in Lady Macbeth and Volumnia; and fatherless, these sons are terribly subject to their power. The initially defining act for both of them thus turns on re-imagining the origin of masculine selfhood: both Macbeth's early victory over Macdonwald and the conquest of Corioli that gives Coriolanus his name figure the decisive masculine act as a bloody rebirth, replacing the dangerous maternal origin through the violence of self-creation. For both heroes, as for Troilus, heroic masculinity turns on leaving the mother behind. Or on seeming to leave her behind: for both plays construct the exaggerated masculinity of their heroes simultaneously as an attempt to separate from the mother and as the playing out of her bloodthirsty will; both enact the paradox through which the son is never more the mother's creature than when he attempts to escape her.

Maternal power in *Macbeth* is not embodied in the figure of a particular mother (as it is in *Coriolanus*); it is instead diffused throughout the play, evoked primarily by the figures of the witches and Lady Macbeth. Largely through Macbeth's relationship to them, the play becomes (like *Coriolanus*) a representation of primitive fears about male identity and autonomy itself, about those looming female presences who threaten to control one's actions and one's mind, to constitute one's very self, even at a distance. When Macbeth's first words echo those we have already heard the witches speak—"So foul and fair a day I have not seen" (1.3.38); "Fair is foul, and foul is fair" (1.1.11)—we are in a realm that questions the very possibility of autonomous identity. As with Richard III, the maternal constitutes the suffocating matrix from which he must break free; and as with Richard, his solution will be to hew his way out with a bloody axe.[2]

This fantasy of escape in fact haunts Macbeth. In its last moments,

---

(*Shakespeare's Development and the Problem Comedies* [Berkeley: University of California Press, 1981], pp. 203–13), each of whom notes that the plays share a common concern with establishing a defensive masculinity; in particular, Kahn's chapter title "The Milking Babe and the Bloody Man in *Coriolanus* and *Macbeth*"—indicates the similarity of our arguments. Linda Bamber also analyzes the two plays together but interprets their similarity differently: for her, the absence of a true feminine Other in both plays prevents the development of true manliness in their heroes (*Comic Women, Tragic Men: A Study of Gender and Genre in Shakespeare* [Stanford, CA: Stanford University Press, 1982], pp. 20, 91–107).

2. In his classic preoedipal account of the failure of differentiation in *Macbeth*, David B. Barron associates the cutting and breaking imagery throughout the play with Macbeth's attempt to "cut his way out of the female environment which chokes and smothers him"; he notes that the choking / suffocating / smothering images find their realization in the witches' "birth-strangled babe" ("The Babe That Milks: An Organic Study of *Macbeth*," originally published in 1960 and reprinted in *The Design Within*, ed. M. D. Faber [New York: Science House, 1970], p. 268). For similar preoedipal readings of the play, see Marvin Rosenberg's *The Masks of Macbeth* (Berkeley: University of California Press, 1978), pp. 81–82, 270–72, and especially Kahn's *Man's Estate*, pp. 151–55, 172–92, Wheeler's *Shakespeare's Development*, pp. 144–49, and David Willbern's "Phantasmagoric *Macbeth*," *English Literary Renaissance* 16 (1986): 520–49, an essay that I saw in an earlier form in 1981.

as Macbeth feels himself increasingly hemmed in by enemies, the stage resonates with variants of his repeated question, "What's he! / That was not born of woman?" (5.7.2–3; for variants, see 5.3.4, 6; 5.7.11, 13; 5.8.13, 31.) Repeated seven times, Macbeth's allusion to the witches' prophecy—"none of woman born / Shall harm Macbeth" (4.1.80–81)—becomes virtually a talisman to ward off danger; even after he has begun to doubt the equivocation of the fiend (5.5.43), mere repetition of the phrase seems to Macbeth to guarantee his invulnerability. And as he repeats himself, his assurance seems to turn itself inside out, becoming dependent not on the fact that all men are, after all, born of woman but on the fantasy of escape from this universal condition.[3] The duplicity of Macbeth's repeated question—its capacity to mean both itself and its opposite—carries such weight at the end of the play, I think, because the whole of the play represents in very powerful form both the fantasy of a virtually absolute and destructive maternal power and the fantasy of absolute escape from this power; I shall argue in fact that the peculiar texture of the end of the play is generated partly by the tension between these two fantasies. For if the unsatisfactory equivocation through which Macduff defeats Macbeth seems to suggest that no man is not born of woman, the play nonetheless re-imagines autonomous male identity only through the ruthless excision of all female presence, its own peculiar satisfaction of the witches' prophecy.

In *Macbeth*, as in *Hamlet*, the threat of maternal power and the

3. Oddly, this fantasy is present in the report of the Earl of Gowrie's attempt to kill King James in 1600, a report that may have influenced Shakespeare in *Macbeth*. James Weimis of Bogy, testifying in 1600 about the earl's recourse to necromancy, reported that the earl thought it "possible that the seed of a man and woman might be brought to perfection otherwise then by the *matrix* of the woman" ("Gowries Conspiracie: A Discoverie of the unnaturall and vyle Conspiracie, attempted against the Kings Maiesties Person at Sanct-Johnstoun, upon Twysday the Fifth of August, 1600," in *A Selection from the Harleian Miscellany* [London: C. and G. Kearsley, 1793], p. 196). The account goes on to suggest the kind of invulnerability the earl sought from the necromancer: searching the dead earl's pockets, James found nothing in them "but a little close parchment bag, full of magicall characters, and words of inchantment, wherein, it seemed, that he had put his confidence, thinking himselfe never safe without them, and therfore ever carried them about with him, being also observed, that, while they were upon him, his wound whereof he died, bled not, but, incontinent after the taking away of them, the blood gushed out in great aboundance, to the great admiration of al the beholders" ("Gowries Conspiracie," p. 196). Stanley J. Kozikowski argues strenuously that Shakespeare knew either this pamphlet, printed in Scotland and London in 1600, or the abortive play on the conspiracy, apparently performed twice by the King's Men and then canceled in 1604 ("The Gowrie Conspiracy Against James VI: A New Source for Shakespeare's *Macbeth*," *Shakespeare Studies* 13 [1980]: 197–211). Although I do not find his arguments entirely persuasive, it seems likely that Shakespeare knew at least the central facts of the conspiracy, given both James's annual celebration of his escape from it and the apparent involvement of the King's Men in a play on the subject. But whether or not Shakespeare knew of and deliberately recalled the conspiracy in *Macbeth*, the pamphlet's figuration of the connection between recourse to necromancy, invulnerability, and escape from maternal origin suggests that this connection would have been culturally and psychically resonant for many in Shakespeare's audience. (See also Steven Mullaney's suggestive use of the Gowrie material as analogous to *Macbeth* in its links between treason and magical riddle ["Lying Like Truth: Riddle, Representation and Treason in Renaissance England," *ELH* 47 (1980): 32, 38].)

crisis it presents for individuated manhood emerge in response to
paternal absence; once again, the death of the father figures the fall
into the maternal realm. But if in *Hamlet* Shakespeare constructs
this fall as the death of the ideally masculine father, here he constructs a revised version in which the fall is the death of the father
as ideally androgynous parent. For Duncan initially seems to combine in himself the attributes of both father and mother: he is the
center of authority, the source of lineage and honor, the giver of
name and gift; but he is also the source of all nurturance, planting
the children to his throne and making them grow. He is the single
source from which all good can be imagined to flow, the source of a
benign and empowering nurturance, the opposite of that imaged in
the witches' poisonous cauldron and Lady Macbeth's gall-filled
breasts. Such a father does away with any need for a mother: he is
the image of both parents in one, threatening aspects of each controlled by the presence of the other.[4] When he is gone, "The wine of
life is drawn, and the mere lees / Is left this vault to brag of" (2.3.93–
94): nurturance itself is spoiled, as all the play's imagery of poisoned
chalices and interrupted feasts implies. In his absence male and
female break apart, the female becoming merely helpless or merely
poisonous and the male merely bloodthirsty; the harmonious relation
of the genders imaged in Duncan fails.

Or so the valorizing of Duncan suggests. But in fact masculinity
and femininity are deeply disturbed even before his death; and he
himself seems strikingly absent before his death. Heavily idealized,
this ideally protective father is nonetheless largely ineffectual: even
while he is alive, he is unable to hold his kingdom together, reliant
on a series of bloody men to suppress an increasingly successful
series of rebellions.[5] The witches are already abroad in his realm;
they in fact constitute our introduction to that realm. Duncan, not
Macbeth, is the first person to echo them ("When the battle's lost
and won" [1.1.4]; "What he hath lost, noble Macbeth hath won"
[1.2.69]). The witches' sexual ambiguity terrifies: Banquo says of

---

4. David Sundelson (*Shakespeare's Restorations of the Father* [New Brunswick, N.J.: Rutgers
University Press, 1983], p. 3), Harry Berger, Jr. ("The Early Scenes of *Macbeth*: Preface
to a New Interpretation," *ELH* 47 [1980]: 26–28), and Willbern ("Phantasmagoric *Macbeth*," pp. 522–23) all see Duncan as an androgynous parent. Murray M. Schwartz and
Wheeler note specifically the extent to which the male claim to androgynous possession
of nurturant power reflects a fear of maternal power outside male control (Schwartz,
"Shakespeare through Contemporary Psychoanalysis," in *Representing Shakespeare*, p. 29;
Wheeler, *Shakespeare's Development*, p. 146). My discussion of Duncan's androgyny is
indirectly indebted to Peter Erickson's rich account of the Duke's taking on of nurturant
function in *As You Like It*, an account that I first heard in 1979, now a chapter in his
Patriarchal Structures in Shakespeare's Drama (Berkeley: University of California Press,
1985); see especially pp. 27–37.
5. Many commentators note that Shakespeare's Duncan is less ineffectual than Holinshed's;
others note the continuing signs of his weakness. See especially Harry Berger's brilliant
account of the structural effect of Duncan's weakness in defining his (and Macbeth's)
society ("The Early Scenes of *Macbeth*," pp. 1–31).

them, "You should be women, / And yet your beards forbid me to interpret / That you are so" (1.3.45–47). Is their androgyny the shadow-side of the King's, enabled perhaps by his failure to maintain a protective masculine authority? Is their strength a consequence of his weakness? (This is the configuration of *Cymbeline*, where the power of the witch-queen-stepmother is so dependent on the failure of Cymbeline's masculine authority that she obligingly dies when that authority returns to him.) Banquo's question to the witches may ask us to hear a counter-question about Duncan, who should be man. For Duncan's androgyny is the object of enormous ambivalence: idealized for his nurturing paternity, he is nonetheless killed for his womanish softness, his childish trust, his inability to read men's minds in their faces, his reliance on the fighting of sons who can rebel against him. Macbeth's description of the dead Duncan— "his silver skin lac'd with his golden blood" (2.3.110)—makes him into a virtual icon of kingly worth; but other images surrounding his death make him into an emblem not of masculine authority but of feminine vulnerability. As he moves toward the murder, Macbeth first imagines himself the allegorical figure of Murder, as though to absolve himself of the responsibility of choice. But the figure of murder then fuses with that of Tarquin:

> wither'd Murther,
> . . . thus with his stealthy pace,
> With Tarquin's ravishing strides, towards his design
> Moves like a ghost. (2.1.52–56)

These lines figure the murder as a display of male sexual aggression against a passive female victim: murder here becomes rape; Macbeth's victim becomes not the powerful male figure of the king but the helpless Lucrece.[6] Hardened by Lady Macbeth to regard maleness and violence as equivalent, that is, Macbeth responds to Duncan's idealized milky gentleness as though it were evidence of his femaleness. The horror of this gender transformation, as well as the horror of the murder, is implicit in Macduff's identification of the king's body as a new Gorgon ("Approach the chamber, and destroy you sight / With a new Gorgon" [2.3.70–71]). The power of this image lies partly in its suggestion that Duncan's bloodied body, with

6. Many note the appropriateness of Macbeth's conflation of himself with Tarquin, given the play's alliance of sexuality and murder. See, for example, Ian Robinson, "The Witches and Macbeth," *The Critical Review* 11 (1968): 104; Dennis Biggins, "Sexuality, Witchcraft, and Violence in *Macbeth*," *Shakespeare Studies* 8 (1975): 269; and Robert N. Watson, *Shakespeare and the Hazards of Ambition* (Cambridge, Mass.: Harvard University Press, 1984), p. 100. Arthur Kirsch works extensively with the analogy, seeing the Tarquin of *The Rape of Lucrece* as a model for Macbeth's ambitious desire ("Macbeth's Suicide," *ELH* 51 [1984]: 269–96). Commentators on the analogy do not in general note that it transforms Macbeth's kingly victim into a woman; Norman Rabkin is an exception (*Shakespeare and the Problem of Meaning* [Chicago: Chicago University Press, 1981], p. 107).

its multiple wounds, has been revealed as female and hence blinding to his sons: as if the threat all along was that Duncan would be revealed as female and that this revelation would rob his sons of his masculine protection and hence of their own masculinity.[7]

In *King Lear*, the abdication of protective paternal power seems to release the destructive power of a female chaos imaged not only in Goneril and Regan but also in the storm on the heath. *Macbeth* virtually alludes to Lear's storm as he approaches the witches in Act IV, conjuring them to answer though they "untie the winds, and let them fight / Against the Churches," though the "waves / Confound and swallow navigation up," though "the treasure / Of Nature's germens tumble all together, / Even till destruction sicken" (4.1.52–60; see *King Lear*, 3.2.1–9). The witches merely implicit on Lear's heath have become in *Macbeth* embodied agents of storm and disorder, and they are there from the start. Their presence suggests that the paternal absence that unleashes female chaos (as in *Lear*) has already happened at the beginning of *Macbeth*. That absence is merely made literal in Macbeth's murder of Duncan at the instigation of female forces: from the start, this father-king cannot protect his sons from powerful mothers, and it is the son's—and the play's—revenge to kill him, or, more precisely, to kill him first and love him after, paying him back for his excessively "womanish" trust and then memorializing him as the ideal androgynous parent.[8] The reconstitution of manhood becomes a central problem in the play in part, I

---

7. Wheeler sees the simultaneously castrated and castrating Gorgon-like body of Duncan as the emblem of the world Macbeth brings into being (*Shakespeare's Development*, p. 145); I see it as the emblem of a potentially castrating femaleness that Macbeth's act of violence reveals but does not create. For an interesting counter-reading, see Marjorie Garber ("Macbeth: The Male Medusa," *Shakespeare's Ghost Writers: Literature as Uncanny Causality* [New York: Methuen, 1987], pp. 87–123); in her account, the gorgon functions throughout *Macbeth* not as the sign of a terrifying femaleness but as the sign of a (more terrifying) gender undecidability *per se*.

8. Many commentators, following Freud, find the murder of Duncan "little else than patricide" ("Those Wrecked by Success," *The Standard Edition of the Complete Psychological Works of Sigmund Freud*, ed. James Strachey [London: The Hogarth Press, 1957], vol. 14, p. 321); see, for example, Rabkin (*Shakespeare and the Problem of Meaning*, pp. 106–9), Kirsch ("Macbeth's Suicide," pp. 276–80, 286), and Watson (*Shakespeare and the Hazards of Ambition*, esp. pp. 85–88, 98–99). (The last two are particularly interesting insofar as they understand parricide as an ambitious attempt to redefine the self as omnipotently free from limits.) In standard oedipal readings of the play, the mother is less the object of desire than "the 'demon-woman,'" who creates the abyss between father and son" by inciting the son to parricide (Ludwig Jekels, "The Riddle of Shakespeare's *Macbeth*," in *The Design Within*, p. 240); see also, for example, L. Veszy-Wagner ("*Macbeth*: 'Fair Is Foul and Foul Is Fair,'" *American Imago* 25 [1968]: 242–57), Norman N. Holland (*Psychoanalysis and Shakespeare* [New York: Octagon Books, 1979], p. 229), and Patrick Colm Hogan ("Macbeth: Authority and Progenitorship," *American Imago* 40 [1983]: 385–95). For Janis Krohn, Lady Macbeth is simultaneously the oedipal mother who incites her son to parricide and the preoedipal mother who betrays him ("Addressing the Oedipal Dilemma in *Macbeth*," *The Psychoanalytic Review* 73 [1986]: 333–37). By emphasizing the degree to which Duncan is absent even before his murder, I mean to suggest the extent to which maternal power—including the power to incite parricide—is a consequence as well as a cause of paternal absence.

think, because the vision of manhood embodied in Duncan has already failed at the play's beginning.

The witches constitute our introduction to the realm of maternal malevolence unleashed by the loss of paternal protection; as soon as Macbeth meets them, he becomes (in Hecate's probably non-Shakespearean words) their "wayward son" (3.5.11). This maternal malevolence is given its most horrifying expression in Shakespeare in the image through which Lady Macbeth secures her control over Macbeth:

> I have given suck, and know
> How tender 'tis to love the babe that milks me:
> I would, while it was smiling in my face,
> Have pluck'd my nipple from his boneless gums,
> And dash'd the brains out, had I so sworn
> As you have done to this. (1.7.54–59)

This image of murderously disrupted nurturance is the psychic equivalent of the witches' poisonous cauldron; both function to subject Macbeth's will to female forces.[9] For the play strikingly constructs the fantasy of subjection to maternal malevolence in two parts, in the witches and in Lady Macbeth, and then persistently identifies the two parts as one. Through this identification, Shakespeare in effect locates the source of his culture's fear of witchcraft in individual human history, in the infant's long dependence on female figures felt as all-powerful: what the witches suggest about the vulnerability of men to female power on the cosmic plane, Lady Macbeth doubles on the psychological plane.

Lady Macbeth's power as a female temptress allies her in a general way with the witches as soon as we see her. The specifics of that implied alliance begin to emerge as she attempts to harden herself

9. For those recent commentators who follow Barron in seeing preoedipal rather than oedipal issues as central to the play, the images of disrupted nurturance define the primary area of disturbance: see, for example, Barron ("The Babe That Milks," p. 255); Schwartz ("Shakespeare through Contemporary Psychoanalysis," p. 29); Kahn (*Man's Estate*, pp. 172–78); Wheeler (*Shakespeare's Development*, pp. 147–48); Berger ("The Early Scenes of *Macbeth*," pp. 27–28); Joan M. Byles ("Macbeth: Imagery of Destruction," *American Imago* 39 [1982]: 149–64); Kirsch ("Macbeth's Suicide," pp. 291–92); Susan Bachmann (" 'Daggers in Men's Smiles'—The 'Truest Issue' in *Macbeth*," *International Review of Psycho-Analysis* 5 [1978]: 97–104); and Willbern ("Phantasmagoric *Macbeth*," pp. 526–32). Among these, Barron, Bachmann, and Kahn see the abrupt and bloody weaning imaged by Lady Macbeth here as the root cause of Macbeth's failure to differentiate himself from the maternal figure and his consequent susceptibility to female influence; Willbern locates in it the psychological point of origin for the failure of potential space that Macbeth enacts. In Peter Erickson's suggestive account, patriarchal bounty itself fails in *Macbeth* in part because it depends on the maternal nurturance that is here disturbed (*Patriarchal Structures*, pp. 116–21). Each of these critics constructs Lady Macbeth as the destructive mother in relation to whom Macbeth is imagined as an infant; Rosenberg notes intriguingly that *Macbeth* has twice been performed with a mother and son in the chief roles (*Masks of Macbeth*, p. 196).

in preparation for hardening her husband: the disturbance of gender
that Banquo registers when he first meets the witches ("you should
be women / And yet your beards forbid me to interpret / That you
are") is played out in psychological terms in Lady Macbeth's attempt
to unsex herself. Calling on spirits ambiguously allied with the
witches themselves, she phrases this unsexing as the undoing of her
own bodily maternal function:

> Come, you Spirits
> That tend on mortal thoughts, unsex me here,
> And fill me, from the crown to the toe, top-full
> Of direst cruelty! make thick my blood,
> Stop up th'access and passage to remorse;
> That no compunctious visitings of Nature
> Shake my fell purpose, nor keep peace between
> Th'effect and it! Come to my woman's breasts,
> And take my milk for gall, you murth'ring ministers. (1.5.40–
>   48)

In the play's context of unnatural births, the thickening of the blood
and the stopping up of access and passage to remorse begin to sound
like attempts to undo reproductive functioning and perhaps to stop
the menstrual blood that is the sign of its potential.[1] The metaphors
in which Lady Macbeth frames the stopping up of remorse, that is,
suggest that she imagines an attack on the reproductive passages of
her own body, on what makes her specifically female. And as she
invites the spirits to her breasts, she reiterates the centrality of the
attack specifically on maternal function: needing to undo the "milk
of human kindness" (1.5.17) in Macbeth, she imagines an attack on
her own literal milk, its transformation into gall. This imagery locates
the horror of the scene in Lady Macbeth's unnatural abrogation of
her maternal function. But latent within this image of unsexing is
the horror of the maternal function itself. Most modern editors follow Johnson in glossing "take my milk for gall" as "take my milk in
exchange for gall" imagining in effect that the spirits empty out the
natural maternal fluid and replace it with the unnatural and poisonous one.[2] But perhaps Lady Macbeth is asking the spirits to take her

1. Despite some over-literal interpretation, Alice Fox and particularly Jenijoy La Belle usefully
   demonstrate the specifically gynecological references of "passage" and "visitings of nature,"
   using contemporary gynecological treatises: see Fox ("Obstetrics and Gynecology in *Macbeth*," *Shakespeare Studies* 12 [1979]: 129) and La Belle (" 'A Strange Infirmity': Lady
   Macbeth's Amenorrhea," *Shakespeare Quarterly* 31 [1980]: 382) for the identification of
   "visitings of nature" as a term for menstruation; see La Belle (p. 383) for the identification
   of "passage" as a term for the neck of the womb. See also Barron, who associates Lady
   Macbeth's language here with contraception ("The Babe That Milks," p. 267).
2. "For" is glossed as "in exchange for" in the following editions, for example: *The Complete
   Signet Classic Shakespeare,* ed. Sylvan Barnet (New York: Harcourt, Brace, Jovanovich,
   1972); *The Complete Works of Shakespeare,* ed. Hardin Craig (Chicago: Scott, Foresman,
   1951), rev. ed. edited by David Bevington, 1973; *The Riverside Shakespeare,* ed.
   G. Blakemore Evans (Boston: Houghton Mifflin, 1974); *William Shakespeare: The Com-*

milk *as* gall, to nurse from her breasts and find in her milk their sustaining poison. Here the milk itself is the gall; no transformation is necessary. In these lines, Lady Macbeth focuses the culture's fear of maternal nursery—a fear reflected, for example, in the common worries about the various ills (including female blood itself) that can be transmitted through nursing and in the sometime identification of colostrum as witch's milk.[3] Insofar as her milk itself nurtures the evil spirits, Lady Macbeth localizes the image of maternal danger, inviting the identification of her maternal function itself with that of the witch. For she here invites precisely that nursing of devil-imps so central to the current understanding of witchcraft that the presence of supernumerary teats alone was often taken as sufficient evidence that one was a witch.[4] Lady Macbeth and the witches fuse at this moment, and they fuse through the image of perverse nursery.

It is characteristic of the play's division of labor between Lady Macbeth and the witches that she, rather than they, is given the imagery of perverse nursery traditionally attributed to witches. The often-noted alliance between Lady Macbeth and the witches constructs malignant female power both in the cosmos and in the family; it in effect adds the whole weight of the spiritual order to the condemnation of Lady Macbeth's insurrection.[5] But despite the superior cosmic status of the witches, Lady Macbeth seems to me

plete Works, ed. Alfred Harbage (Baltimore: Penguin, 1969); *The Complete Works of Shakespeare*, ed. George Lyman Kittredge (Boston: Ginn, 1936), rev. ed. edited by Irving Ribner, 1971). Muir demurs, preferring Keightley's understanding of "take" as "infect" (see the Arden *Macbeth*, p. 30).

3. See Samuel X. Radhill for the identification of colostrum with witch's milk ("Pediatrics," in *Medicine in Seventeenth Century England*, ed. Allen G. Debus [Berkeley: University of California Press, 1974], p. 249). The topic was of interest to King James, who claimed to have sucked his Protestantism from his nurse's milk; his drunkenness was also attributed to her (see Henry N. Paul, *The Royal Play of Macbeth* [New York: The Macmillan Company, 1950], pp. 387–88).

4. Many commentators on English witchcraft note the unusual prominence given to the presence of the witch's mark and the nursing of familiars; see, for example, Barbara Rosen's introduction to her collection of witchcraft documents (*Witchcraft* [London: Edward Arnold, 1969], pp. 29–30). She cites contemporary documents on the nursing of familiars, e.g., on pp. 187–88 and 315; the testimony of Joan Prentice, one of the convicted witches of Chelmsford in 1589, is particularly suggestive: "At what time so ever she would have her ferret do anything for her, she used the words 'Bid, Bid, Bid, come Bid, come Bid, come suck, come suck, come suck' " (p. 188). Katherine Mary Briggs quotes a contemporary (1613) story about the finding of a witch's teat (*Pule Hecate's Team* [New York: Arno Press, 1977], p. 250); see also Wallace Notestein, A *History of Witchcraft in England from 1558 to 1718* (Washington, D.C.: The American Historical Association, 1911), p. 36, and George Lyman Kittredge, *Witchcraft in Old and New England* (New York: Russell and Russell, 1956), p. 179. Though he does not refer to the suckling of familiars, King James believed in the significance of the witch's mark, at least when he wrote the *Daemonologie* (London, 1603; see p. 33). M. C. Bradbrook notes that Lady Macbeth's invitation to the spirits is "as much as any witch could do by way of self dedication" ("The Sources of *Macbeth*," *Shakespeare Survey* 4 [1951]: 43); see also Leslie A. Fiedler, *The Stranger in Shakespeare* (London: Croom Helm, 1973), p. 72.

5. In a brilliant essay, Peter Stallybrass associates the move from the cosmic to the secular realm with the ideological shoring up of a patriarchal state founded on the model of the family ("*Macbeth* and *Witchcraft*," in *Focus on Macbeth*, ed. John Russell Brown [London: Routledge and Kegan Paul, 1982], esp. pp. 196–98).

finally the more frightening figure. For Shakespeare's witches are an
odd mixture of the terrifying and the near-comic. Even without consideration of the Hecate scene (3.5) with its distinct lightening of
tone and it's incipient comedy of discord among the witches, we may
begin to feel a shift toward the comic in the presentation of the
witches: the specificity and predictability of the ingredients in their
dire recipe pass over toward grotesque comedy even while they create
a (partly pleasurable) shiver of horror.[6] There is a distinct weakening
of their power after their first appearances: only in 4.1 do we hear
that they themselves have masters (1.63). The more Macbeth claims
for them, the less their actual power seems: even their power over
the storm—the signature of maternal malevolence in *King Lear*—is
eventually taken from them. By the time Macbeth evokes the cosmic
damage they can wreak (4.1.50–60), we have already felt the presence of such damage, and felt it moreover as issuing not from the
witches but from a divinely sanctioned nature firmly in league with
patriarchal order. The witches' displays of thunder and lightning, like
their apparitions, are merely childish theatrics compared to what we
have already heard: the serious disruptions of natural order—the
storm that toppled the chimneys and made the earth shake (2.3.53–
60), the unnatural darkness in day (2.4.5–10), the cannibalism of
Duncan's horses (2.4.14–18)—are the horrifying but reassuringly
familiar signs of God's displeasure, firmly under His—not their—
control. Partly because their power is thus circumscribed, nothing
the witches say or do conveys the presence of awesome and unexplained malevolence in the way that Lear's storm does. Even the
process of dramatic representation itself may diminish their power:
embodied, perhaps, they lack full power to terrify; "Present fears"—
even of witches—"are less than horrible imaginings" (1.3.137–38).
They tend thus to become as much containers for, as expressions of,
nightmare; to a certain extent, they help to exorcise the terror of
female malevolence by localizing it.

The witches may of course have lost same of their power to terrify
through the general decline in witchcraft belief. Nonetheless, even
when that belief was in full force, these witches would have been

---

6. Wilbur Sanders notes the extent to which "terror is mediated through absurdity" in the
witches (*The Dramatist and the Received Idea* [Cambridge: Cambridge University Press,
1968], p. 277); see also Harry Berger's fine account of the scapegoating reduction of the
witches to comic and grotesque triviality ("Text Against Performance in Shakespeare: The
Example of *Macbeth*," in *The Forms of Power and the Power of Forms in the Renaissance*,
ed. Stephen Greenblatt, *Genre* 15 [1982]: 67–68). Harold C. Goddard (*The Meaning of
Shakespeare* [Chicago: The University of Chicago Press, 1951], pp. 512–13), Robinson
("The Witches and Macbeth," pp. 100–103), and Stallybrass ("*Macbeth* and Witchcraft,"
p. 199) note the witches' change from potent and mysterious to more diminished figures
in act 4. For Fiedler, the witches are "always on the verge of shifting from satanic to
grotesque to fully comic"; Lady Macbeth is "the sole substantial reality behind the shadow
play of stage convention, hallucination, and delusion" in them (*The Stranger in Shakespeare*, pp. 71–72).

less frightening than their Continental sisters, their crimes less sensational. For despite their numinous and infinitely suggestive indefinability,[7] insofar as they are witches, they are distinctly English witches; and most commentators on English witchcraft note how tame an affair it was in comparison with witchcraft belief on the Continent.[8] The most sensational staples of Continental belief from the *Malleus Maleficarum* (1486) on—the ritual murder and eating of infants, the attacks specifically on the male genitals, the perverse sexual relationship with demons—are missing or greatly muted in English witchcraft belief, replaced largely by a simpler concern with retaliatory wrongdoing of exactly the order Shakespeare points to when one of his witches announces her retaliation for the sailor's wife's refusal to share her chestnuts.[9] We may hear an echo of some of the Continental beliefs in the hint of their quasi-sexual attack on the sailor with the uncooperative wife: (the witches promise to "do and do and do," leaving him drained "dry as hay") and in the infanticidal contents of the cauldron, especially the "finger of birth-strangled babe" and the blood of the sow "that hath eaten / Her nine farrow." The cannibalism that is a stable of Continental belief may be implicit in the contents of that grim cauldron, and the various eyes, toes, tongues, legs, teeth, livers, and noses (indiscriminately human and animal) may evoke primitive fears of dismemberment close to the center of witchcraft belief. But these terrors remain largely implicit. For Shakespeare's witches are both smaller and greater than their Continental sisters: on the one hand, more the representation of English homebodies with relatively small concerns; on the other, more the incarnation of literary or mythic fates or sybils, given the power not only to predict but to enforce the future.

7. After years of trying fruitlessly to pin down a precise identity for the witches, critics are increasingly finding their dramatic power precisely in their indefinability. The most powerful statements of this critical topos are those by Sanders (*The Dramatist and the Received Idea*, pp. 277–79), Robert H. West, (*Shakespeare and the Outer Mystery* [Lexington: University of Kentucky Press, 1968], pp. 78–79), and Stephen Booth (*"King Lear", "Macbeth", Indefinition, and Tragedy* [New Haven: Yale University Press, 1983], pp. 101–103).

8. For their "Englishness," see Stallybrass, "*Macbeth* and Witchcraft," p. 195. Alan Macfarlane's important study of English witchcraft, *Witchcraft in Tudor and Stuart England* (New York: Harper and Row, 1970), frequently notes the absence of the Continental staples: if the witches of Essex are typical, English witches do not fly, do not hold Sabbaths, do not commit sexual perversions or attack male potency, do not kill babies (see pp. 6, 160, and 180, for example).

9. Macfarlane finds the failure of neighborliness reflected in the retaliatory acts of the witch the key to the social function of witchcraft in England; see *Witchcraft in Tudor and Stuart England*, especially pp. 168–76, for accounts of the failures of neighborliness—very similar to the refusal to share chestnuts—that provoked the witch to act. James Sprenger's and Heinrich Kramer's *Malleus Maleficarum* (trans. Montague Summers [New York: Benjamin Blom, 1970]) is the *locus classicus* for Continental witchcraft beliefs: for the murder and eating of infants, see pp. 21, 66, 99, and 100–101; for attacks on the genitals, see pp. 47, 55–60, and 117–19; for sexual relations with demons, see pp. 21, 112–14. Or see Reginald Scot's convenient summary of these beliefs (*The Discoverie of Witchcraft* [London, 1584; reprinted, with an introduction by Hugh Ross Williamson, Carbondale: Southern Illinois University Press, 1964], p. 31).

But the staples of Continental witchcraft belief are not altogether missing from the play: for the most part, they are transferred away from the witches and recur as the psychological issues evoked by Lady Macbeth in her relation to Macbeth. She becomes the inheritor of the realm of primitive relational and bodily disturbance: of infantile vulnerability to maternal power, of dismemberment and its developmentally later equivalent, castration. Lady Macbeth brings the witches' power home: they get the cosmic apparatus, she gets the psychic force. That Lady Macbeth is the more frightening figure—and was so, I suspect, even before belief in witchcraft had declined—suggests the firmly domestic and psychological basis of Shakespeare's imagination.[1]

The fears of female coercion, female definition of the male, that are initially located cosmically in the witches thus find their ultimate locus in the figure of Lady Macbeth, whose attack on Macbeth's virility is the source of her strength over him and who acquires that strength, I shall argue, partly because she can make him imagine himself as an infant vulnerable to her. In the figure of Lady Macbeth, that is, Shakespeare rephrases the power of the witches as the wife / mother's power to poison human relatedness at its source; in her, their power of cosmic coercion is rewritten as the power of the mother to misshape or destroy the child. The attack on infants and on the genitals characteristic of Continental witchcraft belief is thus in her returned to its psychological source: in the play these beliefs are localized not in the witches but in the great central scene in which Lady Macbeth persuades Macbeth to the murder of Duncan. In this scene, Lady Macbeth notoriously makes the murder of Duncan the test of Macbeth's virility,[2] if he cannot perform the murder,

1. The relationship between cosmology and domestic psychology is similar *in King Lear;* even as Shakespeare casts doubt on the authenticity of demonic possession by his use of Harsnett's *Declaration of Egregious Popish Impostures,* Edgar / Poor Tom's identification of his father as "the foul Flibbertigibet" (3.4.118) manifests the psychic reality and source of his demons. Characteristically in Shakespeare, the site of blessing and of cursedness is the family, their processes psychological.
2. In an early essay that has become a classic, Eugene Waith established the centrality of definitions of manhood and Lady Macbeth's role in enforcing Macbeth's particularly bloodthirsty version, a theme that has since become a major topos of *Macbeth* criticism ("Manhood and Valor in Two Shakespearean Tragedies," *ELH* 17 [1950]: 262–73). Among the legions, see, for example, Robert B. Heilman, "Manliness in the Tragedies: Dramatic Variations," in *Shakespeare 1564–1964: A Collection of Modern Essays by Various Hands,* ed. Edward A. Bloom (Providence, R.I: Brown University Press, 1964), p. 27; Mathew N. Proser, *The Heroic Image in Five Shakespearean Tragedies* (Princeton, N.J.: Princeton University Press, 1965), pp. 51–91; Michael Taylor, "Ideals of Manhood in *Macbeth,*" *Études Anglaises* 21 (1968): 337–48 (an early foregrounding of cultural complicity in defining masculinity as aggression); D. W. Harding, "Women's Fantasy of Manhood: A Shakespearean Theme," *Shakespeare Quarterly* 20 (1969): 245–53; Paul A. Jorgensen, *Our Naked Frailties: Sensational Art and Meaning in "Macbeth"* (Berkeley: University of California Press, 1971), esp. pp. 147ff.; Jarold Ramsey, "The Perversion of Manliness in *Macbeth,*" *SEL* 13 (1973): 285–300; Carolyn Asp, " 'Be bloody, bold, and resolute': Tragic Action and Sexual Stereotyping in *Macbeth,*" *Studies in Philology* 25 (1981): 153–69; Harry Berger, Jr., "Text Against Performance," esp. pp. 67–75; Robert Kimbrough, "Macbeth: The Prisoner of Gender," *Shakespeare Studies* 16 (1983): 175–90; King-Kok

he is in effect reduced to the helplessness of an infant subject to her rage. She begins by attacking his manhood, making her love for him contingent on the murder that she identifies as equivalent to his male potency: "From this time / Such I account thy love" (1.7.38–39); "When you durst do it, then you were a man" (1.7.49). Insofar as his drunk hope is now "green and pale" (1.7.37), he is identified as emasculated, exhibiting the symptoms not only of hangover but also of the green-sickness, the typical disease of timid young virgin women. Lady Macbeth's argument is, in effect, that any signs of the "milk of human kindness" (1.5.17) mark him as more womanly than she; she proceeds to enforce his masculinity by demonstrating her willingness to dry up that milk in herself, specifically by destroying her nursing infant in fantasy: "I would, while it was smiling in my face, / Have pluck'd my nipple from his boneless gums, / And dash'd the brains out" (1.7.56–58). That this image has no place in the plot, where the Macbeths are strikingly childless, gives some indication of the inner necessity through which it appears. For Lady Macbeth expresses here not only the hardness she imagines to be male, not only her willingness to unmake the most essential maternal relationship; she expresses also a deep fantasy of Macbeth's utter vulnerability to her. As she progresses from questioning Macbeth's masculinity to imagining herself dashing out the brains of her infant son[3] she articulates a fantasy in which to be less than a man is to become interchangeably a woman or a baby,[4] terribly subject, to the wife / mother's destructive rage.

By evoking this vulnerability, Lady Macbeth acquires a power over

Cheung, "Shakespeare and Kierkegaard: 'Dread' in *Macbeth*," *Shakespeare Quarterly* 35 (1984):437–38; and Krohn, "Addressing the Oedipal Dilemma," pp. 334–37. Virtually all these essays recount the centrality of 1.7 to this theme; most see Macbeth's willingness to murder as his response to Lady Macbeth's nearly explicit attack on his male potency. Dennis Biggins ("Sexuality, Witchcraft, and Violence," pp. 255–77) and James J. Greene ("Macbeth: Masculinity as Murder," *American Imago* 41 [1984]: 155–80) see the murder as a sexual act consummating the union of Macbeth and Lady Macbeth; see also Watson, *Shakespeare and the Hazards of Ambition*, p. 90. My account differs from most of these largely in stressing the infantile components of Macbeth's susceptibility to Lady Macbeth.

3. Although "his" was a common form for the as-yet unfamiliar possessive "its," Lady Macbeth's move from "while it was smiling" to "his boneless gums" nonetheless seems to register the metamorphosis of an ungendered to a gendered infant exactly at the moment of vulnerability, making her attack specifically on a male child. That she uses the ungendered "the" a moment later ("the brains out") suggests one alternative open to Shakespeare had he wished to avoid the implication that the fantasied infant was male; Antony's crocodile, who "moves with it own organs" (*Antony and Cleopatra*, 2.7.42) suggests another. (*OED* notes that, although "its" occurs in the Folio, it does not occur in any work of Shakespeare published while he was alive; it also notes the various strategies by which authors attempted to avoid the inappropriate use of "his.")

4. Lady Macbeth maintains her control over Macbeth through 3.4 by manipulating these categories: see 2.2.53–54 ("'tis the eye of childhood / That fears a painted devil") and 3.4.57–64 ("Are you a man? . . . these flaws and starts . . . would well become / A woman's story"). In his response to Banquo's ghost, Macbeth invokes the same categories and suggests their interchangeability: he dares what man dares (3.4.98); if he feared Banquo alive, he could rightly be called "the baby of a girl" (3.4.105).

Macbeth more absolute than any the witches can achieve. The play's central fantasy of escape from woman seems to me to unfold from this moment: for if Macbeth's bloodthirsty masculinity is partly a response to Lady Macbeth's desire, in effect an extension of her will, it simultaneously comes to represent the way to escape her power. We can see the beginnings of this process in Macbeth's response to her evocation of absolute maternal power. Macbeth first responds by questioning the possibility of failure ("If we should fail?" [1.7.59]). Lady Macbeth counters this fear by inviting Macbeth to share in her fantasy of omnipotent malevolence: "What cannot you and I perform upon / Th'unguarded Duncan?" (1.7.70–71). The satiated and sleeping Duncan takes on the vulnerability that Lady Macbeth has just invoked in the image of the feeding, trusting infant;[5] Macbeth releases himself from the image of this vulnerability by sharing in the murder of this innocent. In his elation at this transfer of vulnerability from himself to Duncan, Macbeth imagines Lady Macbeth the mother to infants sharing her hardness, born in effect without vulnerability; in effect, he imagines her as male and then reconstitutes himself as the invulnerable male child of such a mother:

> Bring forth men-children only!
> For thy undaunted mettle should compose
> Nothing but males. (1.7.73–75)

Through the double pun on *mettle / metal* and *male / mail*, Lady Macbeth herself becomes virtually male, composed of the hard metal of which the armored male is made.[6] Her children would necessarily be men, composed of her male mettle, armored by her mettle, lacking the female inheritance from the mother that would make them vulnerable. The man-child thus brought forth would be no trusting infant; the very phrase "men-children" suggests the presence of the adult man even at birth, hence the undoing of childish vulnerability.[7]

---

5. Willbern notes the extent to which the regicide is re-imagined as a "symbolic infanticide," so that the image of Duncan fuses with the image of Lady Macbeth's child murdered in fantasy ("Phantasmagoric *Macbeth*," p. 524). Macbeth's earlier association of Duncan's power with the power of the "naked new-born babe, / Striding the blast" (1.7.21–22) prepares for this fusion: whatever their symbolic power, the literal babies of this play and those adults who sleep and trust like infants are hideously vulnerable. That Duncan is simultaneously female (Lucrece or Gorgon) and infantile suggests the degree to which these categories fuse in defining adult masculinity by opposition.

6. Kahn's reading of this passage is very similar to mine (*Man's Estate*, p. 173); for Jan Groen, the passage indicates Macbeth's attempt to identify with the split-off bad-mother part of himself, which is then defined as masculine ("Women in Shakespeare with Particular Reference to Lady Macbeth," *The International Review of Psycho-Analysis* 12 [1985]: 476). Cheung notes the puns, seeing in them the signs not of Lady Macbeth's fantasied maleness but of Macbeth's own equation of masculinity and aggression ("Shakespeare and Kierkegaard," p. 438).

7. Shakespeare's only other use of "man-child" is in *Coriolanus,* when Volumnia tells Virgilia, "I sprang not more in joy at first hearing he was a man-child, than now in first seeing he had proved himself a man" (1.3.16–18); this isolated repetition suggests the extent to which Shakespeare reworks similar concerns in that play.

The mobility of the imagery—from male infant with his brains dashed out, to Macbeth and Lady Macbeth triumphing over the sleeping, trusting Duncan, to the all-male invulnerable man-child—suggests the logic of the fantasy: only the child of an all-male mother is safe. We see here the creation of a defensive fantasy of exemption from the woman's part: as infantile vulnerability is shifted to Duncan, Macbeth creates in himself the image of Lady Macbeth's hardened all-male man-child; his murder of Duncan thus becomes the sign of his distance from the infant whom Lady Macbeth could destroy, the sign of the mettle that composes him.

Macbeth's temporary solution to the infantile vulnerability and maternal malevolence revealed by Lady Macbeth is to imagine Lady Macbeth the all-male mother of invulnerable infants and to imagine himself as such an infant, in effect doing away with vulnerability by doing away with the female site of origin. The final solution, both for Macbeth and for the play itself, though in differing ways, is an even more radical excision of the female site of origin: it is to imagine a birth entirely exempt from women, to imagine in effect an all-male family, composed of nothing but males, in which the father can be fully restored to power. Overtly, of course, the play denies the possibility of this fantasy: Macduff carries the power of the man not born of woman only through the equivocation of the fiends, their obstetrical joke that quibbles with the meaning of "born" and thus confirms circuitously that all men come from women after all. Even Macbeth, in whom, I think, the fantasy is centrally invested, knows its impossibility: his false security depends exactly on his common-sense assumption that everyone is born of woman. Nonetheless, I shall argue, the play curiously enacts the fantasy that it seems to deny: punishing Macbeth his participation in a fantasy of escape from the maternal matrix, it nonetheless allows the audience the partial satisfaction of a dramatic equivalent to it. The equivocating ending of *Macbeth* seems to me to play out this dual process of repudiation and enactment, uncreating any space for the female even while it seems to insist on the universality of maternal origin.

The witches prophesy invulnerability for Macbeth insofar as all are born of women:

> Be bloody, bold, and resolute: laugh to scorn
> The power of man, for none of woman born
> Shall harm Macbeth. (4.1.79–81)

But the prophecy has the immediate force of psychic relevance for Macbeth in part because it so perfectly fits with the fantasy constructions central to 1.7: even as it depends on the vulnerability of all others, it ambiguously constructs Macbeth as exempt from this vulnerability. For the witches here invite Macbeth to make himself into the bloody and invulnerable man-child he has created as a defense against maternal malevolence in 1.7. The creation of this man-child is recalled by the apparition of the Bloody Child that accompanies the witches' prophecy: the apparition alludes at once to the bloody vulnerability of the infant destroyed in fantasy by Lady Macbeth and to the bloodthirsty masculinity that seems to promise escape from this vulnerability, the bloodiness the witches urge Macbeth to take on. The doubleness of the image thus epitomizes exactly the doubleness of the prophecy itself, which constructs Macbeth's invulnerability in effect from the vulnerability of maternal origin in all other men. Macbeth does not question this prophecy, even after the experience of Birnam Wood should have taught him better, partly because it so perfectly meets his needs: in encouraging him to "laugh to scorn / The power of man" the prophecy seems to grant him exemption from the condition of all men, who bring with them the liabilities inherent in their birth. As Macbeth carries the prophecy as a shield onto the battlefield, his confidence in his own invulnerability increasingly reveals his sense of exemption from the universal human condition. Repeated seven times, the phrase "born to woman" with its variants begins to carry for Macbeth the meaning "vulnerable," as though vulnerability itself were the taint deriving from woman; his own invulnerability comes therefore to stand as evidence for his exemption from that taint. This is the subterranean logic of Macbeth's words to Young Siward immediately after Macbeth killed him:

> Thou wast born of woman:—
> But swords I smile at, weapons laugh to scorn,
> Brandish'd by man that's of a woman born. (5.7.11–13)

Young Siward's death becomes in effect proof that he was born of woman; and in the logic of Macbeth's psyche, his own invulnerability is the proof that he was not. The "but" records this fantasied distinction: it constructs the sentence, "You, born of woman, are vulnerable; but I, not born of woman, am not."[8]

Insofar as this is the fantasy embodied in Macbeth at the play's end, it is punished by the equivocation of the fiends: the revelation that Macduff derives from woman, though by unusual means, mus-

---

8. De Quincy seems to have intuited this process: "The murderers are taken out of the region of human things, human purposes, human desires. They are transfigured: Lady Macbeth is 'unsexed'; Macbeth has forgot that he was born of woman" ("On the Knocking at the Gate in 'Macbeth,'" in Shakespeare Criticism: A Selection, 1623–1840, ed. D. Nichol Smith [London: Oxford University Press, 1946], p. 335). Critics who consider gender relations central to this play generally note the importance of the witches' prophecy for the figure of Macduff; they do not usually note its application to Macbeth. But see Kahn's suggestion that the prophecy sets Macbeth "apart from women as well as from men" (Man's Estate, p. 187) and Gohlke / Sprengnether's central perception that, "To be born of woman, as [Macbeth] reads the witches' prophecy, is to be mortal" ("'I wooed thee with my sword,'" p. 176).

ters against Macbeth all the values of ordinary family and community that Macduff carries with him. Macbeth, "cow'd" by the revelation (5.8.18),[9] is forced to take on the taint of vulnerability; the fantasy of escape from the maternal matrix seems to die with him. But although this fantasy is punished in Macbeth, it does not quite die with him; it continues to have a curious life of its own in the play, apart from its embodiment in him. Even from the beginning of the play, the fantasy has not been Macbeth's alone: as the play's most striking bloody man, he is in the beginning the bearer of this fantasy for the all-male community that depends on his blood prowess. The opening scenes strikingly construct male and female as realms apart; and the initial description of Macbeth's battles construe his prowess as a consequence of his exemption from the taint of woman.

In the description of his battle with Macdonwald, what looks initially like a battle between loyal and disloyal sons to establish primacy in the father's eyes is oddly transposed into a battle of male against female:

> Doubtful it stood;
> As two spent swimmers, that do cling together
> And choke their art. The merciless Macdonwald
> (Worthy to be a rebel, for to that
> The multiplying villainies of nature
> Do swarm upon him) from the western isles
> Of Kernes and Gallowglasses is supplied;
> And Fortune, on his damned quarrel smiling,
> Show'd like a rebel's whore: but all's too weak;
> For brave Macbeth (well he deserves that name),
> Disdaining Fortune, with his brandish'd steel,
> Which smok'd with bloody execution,
> Like Valour's minion, carv'd out his passage,
> Till he fac'd the slave;
> Which ne'er shook hands, nor bade farewell to him,
> Till he unseam'd him from the nave to th'chops,
> And fix'd his head upon our battlements. (1.2.7–23)

The two initially indistinguishable figures metaphorized as the swimmers eventually sort themselves out into victor and victim, but only by first sorting themselves out into male and female, as though Macbeth can be distinguished from Macdonwald only by making Macdonwald functionally female. The "merciless Macdonwald" is initially firmly identified; but by the time Macbeth appears, Macdonwald has temporarily disappeared, replaced by the female figure of Fortune, against whom Macbeth seems to fight ("brave Macbeth, . . . Disdaining Fortune, with his brandish'd steel"). The meta-

---

9. See Kahn's rich understanding of the function of the term "cow'd" (*Man's Estate*, p. 191).

phorical substitution of Fortune for Macdonwald transforms the battle into a contest between male and female; in effect, it makes Macbeth's claim to his name—"brave Macbeth"—contingent on his victory over the female. We are prepared for this transformation by Macdonwald's sexual alliance with the tainting female, the whore Fortune,[1] Macbeth's identification as valor's minion redefines the battle as a contest between the half-female couple Fortune / Macdonwald and the all-male couple Valor / Macbeth. Metaphorically, Macdonwald and Macbeth take on the qualities of the unreliable female and the heroic male; Macbeth's battle against Fortune turns out to be his battle against Macdonwald because the two are functionally the same. Macdonwald, tainted by the female, thus becomes an easy mark for Macbeth, who demonstrates his own untainted manhood by unseaming Macdonwald from the nave to the chops: simultaneously castrating and performing a caesarian section on him, Macbeth remakes Macdonwald's body as female, revealing what his alliance with Fortune has suggested all along.

In effect, then, the battle that supports the father's kingdom plays out the creation of a conquering all-male erotics that marks its conquest by its triumph over a feminized body, simultaneously that of Fortune and Macdonwald. Hence, in the double action of the passage, the victorious unseaming happens twice: first on the body of Fortune and then on the body of Macdonwald. The lines descriptive of Macbeth's approach to Macdonwald—"brave Macbeth . . . Disdaining Fortune, with his brandish'd steel, / . . . carv'd out his passage"—make that approach contingent on Macbeth's first carving his passage through a female body, like Richard III hewing his way out (3 *Henry VI*, 3.2.181). The language here perfectly anticipates Macduff's birth by caesarian section, revealed at the end of the play: if Macduff is ripped untimely from his mother's womb, Macbeth here manages in fantasy his own caesarian section,[2] carving his passage out from the unreliable female to achieve heroic male action, in effect carving up the female to arrive at the male. Only after this rite of passage can Macbeth meet Macdonwald: this act of aggression toward the female body, with its accompanying fantasy of self-birth, marks Macbeth's passage to the contest that will define his maleness partly by attributing tainted femaleness to Macdonwald. For the all-male community surrounding Duncan, then, Macbeth's victory is

1. Many comment on this contamination: see, for example, Berger, "The Early Scenes of *Macbeth*," pp. 7–8; Hogan, "Macbeth," p. 387; Rosenberg, *The Masks of Macbeth*, p. 45; and Biggins, "Sexuality, Witches, and Violence," p. 265.
2. Watson notes the suggestion of caesarian section here (*Shakespeare and the Hazards of Ambition*, p. 100) and in *Coriolanus*; but in part because he understands self-birth in oedipal rather than preoedipal terms, he fails to note the aggression toward the female at its root (see Chapter 1, n. 3). I am specifically indebted to Willbern's reading of the caesarian implications of the unseaming from nave to chops ("Phantasmagoric *Macbeth*," pp. 528–29).

allied with his triumph over femaleness; selfborn, he becomes invulnerable, "lapp'd in proof" (1.2.55) like one of Lady Macbeth's armored men-children.[3] Even before his initial entry into the play, that is, Macbeth becomes the bearer of the shared fantasy that secure male community depends on the prowess of the man not born of woman, the man who can carve his own passage out, the man whose very maleness is the mark of his exemption from maternal origin and the vulnerabilities that are its consequence.[4]

Ostensibly, the play rejects the version of manhood implicit in the shared fantasy of the beginning. Macbeth himself is well aware that his capitulation to Lady Macbeth's definition of manhood entails his abandonment of his own more inclusive definition of what becomes a man (1.7.46); and Macduff's response to the news of his family's destruction insists that humane feeling is central to the definition of manhood (4.3.221). Moreover, the revelation that even Macduff had a mother sets a limiting condition on the fantasy of a bloody masculine escape from the maternal matrix and hence on the kind of manhood defined by that escape. Nonetheless, even at the end, the play enables one version of the fantasy that heroic manhood is exemption from the female even while it punishes that fantasy in Macbeth. The key figure in whom this double movement is vested at the end of the play is Macduff; the unresolved contradictions that surround him are, I think, marks of ambivalence toward the fantasy itself. In insisting that mourning for his family is his right as a man, he presents family feeling as central to the definition of manhood; and yet he conspicuously leaves his family vulnerable to destruction when he goes off to offer his services to Malcolm. The play moreover insists on reminding us that he has inexplicably abandoned his family: both Lady Macduff and Malcolm question the necessity of this abandonment (4.2.6–14, 4.3.26–28), and the play never allows Macduff to explain himself. This unexplained abandonment severely qualifies Macduff's force as the play's central exemplar of a healthy manhood that can include the possibility of relationship to women: the play seems to vest diseased familial relations in Macbeth and the

---

3. The reference to Macbeth as "Bellona's bridegroom" anticipates his interaction with Lady Macbeth in 1.7: only the murderous man-child is fit mate for either of these unsexed, quasi-male figures.
4. To the extent that ferocious maleness is the creation of the male community, not of Lady Macbeth or the witches, the women are scapegoats who exist partly to obscure the conflicts in that male community. For fuller accounts of this process, see Veszy-Wagner ("Macbeth," p. 244), Bumber (*Comic Women*, pp. 19–20), and especially Berger ("Text Against Performance," pp. 69–75); for a more recent version, see Dianne Hunter ("Doubling, Mythic Difference, and the Scapegoating of Female Power in *Macbeth*," *The Psychoanalytic Review* 75 [1988]: 129–52). But whether or not the women are scapegoats falsely held responsible for Macbeth's murderous maleness, fear of the female power they represent remains primary (not secondary and obscurantist) insofar as the male community and to some extent the play itself construct maleness as violent differentiation from the female.

possibility of healthy ones in Macduff; and yet we discover dramatically that Macduff has a family only when we hear that he has abandoned it. Dramatically and psychologically, he takes on full masculine power only as he loses his family and becomes energized by the loss, converting his grief into the more "manly" tune of vengeance (4.3.235); the loss of his family here enables his accession to full masculine action even while his response to that loss insists on a more humane definition of manhood.[5] The play here pulls in two directions; and it then reiterates this doubleness by vesting in Macduff its final fantasy of exemption from woman. The ambivalence that shapes the portrayal of Macduff is evident even as he reveals to Macbeth that he "was from his mother's womb / Untimely ripp'd" (5.8.15–16): the emphasis on untimeliness and the violence of the image suggest that he has been prematurely deprived of a nurturing maternal presence; but the prophecy construes just this deprivation as the source of Macduff's strength.[6] The prophecy itself both denies and affirms the fantasy of exemption from women: in affirming that Macduff has indeed had a mother, it denies the fantasy of male self-generation; but in attributing his power to his having been untimely ripped from that mother, it sustains the sense that violent separation from the mother is the mark of the successful male. The final battle between Macbeth and Macduff thus replays the initial battle between Macbeth and Macdonwald. But Macduff has now taken the place of Macbeth: he carries with him the male power given him by the caesarian solution, and Macbeth is retrospectively revealed as Macdonwald, the woman's man.

5. A great many critics, following Waith ("Manhood and Valor," pp. 266–67), find the play's embodiment of healthy masculinity in Macduff. They often register some uneasiness about his leaving his family, but they rarely allow this uneasiness to complicate their view of him as exemplary. But critics interested in the play's construction of masculinity in part as a defense against the fear of femaleness tend to see in Macduff's removal from family a replication of the central fear of women that is more fully played out in Macbeth. See, for example, Wheeler (Shakespeare's Development, p. 146), Berger ("Text Against Performance," p. 70), and Krohn ("Addressing the Oedipal Dilemma," p. 343). For these critics, Macduff's flight is of a piece with his status as the man not born of woman.

6. Critics interested in gender issues almost invariably comment on the centrality of Macduff's fulfillment of this prophecy, finding his strength here in his freedom from contamination by or regressive dependency on women: see, for example, Harding ("Women's Fantasy," p. 250), Barron ("The Babe That Milks," p. 272), Fiedler (Stranger, p. 53), Myra Glazer Schotz ("The Great Unwritten Story: Mothers and Daughters in Shakespeare," in The Lost Tradition: Mothers and Daughters in Literature, ed. Cathy N. Davidson and E. M. Broner [New York: Frederick Ungar, 1980], p. 46), Berger ("The Early Scenes," p. 28), Bachmann ("Daggers," p. 101), Kirsch ("Macbeth's Suicide," p. 293), Kahn (Man's Estate, pp. 172–73), Wheeler (Shakespeare's Development, p. 146), and Victor Calef ("Lady Macbeth and Infanticide or 'How Many Children Had Lady Macbeth Murdered?' " Journal of the American Psychoanalytic Association 17 [1969]: 537). For Barron and Harding, Macduff's status as the bearer of this fantasy positively enhances his manhood; but for many of these critics, it qualifies his status as the exemplar of healthy manhood. Perhaps because ambivalence toward Macduff is built so deeply into the play, several very astute critics see the fantasy embedded in Macduff here and nonetheless continue to find in him an ideal manhood that includes the possibility of relatedness to the feminine. See, for example, Kahn (Man's Estate, p. 191) and Kirsch ("Macbeth's Suicide," p. 294).

The doubleness of the prophecy is less the equivocation of the fiends than Shakespeare's own equivocation about the figure of Macduff and about the fantasy vested in him in the end. For Macduff carries with him simultaneously all the values of family and the claim that masculine power derives from the unnatural abrogation of family, including escape from the conditions of one's birth. Moreover, the ambivalence that shapes the figure of Macduff similarly shapes the dramatic structure of the play itself. Ostensibly concerned to restore natural order at the end,[7] the play bases that order upon the radical exclusion of the female. Initially construed as all-powerful, the women virtually disappear at the end. Increasingly cribbed and confined by the play, Lady Macbeth's psychic power and subjectivity are increasingly written out of it. At first a source of terror, she increasingly becomes the merely helpless wife, alienated from her husband's serious business, pleading with him to come to bed, cooperatively dying offstage in her separate sphere, amidst a cry of women. Even when she is at the center of the stage, her own subjectivity is denied her: the broken object of others' observation in the sleep-walking scene, she has become entirely absent to herself. By the end, she is so diminished a character that we scarcely trouble to ask ourselves whether the report of her suicide is accurate or not. At the same time, the witches who are her avatars disappear from the stage and become so diminished in importance that Macbeth never alludes to them, blaming his defeat only on the equivocation of their male masters, the fiends. Even Lady Macduff exists only to disappear.

With the excision of all the female characters, nature itself can in effect be reborn male. The bogus fulfillment of the Birnam Wood prophecy emphasizes the extent to which the natural order of the end depends on this excision of the female. Critics sometimes see in the march of Malcolm's soldiers bearing their green branches an allusion to the Maying festivals in which participants returned from the woods bearing branches, or to the ritual scourging of a hibernal figure by the forces of the oncoming spring.[8] The allusion seems to

---

7. The triumph of the natural order has of course been a commonplace of criticism since the classic essay by G. Wilson Knight ("The Milk of Concord: An Essay on Life-Themes in *Macbeth*," *The Imperial Theme* [London: Methuen, 1965], especially pp. 140–53). The topos is so powerful that it can cause even critics interested in gender issues to praise the triumph of nature and natural sexuality at the end without noting the exclusion of the female; see, for example, Greene ("Macbeth," p. 172). But Rosenberg, for example, notes the qualifying effect of this exclusion (*Masks of Macbeth*, p. 654).

8. See, for example, Goddard (*The Meaning of Shakespeare*, pp. 520–21); Jekels ("Riddle," p. 238); John Holloway (*The Story of the Night* [London: Routledge and Kegan Paul, 1961], p. 66); Rosenberg (*Masks of Macbeth*, p. 626); and Watson (*Shakespeare and the Hazards of Ambition*, pp. 89, 106–16). Even without sensing the covert presence of a vegetation myth, critics often associate the coming of Birnam Wood with the restoration of spring and fertility; see, for example, Knight ("Milk of Concord," pp. 144–45) and Greene ("Macbeth," p. 169). Only Bamber demurs: in her account Birnam Wood rises up in aid of a male alliance, not as the Saturnalian disorder of the Maying rituals (*Comic Women*, p. 106). My view coincides with hers.

me clearly present; but it serves I think to mark precisely what the
moving of Birnam Wood is not. Malcolm's use of Birnam Wood is a
military maneuver. His drily worded command (5.4.4–7) leaves little
room for suggestions of natural fertility or for the deep sense of the
generative world rising up to expel its winter king; not does the play
later enable these associations except in a scattered and partly ironic
way.[9] These trees have little resemblance to those in the Forest of
Arden; their branches, like those carried by the apparition of the
"child crowned, with a tree in his hand" (4.1.86), are little more than
the emblems of a strictly patriarchal family tree.[1] This family tree,
like the march of Birnam Wood itself, is relentlessly male: Duncan
and sons, Banquo and son, Siward and son. There are no daughters
and scarcely any mention of mothers in these family trees. We are
brought as close as possible here to the fantasy of family without
women.[2] In that sense, Birnam Wood is the perfect emblem of the
nature that triumphs at the end of the play: nature without generative possibility, nature without women. Malcolm tells his men to
carry the branches to obscure themselves, and that is exactly their
function: insofar as they seem to allude to the rising of the natural
order against Macbeth, they obscure the operations of male power,
disguising them as a natural force; and they simultaneously obscure

---

9. When Malcolm refers to planting (5.9.31) at the play's end, for example, his comment
   serves partly to reinforce our sense of his distance from his father's generative power.
1. Paul attributes Shakespeare's use of the imagery of the family tree here to his familiarity
   with the cut of the Banquo tree in Leslie's *De Origine, Moribus, et Rebus Gestis Scotorum*
   (*Royal Play*, p. 175). But the image is too familiar to call for such explanations; see, for
   example, the tree described in *Richard II* (1.2.12–21).
2. As Wheeler notes, the description of Malcolm's saintly mother makes him "symbolically
   the child of something approximating virgin birth" (*Shakespeare's Development*, p. 146)—
   in effect another version of the man not quite born of woman. Stallybrass calls attention
   to the structure of antithesis through which "(virtuous) families of men" are distinguished
   from "antifamilies of women" ("*Macbeth* and Witchcraft," p. 198). Berger comments on
   the aspiration to be "a nation of bachelor Adams, of no woman born and unknown to
   women" ("Text Against Performance," p. 72) without, however, noting the extent to which
   this fantasy is enacted in the play; for Krohn, the solution to the oedipal dilemma—
   "eliminate mothers"—is repeatedly portrayed by Shakespeare ("Addressing the Oedipal
   Dilemma," pp. 334–35). The fantasy of escape from maternal birth and the creation of
   all-male lineage would probably have been of interest to King James, whose problematic
   derivation from Mary, Queen of Scots, must occasionally have made him wish himself not
   born of (that particular) woman, no matter how much he was publicly concerned to reha-
   bilitate her image. See Jonathan Goldberg's account of James's complex attitude toward
   Mary (*James I and the Politics of Literature* [Baltimore, Johns Hopkins University Press,
   1983], pp. 11–17, 25–26, and 119) and his later speculations on Mary and the fantasy of
   parthenogenesis in *Macbeth* ("Speculations: *Macbeth* and Source," in *Shakespeare Repro-
   duced: The Text in History and Ideology*, ed. Jean E. Howard and Marion F. O'Connor
   [New York and London: Methuen, 1987], p. 259); the later essay came to my attention
   only after my own speculations on this subject were published. Stephen Orgel finds a
   similar configuration in *The Tempest*: James "conceived himself as the head of a single-
   parent family," as a paternal figure who has "incorporated the maternal," in effect as a
   Prospero; the alternative model is Caliban, who derives his authority from his mother
   ("Prospero's Wife," *Representations* 8 [1984]: 8–9). Perhaps *Macbeth* indirectly serves a
   cultural need to free James from entanglement with the problematic memory of his witch-
   mother (portrayed thus, for example, by Spenser in Book 5 of *The Faerie Queene*), tracing
   his lineage instead from a safely distanced and safely male forefather, Banquo.

the extent to which natural order itself is here reconceived purely as male.[3]

If we can see the fantasy of escape from the female in the play's fulfillment of the witches' prophecies—in Macduff's birth by caesarian section and in Malcolm's appropriation of Birnam Wood—we can see it also in the play's psychological geography. The shift from Scotland to England is strikingly the shift from the mother's to the father's terrain.[4] Scotland "cannot / Be call'd our mother, but our grave" (4.3.165–66), in Rosse's words to Macduff: it is the realm of Lady Macbeth and the witches, the realm in which the mother *is* the grave, the realm appropriately ruled by their bad son Macbeth. The escape to England is an escape from their power into the realm of the good father-king and his surrogate son Malcolm, "unknown to woman" (4.3.126). The magical power of this father to cure clearly balances the magical power of the witches to harm, as Malcolm (the father's son) balances Macbeth (the mother's son). That Macduff can cross from one realm into the other only by abandoning his family suggests the rigidity of the psychic geography separating England from Scotland. At the end of the play, Malcolm returns to Scotland mantled in the power England gives him, in effect bringing the power of the fathers with him: bearer of his father's line, unknown to woman, supported by his agent Macduff (himself empowered by his own special immunity from birth), Malcolm embodies utter separation from women and as such triumphs easily over Macbeth, the mother's son.

The play that begins by unleashing the terrible threat of destructive maternal power and demonstrates the helplessness of its central male figure before that power thus ends by consolidating male power, in effect solving the problem of masculinity by eliminating the female. The play's recuperative consolidation of masculinity answers the maternal threat unleashed and never fully contained in *Hamlet* and *King Lear*: here, maternal power is given its most virulent sway and then handily abolished. In the end, we are in a purely male realm, founded—as Prospero's will be—on the excision of maternal origin; here, mothers no longer threaten because they no longer exist. But this solution is inherently unstable: the ending of *Coriolanus* will undo the ending of *Macbeth*, bringing back the mother with a vengeance.

3. Although neither Berger nor Stallybrass discuss the function of Birnam Wood specifically, I am indebted here to their discussions of the ideological function of the play's appeal to cosmology in the service of patriarchy, Berger seeing it as "a collective project of mystification" ("Text Against Performance," p. 64), Stallybrass as "a returning of the disputed ground of politics to the undisputed ground of Nature" ("*Macbeth* and Witchcraft," pp. 205–6). If, as Bradbrook suggests, witches were thought able to move trees ("Sources," p. 42), then we have in Malcolm's gesture a literal appropriation of female power, an act of making the unnatural natural by making it serve patriarchal needs.

4. See Erickson's fine discussion of this geographic distinction (*Patriarchal Structures*, pp. 121–22).

A. R. BRAUNMULLER

'What do you mean?': The Languages of *Macbeth*†

At least since the Restoration diarist Samuel Pepys recorded attending *Macbeth*—'a pretty good play, but admirably acted'[1]—on the fifty-ninth anniversary of the Gunpowder Plot, 5 November 1664, and undoubtedly long before that, audiences have enjoyed its theatrical spectacle, its marvels and magic—what Pepys later called 'variety' and 'divertisement'[2] Shakespeare's play has equal pleasures for the listening imagination.

Despite the play's exciting linguistic variety, hostile comments from the seventeenth and the twentieth century attack its language. On unknown authority, John Dryden cited Ben Jonson, Shakespeare's greatest rival and (at least by the time he wrote a fine commendatory poem for the 1623 First Folio) eloquent admirer: 'In reading some bombast speeches of *Macbeth*, which are not to be understood, he [Jonson] used to say that it was horror; and I am much afraid that this is so.'[3] Dryden himself asserted:

> he [Shakespeare] often obscures his meaning by his words, and sometimes makes it unintelligible . . . the fury of his fancy often transported him beyond the bounds of judgement, either in coining of new words and phrases, or racking words which were in use into the violence of a catachresis. 'Tis not that I would explode the use of metaphors from passions . . . but to use 'em at every word, to say nothing without a metaphor, a simile, an image, or description, is I doubt to smell a little too strongly of the buskin.[4]

---

† From *Macbeth*, ed. A. R. Braunmuller (Cambridge: Cambridge University Press, 1997), 43–56. Reprinted by permission of Cambridge University Press. Some of the author's footnotes have been omitted. Footnotes are by the author of this article, unless otherwise indicated.

1. Robert Latham and William Matthews (eds.), *The Diary of Samuel Pepys*, 11 vols., 1970–83, V, 314. On this anniversary of the Gunpowder Plot, Pepys almost certainly saw William Davenant's adaptation, quite possibly its première; see Arthur H. Scouten, 'The premiere of Davenant's adaptation of *Macbeth*', in W. R. Elton and William B. Long (eds.), *Shakespeare and Dramatic Tradition*, 1989, pp. 286–93.

2. Pepys, VII, 423 (28 December 1666), and VIII, 7 (7 January 1667); Pepys describes William Davenant's adapted text which indeed contained, as he said, 'variety of dancing and music' (VIII, 171; 19 April 1667).

3. John Dryden, 'Defence of the epilogue', in George Watson (ed.), *Of Dramatic Poesy and Other Critical Essays* 2 vols., 1962, I, 173. Dryden may be putting words in an elder and deeply respected playwright's mouth here, but 'it was horror' is none the less a peculiar phrase, allowing one to imagine Dryden's 'Jonson' saying that the play's occasional linguistic confusion conveys 'horror' rather than that the play's language is horribly confused.

4. 'The grounds of criticism in tragedy', prefixed to *Troilus and Cressida* (1679), in Watson (ed.), *Of Dramatic Poesy*, I, 257. Dryden gives no examples, but *Macbeth* is full of evocative but logically confusing (and therefore neo-classically offensive) figurative language: 'Was

A. C. Bradley, a sympathetic late-Victorian reader of *Macbeth*, partly agrees: 'The diction has in places a huge and rugged grandeur, which degenerates here and there into tumidity.'[5] Almost two-and-a-half centuries after Dryden's death, James Thurber imagined himself marooned in a hotel with reading matter as random and ill-assorted as that found in a dentist's waiting-room. One fellow-resident was stuck with *Macbeth*, which she found, Thurber says, 'a Murder Mystery'. She especially notes the moment when Macduff describes finding Duncan's body:

> 'Macduff discovers it,' she said, slipping into the historical present. 'Then he comes running downstairs and shouts, 'Confusion has broke open the Lord's anointed temple' and 'Sacrilegious murder has made his masterpiece' and on and on like that.' The good lady tapped me on the knee. 'All that stuff was *rehearsed*,' she said. 'You wouldn't say a lot of stuff like that, offhand, would you—if you had found a body? . . . You wouldn't! Unless you had practiced it in advance. 'My God, there's a body in here!' is what an innocent man would say.[6]

The lady's complaint echoes Dr Johnson on Milton's *Lycidas*: 'Where there is leisure for fiction there is little grief.' Here, Thurber's reader concludes, where there is leisure for personification there is little personal feeling.

Dryden's possibly fictitious Jonson, and Dryden himself, and Bradley, and Thurber's imaginary reader all hear the play's linguistic, especially metaphorical, volatility, a volatility that sometimes reaches near-incomprehensibility in marvellous but unparaphrasable language:

> this Duncan
> Hath borne his faculties so meek, hath been
> So clear in his great office, that his virtues
> Will plead like angels, trumpet-tongued against
> The deep damnation of his taking-off.
> And pity, like a naked newborn babe
> Striding the blast, or heaven's cherubin horsed
> Upon the sightless couriers of the air,
> Shall blow the horrid deed in every eye,

---

the hope drunk / Wherein you dressed yourself? Hath it slept since? / And wakes it now to look so green and pale / At what it did so freely?' (1.7.35–8), for example.

5. Bradley [*Shakespearean Tragedy*, 1904], p. 256; in a later (p. 310) comparison of *Macbeth* with Seneca, Bradley describes some of the play's language as 'turgid bombast'.

6. James Thurber, *My World—And Welcome To It*, 1942, pp. 35–6. George Bernard Shaw achieves a similar effect in a burlesque of Act 1, Scenes 5 and 7, where Lady Macbeth's lines are mostly intact and Macbeth's are modern and colloquial (e.g., 'What the devil is a limbec?'); see Bernard Dukore (ed.), George Bernard Shaw, 'Macbeth skit', *Educational Theatre Journal* 19 (1967), 343–8.

That tears shall drown the wind. (1.7.16–25)
                    Come, seeling night,
Scarf up the tender eye of pitiful day
And with thy bloody and invisible hand
Cancel and tear to pieces that great bond
Which keeps me pale. Light thickens,
And the crow makes wing to th'rooky wood;
Good things of day begin to droop and drowse,
Whiles night's black agents to their preys do rouse. (3.2.46–
    53)

Writers bold enough to comment on these speeches have generally
admitted both defeat and admiration. Of the first passage, Dr Johnson said, 'the meaning is not very clear; I have never found the read-
ers of Shakespeare agreeing about it'[7] The play has language to
puzzle not only Johnson, but anyone.

Rather than offer yet another interpretation of Macbeth's extraordinary speech on 'pity, like a naked newborn babe', a speech elo-
quently discussed by Cleanth Brooks and Helen Gardner among
many others,[8] I offer a shorter example, equally condensed and
equally typical of the play's most complex way with words. When
Ross and Angus ceremonially announce that Duncan has granted
Macbeth a new title, 'Thane of Cawdor' (1.3.87–105), Macbeth
divides into a public man, publicly acknowledging a deliberately public honour—'Thanks for your pains', 'I thank you, gentlemen'
(1.3.116, 128)—and into a musing, reflective mind seeking the links
among sudden, new honour and the sisters' earlier predictions:

                    Two truths are told,
As happy prologues to the swelling act
Of the imperial theme. (1.3.126–8)

This small portion of Macbeth's speech shows the way the play's
language, or, more precisely, the way this character's language, shifts
from one verbal register or matrix to another. One matrix is the language of the theatre: 'prologues' are familiar introductory or explanatory figures who preface an entire play or an 'act' of one; after the
prologue, an audience would expect the stage to fill (or 'swell') with
other actors representing the persons and enacting the events the
prologic character predicted or promised. Another matrix is the lan-

---

7. On the first speech, see also Cleanth Brooks, *The Well Wrought Urn*, 1947, pp. 21–46.
   On the second speech, see William Empson, *Seven Types of Ambiguity*, 1930, 3rd edn,
   1953, pp. 18–20 and 81–2, and R. A. Foakes, 'Poetic language and dramatic significance
   in Shakespeare', in Philip Edwards *et al.* (eds.), *Shakespeare's Styles*, 1980, pp. 79–83. On
   their Hebridean walking tour, Samuel Johnson had to endure James Boswell's numerous
   quotations of *Macbeth*; see James Boswell, *Journal of a Tour to the Hebrides*, ed. Frederick
   A. Pottle and Charles H. Bennett, 1961, *passim*, but esp. the entry (29 August 1773)
   recording their visit to 'Macbeth's Castle'.
8. See Brooks, pp. 21–46, and Helen Gardner, *The Business of Criticism*, 1959, pp. 52–61.

guage of rhetoric and of music: 'theme' is a speaker's or thinker's subject or topic, or possibly (the meaning is barely established in the late sixteenth century) a recognisable—'hearable'—set of repeated or varied notes.[9] 'Two truths', Macbeth says, introduce an extended passage (of thought, argument, music) leading metaphorically to empery or kingship, and the 'imperial theme' turns from static to active, from contemplation to incitement. From mentally debating what it might be like to be king, Macbeth's reflection (or rather the highly compressed language Shakespeare gives the character) now introduces the possibility of acting to achieve kingship.[1] A final linguistic matrix arises from the 'swelling' of a pregnant woman's body. Speaking to Banquo—'Thou shalt get kings, though thou be none' (1.3.65)—the sisters raise the play's most intractable and profound issue, the questions of generation, children, inheritance, the prolonging of a familial line. Their emphasis is almost but not quite unremarked—'Do you not hope your children shall be kings, / When those that gave the Thane of Cawdor to me / Promised no less to them?' (1.3.117–19)—but with 'swelling' (of pregnancy or of impregnating penis) this brief passage acknowledges the possibility that the 'imperial' or royal goal might be barren, that the sisters 'Upon my head . . . placed a fruitless crown / And put a barren sceptre in my gripe' (3.1.62–3).

In these passages, the play's language moves rapidly among many images and many linguistic possibilities; this shifting brings together the eloquent, the homely, the proverbial, and the brilliantly theatrical helter-skelter. Among many extraordinary verbal effects in Macbeth's reflection upon killing Duncan (1.7.12ff.), for example, '*naked newborn babe*' subtly patterns the sounds of *n* and of *b*, making a rhetorical chiasmus of the middle term, 'newborn', where the sounds 'cross' and coexist.[2]

This later passage, when Macbeth has determined to kill Banquo and Fleance, begins with Macbeth's intimate endearment, 'Be innocent of the knowledge, dearest chuck, / Till thou applaud the deed' (3.2.45–6). If a 'noble' hero may be so tender amidst the slaughter past and to come, and so bourgeois as to use 'chuck', a 'citizen' term, then so too the man and child he would kill employ an innocently 'humble' diction:

9. On the musical meaning of 'theme', dated to 1597, see *OED* Theme 4; the rhetorical meaning * * * is far older.
1. This shift or glide from a more or less abstract and static mental consideration to an active intention occurs often in the play; see, e.g., 1.5.14–23.
2. A similar, more extended antimetabole [repetition in reverser order] using *d* and *b* appears in 'I will not be afraid of *d*eath and *b*ane / Till *B*irnam Forest come to *D*unsinane' (5.3.60–1). Compare the different but similar auditory experience of '*b*ear [bare?] the knife myself' (16) and '*b*orne his faculties' (17).

> BANQUO How goes the night, boy?
> FLEANCE The moon is down; I have not heard the clock.
> BANQUO And she goes down at twelve.
> FLEANCE I take't, 'tis later, sir.
>   (2.1.1–3)

And when Banquo dies, a single pentameter unites a passing comment about the weather with the command for his death:

> BANQUO It will be rain tonight.
> FIRST MURDERER Let it come down. (3.3.18)

With little help from the dialogue, the actor playing Lady Macbeth must shift the audience's imagination from plot-orientated fact to gnawing moral self-examination:

> LADY MACBETH Is Banquo gone from court?
> SERVANT Ay, madam, but returns again tonight.
> LADY MACBETH Say to the king, I would attend his leisure
>   For a few words.
> SERVANT Madam, I will. *Exit*
> LADY MACBETH Nought's had, all's spent
>   Where our desire is got without content.
>   'Tis safer to be that which we destroy
>   Than by destruction dwell in doubtful joy. (3.2.1–7)

Almost at once, Lady Macbeth must turn from self-reflection and seek to assuage Macbeth's scorpion-filled mind.

Lady Macbeth's couplets (3.2.4–7) have a quasi-proverbial force, and many well-known lines quote proverbs or have a substratum of proverbial language or thought. One proverb, 'Things done cannot be undone', contributes to three strategically placed moments, at the beginning, the middle, and the end of the play:

> If it were done when 'tis done, then 'twere well
> It were done quickly. (1.7.1–2)
>   Things without all remedy
> Should be without regard; what's done, is done. (3.2.11–
>   12)[3]
> Come, come, come, come, give me your hand; what's done
>   cannot be undone. To bed, to bed, to bed. (5.1.57–8)

Sedimented, even ossified, commonplaces of wisdom or observation, proverbs and proverbial language make ordinary the play's events and the speakers' reactions while simultaneously and starkly showing how far beyond the ordinary, the proverbial, the stony, these events and attitudes are: proverbs toll through important moments in Act

---

3. These lines include another proverb: 'Where there is no remedy it is folly to chide.'

3—'Men are but men'; 'Fair face foul heart'; 'And there's an end'; 'Blood will have blood.'

The language of *Macbeth* combines sublime magniloquence— which the neoclassical critics Ben Jonson, Dryden, and Dr Johnson found distasteful—with everyday language that also has great theatrical power. After Duncan's murder is discovered, Macbeth has two speeches that certainly 'say nothing without a metaphor, a simile, an image':

> Had I but died an hour before this chance,
> I had lived a blessèd time, for from this instant,
> There's nothing serious in mortality.
> All is but toys; renown and grace is dead,
> The wine of life is drawn, and the mere lees
> Is left this vault to brag of. (2.3.84–9)

And then:

> Who can be wise, amazed, temp'rate, and furious,
> Loyal and neutral, in a moment? No man.
> Th'expedition of my violent love
> Outran the pauser, reason. Here lay Duncan,
> His silver skin laced with his golden blood
> And his gashed stabs looked like a breach in nature,
> For ruin's wasteful entrance. There the murderers,
> Steeped in the colours of their trade; their daggers
> Unmannerly breeched with gore. Who could refrain,
> That had a heart to love and in that heart
> Courage to make's love known? (2.3.101–111)

These speeches mix Macbeth's sorrow, which may be genuine, or partly so, with the lies needed to conceal guilt and win the kingship.

In the brief interval between Duncan's murder and its discovery, Shakespeare faced a different dramatic problem. As in the aftermath of the discovery, Macbeth must conceal and deceive, but here— before Duncan's death is known—the problem is more acute because the moment (the porter with a hangover, the impatient noblemen) has a lower emotional temperature. Plainer, everyday language and rhetoric must convey the deceit. Thus, Macbeth's simple answer to Macduff's 'Is the king stirring, worthy thane' so perfectly mixes deceit and truth that it deserves the gasp the line sometimes earns: 'Not yet' (2.3.38). 'Not yet' means, of course, both 'Duncan has not awakened until now' and 'Duncan will never again stir.' ('Not yet' = 'not so far' and 'no longer'.) The effect is repeated and intensified when Lennox asks, 'Goes the king hence today?', and Macbeth replies, 'He does—he did appoint so.'[4] Once again, Macbeth deceives

---

4. 'Goes the king hence' is a euphemism for 'Does the king die.'

and tells the truth as the witches do. He is the serpent but looks like the flower. The nerve-wrenching sequence concludes with Lennox's grand catalogue of portents, to which Macbeth replies truthfully and laconically, 'Twas a rough night' (2.3.53).[5]

In the following act, similarly complex verbal simplicity greets the murderers: 'Well then, now have you considered of my speeches?' (3.1.77). Those first three words offer the actor an enormous range of possibilities.[6] Are they off-hand conversational filler ('Stand at ease', or 'Please be seated', or 'Listen to me', or 'Thank you for coming'), or the hesitant stutterings of a man ordering death, or the abrupt autocratic directions of a feared tyrant? At Stratford in 1955, Laurence Olivier

> stood centre-stage . . . The murderers stood down-stage, left and right respectively. Olivier glanced arrogantly from one to the other, crooked the index finger of each hand in terrible invitation and made 'well' into a question. He paused. The murderers looked at one another. The index fingers swept downwards and pointed straight at the floor on each side of him. He said 'then' as a command. They moved slowly towards him like frightened stoats. Almost humorously, but with an edge of impatience, he said 'now', and an act of hypnosis was completed.[7]

Simple language, particularly euphemistic or indefinite language, continually counterpoints the play's extravagant rhetoric and dense metaphor. Thus, murder appears as 'it'—'If it were done' (1.7.1), 'so, it will make us mad' (2.2.37), 'Thou canst not say I did it' (3.4.50)—and the grooms' guilt-dispelling drunkenness joins Lady Macbeth's half-manic excitement at committing murder as 'that'—'That which hath made them drunk, hath made me bold' (2.2.1). Later, death is 'absence' (3.1.135) and 'safe' (3.4.25), and 'sent to peace' (3.2.20), dead.

A related linguistic register makes such indefinition a source of comedy: millions of obscene jokes and hundreds of dramatic scenes turn upon double, triple, or uncertain referents for 'it', or 'that', or equally innocuous words and phrases. While *Macbeth* has few comic moments and its wordplay is more often grim than fanciful, the way language blurs rather than clarifies, confuses rather than makes

---

5. Speaking this line, David Garrick 'shew[ed] as much self-condemnation, as much fear of discovery, as much endeavour to conquer inquietude and assume ease, as ever was infused into, or intended for, the character' (Thomas Wilkes, *A General View of the Stage*, 1759, p. 249).
6. Their punctuation, or editorial repunctuation, is therefore uncertain.
7. Gareth Lloyd Evans, 'Macbeth in the twentieth century', *TQ* 1, 3 (1971), 39. After Olivier drew the Murderers to him, 'the three figures stood in a black-cloaked huddle, looking as sinister a group as the three Witches of Act I' (R. A. Foakes (ed.), *Macbeth*, 1968, p. xxiv).

plain, connects paltering sisters and self-deceiving criminals and jokey Porter. Thus, the Porter's words 'come in', 'stealing out', 'it' (again), 'lie' (and 'lye'), 'shift'- duplicate, make more intense and trivial and painful, the same linguistic acts when Macbeth and his lady speak them.

Appropriately for a play where prophecy and misunderstanding propel the action, paradox, oxymoron, antithesis, and self-contradiction fill the dialogue:

> One of the play's most haunting and pervasive stylistic characteristics is a speech-rhythm that constantly contracts into self-checking half-rhyming half-lines: a device, surely, that realizes the foreshortening, the terrible presentness which Macbeth forces on himself, an existence without breadth and without perspective.[8]

Macbeth echoes the 'paltering' sisters—'Fair is foul, and foul is fair' (1.1.12)—when he observes that the pathetic fallacy has failed: 'So foul and fair a day I have not seen' (1.3.36). It is a stormy yet victorious day, but victory and storm has each its place, its category, and neither can influence or change the other. They coexist, but they do not interpenetrate, and only the musing mind would or could find sunshine and victory appropriate, if unpredictable, companions. By contrast, the words Macbeth unconsciously echoes are not a stable antithesis, a conversational *bon mot* as his remark is, but rather a worrying, endless, finally 'tedious' (3.4.138) and idiot-like (see 5.5.26) alternation: 'Fair is foul, and foul is fair' (1.1.12). For the witches, distinction exists only in its annihilation by or in alternation with its opposite. Categories—fair, foul—exist, but rather than being defined by difference or opposition, each *is* the other.

Macbeth's speech absorbs the 'sickening see-saw rhythm'[9] of witch-language—'This supernatural soliciting / Cannot be ill, cannot be good' (1.3.129–30)—and he accurately echoes witch-thinking when he claims, 'nothing is, / But what is not' (1.3.140–1), a formulation precisely anticipating the Second Apparition's promise that 'none of woman born / Shall harm Macbeth' (4.1.79–80) and encapsulating at this moment and the later one time, birth, imagination, ambition, and their various defects. The initial paradox (how can one predicate anything of 'nothing'?) is explained by a further paradox (all that is, is not), and both are understood when we recognise that Macbeth speaks of the difference between 'present' conditions and

---

8. [Barbara] Everett [*Young Hamlet*, 1989], p. 89. See also [Terry] Eagleton, *William Shakespeare*, pp. 2–4; Margaret D. Burrell, '*Macbeth*: a study in paradox', *Shakespeare Jahrbuch* 90 (1954), 167–90; Madeleine Doran, 'The *Macbeth* music', *S.St.* 16 (1983), 156.
9. [L. C.] Knights [*Explorations*, 1946], p. 20.

'imaginings' of the, future, though the former are 'fears' and the latter 'horrible'[1] None the less, his phrase denies reality or existence to both that which is and that which is not, to what he fantasises and what he imagines, to killing the king and being the king. In a play where submitting to or commanding time becomes a dominant issue, rhetorical conflict invades even the act of telling the time: echoing Banquo (2.1.1), Macbeth asks, 'What is the night?', and his wife replies, 'Almost at odds with morning, which is which' (3.4.126–7). Struggling with time and its consequences—birth and death, usurpation and punishment—Lord and Lady Macbeth sense time 'at odds' with itself, time *now* conflicting with time *then* and time *to come*.

Lady Macbeth's 'which is which' echoes the play's varied use of repetition, ranging from alliteration and assonance to repeated words and phrases, and rhyme.[2] Rhymes are the most easily heard and most easily remembered repetitions. They fill the sisters' speeches, which generally use trochaic tetrameter couplets, 'the fairy dialect of English literature', and *Macbeth* has more scenes that end with one or more couplets than any other Shakespearean play—both a higher proportion of such scenes, and the highest absolute number of them.[3] As well as rhyming, witch-language also alliterates—'nine times nine . . . peak, and pine' (1.3.21–2)—but so does Macbeth's language:

> I had else been perfect;
> Whole as the marble, founded as the rock,
> As broad and general as the casing air:
> But now I am cabined, cribbed, confined, bound in
> To saucy doubts and fears. (3.4.21–5)

Beside the alliteration on *c* ('casing . . . cabined, cribbed, confined') and the abrupt tremor, *ck,* in 'rock', this passage exemplifies many of the play's more subtle verbal effects: the way 'doubts' echoes the *d*s of the past participles and the vowels of 'bound' and 'founded', for example, or the way the *s*-sound runs from 'else' to 'as' to 'casing' to 'saucy' and 'fears'.[4] The word 'perfect' repeats more largely in the

1. Much later, Lady Macbeth speaks a similarly self-cancelling phrase, ''Tis safer to be that which we destroy' (3.2.6). Here, the word 'present', as in 'Present fears', has already been used once of death (1.2.64) and once of the honours Duncan bestows on Macbeth (1.3.53) and therefore represents both foul and fair. In *Poets' Grammar,* 1958, pp. 48–57, Francis Berry argues that 'the whole play is Future minded' and that the future indicative, especially associated with Lady Macbeth, 'drives the play', while Macbeth in this speech and elsewhere (e.g., 1.7.1 ff.) employs the future subjunctive.
2. On verbal repetition, see Maynard Mack, Jr, *Killing the King,* 1973, pp. 160–4, 173–4; Doran, pp. 159–60; G. W. Williams, ' "Time for such a word": verbal echoing in *Macbeth',* S. Sur. 47 (1994), 153–9.
3. See Edwin Guest, *A History of English Rhythms,* ed. W. W. Skeat, 1882, p. 179, and D. L. Chambers, *The Metre of 'Macbeth',* 1903, pp. 19–23.
4. Alliteration, here in Macbeth's speech and later (5.1) in his wife's, is the verbal equivalent of a human's inability to change or evolve through time; the recurrence to a letter or a sound voices an inability to escape a singular act—for Macbeth and Lady Macbeth, that

play and weaves solicitation and over-confidence with guilt and death: it begins in Macbeth's 'Stay, you imperfect speakers' (1.3.68), continues in his letter ('the perfectest report' (1.5.2), reappears in Banquo's death, which will make Macbeth's health 'perfect' (3.1.107) and require 'the perfect spy o'th'time' (3.1.129), and concludes in the Messenger's assurance that he is 'perfect' in Lady Macduff's 'state of honour' (4.2.63).[5] 'Issue' also occurs frequently in the play. Before Act 5, Scene 4, we have heard it five times, each time with the meaning 'progeny' or 'children'; Siward then uses the word to mean 'result, outcome': 'But certain issue strokes must arbitrate. / Towards which, advance the war' (5.4.20–1). At once, varied meanings—children, the future, a dynasty's existence, the outcome of war against a tyrant—coalesce. Macbeth's fear of the 'unlineal hand' (3.1.64) depriving him of a 'fruitless crown' and Banquo's witch-inspired hope of 'children [who] shall be kings' (1.3.84) collide in 'issue', a word that now means not only 'children', but also victory or defeat, the result (the 'issue' and outcome) of an Anglo-Scottish war against Macbeth.

These rhetorical, sonic, and logical devices spin the mind, whirl it into endless oscillation, but the play, brief and with an angrily forceful plot, also imposes a kind of imagistic claustrophobia. A. C. Bradley identified important features of the play's figurative language:

> Darkness . . . even . . . blackness, broods over this tragedy . . . it [gives] . . . the impression of a black night broken by flashes of light and colour, sometimes vivid and even glaring . . . above all, the colour is the colour of blood.[6]

Yet, like other critics eager to see bipolar oppositions in the play's language and structures, Bradley does not notice how complex the colour-associations are. Macbeth's famous

> Will all great Neptune's ocean wash this blood
> Clean from my hand? No: this my hand will rather
> The multitudinous seas incarnadine,
> Making the green one red. (2.2.63–6)

---

act is murder—or move forward in time beyond or after the act. Compare Macbeth's soliloquy, 'Tomorrow, and tomorrow, and tomorrow . . . ' (5.5.18–27).

5. For a discussion of the play's uses of 'clear', see Doran, pp. 163–5. 'Present' is another repeated word; see e.g., 1.2.64, 1.3.53, 1.3.136. Jürgen Schäfer, *Shakespeares Stil: Germanisches and Romanisches Vokabular*, 1973, Appendix 2, details Shakespeare's characteristic pairing of Germanic and romance synonyms in the play. Among many other significantly repeated words in Macbeth, consider 'strange', used in *Macbeth* more frequently (sixteen times) than in any other Shakespearean text except *The Tempest* (eighteen times), and note that both *The Tempest* and *Macbeth* are unusually short Shakespearean plays * * * and that the audience might therefore hear the word's repetition with unusual force. Only *Measure for Measure* (fifteen times), *Antony and Cleopatra* (fourteen times), and *Much Ado About Nothing* (eleven times) use 'strange' more frequently than ten times among the First Folio plays.

6. Bradley, pp. 266–7.

powerfully puns on 'incarnadine', which means 'make red' and 'make flesh' or 'make flesh-coloured'. For a murderer, his own flesh, or his victim's, might be blood-red, or bloody, whatever the colour of the skin that covered that flesh. No simple code will decipher the play's chromatic figures. Black and darkness may often be evil, white and light good, red bloody, but the white of lily and linen is also cowardly, brightness Satanic, red the colour of courage and the 'painting' of a drunkard's nose, and dark night the time of restorative sleep.[7] Shakespeare often uses repeated (or 'iterative') images and 'image clusters',[8] and Macbeth brims with images of light and dark, of contraction and expansion (dwarf and giant, for example), of liquids (water, wine, milk, urine, blood), of horses that throw their riders or eat each other, of birds good and bad (owls, ravens, wrens, sparrows, hawks, eagles, martlets), of clothing (robes, seams, linings, sleeves, breeches), of procreation (children, eggs), and of sounds (knells, crickets, owls, clocks, bells, trumpets, knockings).[9]

Verbal and non-verbal sounds are especially prominent as fact and image in Act 2, Scene 2, where Macbeth hallucinates, it seems, a voice murdering sleep and Lady Macbeth hears both the sounds of nature (the owl's shriek, the crickets' cry) and her husband's steps as he returns from killing Duncan. The uncanny and indefinite 'voice' Macbeth hears (2.2.38) echoes the 'voice' of the crown Lady Macbeth hears, or says or thinks she hears, in Act 1, Scene 5. Later, with a gallantry both futile and ironic, Macduff tries to shield Lady Macbeth from knowledge of her crime:

> O gentle lady,
> 'Tis not for you to hear what I can speak.
> The repetition in a woman's ear
> Would murder as it fell. (2.3.76–9)

'Repetition in a woman's ear' murders as it falls again and again in Act 5, Scene 1, when Lady Macbeth repeats the echoing Knock of Act 2, Scene 3, and obsessively repeats words and actions:

> No more o'that, my lord, no more o'that . . . To bed, to
> bed; there's knocking at the gate. Come, come, come,

7. Notable productions or adaptations of Macbeth in Africa and elsewhere demonstrate the imagery's malleability; consider e.g., Adrian Stanley's so-called 'Zulu' Macbeth, Glamis (sic!) Stadium, 1961, in what was then Salisbury, Southern Rhodesia (see Johannesburg Star, 5 April 1961, and The Sphere, 3 June 1961); The Black Macbeth, London, March 1972; Natal Theatre Workshop's production of Welcome Msomi's uMabatha, Aldwych Theatre, London, April 1972, which was revived at the Civic Theatre, Johannesburg, June 1995 (see Philip Revzin, 'A Zuluized "Macbeth" ', The Wall Street Journal, 14 June 1995, p. A16). For U.S. examples, see Ruby Cohn, Modern Shakespeare Offshoots, 1976, pp. 60–73, starting with Orson Welles's 'voodoo' Macbeth (New York, 14 April 1936).
8. See Edward Armstrong, Shakespeare's Imagination, rev. edn, 1963.
9. See, generally, Caroline Spurgeon, Shakespeare's Imagery and What It Tells Us (1935), Wolfgang Clemen, The Development of Shakespeare's Imagery (1951), and M. M. Mahood, Shakespeare's Wordplay (1957).

> come, give me your hand; what's done cannot be undone.
> To bed, to bed, to bed. (5.1.37–8, 56–8)

Sound-as-sound and sound-as-image make a brief moment wonderfully evocative. Macbeth reassures his wife:

> ere the bat hath flown
> His cloistered flight, ere to black Hecate's summons
> The shard-born beetle with his drowsy hums
> Hath rung night's yawning peal, there shall be done
> A deed of dreadful note.
>
> LADY MACBETH   What's to be done?
> MACBETH   Be innocent of the knowledge, dearest chuck,
> Till thou applaud the deed. (3.2.40–6)

Before Lady Macbeth may applaud, before she claps as a theatre audience might (or so Macbeth hopes), at the deaths of Banquo and Fleance, husband, wife, and audience must hear an insect's sleepy humming as the sound of a church bell ringing the death of a day's labour, or the death of a parishioner. Tolling, the bell's open 'mouth' seems a human yawn, but its sound—its 'note'—marks and invites murder, the dreadful deed, the 'dreadful note', and the notably infamous. Hearing another, not metaphorical, bell, Macbeth went to an earlier crime:

> The bell invites me.
> Hear it not, Duncan, for it is a knell
> That summons thee to heaven or to hell. (2.1.62–4)

The 'knell' returns twice more, tolling for the dead of Scotland, especially Macduff's family and retainers (4.3.172–3), and then for Siward's son (5.9.17).

With so much else that has become drained of meaning, sound loses its terror for Macbeth when he nears his end. Senses—taste, hearing, vision—marry in death:

> I have almost forgot the taste of fears;
> The time has been, my senses would have cooled
> To hear a night-shriek and my fell of hair
> Would at a dismal treatise rouse and stir
> As life were in't. I have supped full with horrors;
> Direness familiar to my slaughterous thoughts
> Cannot once start me. Wherefore was that cry?
>
> SEYTON   The queen, my lord, is dead.
> MACBETH   She should have died
> hereafter;
> There would have been a time for such a word. (5.5.9–17)

Macbeth's last phrase, 'a time for such a word', joins time with language, timing with speech, and directs us to the characters' recurrent failures to synchronise their words with events. There never should have been a 'time' for a word so infective as 'hail'—'All hail Macbeth, that shalt be king' nor, Macbeth wishes, should there ever have been a time for so profoundly weary a word—'She should have died'—as 'hereafter'. This moment's 'hereafter' became inevitable once there was a time when Macbeth heard the word first: 'All hail Macbeth, that shalt be king *hereafter*' (1.3.48; my italics).

DEREK JACOBI

Macbeth†

Macbeth was the first Shakespeare play I was ever in at school, doubling Fleance and Lady Macbeth, but the offer from Adrian Noble to play the title role came as something of a surprise. I had never really thought of myself for the part, which had always seemed to me a bass role—and I'm a tenor. Physically, too, I'm light to look at, which isn't normal casting for the part. However, Adrian must have felt I had the right potential—just as Terry Hands, the last time I worked for the RSC [Royal Shakespeare Company], had found the anger in me to play Cyrano de Bergerac. Macbeth would have to be found, searched for and projected: and I would have to think hard about the way I would put it together physically, and facially, too. The colour, as it were, had to change. Those who had never seen the play before, I thought, would find it easier to accept me as Macbeth than those who came to it with a great deal of watching Shakespeare behind them.

As always with major productions, there was inadequate opportunity for the actors to be involved with the preliminary concepts and ideas. Discussion before we started rehearsals was not in great depth, really; nor was there much time. I saw the mock-up of the set, but it didn't make a great deal of impact on me: it was basically a big black box, which seemed acceptable. The costumes were to be very eclectic, coming from past, present, and future. Costumes are a strange area for me: as long as they're comfortable, feel like clothing, and leave me free to get on with it, I tend not to worry. They were made of a variety of materials, but with quite a lot of suede, which does not like sweat—and actors sweat. During the run, therefore, the costumes came to look muddy and dirty, which was no bad thing.

† From *Players of Shakespeare 4: Further Essays in Shakespearian Performance by Players with the Royal Shakespeare Company*, ed. Robert Smallwood (Cambridge: Cambridge University Press, 1998), 193–210. Reprinted by permission of Cambridge University Press.

I learned the part before rehearsals began. This is becoming rather more frequent for me and comes of not wanting to waste precious rehearsal time, especially on such a big play. I learn it just simply: no decisions, no inflexions, just the words. During the course of rehearsal I want to find out what those words mean, how I'm feeling and saying them, what I'm doing; but the words are already there. This was very important to me for Macbeth: it's a big part, with a great big fight at the end, and we weren't going to be playing it in the normal RSC repertoire situation but in a single run, for quite a lot of which we would be doing eight performances a week. When we came to work on Macbeth's big set pieces, the soliloquies for example, knowing the words was a great help. I didn't know how to say them, how to think them, but with the words already there, the long hard work we did on them in rehearsal became extraordinarily exciting and stimulating. Looking back I think ultimately I did some of the soliloquies too quickly. My sense as we worked on them was that Macbeth's mind is working with enormous speed and I wanted to reflect that in the speaking; he is thinking very rapidly, all the time, and thought and speech come simultaneously. 'I'm not going to do it'; the thought simply hits him, just like that, until Lady Macbeth comes in; and he's like that all the time, the thoughts coming so fast. Perhaps I made the mistake of trying to reflect this a little too much in the speaking, getting myself into a state of anxiety, as Macbeth does; but my approach to all the speeches was to make them as true as possible, and as light as possible too, so as not to impede the thought. When an audience knows lines well (and in this play a lot of them know what you're going to say before you've said it) it's harder to make them listen to what you are saying, and how you are saying it. I wanted very much to make people listen with new ears to, 'If it were done' and 'Tomorrow'.

I found in rehearsal that the first section of the play, the establishing of who Macbeth was before the start of the deterioration, came quite easily. The ending, trying to show him still aware of what he had lost, realizing where he now was, was wonderful to do but took more searching for. Macbeth didn't seem to me, at the start, to know more of evil than any other soldier of his time who is used to killing people. What caught my imagination was the effect of evil on him, the changes it brings about. We spent a certain amount of time in rehearsal thinking about what is frightening, what is palpably evil, what is out *there*; the forces that seem to lurk malevolently around the world of the play. This was an area we tried to work hard on, with as much psychological depth as possible.

Macbeth is given a tremendous build-up for his first entrance; everyone talks about him in such glowing terms. I wanted to show a man arriving on stage at a pitch of exhilaration at what he's just done:

the fighting, the blood-lust, the victory have put him on a high, which he shares with Banquo. They are together in this moment—together in companionship, in victory, in blood—as the Third Witch says:

> A drum! a drum!
> Macbeth doth come. (1.3.29–30)

I suppose we might have had a cohort of men coming; but we didn't have lots of extras, so I thought I would provide the drum myself, picked up, perhaps, from a corpse on the battlefield. He's banging it, banging it, unaware of his surroundings, drunk with it all. In he comes on this great big wonderful high, this man you've been hearing so much about, this great victor, winner of ten gold medals at the Olympics: in he comes, at the height of his power. I didn't want to show a man in the least exhausted by the battle, but revelling in it; a man in his glory, a great powerhouse. 'So foul and fair a day' (1.3.37) does not, it seems to me, refer to the weather: 'foul' is about those heads he's cut off and bowels he's ripped out; 'fair' is because it was all worth it, for this great victory. That is the state of mind he is in, as, just by chance, he repeats the phrase that the witches have used.

Macbeth is mesmerized by the witches and, to an extent, excited by what they have to say, but instinctively he's afraid of them, though he doesn't know why. Because of his mood of elation, however, he's perfectly ready to try to find out why he fears them, by asking them questions and trying to persuade them to stay. He is startled by their greeting 'that shalt be king hereafter' (line 49) primarily because he's thought about it already—oh, yes, he's certainly thought about it. Why not? It's perfectly natural for a man so near the top as Macbeth to have thought about being king: every member of every cabinet must at some time think about being Prime Minister. When the Third Witch says it, therefore, she is echoing Macbeth's own thoughts, perhaps not particularly present at that moment—though, in his present state of mind, aware that a triumphal entry (at the very least) awaits him, perhaps the idea does occur to him that he could become king because of the victory he has just won. Whatever the reason, the greeting gives him pause, makes him reflect—and that is what Banquo picks up on.

The sudden awareness that Banquo is deeply intrigued and looking at him very searchingly is something I tried to use to whip Macbeth out of his reverie and bring him back into focus. He listens to what the witches prophesy for Banquo and tries to detain them, to hear more, as they begin to leave. I tried to suggest at this point that he attempts to wipe these things from his mind, to make a joke of them with Banquo, their little exchange finishing with them both laughing.

But there is an odd edge to it, because they are not exactly sure what they are laughing at; the end of the conversation is strained and awkward. This is a significant moment, for it marks the beginning of their divergence, of their ceasing to trust each other. It must be plotted, because their relationship is so important, but it must not be overdone. They have been shown as pals (there's just a few seconds to do that), but if you show the distrust here too big and too soon you've got nowhere to go. It is merely a thought at this point. At the end of the scene, after the news of Macbeth's elevation has come from Ross and Angus, Macbeth says to Banquo 'Think upon what hath chanced' (line 153) and it seems as though they are about to talk to each other again in the old way. Then Macbeth says 'Till then, enough', and I tried to suggest that he was about to say something serious and confidential, then paused and instead said 'enough', implying uncertainty about sharing his thoughts with him: the process of separation has gone a little further. Even the final 'Come, friends' seemed to have a double edge: 'Come, . . . '—and what am I to call them? Are they friends? Yes, everyone is a friend at the moment. What *am* I worrying about?

Macbeth's response to the witches' greeting is hesitant and interrogative. He considers the idea, the pause I used on the word *king* in 'to be king / Stands not within the prospect of belief' (1.3.72–73) seeming to hold it up for momentary examination. To the news from Ross and Angus, on the other hand, his reaction is much more fearful. The very thought of it makes his heart beat and his hair stand on end. This was very important to me, one of the through-lines for Macbeth. I went through the play marking the times he speaks of fear, particularly in relation to himself. He does so in every scene: it is paramount for him; the man is constantly fearful. He says so to himself, he says so to his wife: it never changes. When the witches said he was going to be king, I had dropped the dagger which I'd been using to beat the drum and bent to pick it up and put it away. I took it out again in the middle of Macbeth's long aside (1.3.126ff.) and was very conscious of it on 'Present fears / Are less than horrible imaginings' (lines 136–7) because those imaginings are already of killing the king. It was only a momentary thing, but still the dagger came out when he thought of being king. The dagger was a constant emblem for me: the physical dagger, one of his essential accoutrements for battle, was from the beginning connected with the idea of his kingship, leading inevitably to 'Is this a dagger that I see before me?' (2.1.33) and to the drawing of the dagger in earnest to commit the terrible murder. Obviously this is just an actor's finessing: it doesn't have to be there for this aside, but it seemed to me to create a link with the next stage of the play—and it was no doubt useful for the other actors, biding my soliloquizing, to look across at Macbeth and see that he has a dagger in his hand that he is twisting and looking at and yet not really seeing.

Macbeth, then, before the end of his first scene, has faced the thought of killing the king. 'Why do I yield to that suggestion', he asks (line 133), and the word is *yield*. The thought could have been repulsed immediately, but it's not repulsed, it's accepted. And the thought terrifies him. He is in an extraordinary mood; the adrenalin is coursing through him and he's not thinking totally straight. Because of the victory he is in a state of high excitement and of emotional exhaustion. He has been killing all day: he is covered with blood. In this state he gets the news: in this state he must react to it. The speed with which things happen in the next phase of the play is to a large extent conditioned by Macbeth's physical and mental state when he receives the witches' greeting.

In his next scene Macbeth meets Duncan. I don't think they are in any sense bosom pals. 'Duncan comes here tonight' (1.5.58) sounds to me surprised: I don't believe Duncan has stayed in Macbeth's house before. There has always been a certain distance between them: the lack of prowess on the battlefield shown by Duncan's sons would have been noted by Macbeth. He would see it, of course, as his absolute duty to uphold Duncan's power, his tenure of the throne. Macbeth is, I think, in awe of the whole concept of kingship, but attracted to it too, and fascinated by it. He is now, obviously, the man of the hour, being publicly honoured by Duncan for the first time; and he revels in the situation. Before he was one of the many; now he's the top man, a Field-Marshall. There they all are, applauding him, and he's acknowledging the applause, loving it, hugely enjoying being on the winner's podium. At the same time, however, and because of the scene before, he notices that Duncan actually touches Banquo: 'let me enfold thee / And hold thee to my heart' (2.4.32–33). He didn't do that to Macbeth: he was much more formal with him. I was aware that Banquo was getting the hug, and the kiss, and that I wasn't.

Moments later Duncan has declared Malcolm heir to the throne as Prince of Cumberland. Banquo and I had a glance at each other at this point, and a little grin: 'I know what you're thinking; you know what I'm thinking; we're both thinking the same thing.' But there is as yet no serious rift between them. At the beginning of my Prince of Cumberland soliloquy I went over to Malcolm and did what Duncan had just done to Banquo—gave him a big manly hug and patted him on the face: 'Great that you're around, Prince of Cumberland, absolutely great . . . You little bastard'. That got a laugh at most performances, which I loved. There aren't many laughs for Macbeth, and I meant this one here, and the bathos of it. All that it means to be a king is here visible to Macbeth, and to the audience. It is no accident that the play moves him directly from that first soliloquy of thoughts of kingship into the royal presence, to being touched by the king's hand, irradiated by the king's electric field. By the end of the scene his thoughts are racing: perhaps there is a possibility, perhaps there is; I must tell my wife; I must write; where is the messenger to take the letter. And then he gets on his horse and tears off to her. By the time he gets to her she is in a state that he was not expecting: the letter has had an effect way beyond what he had supposed. He had, of course, imagined that she would be glad at what has happened to him, but he never realized that the idea of his becoming king would affect her as it has.

I'm sure the play's time-scheme is here very fast and that only hours have elapsed before we see the Macbeths together. We wanted to present a couple much in love and comfortable with each other. We also wanted to show the contrast between Macbeth the warrior, whose duty is killing and maiming, and Macbeth the husband, the lover, the domestic, cultured man who dances and listens to music. Off the battlefield he isn't in the least gruff or brutal in his behaviour. There is quite another side to him, a much gentler side: the fact that he fights well does not imply that he is a hoodlum, a yob. He is a man of enormous imagination, who has a life going on all the time in his head. He doesn't say very much in the letter scene. His first words are 'My dearest love' (1.5.56), a very romantic phrase, which he doesn't use again—his language to his wife becomes, indeed, progressively less endearing. To her question (line 57) 'And when goes hence?' his reply ('Tomorrow, as he purposes') can be understood in any way one likes. I took it to mean that he was surprised by the question, and by her asking it; then, realizing why she had asked it, I saw that she was thinking what I wanted her to think and that we knew each other better, perhaps, than we had thought. And then, as he wonders tentatively what they may be thinking and saying, very suddenly, she lets him know with astonishing directness: 'O, never / Shall sun that morrow see' (lines 58–9). The phrase a little later in her speech (line 63) about his looking 'like the innocent flower' always seemed to me to tie in with my worries about whether or not I looked right for the part. I felt that she was describing what she saw when she looked at him. She has been going on about his abilities and his talents, about his desire to be great but his lack of the 'illness should attend it' (1.5.18), about his deficiency in that little streak of nastiness that allows you to get to the top. And now she looks at him again, and sees the 'innocent flower' and knows that he will get nowhere without 'the serpent under it'. He needs all this if he is to rise higher; and again his reaction is not to say 'forget it', but rather 'We will speak further' (1.5.69).

Time for such further thought is hardly available, however: if Duncan is to be killed, it must be done that night. The swiftness of the time scheme is reflected in the swiftness of the language. Sometimes it is almost telegrammatic. The actor will wish to get his point across, his interpretation of a particular line, but it's not always easy because it's all so densely written. There may well be six images in a line and you have to choose only one or two—you can't do them all, you can't play everything. (One is frequently criticized for not playing one of the possibilities as though one hadn't been aware of it; the fact that one didn't play something does not, however, mean that it wasn't considered, but rather that on this occasion the other road was chosen; it would be nice if critics were more often willing to recognize this.) The density of the language is all part of Macbeth's thought-process: he is thinking at the speed of light as he begins his soliloquy, 'If it were done when 'tis done' (1.7.1ff.). He is the host; he is providing for the king and his retinue; and yet he has left the banqueting room. It's all going on back there, but somehow he has extricated himself. How has he got out of that room? Presumably he's been sitting next to the king with the knowledge that if it's to happen, if he's actually going to do it, it's got to be very soon: 'How many hours have I got before I must do it? It's got to be now.' He's been sitting there thinking like that and his head's coming off with the thought; he's been boiling and sweating, and he's absented himself because he's just got to get out to breathe, to be on his own. Perhaps he excuses himself because he's had a hard couple of days, with all the fighting. However he achieves it, he leaves; and now, alone, he talks himself, quite rapidly, out of the idea. What has been spurring him on, he wonders: only 'vaulting ambition' (1.7.27) is prompting him, and that implies landing on your arse on the other side. He reaches his decision—and then Lady Macbeth comes in. If she had not come in at this point I do not believe he would have gone through with it. She uses all the predictable arguments—'When you durst do it, then you were a man' (line 49)—and if you presuppose, as we did, that they are in love, then of course it's very difficult for him to take. Without her arrival at that moment, he would never have done it.

The soliloquy is full of extraordinary images—'pity, like a naked newborn babe', and so on—all occurring to him on the instant. He is a highly intelligent, imaginative, articulate man, quite unlike the brutal, nonthinking slasher of the battlefield, the tried, and honed, killing machine. Here we are in contact with that other side of him, the great contrast with his life as a soldier; in his own head he lives in an astonishing imaginative world which he is able to express sensationally and beautifully. His head is full of the mixture of good and evil. At this moment the evil side of him, which we all possess, is getting the upper hand and in order to balance it he brings up the best, the purest, the most innocent of images, of angels, and new-born babies, and the sky. They are all pure, unsullied, wonderful images; goodness pours out of them; they're shining. And on the other side are the dark, blood-driven, evil, dank thoughts. Eventually in this soliloquy he chooses good; the good images win—until Lady Macbeth comes in and taunts his manliness. It is her intimation that he's a coward, that he has no balls, that turns him. She goes for the jugular. She has always been his inspiration. Before a battle I'm sure that his thoughts were always with her. She makes him the man he is, encourages him, stirs up his testosterone. Without her he would never be so rampant. He needs her. And in this very short scene she quickly forces him back onto the path.

We had decided that somewhere in the past of their relationship they had lost a child. There are many other possible interpretations, but you have to decide for one. It's something that really needs a programme note: you can't act it, really, though you can think it. When she mentions having 'given suck' (line 54) I immediately went towards her, to stop her talking about it, as if to say 'Don't talk about it; you know what it does to us.' And she does know, of course, which is why she brings it up here. It's a vulnerable point for him. The moment the subject is mentioned he's automatically on the defensive and she uses all that. She is very clever, brilliantly manipulative, as she is in their first scene—and no doubt always has been with him. The appalling image of the braining of the child comes from the hardness that is within her, the hardness that she wishes him to share, that soon he will more than share.

Then she comes very close to making a mistake. 'When Duncan is asleep', she says, and if Macbeth is the man I think he is trying to be he must feel 'O, no, I've got to kill him with his eyes open. I've got to give him a bit of a chance. An old man, the king, a guest in my house, unguarded, and asleep: that is pure cowardice, murder of the innocents.' And the extraordinary thing about this image of Duncan asleep is that from this moment on it is going to be Macbeth who cannot sleep and Lady Macbeth who is unable to wake up. That becomes the symbol of their partnership.

On his way to Duncan's chamber Macbeth meets Banquo. Banquo is no fool and is keeping his eye on Macbeth. I enjoyed this scene: I enjoyed its surprises, and Banquo's obvious relish of the moment when he gives Macbeth the king's gift. Lady Macbeth has made great efforts to screw his courage to the sticking place; he's on his way to do the deed; everybody is supposed to be in bed; and of all people he meets Banquo. He shows his surprise at the meeting, and at the king's present, and with his surprise he shows his tension, just an inkling of it. And Banquo senses it, straightaway, because he's got to suspect him—got to, otherwise the part doesn't make sense. In this moment Macbeth gives himself away and Banquo makes it clear that he knows what is happening and that he wants no part of it: 'I . . . keep / My bosom franchised and allegiance clear' (2.1.26–28).

'Is this a dagger' (2.1.33), like 'To be or not to be' [*Hamlet*, 3.1.58ff.], is the line they're all waiting for. Once again it's a question of choice. Is he surprised to see the dagger or did he expect it to be there? Has he seen it before? Is he frightened of it? Do his eyes attract him to it? Does his choice of the word 'clutch' mean that the dagger is pulling him forward, or is it repelling him as he tries to grasp it? (I think I tried for both—a bit of repel, a bit of attract.) Does 'let me clutch thee' mean 'dare I clutch thee'? And so on—all choices. Again I tried to give him a last-minute reprieve: right at the end of the soliloquy there's a moment when he speaks of taking 'the present horror from the time' (line 59). I paused here as I had him going towards the door but still not being able to go through it. 'Whiles I threat, he *lives*', he says, and adds 'Words to the heat of deeds too cold breath gives' (lines 60–1)—'while I'm still talking about it I'm putting off doing it'. And at that moment Lady Macbeth appears: 'appears' in the ringing of the bell. The bell is her; she is ringing it. It's not the bell he hears; he hears her ringing the bell. That's what propels him through the door.

He comes out of it a changed man. Never can he be the same man again. There is not a single moment that he enjoys the thought of killing. It torments him, though it also impels him. And never does he enjoy the fruit of his killing. He comes out of that room demented. He went into it terrified, as he says all the time; he comes out of it crazy. Lady Macbeth has never before seen the man who comes out of that door; he is a stranger to her. They have stopped communicating and there is no way that they will ever communicate again. She had no idea that that was going to happen. He did it only to please her, to prove himself to her. Had she been other than she was he would not have done it. The thought may have been present, but so was the fear of the thought: the first time we see him think it his hair stands on end. Always the thought strikes fear into him. The moment before he does the murder he is afraid—the dagger speech is a fearful speech, the utterance of a terrified man. He does the murder for her, and it destroys them both.

He has no idea what he has done with the daggers. They are simply there; he's not conscious of them at all. It's only when she asks 'Why did you bring these daggers from the place?' (2.2.48) that he realizes that they are on the ends of his hands. I tried to throw them away, but they wouldn't go; he can't physically get rid of them because the blood on them is sticking to his hands. Again he talks of fear: 'I am afraid to think what I have done' (line 51). I wanted to emphasize that, because I think it's an answer to her rather than a statement

of his own feelings. She goes on and on about him being fearful and
he says 'Yes, I *am* afraid. You're absolutely right. I'm quaking to think
what I've done. I *am* afraid. Look what a state I'm in now.' Up to this
point he has spoken of being afraid only to himself; to her he has
wanted to appear always the man. But here he confesses his fear to
her, the first indication of the new state of their relationship.

Macbeth then has a short time off stage, during which the actor
is doing precisely what the character himself would be doing: trying
to wash all the blood off, and changing his costume. He comes back
on again into the public scene of the discovery of Duncan's murder.
Intelligent and imaginative man that he is, and having had his hysterical, terrified scene after the murder, he now has to think quickly,
and rationally, if he is going to survive. This is going to be a very
tricky moment for both him and Lady Macbeth, but from the audience's point of view he seems fine at the start, totally calm. He shows
Macduff the door to Duncan's chamber: he doesn't offer to take him
in himself. Then he's left with Lennox, though of course his mind
isn't on the conversation at all: it's on what Macduff is about to see.
He spent all that time with the dagger, terrified, before going into
that room. In the preceding scene he refused to return there—'Look
on't again I dare not' (2.2.52). Now he has to face it; he plucks up
his courage and follows Lennox into the room.

When he comes out he is absolutely riven by it. What he says is
real, and genuine: 'Had I died an hour before this chance, / I had
lived a blessed time' (2.3.88–89). He means it; it is the simple truth.
Then he makes the mistake of saying that he killed the grooms. He
has to cover up and he starts to get hysterical again, as he was over
the daggers. The silver skin and the golden blood and the gashes all
come into his imagination, and then the crucial image: 'their
daggers / Unmannerly breeched with gore' (lines 112–13). He is
working himself up again, just as he did after the murder; it's all
tumbling out and she thinks 'O, Christ, what is he going to say?' One
passage of the speech seems to me specifically directed at her:

> . . . Who could refrain,
> That had a heart to love, and in that heart
> Courage to make's love known. (lines 113–15)

I don't think he's saying that he loved the king so much that he had
to murder his grooms. I think he is saying to Lady Macbeth, eye to
eye: 'I proved my love to you by killing the king. O, yes, my heart
loved you, and in that heart was courage. You said I hadn't got courage, but I had courage to make my love known to you. In fact I killed
him to show you how courageous I was.' She knows what he means:
he's looking directly at her, and she's terrified at what he might say
next. And so, manipulative and resourceful as ever, she faints. It's

the only thing she can do. He's getting himself into a terrible state: he can't speak (he's silent, in fact, for nearly twenty lines): he's hyperventilating. The rest might take it as grief for the king, but she knows it's something else and creates a diversion to get him out of it.

The next time we see them together they are king and queen. Time has elapsed—time enough (we learn from Macduff) for them to have been to Scone to be crowned. How much time was a question we ultimately decided we couldn't bother about. It's stage time, which is continuous (unless you deliberately pause to indicate the passage of time), and the speed with which this play moves—and we did it without an interval—is remarkable. But clearly there has been time for a further change in their relationship: he is now dismissing her from his company. The moment is preceded by the last meeting with Banquo. Both Macbeth and Banquo know what has happened; neither is saying, but both know. That, anyway, is how we played it: he knows; I know that he knows. As he left, Banquo turned to look at me and suddenly Macbeth wants everybody else out: he wants to get rid of them all, to be alone. He's also arranged his meeting with the murderers. I went up to Lady Macbeth and when I reached her said 'We will keep ourself till supper-time alone' (3.1.43), with *alone* said straight to her: 'that includes you'. As she stood her ground I looked at her and called Seyton behind me. She tried to stay, but for the first time the boot is on the other foot and she has to go. For the first time she has to do what he tells her.

After his scene with the murderers she comes back and more or less has to ask Seyton's permission to speak to him. She can't understand the new situation: 'Why do you keep alone?' (3.2.8). After a while he gives in a little: 'O full of scorpions is my mind, *dear* wife' (line 36). I wanted to show the pull of that other side, that the forces which are dragging him in one direction are still meeting with some resistance. This is the last relic of 'my dearest love' earlier. For one moment he's gentle with her; he clasps her and they're cheek to cheek and there is love between them again. But immediately the fact that Banquo knows the truth about him comes back into his mind—and he's off again. She tries to be reassuring: 'nature's copy's not eterne' in Banquo (3.2.38), but it's not enough for him, though the moment when they were together again has had its importance. At the end of the scene, as he hints at the murder of Banquo, he says to her 'prithee go with me'. I'm sure this doesn't just mean 'Go with me from this room'. It's much more of an appeal: 'Go along with me, support me in what I'm doing. I'm terrified: don't desert me and leave me to do this on my own.' But she does desert him, of course. He deals with the murder of Banquo alone and he's alone from then on.

The banquet scene marks the next stage in the decline of their relationship. Such lines as 'Our hostess keeps her state; but in best time / We will require her welcome' (3.4.5–6) are said directly to her, with the implication: 'You're making me do all the work, love. Isn't it time you did a bit of queenly acting—I'm doing all the kingly acting up my end of the table?' It has ceased to be a nice relationship: in our production he tried to kiss her and she turned her face away. After the murderer had reported the death of Banquo (and the escape of Fleance) I spoke the lines 'Here had we now our country's honour roofed, / Were the graced person of our Banquo present' (3.4.39–40) directly to her rather than to the table generally, with the meaning 'I told you I'd kill him, didn't I—and I have, haven't I?' He's trying to get her to react; it will mean so much more if she shares it. Meanwhile he's desperately trying to be one of the party, one of the boys. I went round the table filling the glasses, trying to get the evening to go with a swing, and she not helping at all.

I think the audience is cheated if they don't see the ghost of Banquo—the chase round the table and all. We always intended that he should be there. And when the ghost has gone, and she's done her best to excuse him (and she's only just able to keep herself together), and the end of the scene has been reached and the awful realization that

> . . . I am in blood
> Stepped in so far, that, should I wade no more,
> Returning were as tedious as go o'er (3.4.135–37)

there is a kind of terrible regret in them both. The man still has that extraordinary imagination; it's never deserted him, right through the killing. He knows where he's reached, he knows what he's lost, and he knows what it entails. What I called on God, and on the images of the naked new-born babes, to stop me doing, what I desperately tried to persuade myself not to do, I have done. I have given in to the evil that I fought not to give in to and it has grown like a cancer within me. It is now terminal and in order to survive at all I have got to be wholly taken over by it, and quickly. I thought more than twice about the shedding of innocent blood, but now I must be constant about it, do it again and again, if I am going to survive. 'We are yet but young in deed' (line 143): it is awful, awful, coming from that man. He is not someone who enjoys what he has to do, but he knows what now has to be done. If Macbeth is a monster, the out-and-out black-hearted monster that they all say he is later on, then much of the heart of the play is missing. We were trying in our production to show the audience the other side of this man. The people who are the victims of his monstrosities will, of course, call him a monster, but it was the other side that I wanted to show—and particularly with me playing Macbeth, for that is a side that is part of me anyway.

I wanted him to appear as a man driven, sent mad by what he experiences, but still with the imagination to see clearly where he has come from, where he is now, where he has to go to, but, above all, what he has lost. 'Honour, love, obedience, troops of friends' (5.3.25), these are not to be his any more, he now knows that. But they *could* have been: at the beginning he had them all, all of them, and, wilfully, he has got rid of them, cast them away. His wife's death makes him again aware of these things, and of his great love for her, but by then he has become more or less catatonic, living only inside his own head, thinking neither very long, nor very far.

Before then, however, he has a journey to travel, and the next stage on it is his second visit to the witches. They were very up-front with what they had to say to him last time, but on this second occasion they're rather more cagey. He is no longer afraid of them—not at all afraid to go back. He says later (5.4.9) that he has 'almost forgot the taste of fears', a line I tried to do as a kind of revelation: 'I always used to be afraid; I've been frightened for so long, but now I seem not to be. What's happening?' The route to that is through the ossifying of the mind and emotions, and we see that in this second encounter with the witches. He is truculent with them, and ready to believe in their obviously riddling prophecies—as he has to, as justification for it all. At the end of the scene he can say quite dispassionately that he is going to have Macduff's wife and babes put to the sword—and in our production go and carefully check that it's been done. He gives the order with no sense of the before and after, with no emotion. That is the true monstrousness; it is that appalling lack of emotion that he has to come to terms with at the end.

Shakespeare gives Macbeth a short rest while the English scene is in progress. I had a costume and wig change during it but I tried to use the time to think myself into the sort of stillness and quietness that is needed on Macbeth's return. Perhaps I erred a little too much on the side of loudness earlier, but I certainly wanted to show him a very different figure at the end. He has aged in the interim and returns an older and a physically different man. There is a slowness about him, as though everything has collapsed. The hands are still, the speech is quieter and slower. It's as though his blood has been let, as though the leeches have been at him. Great swathes of time have passed for Macbeth, if not for everyone else. This seemed very important to me, though I think some people who saw the production were puzzled by it. I wanted a huge contrast with his behaviour at the beginning, leaping onto the stage, banging his drum, his blood coursing through his veins; now he comes on with seemingly no blood flowing at all. I played with the dagger again; it never left my hands throughout this final sequence as I turned it obsessively in my gloved fingers—the gloves concealing the fact that his hands are as blood-covered as Lady Macbeth's. Two acts earlier he had gone off washing his hands as she had taken the daggers; now here he is with gloves on, constantly playing with a dagger, his figure bloodless.

I took 'I have lived long enough' (5.3.22ff.) as a momentary consideration of the possibility of suicide. I had the dagger in my hand and the idea occurred of simply ending it all—'I wonder why I don't just kill myself'—until the thought was interrupted by Seyton's entrance and a little of the old blood starts coursing around again. Macbeth knows he is defending a lost cause, in spite, of the witches' prophecies—for I suspect that, deep down, he has never really believed in them, however desperately he hoped they were true. At the end, when their falsity is revealed, he speaks of the 'juggling fiends' that 'palter with us', and of their breaking 'the word of promise to our . . . hope' (5.6.58–61): he hoped, but he didn't ever fully believe; Macbeth is too intelligent really to have believed. There is a kind of pathos about the way he has almost knowingly deluded himself. He knows about what Hamlet calls his 'god-like reason . . . looking before and after' [*Hamlet*, 4.4.28ff.], but because of his enthralment to Lady Macbeth he chooses to ignore it. And he *is* in thrall to her: she has played continuously on his status as a man and that has made him go the way he has. 'Honour, love, obedience, troops of friends' were his as the successful general of the beginning of the play; in 'Tomorrow and tomorrow' he faces the fact that they will never be his again.

I do not think Macbeth is mad at the end of the play, though he encountered madness during the banquet scene. The horrors of that experience for him were palpable; he could not understand why no-one else perceived them and he lost his reason completely. He lives partly in this terrifying world of the imagination, but he lives also in a world of the senses, and at the end of the banquet scene his reason starts to take over again. There is no escape into madness for him at the end. His soliloquies before he dies record with grim sanity the emotionless state at which he has arrived.

The hint at the idea of suicide on 'I have lived long enough' was in part preparation for Macbeth's death. Suicide is clearly in his mind: 'I 'gin to be aweary of the sun' (5.5.49); 'Why should I play the Roman fool' (5.6.40)—he keeps using phrases that incorporate it. I wanted to show this at the end. Adrian Noble had made an early decision (with which I was perfectly content) that I should die on stage, not go off and have my head chopped off and have it brought back on again. So, with the co-operation of Michael Siberry as Macduff, we worked out a death sequence in which Macbeth and Macduff fight (and fight, and fight), and then he disarms me and I pull his sword into myself. Macbeth's last words 'And damned be he that first cries "Hold, enough"' (5.6.73) seem to me to be about damnation. Whether the line can bear this interpretation I don't know, but in my own head I was saying 'damned be he' (pointing upwards—'damned be He') 'who first says to you "Hold" '. And then 'Now, now'; and I pulled the sword into me, so that there was a degree, in his last moments, just a degree, of the old magnificence that he had had at the beginning. Some of that old strength came back and he spoke here of his own damnation, aware of the powers that had caused it, and, with something of his old dignity, accepting it.

Macbeth is an exhausting role—psychologically, mentally, emotionally and physically. I tried to play him, not as monster but as hero, as flawed hero. I think the man's journey is much more interesting than that of unchanging monster from start to finish. I wanted my Macbeth to be very different at the end from the man we had encountered at the beginning, though with recollections of what he has been that inform so much of what he says in the final stages. I tried to plot his journey from the golden boy of the opening to the burnt-out loser accepting his own damnation of the conclusion.

STEPHEN ORGEL

Macbeth and the Antic Round†

I begin my consideration of Macbeth some years before the Folio, for what seem to me good historical reasons: while it is certainly true, as historians of the book from Stanley Morison to Donald McKenzie and Randall McLeod have insisted, that works of literature do not exist independent of their material embodiment in texts, the printing of Shakespeare's plays is, nevertheless, really incidental. In their inception, in their conception, they are not books but scripts, designed to be realized in performance; and in this form they are not at all fixed by their material embodiment, whether Quarto or Folio (to say nothing of Riverside, Oxford or Norton), but fluid and open-ended. To realize them requires an infinite number of collaborative, often non-authorial, decisions, both textual and interpretive, which in turn eventuate in continual, increasingly non-authorial, revisions, excisions, additions. In this respect, Shakespeare plays have always been the free-floating signifiers of postmodern theory, standing for an infinitely variable range of signifieds. The play, that is, even in print, is always a process.

In the case of Macbeth, we are well into the process from the

† From Shakespeare Survey 52 (Cambridge: Cambridge University Press, 1999), 143–53. Reprinted by permission of Cambridge University Press.

outset, since the earliest surviving version of the play, that included in the Folio, is demonstrably a revision. It includes songs for the witches, given in the text only as incipits ('Come away, come away, etc.'; 'Black spirits, etc.'). These are songs from Middleton's play *The Witch*. In performance they would have been accompanied by dances, which means that in the theatre these scenes took a good deal longer than they do on the page. The manuscript of Davenant's version of the play,[1] prepared around 1664, includes the whole text of the witches' songs from Middleton—these are really musical dialogues, short scenes. The fact that Davenant did not supply his own witches' material at these points, as he did elsewhere, suggests that the Middleton material was already a standard feature of the play (Stanley Wells and Gary Taylor, in the Oxford Shakespeare, assume that the inclusion of all the Middleton material dates from the revision printed in the Folio, and include the complete text of the songs in their edition).

The elaboration of the witches' roles could have taken place anywhere up to about fifteen years after the play was first performed, but the presence of the Middleton songs suggests that Shakespeare was no longer around to do the revising, which presumes a date after 1614. Why, only a decade after the play was written, would augmenting the witches' roles have seemed a good idea? To begin with, by 1610 or so witchcraft, magic and the diabolical were good theatre business—Barnabe Barnes' *The Devil's Charter* was at the Globe in the same season as *Macbeth*, and Marston's *The Wonder of Women*, with its sorcery scenes, was at the Blackfriars. Jonson's *Masque of Queens*, performed at court in 1609, inaugurated a decade of sorcery plays and masques, including *The Tempest, The Alchemist, The Witch, The Witch of Edmonton, The Devil is an Ass*, and the revived and rewritten *Doctor Faustus*.

The ubiquitousness of theatrical magic is perhaps sufficient reason for the elaboration of the witches in *Macbeth*, but for me, it does not account for everything. When Macbeth, after the murder of Banquo, goes to consult the witches, and they show him a terrifying vision of Banquo's heirs, Hecate proposes a little entertainment to cheer him up:

> I'll charm the air to give a sound
> While you perform your antic round,
> That this great king may kindly say
> Our duties did his welcome pay. (4.1.145–8)

The tone of the scene here changes significantly: the witches are not professional and peremptory any more, they are lighthearted,

---

1. See excerpts below, pp. 161–73 [*Editor's note*].

gracious and deferential. We may choose to treat this as a moment of heavy irony, though Macbeth does not seem to respond to it as such; but if it is not ironic, the change of tone suggests that the 'great king' addressed in this passage is not the king on stage, but instead a real king in the audience, Banquo's descendant and the king of both Scotland and England.

The editors of both the recent Oxford and Cambridge editions have resisted the suggestion that this moment in *Macbeth* reflects the local conditions of a court performance, observing that nothing in the scene positively requires such an assumption. This is true enough, but I also see nothing implausible about it, and though there is no record of a court performance, King James surely must have wanted to see a play that included both witches and his ancestors. What are the implications if we assume that the text we have is a revision to take into account the presence of the king, and that his interest in witchcraft also accounts for the augmentation of the witches' scenes, so that the 'filthy,' 'black and midnight hags' become graciously entertaining after they have finished being ominously informative? Such a play would be significantly less author-centred than our familiar text: first because it is reviser-centered—and the presence of the Middleton scenes implies that Shakespeare was not the reviser—and second, because it is patron-centred, taking a particular audience into account. To this extent Shakespeare's *Macbeth* is already, in the Folio version, a significantly collaborative enterprise. But if this is correct, it also means that this version of *Macbeth* is a special case, devised for a single occasion, a performance at court, not the play in repertory, the play for the public.

This leads us to another question: how did this text become the 'standard' version—why was it the right version to include in the Folio? It needs to be emphasized that this is a question whether we assume that a performance before the king is involved or not: there is no denying that this is a revised text with non-Shakespearian material. Most attempts to deal with this issue beg the question, assuming that what we have is indeed the wrong text, and that Shakespeare's first editors would never have included it if they had had any alternative. The right text, the text we want (the prompt-book, or even better, Shakespeare's holograph) must have been unavailable, lost—burned, perhaps, in the destruction of the Globe in 1613, as if only a conflagration could explain the refusal of Hemminge and Condell (who promise, after all, 'the true original copies') to give us what we want. But perhaps it was included precisely because it was the right text—whether because by 1620 this, quite simply, was the play, or, more interestingly, because the best version of the play was the one that included the king.

This would make it an anomaly in the Folio, a version of the play prepared for a single, special occasion, rather than the standard public theatre version. In fact, the play as it stands in the Folio is anomalous in a number of respects. It is a very unusual play textually: it is very short, the shortest of the tragedies (half the length of *Hamlet*, a third shorter than the average), shorter, too than all the comedies except *The Comedy of Errors*. It looks, moreover, as if the version we have has not only been augmented with witches' business, but has also been cut and rearranged, producing some real muddles in the narrative: for example, the scene between Lenox and the Lord, 3.6, reporting action that has not happened yet, or the notorious syntactic puzzles of the account of the battle in the opening scenes, or the confusion of the final battle, in which Macbeth is slain onstage, and twenty lines later Macduff re-enters with his head. Revision and cutting were, of course, standard and necessary procedures in a theatre where the normal playing time was two hours; but if theatrical cuts are to explain the peculiarities of this text, why was it cut so peculiarly, not to say ineptly? Arguments that make the muddles not the result of cutting but an experiment in surreal and expressionistic dramaturgy only produce more questions, rendering the play a total anomaly, both in Shakespeare's work and in the drama of the period.

The very presence of the witches is unusual. Shakespeare makes use of the supernatural from time to time—ghosts in *Richard III*, *Julius Caesar*, and most notably in *Hamlet*, fairies and their magic in *A Midsummer Night's Dream*, Prospero's sorcery in *The Tempest*, Joan of Arc's and Marjory Jordan's in the *Henry VI* plays, and Rosalind's claim to be a magician at the end of *As You Like It*—but there is no other play in which witches and witchcraft are such an integral element of the plot. Indeed, whether or not King James was in the audience, the fact that it is the witches who provide the royal entertainment can hardly be accidental. The king was intensely interested in witchcraft; his dialogue on the subject, *Dæmonology*, first published in Edinburgh in 1597, was reissued (three times) upon his accession to the English throne in 1603. This and the *Basilicon Doron*, his philosophy of kingship, were the two works that he chose to introduce himself to his English subjects, and as I have argued elsewhere, witchcraft and kingship have an intimate relationship in the Jacobean royal ideology.[2] This is a culture in which the supernatural and witchcraft, even for sceptics, are as much part of reality as religious truth is. Like the ghost in *Hamlet*, the reality of the witches in *Macbeth* is not in question; the question, as in *Hamlet*, is why they are present and how far to believe them.

Like the ghost, too, the witches are quintessential theatrical devices: they dance and sing, perform wonders, appear and disap-

---

2. 'Jonson and the Amazons', in Elizabeth D. Harvey and Katharine Eisaman Maus, eds., *Soliciting Interpretation* (Chicago, 1990), pp. 119–39.

pear, fly, produce visions—do, in short, all the things that, historically, we have gone to the theatre to see. They open the play and set the tone for it. On Shakespeare's stage they would simply have materialized through a trap door, but Shakespeare's audience believed in magic already. Our rationalistic theatre requires something more theatrically elaborate—not necessarily machinery, but some serious mystification. For Shakespeare's audience, the mystification is built into their physical appearance, which defies the categories: they look like men and are women. The indeterminacy of their gender is the first thing Banquo calls attention to. This is a defining element of their nature, a paradox that identifies them as witches: a specifically female propensity to evil—being a witch—is defined by its apparent masculinity. This also is, of course, one of the central charges levelled at Shakespeare's theatre itself, the ambiguity of its gender roles—the fact that on Shakespeare's stage the women are really male. But the gender ambiguity relates as well to roles within the play—Lady Macbeth unsexes herself, and accuses her husband of being afraid to act like a man. What constitutes acting like a man in this play: what other than killing? Lady Macbeth unsexing herself, after all, renders herself, unexpectedly, not a man but a child, and thus incapable of murder: 'Had he not resembled / My father as he slept, I had done't' (2.2.12–13). Indeed, the definitive relation between murder and manhood applies to heroes as well as villains. When Macduff is told of the murder of his wife and children and is urged to 'Dispute it like a man,' he replies that he must first 'feel it as a man' (4.3.221–3). Whatever this says about his sensitivity and family feeling, it also says that murder is what makes you feel like a man.

The unsettling quality of the witches goes beyond gender. Their language is paradoxical: fair is foul and foul is fair; when the battle's lost and won. One way of looking at this is to say that it constitutes no paradox at all: any battle that is lost has also been won, but by somebody else. The person who describes a battle as lost and won is either on both sides or on neither; what is fair for one side is bound to be foul for the other. In a brilliantly subversive essay about twenty years ago, Harry Berger, Jr, suggested that the witches are in fact right, and are telling the truth about the world of the play—that there really are no ethical standards in it, no right and wrong sides.[3] Duncan certainly starts out sounding like a good king: the rhetoric of his monarchy is full of claims about its sacredness, about the deference that is due to it, how it is part of a natural hierarchy descending from God, how the king is divinely anointed, and so forth. But in fact

3. 'The Early Scenes of *Macbeth*: Preface to a New Interpretation' [1980, rpt.] in his collection *Making Trifles of Terrors* (Stanford, 1997), pp. 70–97.

none of this is borne out by the play: Duncan's rule is utterly chaotic, and maintaining it depends on constant warfare—the battle that opens the play, after all, is not an invasion, but a rebellion. Duncan's rule has never commanded the deference it claims for itself—deference is not natural to it. In upsetting that sense of the deference Macbeth feels he owes to Duncan, maybe the witches are releasing into the play something the play both overtly denies and implicitly articulates: that there is no basis whatever for the values asserted on Duncan's behalf; that the primary characteristic of his rule, perhaps of any rule in the world of the play, is not order but rebellion.

Whether or not this is correct, it must be to the point that women are the ones who prompt this dangerous realization in Macbeth. The witches live outside the social order, but they embody its contradictions: beneath the woman's exterior is also a man; beneath the man's exterior is also a woman; nature is anarchic, full of competing claims, not ordered and hierarchical; and to acknowledge that is to acknowledge the reality and force and validity of the individual will—to acknowledge that all of us have claims that conflict with the claims about deference and hierarchy. This is the same recognition that Edmund brings into *King Lear* when he invokes Nature as his goddess. It is a Nature that is not the image of divine order, but one in which the strongest and craftiest survive—and when they survive, they then go on to devise claims about Nature that justify their success, claims about hierarchies, natural law and order, the divine right of kings. Edmund is a villain, but if he were ultimately successful he would be indistinguishable from the Duncans and Malcolms (and James I's) of Shakespeare's world.

Here is a little history: the real Macbeth was, like Richard III, the victim of a gigantic and very effective publicity campaign. Historically, Duncan was the usurper—that is what the rebellion at the beginning of the play is about, though there is no way of knowing it from Shakespeare. Macbeth had a claim to the throne (Shakespeare does know this: Duncan at one point in the play refers to him as 'cousin' (1.4.14)—they were first cousins, both grandsons of King Malcolm II). Macbeth's murder of Duncan was a political assassination, and Macbeth was a popular hero because of it. The legitimate heir to the throne, whose rights have been displaced by the usurping Duncan, was Lady Macbeth. When Macbeth ascended the throne, he was ruling as Protector or Regent until Lady Macbeth's son came of age (she did have children—it is Shakespeare who deprives her and Macbeth those heirs). Macbeth's defeat at the end of the play, by Malcolm and Macduff, constituted essentially an English invasion—the long-term fight was between native Scottish Celts and Anglo-Norman invaders, with continental allies (such as the

Norwegian king) on both sides. One way of looking at the action is to say that it is about the enforced anglicization of Scotland, which Macbeth is resisting.

Shakespeare knows some of this. In Holinshed, Macbeth not only has a claim to the throne, he also has a legitimate grievance against Duncan. Moreover, in Shakespeare's source, Banquo is fully Macbeth's accomplice, and the murder of Duncan has a good deal of political justification. All this would be very touchy for Shakespeare, because Banquo is King James's ancestor, and if Duncan is a saint, then Banquo is a real problem, the ancestor one wants to forget. Shakespeare's way of handling Banquo fudges a lot of issues. Should he not, as a loyal thane, be pressing the claim of Malcolm, the designated heir, after the murder? Should he remain loyal to Macbeth as long as he does? In fact, this is precisely the sort of question that shows how close the play is to *Hamlet*: in both plays, the issue of legitimacy remains crucially ambiguous. Nobody in *Macbeth* presses the claim of Malcolm until Malcolm reappears with an army to support him, any more than anyone in *Hamlet* presses the claim of Hamlet. In both plays, there is deep uncertainty about the relation between power and legitimacy—about whether legitimacy constitutes anything more than the rhetoric of power backed by the size of its army. Duncan tries to legitimize his son's succession by creating Malcolm Prince of Cumberland on the analogy of the Prince of Wales, thus declaring him heir to the throne. But this is not the way the succession works in Scotland—Cumberland is an English county, which was briefly ceded to the Scottish crown, and Malcolm's new title is the thin edge of the English invasion. James I himself became king of England not because he was the legitimate heir (he was one of a number of people with a distant claim to the throne), but because he was *designated* the successor by Queen Elizabeth; or at least several attendants at her death claimed that he was, and the people in control supported him. This is much closer to the situation in *Hamlet* and *Macbeth* than it is to any system of hereditary succession. And Macbeth is, even in the play, a fully legitimate king, as legitimate as Duncan: like Hamlet's Denmark, this is not a hereditary monarchy; Macbeth is *elected* king by the thanes, and duly anointed. The fact that he turns out to be a bad king does not make him any less the king, any more than the rebellion that opens the play casts doubt on Duncan's right to the throne.

Let us return to the witches' royal entertainment, with its songs and dances from Middleton. *The Witch* was written between 1610 and 1615; so by that time there was felt to be a need for more variety in the play, of a specifically theatrical kind, singing and dancing. I have suggested that witchcraft was good theatrical capital, but this does not really account for the revisions. Witchcraft was good theatre no matter what the witches did—spells, incantations, visions, appearances and disappearances, diabolical music were their stock in trade. It would not have been at all necessary to transform them into the vaudevillians they become for Macbeth's entertainment. If variety was required, Duncan's hosts could have entertained him at dinner as the King of Navarre entertains the Princess of France, with dances and a disguising; or Banquo's ghost, like Puck or Hamlet, could have interrupted a play within the play; or like Prospero, Duncan could have presented a royal masque to celebrate his son's investiture as Prince of Cumberland. Why bring the witches into it? But, to judge from the play's stage history, the vaudevillian witches constituted a stroke of theatrical genius.

Or did they? Consider the play's stage history. How successful, in fact, was Macbeth in its own time? Though it seems inconceivable that King James would not have been interested in the play, there is, as I have said, no record of a court performance—nor is there, in fact, any record of any pre-Restoration performance other than the one Simon Forman saw at the Globe in 1611, and reported in his diary. The Shakespeare Allusion Book records only seven other references to the play before 1649; of these, only three, all before 1677, seem to me allusions to performances. A fourth, from 1642, is quoting it as a classic text. The remaining examples merely refer to the historical figure of Macbeth.[4] This, it must be emphasized, is a very small number of allusions: for comparison, there are fifty-eight to Hamlet, thirty-six to Romeo and Juliet, twenty-nine to the Henry IV plays, twenty-three to Richard III, nineteen to Othello.

This is all we know of the stage history of the play up to the Restoration. So perhaps reinventing the witches was not a stroke of theatrical genius after all; perhaps all it did was undertake, with uncertain success, to liven up an unpopular play. When Davenant revised Macbeth for the new stage, he inserted the whole of the singing and dancing scenes from Middleton—this is, as I have indicated, at least arguably how the play had been performed on the public stage for two decades or more before the closing of the theatres in 1642, and it would thus have been this version of the play that Davenant saw throughout his youth. (Davenant was born in 1606, so he was going to the theatre in the 1620s and thirties). Indeed, since The Witch remained unpublished until 1778, it is likely that Davenant took his text not from Middleton at all, but directly from the

---

4. The book tabulates seven allusions, but in fact includes eight. The Knight of the Burning Pestle and a play called The Puritan refer pretty clearly to Banquo's ghost, and The Two Maids of Mortlake, a parodic play by Robert Armin, the principal clown in Shakespeare's company, recalls Macbeth's 'Will all great Neptune's ocean wash this blood / Clean from my hands' Since Armin's play was published in 1609, this must be a recollection of Macbeth, on the stage. Sir Thomas Browne in 1642 saying that he begins 'to be weary of the sun' is more likely a recollection of the printed text.

King's Men's performing text of *Macbeth*. Pepys provides a good testimony to the success of these and Davenant's other additions.
Between 1664 and 1669 he went to the play nine times. The first
time he found it only 'a pretty good play, but admirably acted'—the
admirable Macbeth was Betterton at the outset of his career. What
Pepys saw on this occasion was certainly the folio text, with its Middleton additions. Thereafter he saw the play as Davenant refurbished
it, and his response changed dramatically. It was, at various times,
'a most excellent play for variety'; 'a most excellent play in all
respects, but especially in divertisement, though it be a deep tragedy;
which is a strange perfection in a tragedy, it being most proper here
and suitable'; and finally, 'one of the best plays for a stage, and a
variety of dancing and music, that I ever saw.'[5]

The interesting point here is the relation between 'deep tragedy'
and 'divertisement,' which clearly for Pepys is a critical one. It is
what he likes best about the play—indeed, it is what makes him
revise his opinion of the play from 'pretty good' to 'most excellent.'
And what Davenant added to the play—songs, dances, spectacle—
is not simply something to appeal to Restoration taste. He expanded
and elaborated elements that were already being added even before
the folio text was published in 1623. So that is something to pause
over: the really striking theatricality of the tragedy, its emphasis not
just on visions and hallucinations, but on spectacle of all kinds, and
even overtly in scenes like the witches' dances—on entertainment,
and its move toward the court masque. We see *Macbeth* as the most
intensely inward of Shakespeare's plays, in which much of the action
seems to take place within Macbeth's head, or as a projection of his
fears and fantasies. But if we look again at the text we have, and fill
in the blanks, we see that, as far back as our evidence goes, a great
deal of the play's character was always determined by what Pepys
called 'variety' and 'divertisement.' Perhaps for early audiences, then,
these elements were not antithetical to psychological depth after all.
In this respect *Macbeth* resembles *The Tempest* more than it does
the other tragedies.

The play's 'divertisement' is a quality that is largely lost to us, partly
because it is only hinted at in the folio text, which merely indicates
that the songs are to be sung, but does not print them, and partly
because it is so difficult to imagine doing the full-scale grotesque
ballet they imply in a modern production. Pepys thought divertisement should have seemed radically indecorous too; but, to his surprise, he did not find it so. What is the relation between tragedy and
the antic quality of the witches? Why does that antic quality keep

5. For a fuller discussion of Pepys's response to the play, see my essay 'Shakespeare and the
Kinds of Drama', *Critical Inquiry* 6: 1 (Autumn, 1979), 107–23.

increasing in size and importance in the stage history of the play from the seventeenth through the nineteenth century? Addison, for example, recalls his attention being distracted at a Betterton performance by a woman loudly asking 'When will the dear witches enter?'[6] Garrick, despite his claim to have returned to the text as originally written by Shakespeare, kept all Davenant's witch scenes; and in 1793, when Mrs Siddons was the Lady Macbeth, Hecate and her spirits descended and ascended on clouds, and the cauldron scene constituted a long interpolated pantomime.[7] Clearly Mrs Siddons did not think she was being upstaged. Can we imagine similar elements playing a similarly crucial role in the stage history of *Lear* or *Hamlet*?

In fact, we can: in *Lear*, if it is the antic quality we are concerned with, there are Lear's mad scenes and the fool's zany speeches, which we find so hard to understand and pare down to a minimum, but which must have been popular in Shakespeare's time because new ones were added between the 1608 quarto and the 1623 folio. As for *Hamlet*, perhaps the witches externalize that anarchic quality that makes the prince so dangerous an adversary to the guilty king.

Suppose we try to imagine a *Hamlet* written from Claudius' point of view, in the way that *Macbeth* is written from Macbeth's. Look at it this way: the murder Claudius commits is the perfect crime; but the hero-villain quickly finds that his actions have unimagined implications, and that the world of politics is not all he has to contend with. Even as it stands, *Hamlet* is a very political play, and does not really need the ghost at all: Hamlet has his suspicions already; Claudius tries to buy him off by promising him the succession, but this is not good enough. It turns out that the problem is not really conscience or revenge, it is Hamlet's own ambitions—he wanted to succeed his father on the throne; Claudius, Hamlet says, 'Lept in between the election and my hopes' [*Hamlet*, 5.2.66]. The ghost is really, literally, a deus ex machina. But in a *Hamlet* that did not centre on Hamlet, Claudius' guilty conscience, which is not much in evidence in the play, would have a great deal more work to do. So would the ghost—who should, after all, logically be haunting Claudius, not Hamlet. This play would be not about politics but about how the dead do not disappear, they return to embody our crimes, so that we have to keep repeating them—just like *Macbeth*. In this version of *Hamlet*, Hamlet is hardly necessary, any more than in *Macbeth*, Malcolm and Macduff are necessary—the drama of *Macbeth* is really a matter between Macbeth and his ambition, Macbeth and the witches and his wife and his hallucinations and his own

6. *Spectator* 45 (1711).
7. *The Dramatic Mirror*, quoted in Gāmini Salgādo, *Eye-witnesses of Shakespeare* (Sussex, 1975), p. 299.

tortured soul, the drama of prophecies and riddles, and how he understands them, and what he decides to do about them, and how they, in themselves, constitute retribution.

What, then, about the riddles, those verbal incarnations of the imperfect speakers the witches? Macbeth is told that he will never be conquered till Birnam Wood comes to Dunsinane; and that no man of woman born will harm him. Are these paradoxical impossibilities realized? Not at all, really: the Birnam Wood prophecy does not come true, it just appears to Macbeth that it does—the wood is not moving, it merely looks as if it is. Or alternatively, we could say that 'Birnam Wood' is a quibble: Macbeth assumes it means the forest, but it could mean merely wood from the forest, the branches the soldiers are using for camouflage—it comes true merely as a stage device. As for 'no man of woman born,' maybe the problem is that Macbeth is not a close enough reader: he takes the operative word to be 'woman,'—'No man of *woman* born shall harm Macbeth'—but the key word turns out to be 'born'—'No man of woman *born* shall harm Macbeth.' If this is right, we must go on to consider the implications of the assumption that a Caesarian section does not constitute birth. This is really, historically, quite significant: a vaginal birth would have been handled by women, the midwife, maids, attendants, with no men present. But surgery was a male prerogative— the surgeon was always a man; midwives were not allowed to use surgical instruments—and the surgical birth thus means, in Renaissance terms, that Macduff was brought to life by men, not women: carried by a woman, but made viable only through masculine intervention. Such a birth, all but invariably, involved the mother's death.

Macbeth himself sees it this way, when he defies Macduff and says,

> . . . though Birnam Wood be come to Dunsinane,
> And thou opposed being of no woman born, (5.10.30–1)

where logically it should be 'being not of woman born': the key concept is not 'no woman' but 'not born.' But Shakespeare seems to be conceiving of a masculine equivalent to the immaculate conception, a birth uncontaminated by women, as the Virgin's was uncontaminated by man.

So this riddle bears on the whole issue of the place of women in the play's world, how very disruptive they seem to be, even when, like Lady Macduff, they are loving and nurturing. Why is it so important, for example, at the end of the play, that Malcolm is a virgin? Malcolm insists to Macduff that he is utterly pure, 'as yet / Unknown to woman' (4.3.126–7), uncontaminated by heterosexuality—this is offered as the first of his qualifications for displacing and succeeding Macbeth. Perhaps this bears too on the really big unanswered question about Macduff: why he left his family unprotected when he went to seek Malcolm in England—this is what makes Malcolm mistrust him so deeply. Why would you leave your wife and children unprotected, to face the tyrant's rage, unless you knew they were really in no danger?

But somehow the question goes unanswered, does not need to be answered, perhaps because Lady Macduff in some way is the problem, just as, more obviously, Lady Macbeth and the witches are. Those claims on Macduff that tie him to his wife and children, that would keep him at home, that purport to be higher than the claims of masculine solidarity, are in fact rejected quite decisively by the play. In Holinshed, Macduff flees only *after* his wife and children have been murdered, and therefore for the best of reasons. Macduff's desertion of his family is Shakespeare's addition to the story. Maybe, the play keeps saying, if it weren't for all those women . . . ? It really is an astonishingly male-oriented and misogynistic play, especially at the end, when there are simply no women left, not even the witches, and the restored commonwealth is a world of heroic soldiers. Is the answer to Malcolm's question about why Macduff left his family, 'Because it's *you* I really love'?

So, to return to the increasingly elaborate witches' scenes, the first thing they do for this claustrophobic play is to open up a space for women; and it is a subversive and paradoxical space. This is a play in which paradoxes abound, and for Shakespeare's audience, Lady Macbeth would have embodied those paradoxes as powerfully as the witches do: in her proclaimed ability to 'unsex' herself, in her willingness to dash her own infant's brains out, but most of all, in the kind of control she exercises over her husband. The marriage at the centre of the play is one of the scariest things about it, but it is worth observing that, as Shakespearian marriages go, this is a good one: intense, intimate, loving. The notion that your wife is your friend and your comfort is not a Shakespearian one. The relaxed, easygoing, happy time men and women have together in Shakespeare all takes place before marriage, as part of the wooing process—this is the subject of comedy. What happens after marriage is the subject of tragedy—Goneril and Regan are only extreme versions of perfectly normative Shakespearian wives. The only Shakespearian marriage of any duration that is represented as specifically sexually happy is the marriage of Claudius and Gertrude, a murderer and an adulteress; and it is probably to the point that even they stop sleeping together after only four months—not, to be sure, by choice.

In this context, Macbeth and Lady Macbeth are really quite well matched. They care for each other and understand each other deeply, exhibiting a genuine intimacy and trust of a sort one does not find, for example, in the marriage of the Capulets, or in Iago and

Emilia (to say nothing of Othello and Desdemona), or in Coriolanus and Virgilia, or in Cymbeline and his villainous queen (who is not even provided with a name), or in Leontes and Hermione. The prospects for life after marriage in Shakespeare really are pretty grim. And in this respect, probably the most frightening thing in the play is the genuine power of Lady Macbeth's mind—not just her powers of analysis and persuasion, but her intimate apprehension of her husband's deepest desires, her perfect understanding of what combination of arguments will prove irresistible to the masculine ego: 'Be a man,' and 'If you really loved me you'd do it.'

But can the play's action really be accounted for simply by the addition of yet another witch? Macbeth's marriage is a version of the Adam and Eve story, the woman persuading the man to commit the primal sin against the father. But the case is loaded: surely Lady Macbeth is not the culprit, any more than Eve is—or than the witches are. What she does is give voice to Macbeth's inner life, release in him the same forbidden desire that the witches have called forth. To act on this desire is what it means in the play to be a man. But having evoked her husband's murderous ambition, having dared him to stop being a child, she suddenly finds that when he *is* a man she is powerless. Her own power was only her power over the child, the child she was willing to destroy to gain the power of a man.

Davenant, redoing the play, does some really interesting thinking about such issues. His version has had a bad press from critics since the nineteenth century, but like all his adaptations, it starts from a shrewd sense not merely of theatrical realities, but of genuine critical problems with the play—problems of the sort that editors and commentators lavish minute attention on, but directors and performers simply gloss over or cut. Many of his changes have to do with elucidation, clarifying obscurities in Shakespeare's text, especially in the opening scenes. There is also a move toward theatrical efficiency in casting. In the opening, for example, Macduff becomes Lenox, Seyton becomes the Captain—it is difficult to see why these are not improvements. Davenant also worries a lot, to our minds unnecessarily, about the location of scenes and the topography of the action, matters Shakespeare is resolutely vague about. Thus when Lady Macduff fears that she is lost, her servant is able to reassure her that 'this is the entrance o' the heath' (2.5.3)[8]—do heaths even have entrances? Such moments are the price of adapting the play to a stage where topography is realized, location materialized in scenery.

The most interesting aspects of the revision involve the women. It

8. Davenant's *Macbeth* is quoted from Christopher Spencer's edition, *Davenant's* Macbeth *from the Yale Manuscript* (New Haven, 1961).

has often been observed that since the Restoration theatre employed actresses, it made sense to increase the women's parts; but this is hardly adequate to account for Davenant's additions: for one thing, the witches continued to be played by men. It is the moral dimension of the woman's role that Davenant rethinks. Thus in a domestic scene that has no parallel in the folio, Lady Macduff sharply questions Macduff's motives, accusing him of ambition: 'I am affraid you have some other end / Than meerely Scottland's freedom to defend' (3.2.18–19)—doesn't he really want the throne himself? Lady Macduff here articulates the same critique of her husband that Hecate does of Macbeth, that he is out for himself alone. Her fear articulates that perennial problem in the play, Malcolm's question about Macduff that never gets answered—where are your real loyalties; why is coming to England to join my army more important than the lives of your wife and children? The problem remains in Davenant, but is mitigated by the fact that Lady Macduff encourages Macduff to flee after the murder of Banquo. If it was a mistake, it was her mistake as well as his. Davenant's Lady Macduff also expresses a conservative royalist line, insisting that the only thing that can justify Macduff's rebellion will be for him to place the true heir, Malcolm, on the throne, rather than claiming it himself—the women, for Davenant, consistently articulate the moral position. Even Lady Macbeth, in a scene of love and recrimination inserted before the sleepwalking scene, accuses Macbeth of being like Adam, following her when he should have led her. But as Davenant's women are more important, they are also less dangerous: the Restoration Malcolm does not claim to be a virgin.

Revisers and performers have never been happy with the way Lady Macbeth simply fades out, and Macbeth is perfunctorily killed. The play does not even provide its hero with a final speech, let alone a eulogy for Shakespeare's most complex and brilliant studies in villainy. Malcolm dismisses the pair succinctly as 'this dead butcher and his fiend-like queen.' Davenant added a rather awkward dying line for Macbeth ('Farewell vain world, and what's most vain in it, ambition,' 5.7.83), and tastefully resolved the problem of Macbeth's double death by leaving the body on stage and having Macduff re-enter with Macbeth's sword, instead of his head. By the mid-eighteenth century, Garrick—who was claiming to be performing the play 'as written by Shakespeare'—had inserted an extended death speech for the hero:

> 'Tis done! The scene of life will quickly close.
> Ambition's vain, delusive dreams are fled,
> And now I wake to darkness, guilt and horror;

> I cannot bear it! Let me shake it off—
> 'Twill not be; my soul is clogged with blood—
> I cannot rise! I dare not ask for mercy—
> It is too late, hell drags me down; I sink,
> I sink—Oh!—my soul is lost forever!
> Oh!

This Faustian peroration went on being used until well into the nineteenth century.

The editors of Bell's Shakespeare in 1774 declared themselves pleased with the play's ending, observing, with characteristic condescension, that Shakespeare, 'contrary to his common practice . . . has wound up the plot, punished the guilty, and established the innocent, in such a regular progression of important events, that nothing was wanting but very slight alterations . . . [9] But there is a puzzling element in Shakespeare's conclusion, which is less symmetrical and more open-ended than this suggests. Why, in a play so clearly organized around ideas of good and evil, is it not Malcolm who defeats Macbeth—the incarnation of virtue, the man who has never told a lie or slept with a woman, overcoming the monster of vice? In fact, historically, this is what happened: Macbeth was killed in battle by Malcolm, not Macduff: Shakespeare is following Holinshed here, but why, especially in a play that revises so much else in its source material? Davenant recognizes this as a problem, and, followed by Garrick, gives Macduff a few lines of justification as he kills Macbeth: 'This for thy Royall Master Duncan / This for my Dearest freind my wife, / This for those pledges of our Loves; my Children . . . Ile as a Trophy bear away his sword / To wittness my revenge' (5.7.76–82). The addition is significant, and revealing: in Shakespeare, Macduff, fulfilling the prophecy, is simply acting as Malcolm's agent, the man not born of woman acting for the king uncontaminated by women. But why does virtue need an agent, while vice can act for itself? And what about the agent: does the unanswered question about Macduff abandoning his family not linger in the back of our minds? Does his willingness to condone the vices Malcolm invents for himself not say something disturbing about the quality of Macduff as a hero? Is he not, in fact, the pragmatic soldier who does what needs to be done so that the saintly king can stay clear of the complexities and paradoxes of politics and war? Davenant does not quite succeed in disarming the ambiguities of the ending. What happens next, with a saintly king of Scotland, and an ambitious soldier as his right hand man, and those threatening offspring the heirs of Banquo still waiting in the wings?

---

9. *Bell's Edition of Shakespeare's Plays* (London, 1774), vol. 1, p. 71.

PETER HOLLAND

"Stands Scotland Where It Did?": The Location of *Macbeth* on Film†

In 1997 Michael Bogdanov, the energetic and irreverent English theater director and co-founder of the English Shakespeare Company, directed a production of *Macbeth* for the British independent television company Channel 4. Made originally for their schools programming and aimed at the United Kingdom equivalent of high school students, this *Macbeth* was first screened in a number of bite-sized segments before the film was broadcast as a complete work, the programming was Shakespeare made palatable for schools' consumption, but the production itself was anything but, offering instead a finely crafted vision of a thuggish world. Bogdanov, whose visual resources for theater or television productions are nothing if not eclectic, placed his weird sisters in the detritus of an urban world, the garbage of inner-city chaos, complete with smashed televisions, heaps of black trash bags, and a number of shopwindow mannequins, but this vision of the decay of late-twentieth-century civilization was displaced into a rural landscape, across which Macbeth and Banquo rode on motorbikes for their encounter with the women.

Placing Macbeth's court meeting in a wonderfully decaying cathedral, full of grand arches and peeling walls, and the final battle in a derelict factory complex, firmly planted Bogdanov's version in a contemporary world. Bogdanov's version was not created as a patronizing gesture of contemporary relevance to make schoolkids feel comfortable with the horrors of having to study Shakespeare but instead as a part of Bogdanov's serious and thoughtful commitment to help them understand Shakespeare as our contemporary and the play as a political commentary on the methods of the modern state.

But Bogdanov's playful bricolage of postmodern fragments also allowed for a lurking presence of the signs of Scotland, those iconic cultural devices that key in the ostensible location of the play's fiction. Some of the military figures in the opening scenes wore plaid scarves over their uniforms as if their regimental allegiance was best encoded by their clan membership. Lady Macbeth announced that "Nought's had, all's spent / Where our desire is got without consent" (3.2.6–7) while wearing an immensely stylish, close-fitting jacket of tartan material, the kind of outfit one finds at an expensive shop

---

† In an essay written for this collection, Peter Holland examines varying depictions of Scotland and England in five film versions of *Macbeth*. Used by permission of the author.

catering to the businesswoman's wardrobe. In the English scene
(4.3), set in the grand formal gardens of a nineteenth-century
English country house (though Scottish country houses have formal
gardens too), Macduff was wearing a kilt, that belated invention of
Queen Victoria's Highland culture, as if Macduff needed to fore-
ground his otherness in the polite English gentility of tea on the
lawn. The Scottish doctor in Act 5 had an appropriately Scottish
accent, though, since the English doctor was, as so often, cut, the
contrast was not needed. Most wittily, while Fife Macduff's children
were eating bowls of porridge that quintessentially Scottish staple
the eldest child, angry at the murderer's comments, flicked a spoon-
ful of his porridge straight into the murderer's face, to the guffaws
of his partner.

Scotland leaves its traces on the film, as if it is only as trace could
that country exist. As a nation-state Scotland had little meaning in
the mid-1990s, even though the film was made, unknowingly, on the
verge of the reestablishment of a Scottish parliament in the devolved
structures of the nation Britain shortly afterwards. Had he made the
film a year or two later or for a less educational context, perhaps
Bogdanov would not have allowed the Scottish presence to be quite
so jokingly allusive and quite so politically vestigial.

But at least Bogdanov's film sees Scotland as a commercial entity
of food and clothing, a former nation now commodified into tartan
couture and Scott's Porridge Oats, a set of visual relics of a national
past. Jeremy Freeston's film of 1996 for Cromwell Productions,
never, as far as I know, given a theater release but sent straight to
video (and quite probably made for the TV / video market), is a low-
budget attempt to film Shakespeare, in part financed by Grampian
Television (a Scottish independent channel). Scotland, that is, exists
as a source of funding for a company committed to making films
about Scottish history, as in *The Bruce* (1996). Though the video's
blurb announces that the film is "[a]uthentically set in eleventh-
century Scotland"—without ever quite saying to what it is being
authentic, since Shakespeare's play is hardly marked by anything
much constituting historical authenticity—the visual style of the film
is much more heavily dependent on the twin conventions of film
costume-drama and nineteenth-century theater spectacle. For all the
freshness of Jason Connery's Macbeth, son of a father who so brilliantly turned a Scots voice into a superbly manipulated film tool,
the visual language of this film is locked into a set of conventions
that it never questions or extends, but only absorbs.

The two films both watched by consumers, define a kind of overly
neat polarity in the representation of place. The blandness of Freeston's acceptance of the accumulated modes of filmic history can be
set against the pleasurable provocations and the analytic invitations

of Bogdanov's method. Bogdanov's film, that is, demands response to its method—where Freeston's only emphasizes the watcher's passivity, as if visual context can be left unquestioned, resting in a cliché aesthetic of landscape and the material texture of supposedly historicized—but non-national—clothing.

Since Scotland does not continue to stand "where it did"—indeed, since Shakespeare's Scotland is so self-evidently a construction of a convergence of twin histories, the constructed past of Holinshed and others and a present, as it were, under King James's construction—how various *Macbeth* films have created their worlds, the visual and aural definitions of their fictive placings, becomes a location of the films' locations, a definition of their senses of the play's landscapings. Precisely because film invites the presentation of a contextual real, an emphasized background contextualisation of the immanence of place, the choices of place made by Shakespeare films create meanings against which the action is played out. The meaning of Branagh's *Hamlet* (1996), for example, appears to be consequent on its setting against the exterior of Blenheim Palace, as grand a building as any post-early-modern castle could be. Film locations become dominant signals for the readings of the play they construct.

In the five films with which I shall be principally concerned, the range of meanings accorded to place sculpts the play's worlds into widely varying forms, enabling the particularities of Shakespeare's politics of nation to stand even clearer. Whether involving a space that includes Chicago gangsters or Japanese samurai, whether the territories are fought over by Italian-American mafiosi or between rival forms of religious practice, the Scotland of *Macbeth* films is always aware of the limits of its power as well as of its geography. The geography is dependant on precisely that sense of adjacency that leads Shakespeare to move the action here, (just as in the tantalizing incompleteness of the hero's comparable journey in *Hamlet*), from the place beyond (Scotland, Denmark) towards England, to that land imaged in *Macbeth* as a quasi-heavenly realm of calm and support.

What is at stake in the quest for the throne, be it by Macbeth or Malcolm, becomes present on film as things seen, whereas in theater the quest can rarely be more visibly defined than in the symbolic aspiration for "The sweet fruition of an earthly crown," as Marlowe's Tamburlaine calls it,[1] or potently heard in the play's dozen uses of the word Scotland. Significantly, after an initial reference to Duncan ("Mark, King of Scotland," 1.2.28), the word disappears until the English scene, where it chimes eight times to indicate that other place from which Malcolm and Macduff are temporarily exiled. Then it is heard in its final occurrences in the shout and echo that mark

1. Christopher Marlowe, *"Doctor Faustus" and Other Plays*, ed. David Bevington and Eric Rasmussen (Oxford: Oxford University Press, 1995), *Tamburlaine, Part 1*, 2.6.29.

the new king ("Hail, King of Scotland!/Hail, King of Scotland!"
5.8.59) and in the new, more English world of earls, "the first that
ever Scotland/In such an honor named" (5.8.63–64), rather than
the more particular Scottishness of thanes. However we conceive of
the territory over which Macbeth is king, the play never allows him
to be named King of Scotland. What we see him achieve is dominion
but not connection, authority but not a title, power displaced from
its geographic and conceptual boundaries, those borders of the physical space and the imaginative existence of nation that will prove to
be permeable, penetrable and vulnerable—like so much else in the
play, from the opening battle against invaders and rebels to the last
moments of turning Scotland into something more akin to England.
Where Scotland precisely stands and what it looks like, its relation
to England and the nature of its physical landscape, charts the films'
senses of the play's political analysis. Location enables the film audience to read the play.

Scotland, IL

In 2001 Billy Morrissette wrote and directed his first feature film,
Scotland, Pa., a parodic displacement of *Macbeth* into a bleakly and
blackly comic tale of ambition in a 1970s roadside fast-food restaurant in small-town Pennsylvania, where Joe "Mac" McBeth and his
wife Pat take over Norm Duncan's eatery by murdering the owner,
spurred on by the prophecies of the three hippies Joe encountered
at a fair. Morrissette probably found the name of his comic hero in
the title of a film that had moved Scotland to a location in the United
States many years earlier: *Joe Macbeth.*

Joe Macbeth was made in England in 1955 for Columbia Studios,
the third in their Shakespeare adaptations from this period (*House
of Strangers* [1949]), directed by Joseph Mankiewicz and derived
from *King Lear,* and *Lear's* transformation into a Western as *Broken
Lance* [1954], directed by Edward Dmytryk). All three were ostensibly scripted or derived from work by Philip Yordan, though, as Tony
Howard points out, Yordan "was often a 'front' for blacklisted writers,
and the precise nature of his role was not always clear."[2] At a time
in which Hollywood was extremely wary of anything that might be
seen as straight Shakespeare (especially after the comparative failure
of Orson Welles's 1948 *Macbeth* and in spite of the comparative
success of Joseph Mankiewicz's 1953 star-studded *Julius Caesar*),
Columbia saw that Shakespeare as script-resource was well worth
pursuing.

---

2. Tony Howard, "Shakespeare's Cinematic Offshoots," in Russell Jackson, ed., *The Cambridge Companion to Shakespeare on Film* (Cambridge: Cambridge University Press,
2000), 312.

Directed by Ken Hughes, who had established his modest reputation in a series of Scotland Yard detective thrillers hosted by Edgar
Lustgarten, *Joe Macbeth* cast a number of British actors opposite
some Americans with reputations even more modest than the director's. Low budget in the extreme, the film uses the conventions of
film noir as far as possible to disguise its necessary economies. Early
reviews, wedded to the traditional high-culture notion of the tran-
scendental status of both Shakespeare and his characters, often
mocked the film as, for instance, "a comic-book version of an immortal piece of literature"[3] while "the sordid gangsters, realistically
treated, are no parallels for Shakespeare's exalted personages, whose
characters are illumined by great poetry."[4] But Columbia's primary
aim was to capitalize on the moviegoers' appetite for gangster movies
rather than to make a statement about the banality of evil in Shakespeare's play. This is *Macbeth* set in a Chicago whose skyline is outlined behind the credits and whose grand Lakeshore Drive becomes
the Lakeview Drive that Joe Macbeth rules.

Yet *Joe Macbeth,* from its title on, does nothing to disguise its
relationship to Shakespeare. The opening action is played after a title
quoting from Shakespeare ("Never in the Legions of Horrid Hell /
Can come a Devil more damn'd / In evils to top Macbeth"[5] carefully
ascribed to "*ACT 4, SCENE 3, MACBETH, WILLIAM SHAKESPEARE*"). The
final sounds of sirens and gunfire suggest the continuation of the
action now in tension with the otherwise invisible forces of law and
order accompany a title quoting "It will have blood they say. / Blood
will have blood."[6] Shakespeare's play is being invoked to suggest both
the scale of the gangsters' actions and the universalism of Shakespeare's action in terms that ought to have endeared the film to the
reviewers. With Banky as his partner, Mr. "The Duke" del Duca as
the Duncan he will murder, and the three stages of Macbeth's ascent
defined as "Baron of the West Side," "Lord of Lakeview Drive," and
"King of the City," a game of allusion is played out that sees modern
forms of power and their consequential quests for control as only
being explicable in terms of a gang's territory.

But Shakespeare's play is more than a discreet presence offering
a grand allusive parallel for the action; *Macbeth* is also present as a
precise echo of performance. Rosie, the ageing flower-seller who
interrupts Joe's quiet wedding celebration *à deux* with his new wife
Lily (a wedding delayed because Joe had to wait for Tommy, Duca's

---

3. Review in *America,* 3 December 1955, quoted by Robert F. Willson, Jr., *Shakespeare in
    Hollywood, 1929–56* (Madison, NJ: Fairleigh Dickinson University Press, 2002), 101.
4. Review in *National Parent Teacher,* March 1956, quoted in Willson, 101.
5. I preserve here the film's odd choices for capitalization.
6. Willson reads the ending sounds as "imply[ing] that the last of the gangsters has been
    destroyed" (96), but there seem in the film to be precious little grounds for seeing such a
    moralistic ending.

former right-hand hitman, to die—and, as Joe tells the dying Tommy over the phone in the film's remarkably brutal opening, "that Tommy sure hates to die") tells Joe's fortune using tarot cards that "came off the body of a hanged murderer." But Rosie greets Joe first with a theatrical salutation of "Ah, noble Macbeth," not because the screenwriter wanted some vestigial echo of Shakespeare but because Rosie had been an actress: as Joe says, "I would sure like to seen you when you played opposite Barrymore." This weird sister is an out-of-work actress, her theatricality some sign of the inappropriateness of theater as career but also of the irrelevance of *Macbeth* as play in a world even more violent and driven by ambition than Shakespeare's.

Rosie, later seen selling chestnuts in the street because the flower business is not going well, begins her second encounter with Joe by asking "Well, since we last met, how heavy hangs the crown?"—not a quote from *Macbeth* or elsewhere in Shakespeare but resoundingly Shakespearean—before warning him that "Banky casts a shadow over you . . . Nothing to fear from Banky, only his shadow," again a Shakespearean portent, especially since the film shows no concern with Malcolm. Retribution comes from Banky's son, Lenny, a Fleance who is able to exact revenge that only subsequent generations of Banquo's descendants will wreak on Shakespeare's Macbeth. The landscape of *Joe Macbeth* is, then, one in which Shakespeare is present as cultural artifact, the source of the voicing of the control over the narrative that prophecy provides. Other echoes of the play occur in the wheeling birds, for example, that are seen from time to time, a recurrent motif in the natural world of *Macbeth* films, and which Rosie sees in her crystal ball as a good omen.[7] Or the potent effect of the bell on the lake that stops Joe from sleeping ("Does it go on all night? Can a guy ever get any sleep?"). Both these motifs are naturalized into the fabric of the film, not calling attention to their status as echoes or allusions unless we wish them to be. Rosie and the consciously Shakespearean diction she uses summon up *Macbeth* as presence behind Joe's actions, the gaps between Macbeth and Joe being part of the film's reading of its own action.

Joe Macbeth is as striking for its careful and thoughtful adjustments to the hierarchies of Scotland as for its general vague faith-

---

7. "I saw birds—they were flying away. . . . Someone will die in this house. But the birds were all flying in one direction. That's a good omen. . . . With every death in this house, Macbeth shall rise." This scene, where Rosie reads her crystal ball for Lily, associates her tightly with the film's Lady Macbeth, much to Joe's annoyance: "I don't want that hag round here." Compare also Duca's comments on birds, the film's wryly witty transmutation of the "temple-haunting martlet" (1.6.4):

LENNY Did you ever see so many birds flying around outside. I guess they like it here.
DUCA Birds don't know from nothing. They're like people: they eat out of your hand one minute, bite it off the next.
BANKY You know, boss, you should a been a preacher.
DUCA I never got the call.

fulness. The opening murder of Tommy, the film's Thane of Cawdor, raises Joe's status in a sequence that Lily has no difficulty presenting as a continuous cycle of eliminated potential rivals (like Tommy's unseen predecessor, Little Mike), something without Shakespearean parallel. If Joe clings to values of loyalty and modest ambition ("I'm as far as I want to go right now"), such traditional morality is seen as cowardice in a world in which the "air-drawn dagger" (3.4.63) becomes a knife that Lily hands Joe: "The knife knows where to go, Joe. Just follow it." There is nothing fully supernatural in *Joe Macbeth*'s world, but there is an eeriness, embodied by Angus, the unnerving butler who comes with the Lakeview mansion. His offer of the housekeys to Lenny, Joe's apparent successor, is firmly rejected in the film's last lines of dialogue: "I suppose this means that you'll be the new master of the house, sir." "No, Angus. This is the end of the line. Better lock up and get yourself a new job."

The violent world of gangsterism is, though, seen as oddly beyond Joe. The murder of Lenny's wife and child (as it were, Lady Macduff and her son) is not planned by Joe but is a hostage-taking that went wrong when she refused to come meekly along and for which Joe is furious with the thugs who killed them. But such actions seem only too easy for Lenny, who moves in the film from being the nervy son who does not belong "in the racket," shooting his mouth off about his father's rights of succession (and earning a punch from his father in the process), into the dedicated avenger stalking his prey. If, as the doctor advises, it makes sense to treat Lily's ravings the modern way ("If you'll take my advice, you'll send for a psychiatrist"), then Lenny's neurotic, near-hysterical aggression deserves the same treatment.

If Lenny is the play's future, a continuation in a new guise of the film's view of the mobs, then the territory that is being fought over is defined as the nightclub, the mansion, and the continuing threat from neighbouring mob leaders, here the richly comic portrait of Dutch whose people muscle in on the Duke's land, burn out his club, and are only stopped when Dutch's crepes suzette are poisoned—and his greed stops Dutch from letting his personal taster try them first. Dutch, who calculates for Joe how many oysters he has eaten in his lifetime (given that he consumes five dozen a night), suggests the fragility of the borders of the Duke's land, how little he is able effectively to be "kingpin" or "King of the City." With borders unmarked on any map, the limits of this state—the Chicago Scotland,—appear, in the joke of Dutch's name, to neighbour Holland as well as Capone's.

But the state also exists within another, as if Illinois has another state of Duca or Macbeth or Dutch within it. In a film that manages so completely and so effectively to suppress the rest of the community within which and alongside which the gangster world is formed and run, the sense of states within states, countries and territories within others, is a disturbing effect. *Joe Macbeth* is not a great film: for all the cleverness of some of its thinking it is often poorly acted and weakly shot.[8] But the transpositions of place (not least from Macbeth's castle to the bleak rich style of the Lakeview mansion) redefine how modern territories are formed.

Scotland, NY

In the wake of the success of Coppola's *Godfather* trilogy, and especially Coppola's use of *King Lear* as an informing presence in the third part (1990), the combination of Shakespeare and the mafia must have seemed ripe for reconsideration. William Reilly, in his first and only film as writer / director, rethought the virtues of *Joe Macbeth* as *Men of Respect* (1991), set in New York. It is superbly acted, especially by John Turturro as Michael Battaglia (whose very name makes him the man of battles) and Katherine Borowitz as his wife Ruthie, and Reilly achieves a remarkably neurotic transposition, as if the edginess of *Joe Macbeth*'s had penetrated the leading roles. Turturro's wide-eyed stare is terrifying both in its danger to others and its revelation of the permanent edge of fear with which Mikey lives. Openly credited as "adapted" from *Macbeth, Men of Respect* uses the possibilities of allusion, with continuous potency. The film begins with the precredit sounds of news reports. Half-heard among the stories of the KGB plotting to kill the Pope (a KGB defector is quoted as saying "No secret lasts forever") or of heroin in an "unusually pure and smokeable form" on the streets ("local police forces are powerless to stem the tide") is a report that "unusual weather patterns continue to plague the metropolitan area." Throughout, lines are transposed, their idiom changed but retaining a curious power: it is not so long a journey from "then, as his host, / Who should against the murderer shut the door, / Not bear the knife myself" (1.7.14–16) to "I should be watching his back, not sticking in the knife myself." Or from "If it were done when 'tis done, then 'twere well / It were done quickly" (1.7.1–2) to "If it's gonna get done, it better get done quick." Reilly wrote, as it were, with an open copy of *Macbeth* on his desk, and the film asks to be watched with a sustained awareness of Shakespeare's play.

Macbeth's opening war has here become an attack on the territory of "Charles 'the little Padrino' d'Amico" (Rod Steiger) by a rival

---

8. Though it has nothing to do with the topic of this article, it is worth mentioning that this is the only version of *Macbeth* known to me in which Macbeth kills his wife: when Joe is preparing for the final shoot-out he forgets the gun by his bedside; Lily, the devoted wife, brings it to him and, reacting to an unexpected noise, Joe shoots, only to discover he has killed her—a neat and bleak ironic twist.

mafioso, Cordero. The tide is turned by Battaglia's murder of a number of people at a restaurant table. When the news comes to d'Amico, suspicious of who might be a loyal and who a traitor, he sends out men to find Battaglia: "When you find him, you treat him as a Man of Respect, is that clear? . . . Cordero's loss, that's Battaglia's gain." Battaglia and his partner, Banky Como, encounter the witches (a campy young man, a dapper middle-aged man, and the woman who utters the prophecies in a semi-trance) in a shuttered room on some wasteland. Battaglia, who is told he will become "capo regime" and that "the time comes when you will be called Padrino, Padrino Battaglia," wonders "What do I have to do for this to happen?" "You only have to be yourself, to do what you're thinking." The awareness of the will is all-important; the self creates its own futures. By contrast, Banky's reaction to the news that "your son will be Padrino" is a brusque rejection: "My son Philly in this business. Over my dead body."

What in *Joe Macbeth* had been barely glimpsed becomes in *Men of Respect* a fully fledged exploration of the state within the state. Battaglia is admitted as a Man of Respect in a solemn ceremony: "We are a fraternity of great honour and we welcome only men of strength, courage and loyalty, men of respect. Our way comes before anything else in life, before God, before country, before family." Mikey has, Charlie tells him, "earned yourself a very special place in our thing." The creation of the ritual, especially after the scene with the "weird sisters" has been so full of Catholic religious images (crosses, icons, small statues, candles, offerings), suggests the interconnection of religious practice and a murderous subculture. Whereas Rosie's reading tarot cards could be ignored, here the full-blown potency of the supernatural solicitings is embedded in the culture it affects.

Men of Respect deserves full-scale examination and praise for its often brilliant re-imaginings: the mad Ruthie doggedly scrubbing at the bathtub to remove the long-gone bloodstains from Charlie's murder or the transformation of Birnam Wood into the prophecy that "not till the stars fall from the heavens will Battaglia's blood be shed," which comes true when there is a massive fireworks display. But if Scotland is only present as a joke (Battaglia at his "coronation" party as Padrino is given a tip for a horse called "Great Scot"), the exploration of "England" and of the future movement of this version of the nation-state is thoughtful and provocative. When d'Amico's power seems ebbing he becomes suspicious of Duffy, "a mean fucking Irishman." This criminal world is not wholly Italian-American— there is room for another nationality's involvement: we are encouraged to see Duffy as a representative of another Catholic nation since his name comes from Father Duffy who ran the orphanage on 149th

Street in the Bronx outside which his dying mother was found in labour ("The intern ripped the little fucker from her belly."). D'Amico's *consigliere,* Carmelo Rossi, the film's Cawdor, urges d'Amico to retire to Florida. After defeating his enemies, d'Amico sends Rossi there. Not executed, this Cawdor will reappear later in "England."

Where *Joe Macbeth* eliminated Malcolm completely, *Men of Respect* leaves him in place as Mal (Stanley Tucci). Mal and his brother have fled not to England and Ireland but to Toronto (Canada as the American Ireland?) and Miami. Now, in the other space that constitutes this film's vision of that land outside Scotland, Mal consults with Cordero and Rossi, who agree to become Mal's *consigliere:* "I do not rest until we all spit on the grave of your father's murderer." In a switch from this increasingly murky world of deals in comfortable lounges, the conspirators meet Duffy in a bright garden, accompanied by troops of loyal men. Battaglia had been warned about Duffy by the "weird sister": "A large man with a red face . . . the complexion. An Irishman?" "Duffy." "This man is very dangerous to you. He doesn't respect you." Battaglia's response had been to blow up Duffy's car, killing his wife and child whom Duffy was taking for an outing at the zoo. Now Duffy promises to provide the muscle for the hit on Battaglia. Whatever else the film achieves, Reilly's revisioning of England into a conspiracy of rivals rather than as a repository for some ordered, blessed other concept of the state marks a considerable and effective act of imagination.

But it is less Mal d'Amico than Philip Como who shows the film's sense of a changing political order, a future that will relocate the nature of this Scotland, this world of violent power. If gangsters and hitmen are modern equivalents of the soldiers who can mean "to bathe in reeking wounds, / Or memorise another Golgotha" (1.2.39–40), then the new Scotland of Malcolm's intention becomes in *Men of Respect* the new way not of Mal but Philip. House-sharing with his father ("He cooks, I clean," says Banky proudly), Philip is not in the business as a hit man (as *Joe Macbeth*'s Banky had wanted to keep Lenny out of his world) but is, as his father even more proudly announces, "MBA Baruch." Banky urges Michael to talk with Philip, who can show new routes to legal profit, offering an echo of Coppola's Michael (Al Pacino), who desperately wants the Corleone family to be completely legitimate. If Duncan's world is unquestionably legitimate it is still founded on a culture and cycle of violence against which Malcolm's new regime may stand. Charlie and Mal come from and remain within a world of violence against which Philip offers an alternative. But when Philip is seen lurking behind the door while Mal plots with Rossi, spoken of as a useful man with a head for

numbers, and when he is, in the film's final sequence, inducted as
a Man of Respect, his final chilling smile indicates the new direction
he will eventually take the thing when he becomes Padrino. Cor-
porate America, rather than Jacobean England, is the destiny
towards which this line of *padrini* will stretch.

Scotland, Japan

Both *Men of Respect* and *Joe Macbeth* are underrated achieve-
ments. Akira Kurosawa's version of *Macbeth*, known in English-
speaking countries as *Throne of Blood*, though its Japanese title
means *Cobweb Castle*,[9] has been accorded the proper respect due to
its immense brilliance. The third of the cultural displacements I am
considering, *Throne of Blood* (dis / re)places *Macbeth* into the Sen-
goku period of civil wars in Japan (1467–1568). Far from *Macbeth*'s
suggestion of a previous period of relative stability and a subsequent
history leading towards James, Kurosawa's film deliberately chooses
a period of disruption in samurai culture and of continuous instability. As many critics have commented, Kurosawa's choice transforms the regicide from a profoundly transgressive act into one of
almost routine occurrence. And as James Goodwin notes, the period
was one "when there were frequent incidents of *gekokujo*, the overthrow of a superior by his own retainers."[1] Just as Lily warns Joe
Macbeth that Duca will have him killed if he doesn't eliminate him,
so Asaji (Lady Macbeth) warns Washizu (Macbeth) that "Only two
choices exist . . . sitting and waiting to be killed by our lord . . . or
killing our lord to become Lord of Kumonosu Castle yourself."[2]

Asaji's argument depends on the risk of Miki's (Banquo) revealing
the prophecy of the single witch the two have met in the enigmatic,
labyrinthine space of Cobweb Forest:

9. The subtitles and the published screenplay both use this form but it sounds to me too
   much like a novel by the eighteenth-century novelist Thomas Love Peacock. "Spider's-
   Web Castle" might be better, if less alliterative. See Akira Kurosawa, *"Seven Samurai" and
   Other Screenplays* (London: Faber and Faber, 1992). There is a large and ever-growing
   critical literature on Kurosawa's film. I note, as particularly helpful with my thinking about
   its accomplishments, Anthony Davies, *Filming Shakespeare's Plays* (Cambridge: Cambridge University Press, 1988), 152–66; John S. Collick, *Shakespeare, Cinema and Society*
   (Manchester, Eng.: Manchester University Press, 1989); Peter S. Donaldson, *Shakespear-
   ean Films / Shakespeare Directors* (Boston: Unwin Hyman, 1990) 69–92; James Goodwin,
   Akira Kurosawa and Intertextual Cinema (Baltimore: Johns Hopkins University Press,
   1994); Robert Hapgood, "Kurosawa's Shakespeare Films: *Throne of Blood, The Bad Sleep
   Well,* and *Ran,*" in Anthony Davies and Stanley Wells, eds., *Shakespeare and the Moving
   Image* (Cambridge: Cambridge University Press, 1994), 234–49; and Donald Richie, *The
   Films of Akira Kurosawa* (3rd ed., expanded with a new epilogue; Berkeley: University of
   California Press, 1998).
1. Goodwin, 176.
2. Kurosawa, *"Seven Samurai" and Other Screenplays,* 237 (ellipses original). The screenplay
   and the subtitles are rarely the same; unless otherwise noted I quote from the screenplay,
   even though it represents the script at an earlier stage of development from the shooting
   script.

> If . . . General Yoshiaki Miki should reveal the prophecy . . .
> then, we won't be left as we are. Our lord, taking you for a
> usurper threatening his throne . . . he will surely besiege the
> North Castle with his men without delay.[3]

It is not, of course, that killing one's superior becomes permissible:
as Washizu responds, "It is high treason to kill our lord!" But in the
system that Kurosawa is exploring through Asaji's voice, the process
can be cyclical: "he himself ascended the throne by killing his previous lord, as you well know."[4]

The historical-political context, then, deliberately weakens the disruptive effect of the murder of the ruler. Only success matters, and
the consequences have nothing to do with divine retribution and
everything to do with holding one's nerve. But the conflicts are not
only internal. Neither Duncan nor his successors seem to want to
take further action against Sweno, the King of Norway who, helped
by Cawdor, had besieged Fife. The defeat is so complete that Sweno
"craves composition" and pays "Ten thousand dollars to our general
use" before even being allowed to bury his dead (1.2.60–63). But
Inui (Sweno), who had been helped by Fujimaki (Cawdor), poses a
threat that is not resolved by the comparable victory. Clearly contig-
uous as landmass, Inui's territory is one from which he can invade
easily—at the opening of the film he has crossed with four hundred
men to besiege the First Fort, taking the opportunity created by seeing the success of Fujimaki's campaign against the Fifth and Fourth
Forts. With Washizu's victory, Kuniharu's (Duncan) response is to
order the border defences to be strengthened against future incur-
sions.

Asaji's encouragement to murder Kuniharu is immediately met by
the arrival at the North Castle (Inverness) of Kuniharu and a large
army, ostensibly on a hunting expedition. There is no notion here
that the opportunity for the regicide happens because Duncan
wishes to accord Macbeth honor by visiting him. Instead the arrival
of the troops, totally and unnervingly unexpected by Washizu, is part
of a secret plan to crush Inui because, as Kuniharu says, "I can
endure Inui's behaviour no longer." The political aftermath of the
murder is that Kuniharu's son (Malcolm) will take refuge with Inui,
that Washizu will claim Miki was murdered by a spy sent by Inui,
that Miki's son (Fleance) will also turn to Inui, and that the invading
army at the end, under the direct command of Noriyasu, Kuniharu's
senior general (a figure who has no exact equivalent in *Macbeth*),
will also be Inui's. At the end of *Ran,* Kurosawa's 1985 rethinking
of *King Lear,* it is clear that the chaos (the meaning of the title)

3. Kurosawa, 237.
4. Kurosawa, 238.

brought about in Hidetora's (Lear's) state will result in the invasion by neighboring lords whose troops are seen watching the final battles, ready to move in. By in effect, conflating Sweno and Edward the Confessor in *Throne of Blood*, Kurosawa makes Inui's land a physically adjacent geographic space as well as edged by a fluid border across which invasion can move in either direction. Just as in *Hamlet* Denmark is finally absorbed into the Norwegian empire, so in *Throne of Blood* it is the film's unseen equivalent of Norway that seems most likely to triumph.

But the political geography of the landscape in Kurosawa's film seems less significant than the physical geography. A film that makes castles appear and disappear in mists as it moves from the opening image of the site of the castle to its reality, proves profoundly to be exploring the natural landscape as a feature of human action in ways that we could call—for lack of a better word—Shakespearean. As Peter Donaldson has shown, Kurosawa's research on castles from the period taught him that some castles had mazes of forests deliberately grown in front of them.[5] The space in which Washizu and Miki encourage the spirit, one whose paths they ought to know, is a man-made defense mechanism, midway, as it were, between the human and the natural. The castle of the spider's web is protected by a forest whose intricately branching paths are the source of the castle's name.

For *Macbeth*s set in the twentieth-century city, like *Joe Macbeth* and *Men of Respect*, the nonurban is merely vestigial: the overgrown wasteland in which Battaglia will find the witches; the courtyard garden behind his restaurant, complete with stone birdbath for Ruthie's hand-washing in the sleepwalking scene, a space in which Mikey throws parties; the lake behind the Lakeview mansion in which Duca takes an early morning swim and where Joe murders him. If the play's emphasis on birds always seems to produce a corresponding avian excess in films, the nonhuman is only an echo of a landscape imagined beyond the city. But in *Throne of Blood* the human world plants itself squarely, though vulnerably, in a rolling landscape, the bare space across which woods can move.

If filmed *Macbeth*s have a natural yearning to produce swirling mists, Kurosawa's vision makes mist a sign of nature's wiping out of the human, the device that takes the film from the present, where Cobweb Castle is nothing more than a single pillar describing it as the castle's vestigial site, to the historic past of the film's main action. The unseen chorus intones a moral lesson that "The devil's path will always lead to doom," but it also defines the link of castle to human: "A proud castle stood in this desolate place / Its destiny wedded to a

5. Donaldson, 72.

mortal's lust for power."[6] The castle and control over it is the path of human desire, given that Washizu's rise is charted as a move from fort to fort, much to the delight of his household (as Kurosawa makes clear in a series of short exchanges between the serving men, a workers' commentary that Shakespeare might well have admired). But the mist becomes also the defining feature of the fogginess of the maze. As they ride towards the castle, Washizu and Miki are lost in the rain-soaked forest, a labyrinth that even they, the great defenders of the castle's ruler, cannot penetrate by keeping to its confusing paths: its forest-spirit holds them, bringing them to the meeting with the witch. Whatever its origins, the forest is now not within human control but is, instead, the location of the supernatural. Following the prophecies, the spirit's hut, (the hut is a bamboo form that mediates the natural into the ambiguous, with its open walls) vanishes, while Washizu and Miki find the heaps of skulls and armour that seems the true end of their inquiry. But Kurosawa then makes their journey toward the castle defined by mist, not a wooded landscape. In the film's most famous and virtuosic sequence, the two horsemen ride to and fro, towards the camera and away from it, at diagonals to it and across its plane of depth, each time coming out of and back into mists as mazey as any forest trail. If the labyrinth of the spider's web forest is human in origin, this mistiness is most emphatically not, a murky feature of the film's supernatural. Mist and forest are the same thing: the space that confuses and disorients the riders—and the viewers.

It is hardly surprising then that the moving wood at the end should be accompanied by dawn mists, but Kurosawa also displaces the equivalent of Malcolm's instruction "Let every soldier hew him down a bough" (5.4.4) until after Washizu's death, when Noriyasu gives the order "Conceal yourselves among the branches"[7] What Washizu sees, the unnerving sight of "a moving grove" (5.5.38), is as inexplicable to the spectators as to Washizu and his men. The natural really does seem to be moving, like some version of Tolkien's Ents, and it will lead directly towards the hail of arrows that will turn Washizu into a human pincushion. The film's buildings are all wooden, extensions and transmutations of the forest, and the arrows are as well. The final arrow that so memorably transfixes Washizu through the neck comes, as Donaldson accurately notes,

> from a place to which we have seen no archers ascend: offscreen right . . . The shot is not merely unexpected, then, but hints at a supernatural retribution. . . .[8]

6. Subtitles. The published screenplay's text is radically different here.
7. Kurosawa, 266.
8. Donaldson, 87.

Washizu, clattering down the ladders to the ground level of the mass of his troops, falls before them in a cloud of dust, as if the mists are enveloping him again and finally. It is only a short step from these mists to the ones that will take us back through time to the present, as if the natural and supernatural have swallowed up almost all traces the human world can leave on this landscape, leaving only those markers of former glory.

The moving wood is part of the merging of the nonhuman and human, but this merger is also established by Noriyasu's wise response to the barrier that the forest poses. If the forest paths are a maze controlled by the spirit world far more than as a man-made defense, then the answer is to ignore them: "Don't take the roads where you will go astray. When you have once entered the forest, proceed through the trees straight ahead."[9] When the army, spread out line abreast, enters the forest, it poses no problem, absorbing the army and eventually, as mobile camouflage, simply blends seamlessly with the army; the restorers of moral order and the natural are now intermingled. This disturbance of the separation between human and natural will also send its own message to the castle when, during the night before the siege, the castle is invaded by "a flock of wild birds,"[1] an ominous occurrence that Washizu tries unconvincingly to read as benign. The vulnerable borders of the state's political geography and the permeable divisions between the human and nonhuman are then explored by Kurosawa as structural parallels, dense signs of the fragility of the human will.

Only in one place in the film's locations does the human make a quasi-permanent mark: in the room in the North Castle where Fujimaki killed himself, leaving a bloodstain that cannot be scraped off, a mark seen on the room's wall. It is from this room, displaced from their own room by the need for Kuniharu to sleep in the castle's best room, that Asaji and Washizu will move to the murder, as if Fujimaki's blood produces a dynamic towards further bloodletting. The indelible trace of Fujimaki is a combination of the human and the supernatural, a sign that "blood will have blood" (3.4.124) here too.

But it is also only in one place in the film that the human makes what one might define as a normative mark on the landscape: when Kuniharu and his "hunting party" ride towards Washizu's castle, they move through rice fields, the film's only signs of agriculture, of the cultivation of the natural for other than warlike ends.

9. Kurosawa, 259. The screenplay describes the advancing army here as a "formation of troops . . . shaped like the wings of a crane", something that I cannot see on the film but which may be recognizable to a Japanese viewer.
1. Kurosawa, 262.

Scotland, Wales

Of the five films, by far the most conventional in its approach to both a traditional view of the play and the realist modes of film is Roman Polanski's 1971 *Macbeth*.[2] The film's location work was shot in Wales (and, to a lesser extent, in England), creating a mostly predictable and uninteresting context of the real as the countryside behind the action. Scotland is only strongly marked in the king's banners and in the use of music (the sword dance at Macbeth's castle and the Celtic inflections of the unremittingly dreadful film score by the Third Ear Band) or in the occasional Scottish inflection of a voice (for example, Frank Wylie's Menteith). Otherwise it is no more than the cliched vague place of historical costume-drama, barely more interesting than that of Jeremy Freeston's 1996 film.

The locations' only special emphasis is a dirtiness, typified by the mud that covers the hems of everyone's robes and which weighs down Macbeth's nightgown as he leads Macduff to the discovery of Duncan's body. As much symbolic as authentic, the dirt is part of the sordid society Polanski charts, a world in which the Macbeth's evils are generated by a social practice of murder—for example, in the first shot after the credits where a soldier, finding that a facedown figure on the battlefield is not quite dead, promptly and brutally dispatches him.

Polanski chose to film in Britain because "I needed the kind of brooding, gray, autumnal skies so typical of the British Isles," but the filming in Wales enveloped the cast and crew

> in an icy, almost incessant downpour . . . [in which] makeup ran, beards came unstuck, horses panicked. When the rain stopped, fog reduced visibility to a few yards. The locations we'd chosen for the witches' scenes became accessible only to four-wheel-drive vehicles capable of crossing the sea of rich, greasy mud in which we spent our days.[3]

Not all the film's pervasive dampness is then deliberate, though Polanski is prone to heavy-handed weather symbolism like the thunderclaps that accompany Lady Macbeth's welcoming Duncan to Inverness, an overly portentous device inadequately naturalized into

---

2. Most work on Polanski's film has been pruriently obsessed by the connections with the Manson family's murder of Polanski's wife, Sharon Tate: see, for example, Bryan Reynolds, "Untimely Ripped: Mediating Witchcraft in Polanski and Shakespeare," in Lisa L. Starks and Courtney Lehmann, eds., *The Reel Shakespeare* (Madison, NJ: Fairleigh Dickinson Press, 2002), 143–64. But see the fine account of the successive scripts of the film in Bernice W. Kliman, "Gleanings: The Residue of Difference in Scripts: The Case of Polanski's *Macbeth*," in Jay L. Halio and Hugh Richmond, eds., *Shakespearean Illuminations* (Newark: University of Delaware Press, 1998), 131–46.
3. Roman Polanski, *Roman by Polanski* (London: Heinemann, 1984), 293–94. On the making of the film, see also Barbara Leaming, *Polanski: His Life and Films* (London: Hamish Hamilton, 1982), 76–89.

the real by the subsequent sudden downpour. If the film's first shot offers a similarly over-elaborated natural image in the blood-red sun spreading its potent color across the landscape, the location itself— the foreshore of an endless beach in which the weird sisters bury a hangman's noose, a severed arm, and a dagger, marking the spot with blood at least until the tide will obliterate the site—functions as a marginal space, a liminal transition that is ambiguously sea and land and where foul and fair might well be indistinguishable. It is in this space that the slaughter of the battle has taken place, and the bleak landscape seems appropriate for such pervasive human brutality: Macbeth is almost inevitably first seen supervising, with Banquo, the mass hanging of rebel soldiers, before he rides off (bored? disgusted?), and Banquo has to wheel and follow him.

Polanski's witches—one elderly and blind from birth, one middle-aged, and one young and dumb[4]—are not in the least spirits but instead poor women who are self-evidently extra-social, exactly the kind who were burnt as witches throughout early modern Europe. Kenneth Tynan, the English theater critic who collaborated with Polanski on the script, thought that "they should be presented in such a way that any sensible person in the audience might also find them trustworthy . . . more like spiritualist mediums than demons— morally neutral creatures who may inspire us with a faint twinge of unease but certainly should not make us shudder with revulsion."[5] But the result is nothing like the "Hindu holy men in loincloths with matted hair" Tynan envisaged. Though apparently semi-domesticated, living in a hovel, these weird sisters live beyond community. They do, however, become part of a greater network of female culture: Macbeth's second encounter with them begins with a young witch leading him into the underground hovel, a hell that is filled with naked women who prepare the cauldron brew and give it to him to drink, as if its psychotropic powers are a belated example of 1960s drug counterculture. The scene is a remarkable combination of a conservative revulsion of hippiedom mixed with visual cliches of female heterodox activity.

What little remains of the "English" scene in the screenplay is not played in England at all but instead among the tents where the English troops are preparing for the war. Polanski also adds a scene where the English army unites with a Scottish one. There is, in effect, no land beyond Scotland here. What matters instead is the film's rather relentless exploration of the margins between inside and out, the border not of country but of the edge of human construc-

---

4. Did Polanski therefore want to hint that the middle one is deaf? If so, there is no apparent trace in the film.
5. Kenneth Tynan, *Letters*, ed. by Kathleen Tynan (London: Weidenfeld and Nicholson, 1994), 478.

tion. *Macbeth,* of course, makes use of that sense of looking across
the landscape, most obviously in the reported sight of Birnam Wood
("As I did stand my watch upon the hill" [5.5.33]). Shakespeare films
have often been interested in the view from windows, especially in
Olivier's *Henry V* (1944) and his *Richard III* (1955). But Polanski's
Macbeth makes it into an obsessive motif so that Macbeth can only
anticipate Banquo's murder by opening the window and looking
across the countryside towards the spot where the murder will take
place. While the film also emphasizes its castles' gates—like the
gates Ross silently instructs Lady Macduff's servant to leave open
for the murderers to enter or the one Macbeth's deserting soldiers
unbar as they leave with their loot—windows function determinedly
as signs of the look beyond, the means of connecting the closed inner
world to the outer. Hence, for instance, Polanski signals Lady Macbeth's madness by having her slumped asleep on a stool at right
angles to a window, making no attempt to look through it, her with-
drawal defined by this disconnection from the vantage point she usually occupied.

If the film became notorious for the banality of its final sequence,
in which the cyclical character of evil is indicated by having Donalbain, limping like a proto-Richard III, going to consult the witches,
its presentation of the final battle shows a more striking approach to
the conflict between human activity and the unnatural or supernatural of this film's world. The arrival of the besieging army is remarkably bombastic. The moving wood fools no one, except perhaps
Macbeth himself, because the script has transferred "Let every soldier hew him down a bough" (5.4.4) from Malcolm to a glum conversation between two of Macbeth's soldiers who take one look at
the wood on the move and knowingly tell each other "Every soldier
has hewn him down a bough." "It shadows the numbers of their host
and makes discovery err in report of them."[6] The army arrives with
catapults firing flaming missiles and camouflaged battering rams, but
none of this military paraphernalia is necessary since the castle is
now deserted except for Macbeth himself, seated on his throne, waiting for all these men born of women.

The invaders may have "tied me to a stake" (5.7.1), but Polanski
turns Macbeth's self-description as "bear-like" (2) into a literal reference, with Macbeth standing by the metal ring in the pillar to
which the bear was tied as bait for the coronation celebrations.
Polanski had wanted the bear-baiting to be an extensive scene, but
it proved technically impossible.[7] Instead the animal, which, rather
than Banquo, is jokingly identified by Macbeth as "our chief guest"

6. I have printed this as prose since, obviously, it is no longer quite in the rhythms of Shakespeare's verse.
7. For an account of the comic failure to film the scene, see Leaming, 83–84.

(3.1.11), is seen dragged along as a dead carcass, leaving smears of blood across the castle floor. The bloodthirstiness that enjoys bear-baiting reappears at the end in the soldiers' jeering at Macbeth's decapitated head, a sight that Polanski shockingly films from Macbeth's point of view, the last images the dying eyes see.

The world Polanski creates is almost always determinedly secular. Though there is, surprisingly, a trio of rough crosses outside the weird sisters' hovel and a cross is briefly glimpsed in the flames that consume Macduff's castle at Fife, Polanski kept to Tynan's view of the play's secularity: "No Christianity except Banquo in 'the great hand of God' line. There is evil but no organized good in this universe."[8] The coronation of Macbeth takes place in a stone circle and is resolutely non-Christian. This has strange consequences for the film's look: as Pearlman rather pedantically comments, "[i]n order to salvage a dark-age setting, Polanski even falls into the anachronism of juxtaposing late medieval fortifications and armaments to neolithic religion."[9] Its secularism seems to be the social landscape out of which the violence of the film so unrestrainedly emerges. More than any other film of *Macbeth*, Polanski's understands the brutality of Shakespeare's play world.

Some Shakespeare films simply do not wear well over time, and Polanski's *Macbeth* now looks oddly timid in its solutions, trapped by a view of period and space that is too bound by cinematic convention to find anything approximating the demands of the play. Only in the brilliant conflation of various roles to create a version of Ross as the arch traitor, the ever-smiling true villain of the play, and an ironic choice to hail Malcolm as the new king, does the film's reading of the play seem lastingly powerful.[1] The deliberate use of realist location is only one part of a dull film-method that brought Shakespeare too close to costume epic for comfort.

Scotland, UT

In 1947 the Utah Centennial Commission and the American National Theater Association invited Orson Welles to direct and star in a stage production of *Macbeth* in Salt Lake City. Welles was already in negotiation with the Republic Studio to film the play, to make what would be the first American film-studio production of Shakespeare since the Reinhardt/Dieterle *A Midsummer Night's Dream* for Warner Brothers in 1935. Republic, even while defining the film project as one of their premiere projects, still stuck to a

---

8. Tynan, *Letters*, 475.
9. See E. Pearlman, "*Macbeth* on Film: Politics," in Wells and Davies, eds., *op. cit.*, 253; this quotation unfairly represents an otherwise interesting article.
1. Kliman is especially interesting on the late decision to create this character, so superbly acted by John Stride.

budget of only $800,000. The Utah production provided Welles with a number of ways to cut costs. Utilizing primarily the same cast, Welles could obviously economize on rehearsal time—something Shakespeare needed but which film budgets could not tolerate—but he also took more extreme measures: the sound for the film was prerecorded in Utah so that filming was done by the actors lip-synching to the already existing tracks. He also used the Utah sets as the primary locations for the film, leaving very visible shots of their origins all over the film in the flat platforms out of which the rocky structures emerge.

In the end the sound became one of the film's more notorious features. Shot in a mere twenty-three days (by comparison, Olivier's 1948 *Hamlet,* with which Welles's film was always unfavourably compared and whose success at the Venice Film Festival resulted in *Macbeth* being withdrawn from competition, was shot over thirty-two weeks), Welles's *Macbeth*'s rough and ready look was bound to rile critics. Before the film was properly distributed in 1951, the studio took over the product and butchered it, cutting the running time of approximately 107 minutes[2] by about 20 minutes and demanding that the actors' voices be rerecorded to eliminate the remarkable and distinctive timbre Welles wanted. The 1980 UCLA / Folger Shakespeare Library restoration of Welles's original, the only version currently available on video or DVD, still left in the quirky music score by Jacques Ibert that the studio incorporated but cut the explanatory prologue that Welles was made to include for the release print.[3]

Welles chose to record the soundtrack with the actors' using Scottish accents. The results are, to say the least, variable, but Welles's purpose was not primarily driven by the play's location. As Richard Wilson, Welles's assistant, noted,

> We didn't put a Scoth dialect in the picture because Macbeth was laid in Scotland. A Scotch dialect was put in because we determined **after careful tests,** that the intelligibility was greater with the Scotch accent, because it had a tendency to slow the actors down just enough to make it more comprehensible to the ear. The secondary reason was that it absolutely

2. There is some evidence that the film as Welles first delivered it ran for as much as 135 minutes; see Luke McKernan and Olwen Terris, eds., *Walking Shadows* (London: BFI Publishing, 1994), 92.
3. The multiple versions of the film are often discussed in the fine criticism the film has produced. See, for example, Michael Anderegg, *Orson Welles, Shakespeare and Popular Cinema* (New York: Columbia University Press, 1999), 74–97; Bernice W. Kliman, "Welles's *Macbeth,* A Textual Parable," in Michael Skovmand, ed., *Screen Shakespeare* (Aarhus: Aarhus University Press, 1994), 25–37; Pamela Mason, "Orson Welles and Filmed Shakespeare," in Jackson, *op. cit.,* 184–89; Neil Forsyth, "Shakespeare the Illusionist: Filming the Supernatural," in Jackson, *op. cit.,* 274–94, especially 282–86. Anthony Davies's often brilliant analysis of the film (*op. cit,* 82–99) seems to have been made without having seen the restored version, though published in 1988.

made it impossible for the actor to sing his lines ala Shakespearian declamation.[4]

Whatever the aim—and the result is slower, nondeclamatory, and
comprehensible in spite of most actors' inability to sustain the
effect—the result is to underpin the film's gestures towards realist
Scottishness, just as the Caribbean accent of the African-American
actors in Welles's 1937 stage production of the play at the Lafayette
Theater in Harlem both helped the cast and emphasized Welles's
setting in Haiti. The film score uses the distant sound of the skirl of
bagpipes to indicate the advancing Anglo-Scots armies (though there
is no sign of bagpipes in the shots of the troops), and costume often
includes plaids thrown over a shoulder, draped across Macbeth's
head, or, for Malcolm, accompanied by a full-dress kilt. There is no
doubt of the geography with such referentiality.

Yet Welles's visual language for the play is emphatically not that
of realist location. Mostly shot on the sets for the Utah production
(themselves visibly derived as stage-forms from the 1937 designs),
with flat stage-floor and vast rocky outcrops that somehow fore-
ground their papier-mâché origins, the film almost ostentatiously
shows off its cheapness, its sheer staginess. As Michael Anderegg
argues,

> That Macbeth, just before his second encounter with the
> witches, stands in front of what appears to be a blank scrim
> against which, as lightning flashes overhead, we see his shadow
> projected, would not be notable on a stage; in a film, of course,
> it becomes an almost scandalous instance of showing the appa-
> ratus, of "baring the device."[5]

Overhead shots reveal the bold, coarse painting of the stage floor;
scenes in entirely different fictive spaces are plainly shot on exactly
the same set albeit from a slightly different angle; Lady Macduff is
apparently murdered at Macbeth's castle; and Macbeth's throne
seems to be placed on a staircase in the castle courtyard. None of
these disjunctions would surprise in the theater, but all work aggres-
sively against cinematic forms and expectations.

Perhaps the most remarkable sequence in such respects is Macbeth's receiving the report of Banquo's murder and then walking
towards the banquet scene. He appears to be in a subterranean maze
hewn from the rock, with water dripping off the ceiling (and onto
the soundtrack) or cascading down the walls—the water is forceful
enough for Macbeth to wash in it before he emerges for the banquet
from between two inordinately large barrels. Jean Cocteau, in one

4. Quoted Kliman, 33 (emphasis original).
5. Anderegg, 83.

of the most sympathetic readings the film received early in its life, saw the effect as a kind of temporal ambiguity supporting a dream vision:

> Coiffed with horns and crowns of cardboard, clad in animal skins like the first motorists, the heroes of the drama move in the corridors of a kind of dream underground, in devastated caves leaking water, in an abandoned coal-mine . . . at times we ask ourselves in what age this nightmare is taking place, and when we encounter Lady Macbeth for the first time before the camera moves back and places her, we almost see a lady in modern dress lying on a fur couch next to the telephone.[6]

In this form of reading, where the defects of budget become the strengths of the film's constructed meaning, even the voices can be heard as deliberately and effectively odd. Cocteau knew that the sound might be "unbearable to English ears" but thought that "this is what one can expect from these bizarre monsters who express in a monstrous language the words of Shakespeare, which remain their words."[7]

If we see the film's sets as a kind of realist definition of eleventh-century Scottish castles, then it becomes willfully disruptive. If the set is left as a form of expressionist cinema in which place is only meaning and never context, if, that is, space is allowed to be as meta-phorical as anything in the play's densely imagistic spoken language, then Welles's landscape is supremely functional because it denies the realist functionality that landscape on film is supposed to have. For all its frequent banality and even cliché, Welles's use of space in *Macbeth* never fails to provoke. Thus the caverns of the castle are seen as the tunnels of the mind through which Macbeth wanders, a space of deliberate interiority accompanied by voice-over echoes of Banquo's parting lines, a journey of confrontation with what has been done that necessarily conjures up the ghost of Banquo in the next sequence, at a banquet claustrophobically compressed by the canopy that overhangs the entire length of the table. Thought, gen-erates event here and, as Anthony Davies argues persuasively, space and the body are conjoined:

> The spatial substance, in some affinitive way, takes on the invol-untary biochemistry of Macbeth. Its cavernous walls exude drops of moisture just as Macbeth's skin glistens with the torrid sweat of panic.[8]

6. Quoted in Joseph McBride, *Orson Welles* (London: Secker and Warburg, 1972), 112. Compare Claude Beylie's definition of the film as "redolent of both the Paleolithic and atomic eras" (quoted in Anderegg, 84) and Anderegg's own sense of the film's Scotland as "not so much prehistoric as outside history" (84).
7. McBride, 112–13.
8. Davies, 89.

The struggle with the forms of space is part of the film's more generalized struggle to create form. Macbeth and his wife, in particular, are repeatedly threatened by swirling mists that define the lure of formlessness, of an undefined universe in which action becomes freer or at least morally disengaged. André Bazin called Welles's universe prehistoric—a prehistoric "not that of our ancestors, the Gauls or the Celts, but a prehistory of the conscience at the birth of time and sin."[9] The opening shots that move between mists and the bubbling contents of the weird sisters' cauldron resolve into a mass of clay which the witches sculpt into an image of Macbeth (and which they will later crown and decapitate as the action moves forward), a new version of the voodoo doll of the 1937 stage production. Form emerging out of formlessness is thus the witches' landscaping of the play.

Welles's prologue for the release-print spoke of the film's time frame:

> Our story is laid in Scotland, ancient Scotland, savage, half lost in the mist which hangs between recorded history and the time of legends. The cross itself is newly arrived here. Plotting against Christian law and order are the agents of chaos, priests of hell and magic; sorcerers and witches.[1]

If there is little sense in the film of a political alternative (England becomes a stage set of a hillock dominated by a massive stone Celtic cross), the true opposition that underpins the film is between Christianity and the witches' paganism. For Welles, Macbeth was "a member of the Christian community" whom "the forces of evil" that "represent ancient religion, paganism" are "fighting to win . . . over. Even at the end, Macbeth remains a member of the Christian world and continues to fight to save his integrity."[2] Welles here may be retrospectively rewriting his film: borrowing a process that was a fundamental part of his voodoo *Macbeth* of 1937, the witches are present at various unexpected junctures, and the film ends with them outside the castle chanting the displaced line, "Peace, the charm's wound up" (1.3.38). The sheer power of these figures, whose faces are barely seen, clutching their tall two-pronged staves, become explicitly an infernal trinity set against the film's pervasive presence of a Christian alternative. The Scottish soldiers, for example, carry three-pronged, Trinitarian spears; the English army is accompanied by a veritable forest of Celtic crosses; and Malcolm and Macduff have crosses on their helmets.

9. Quoted Davies, 89.
1. Quoted Davies, 87; note Welles's use of mist here.
2. Interview with Richard Marienstras in 1974, reprinted in Mark W. Estrin, ed., *Orson Welles: Interviews* (Jackson, MS: University Press of Mississippi, 2002), 151–52.

Most emphatically of all, where the sordid political world of Polanski's film would be defined by the aggregation of various characters into the smiling Ross, Welles's created character—whom he named the Holy Father, whose lines come from Ross, Angus, and the Old Man—seeps into every aspect of the film. As Duncan arrives to visit the Macbeths, the Holy Father leads the assembled troops in a baptismal catechism ("Dost thou renounce Satan and all his works?") while they stand holding lighted candles. By invoking the need for St. Michael to be "our safeguard against the wiles and wickedness of the devil," the Holy Father becomes the play's sign of a Christian good. At his first appearance, for instance, he sends the witches scurrying for cover; as Macbeth muses aloud whether "This supernatural soliciting / Cannot be ill," he looks at the Holy Father and firmly asserts "cannot be good" (1.3.134), as if otherwise subject to a religious reproof; and it is the Holy Father who warns Lady Macduff and later encourages Macduff to join the invaders. During the siege of Macbeth's castle at the end of the play, Macbeth throws his spear at the Holy Father, killing him and thereby provoking the invaders to burst through the gates, as if this act of "sacrilegious murder" (2.3.62) is an echo from Duncan, a sign of Macbeth's final capitulation to the dark forces of the pagan world. If the Holy Father's wig of long, dangling braids looks now irresistibly comic, his presence is the most profound definition of the moral landscape Welles seeks to create. In the politics of Welles's *Macbeth* the play becomes set in a location of religious conflict, its moral choices ultimately defined as the acceptance of a Christian state religion or its subversive opposite, the demonic powers whose presence in the film's last shots unnervingly suggests the incompleteness of Christianity's triumph. Welles's rejection of a realist landscape, in part forced on him by the exigencies of the tiny budget, result in the creation of an interior moral space, a landscape more congruent with Shakespeare's than that of any other filmmaker.

Selected Bibliography

• indicates works included or excerpted in this Norton Critical Edition.

A standard and engaging biography of Shakespeare is S. Schoenbaum, *William Shakespeare: A Compact Documentary Life* (New York: Oxford University Press, 1977); another deft, readable account of the life and works is Stanley Wells, *Shakespeare: A Dramatic Life* (London: Sinclair-Stevenson, 1994). Katherine Duncan-Jones unsettles received opinions and sheds light on Shakespeare's cultural backgrounds in *Ungentle Shakespeare: Scenes from His Life* (London: Arden Shakespeare, 2001).

On Shakespeare's theaters, E. K. Chambers has written a reference book, *The Elizabethan Stage*, 4 vols. (Oxford: Clarendon, 1923). Andrew Gurr provides much information in *The Shakespearean Stage, 1574–1642* (Cambridge: Cambridge University Press, 1970; 1980; 1992) and *Playgoing in Shakespeare's London* (Cambridge: Cambridge University Press, 1987; 1996); with Mariko Ichikawa, Gurr has written a brief introduction, *Staging in Shakespeare's Theatres* (Oxford: Oxford University Press, 2000).

On these and related issues like authorship, canon, staging, language, genre, sources, printing, and adaptations, the following editions of Shakespeare provide informed accounts and suggestions for further reading: (complete works in one volume) ed. Stanley Wells and Gary Taylor, 1987; ed. David Bevington, updated 5th ed., 2003; ed. G. Blakemore Evans and J. J. M. Tobin, 2nd ed., 1997; ed. Stephen Greenblatt, et al., 1997; (individual works in separate volumes) The Oxford Shakespeare, The New Cambridge Shakespeare, The Arden Shakespeare, The New Folger Library Shakespeare, The Pelican Shakespeare, The Bantam Shakespeare, The Signet Classic Shakespeare, The Bedford Shakespeare (with texts and contexts). There are also a number of helpful companions to Shakespeare that offer sound guidance and rich overviews for beginning and advanced students: *The Bedford Companion to Shakespeare* (with primary documents), ed. Russ McDonald, 2nd ed., 2001; the "companions" edited by David Scott Kastan (Oxford: Oxford University Press, 1999); Michael Dobson and Stanley Wells (Oxford: Oxford University Press, 2001); Margreta de Grazia and Stanley Wells (Cambridge: Cambridge University Press, 2001), and others in the *Cambridge Companion* series, gathering critical essays on Shakespeare and film, the stage, his tragedies, comedies, and histories. The *Oxford Shakespeare Topics* series publishes brief volumes treating Shakespeare and dramatic genres, film, race, reading, the arts of language, the Bible, women, masculinity, and other issues.

The annual bibliographies of *Shakespeare Quarterly* and *PMLA* (*Publications of the Modern Language Association*) provide comprehensive listings of publications.

FURTHER READING AND RESEARCH ON *MACBETH*

• Adelman, Janet. *Suffocating Mothers: Fantasies of Maternal Origin in Shakespeare's Plays,* Hamlet *to* The Tempest. London: Routledge, 1992.

Bartholomeusz, Dennis. Macbeth *and the Players.* Cambridge: Cambridge University Press, 1969.

Berger, Harry, Jr. "The Early Scenes of *Macbeth:* Preface to a New Interpretation." *English Literary History* 47 (1980), 1–31.

Blayney, Peter W. M. *The First Folio of Shakespeare.* Washington: Folger Library Publications, 1991.

• Bradley, A. C. *Shakespearean Tragedy: Lectures on* Hamlet, Othello, King Lear, Macbeth. London: Macmillan & Co., 1904.

• Braunmuller, A. R., ed. *Macbeth.* Cambridge: Cambridge University Press, 1997.

Brooks, Cleanth. *The Well Wrought Urn: Studies in the Structure of Poetry.* New York: Reynal & Hitchcock, 1947.

Brown, John Russell, ed. *Focus on* Macbeth. London: Routledge & Kegan Paul, 1982.

• Campbell, Thomas. *Life of Mrs. Siddons.* 2 vols. London: Effingham Wilson, 1834.

Carroll, William C., ed. Macbeth: *Texts and Contexts.* Boston: Bedford / St. Martin's, 1999.

• Coleridge, Samuel Taylor. *The Literary Remains of Samuel Taylor Coleridge.* Ed. Henry Nelson Coleridge. 4 vols. London: William Pickering, 1836–39.

• Davenant, William. Macbeth, *A Tragedy with all the Alterations, Amendments, Additions, and New Songs.* London, 1674.

• Davies, Thomas. *Dramatic Miscellanies.* 3 vols. London, 1783–84.

Dent, R. W. *Shakespeare's Proverbial Language: An Index.* Berkeley: University of California Press, 1981.

• DeQuincey, Thomas. *Confessions of an English Opium-Eater.* London: Walter Scott, 1886. Ed. John E. Jordan. *DeQuincey as Critic.* Boston: Routledge & Kegan Paul, 1973.

Elliott, G. R. *Dramatic Providence in* Macbeth. Princeton: Princeton University Press, 1960.

• Erasmus, Desiderius. *Collected Works of Erasmus.* Toronto: University of Toronto Press, 1974—.

• Forman, Simon. Manuscript transcribed, E. K. Chambers. *William Shakespeare: A Study of Facts and Problems.* 2 vols. Oxford: Clarendon Press, 1930, rpt. 1951, 2: 337–38.

Gardner, Helen. "Milton's 'Satan' and the Theme of Damnation in Elizabethan Tragedy." *English Association Essays and Studies* 1 (1948), 46–66.

• Garnet, Henry. *A Treatise of Equivocation.* Ed. David Jardine. London, 1851.

Greenblatt, Stephen. "Shakespeare Bewitched." *New Historical Literary Study*. Ed. Jeffrey N. Cox and Larry Reynolds. Princeton: Princeton University Press, 1993. Pp. 108–35.

•Hazlitt, William. *Characters of Shakespeur's Plays*. London, 1817.

Hinman, Charlton, ed. *The Norton Facsimile: The First Folio of Shakespeare*. New York, 1968.

•Holinshed, Raphael. *The First and Second Volumes of Chronicles*. London, 1587.

•*An Homilie agaynst disobedience and wyful rebellion*. London, 1570.

•James I. *Daemonologie*. Edinburgh, 1597.

•———. *Newes from Scotland*. London, 1592.

•Johnson, Samuel. *Miscellaneous Observations on the Tragedy of Macbeth*. London, 1745.

•Jacobi, Derek. "Macbeth." In *Players of Shakespeare 4: Further Essays in Shakespearian Performances by Players with the Royal Shakespeare Company*. Ed. Robert Smallwood. Cambridge: Cambridge University Press, 1998. Pp. 193–210.

Knight, G. Wilson. *The Imperial Theme*. London: Oxford University Press, 1931.

Knights, L. C. "How Many Children Had Lady Macbeth?" *Explorations*. 1933; rpt. New York, 1964.

•Levin, Harry. "Two Scenes from *Macbeth*." *Shakespeare's Craft: Eight Lectures*. Ed. Philip H. Highfill, Jr. Carbondale: Southern Illinois University Press, 1982. Pp. 48–68.

•Mariana, Juan de. *De Rege et Regis Institutione*. Toledo, 1599.

•Montagu, Elizabeth. *An Essay on the Writings and Genius of Shakespeare*. London, 1769.

•Moore, Rush. *Macbeth Travestie, in Three Acts*. Calcutta, 1820.

•Msomi, Welcome. *uMabatha: An Adaptation of Shakespeare's "Macbeth."* Praetoria: Via Afrika / Skotaville Publishers, 1996.

•Muir, Kenneth. "Image and Symbol in *Macbeth*." *Shakespeare Survey* 19. Cambridge: Cambridge University Press, 1966. Pp. 45–54.

———. *The Sources of Shakespeare's Plays*. London: Methuen, 1977.

•N-Town Cycle. *The N-Town Play: Cotton MS Vespasian D.8*. Ed. Stephen Spector. 2 vols. Oxford: Oxford University Press, 1991.

Norbrook, David. "*Macbeth* and the Politics of Historiography." *Politics of Discourse: The Literature and History of Seventeenth-Century England*. Ed. Kevin Sharpe and Steven N. Zwicker. Berkeley: University of California Press, 1987. Pp. 78–116.

•Northall, W. K. *Macbeth Travestie*. New York, 1847.

•Orgel, Stephen. "*Macbeth* and the Antic Round." *Shakespeare Survey* 52. Cambridge: Cambridge University Press, 1999. Pp. 143–53.

Paul, Henry N. *The Royal Play of Macbeth*. New York: Macmillan, 1950.

Rosenberg, Marvin. *The Masks of Macbeth*. Berkeley: University of California Press, 1978.

•———. "Culture, Character, and Conscience in Shakespeare." *Shakespeare and the Triple Play: From Study to Stage to Classroom*. Ed. Sidney Homan. Cranbury, NJ: Associated University Presses, 1988. Pp. 138–49.

Schoenbaum, S., ed. *Macbeth: Critical Essays*. New York: Garland, 1991.

•Scot, Reginald. *The Discouerie of Witchcraft*. London, 1584.

• Seneca. *Seneca His Tenne Tragedies, Translated into Englysh*. Ed. Thomas Newton. London, 1581.

Shaheen, Naseeb. *Biblical References in Shakespeare's Plays*. London: Associated University Presses, 1999.

• Siddons, Sarah. See Campbell, Thomas.

Spurgeon, Caroline F. E. *Shakespeare's Imagery and What It Tells Us*. Cambridge: Cambridge University Press, 1935.

• Talfourd, Francis. *Macbeth Travestie: A Burlesque*. 3rd ed. Oxford, 1850.

Vickers, Brian, ed. *Shakespeare: The Critical Heritage*. 6 vols. London: Routledge & Kegan Paul, 1974–81.

Wills, Garry. *Witches and Jesuits: Shakespeare's* Macbeth. New York: Oxford University Press, 1995.

Wheeler, Thomas. Macbeth: *An Annotated Bibliography*. New York: Garland, 1990.